Ireland

Edited by Brian Bell
Directed and Designed by Hans Hoefer

APA PUBLICATIONS

IRELAND
Second Edition (Reprint)

© 1988 APA PUBLICATIONS (HK) LTD
Printed in Singapore by APA Press Pte. Ltd.
Colour Separation in Singapore by Colourscan Pte Ltd

APA PUBLICATIONS

Publisher: Hans Johannes Hoefer
General Manager: Henry Lee
Marketing Director: Aileen Lau
Editorial Director: Geoffrey Eu
Editorial Manager: Vivien Kim
Editorial Consultants: Adam Liptak (North America)
Brian Bell (Europe)
Heinz Vestner (German Editions)

Project Editors

Helen Abbott, Diana Ackland, Mohamed Amin, Ravindralal Anthonis, Roy Bailet, Louisa Cambell, Jon Carroll, Hillary Cunningham, John Eames, Janie Freeburg, Bikram Grewal, Virginia Hopkins, Samuel Israel, Jay Itzkowitz, Phil Jaratt, Tracy Johnson, Ben Kalb, Wilhelm Klein, Saul Lockhart, Sylvia Mayuga, Gordon MaLauchlan, Kal Müller, Eric Oey, Daniel P. Reid, Kim Robinson, Ronn Ronck, Robert Seidenberg, Rolf Steinberg, Sriyani Tidball, Lisa Van Gruisen, Merin Wexler.

Contributing Writers

A.D. Aird, Ruth Armstrong, T. Terence Barrow, F. Lisa Beebe, Bruce Berger, Dor Bahadur Bista, Clinton V. Black, Star Black, Frena Bloomfield, John Borthwick, Roger Boschman, Tom Brosnahan, Jerry Carroll, Tom Chaffin, Nedra Chung, Tom Cole, Orman Day, Kunda Dixit, Richard Erdoes, Guillermo Gar-Oropeza, Ted Giannoulas, Barbara Gloudon, Harka Gurung, Sharifah Hamzah, Willard A. Hanna, Elizabeth Hawley, Sir Edmund Hillary, Tony Hillerman, Jerry Hopkins, Peter Hutton, Neil Jameson, Michael King, Michele Kort, Thomas Lucey, Leonard Lueras, Michael E. Macmillan, Derek Maitland, Buddy Mays, Craig McGregor, Reinhold Messner, Julie Michaels, M.R. Priya Rangsit, Al Read, Elizabeth V. Reyes, Victor Stafford Reid, Harry Rolnick, E.R. Sarachandra, Uli Schmetzer, Ilsa Sharp, Norman Sibley, Peter Spiro, Harold Stephens, Keith Stevens, Michael Stone, Desmond Tate, Colin Taylor, Deanna L. Thompson, Randy Udall, James Wade, Mallika Wanigasundara, William Warren, Cynthia Wee, Tony Wheeler, Linda White, H. Taft Wireback, Alfred A. Yuson, Paul Zach.

Contributing Photographers

Carole Allen, Ping Amarand, Tony Arruza, Marcello Bertinetti, Alberto Cassio, Pat Canova, Alain Compost, Ray Cranbourne, Alian Evrard, Ricardo Ferro, Lee Foster, Manfred Gottschalk, Werner Hahn, Dallas and John Heaton, Brent Hesselyn, Hans Hoefer, Luca Invernizzi, Ingo Jezierski, Whilhelm Klein, Dennis Lane, Max Lawrence, Lyle Lawson, Philip Little, Guy Marche, Antonio Martinelli, David Messent, Ben Nakayama, Vautier de Nanxe, Kal Müller, Günter Pfannmuller, Van Philips, Ronni Pinsler, Fitz Prenzel, G.P. Reichelt, Dan Rocovits, David Ryan, Frank Salmoiraghi, Thomas Schollhammer, Blair Seitz, David Stahl, Bill Wassman, Rendo Yap, Hashim Youssef.
While contributions to Insight Guides are very welcome, the publisher cannot assume responsibility for the care and return of unsolicited manuscripts or photographs. Return postage and/or a self-addressed envelope must accompany unsolicited material if it is to be returned. Please address all editorial contributions to Apa Photo Agency P.O. Box 219, Orchard Point Post Office, Singapore 9123.

Distributors:

Australia and New Zealand: Prentice Hall of Australia, 7 Grosvenor Place, Brookvale, NSW 2100, Australia. **Benelux:** Utigeverij Cambium, Naarderstraat 11, 1251 AW Laren, The Netherlands. **Brazil and Portugal:** Cedibra Editora Brasileira Ltda, Rua Leonidia, 2-Rio de Janeiro, Brazil. **Denmark:** Copenhagen Book Centre Aps, Roskildeveji 338, DK-2630 Tastrup, Denmark. **Germany:** RV Reise-und Verkehrsuerlag Gmbh, Neumarkter Strasse 18, 8000 Munchen 80, West Germany. **Hawaii:** Pacific Trade Group Inc., P.O. Box 1227, Kailua, Oahu, Hawaii 96734, U.S.A. **Hong Kong:** Far East Media Ltd., Vita Tower, 7th Floor, Block B, 29 Wong Chuk Hang Road, Hong Kong. **India and Nepal:** India Book Distributors, 107/108 Arcadia Building, 195 Narima Point, Bombay-400-021, India. **Indonesia:** Java Books, Box 55 J.K.C.P., Jakarta, Indonesia. **Israel:** Steimatzky Ltd., P.O. Box 628, Tel Aviv 61006, Israel (Israel title only). **Italy:** Zanfi

Editori SRL. Via Ganaceto 121, 41100 Modena, Italy. **Jamaica:** Novelty Trading Co., P.O. Box 80, 53 Hanover Street, Kingston, Jamaica. **Japan:** Charles E. Tuttle Co. Inc., 2-6 Suldo 1-Chome, Bunkyo-ku, Tokyo 112, Japan. **Kenya:** Camerapix Publishers International Ltd., P.O. Box 45048, Nairobi, Kenya. **Korea:** Kyobo Book Centre Co., Ltd., P.O. Box Kwang Hwa Moon 1 658, Seoul, Korea. **Philippines:** National Book Store, 701 Rizal Avenue, Manila, Philippines. **Singapore:** MPH Distributors (S) Pte. Ltd., 601 Sims Drive #03-21 Pan-I Warehouse and Office Complex, S'pore 1438, Singapore. **Switzerland:** M.P.A. Agencies-Import SA, CH. du Croset 9, CH-1024, Ecublens, Switzerland. **Taiwan:** Caves Books Ltd., 103 Chungshan N. Road, Sec. 2, Taipei, Taiwan, Republic of China. **Thailand:** Asia Books Co. Ltd., 5 Sukhumvit Road Soi 61, P.O. Box 11-40, Bangkok 10110, Thailand. **United Kingdom, Ireland and Europe (others):** Harrap Ltd., 19-23 Ludgate Hill, London EC4M 7PD, England, United Kingdom. **Mainland United States and Canada:** Graphic Arts Center Publishing, 3019 N.W. Yeon, P.O. Box 10306, Portland OR 97210, U.S.A. (The Pacific Northwest title only); Prentice Hall Press, Gulf & Western Building, One Gulf & Western Plaza, New York, NY 10023, U.S.A. (all other titles).

French editions: Editions Gallimard, 5 rue Sèbastien-Bottin, F-75007 Paris, France. **German editions:** Nelles Verlag GmbH, Schleissheirner Str. 371b, 8000 Munich 45, West Germany **Italian editions:** Zanfi Editori SLR. Via Ganaceto 121 41100 Modena, Italy. **Portuguese editions:** Cedibra Editora Brasileira Ltda, Rua Leonidia, 2-Rio de Janeiro, Brazil.

Advertising and Special Sales Representatives

Advertising carried in Insight Guides gives readers direct access to quality merchandise and travel-related services. These advertisements are inserted in the Guide in Brief section of each book. Advertisers are requested to contact their nearest representatives, listed below.
Special sales, for promotion purposes within the international travel industry and for educational purposes, are also available. The advertising representatives listed here also handle special sales. Alternatively, interested parties can contact Apa Publications, P.O. Box 219, Orchard Point Post Office, Singapore 9123.

Australia and New Zealand: Harve and Gullifer Pty. Ltd. 1 Fawkner St. Kilda 3181, Australia. Tel: (3) 525 3422; Tlx: 523259; Fax: (89) 4312837.
Canada: The Pacific Rim Agency, 6900 Cote Saint Luc Road, Suite 303, Montreal, Quebec, Canada H4V 2Y9. Tel: (514) 9311299; Tlx: 0525134 MTL; Fax: (514) 8615571.
Hawaii: HawaiianLMedia Sales; 1750 Kalakaua Ave., Suite 3-243, Honolulu, Hawaii 96826, U.S.A. Tel: (808) 9464483.
Hong Kong: C Cheney & Associates, 17th Floor, D'Aguilar Place, 1-30 D'Aguilar Street, Central, Hong Kong. Tel: 5-213671; Tlx: 63079 CCAL HX.
India and Nepal, Pakistan and Bangladesh: Universal Media, CHA 2/718, 719 Kantipath, Lazimpat, Kathmandu-2, Nepal. Tel: 412911/414502; Tlx: 2229 KAJI NP ATTN MEDIA.
Indonesia: Media Investment Services, Setiabudi Bldg. 2, 4th Floor, Suite 407, Jl. Hr. Rasuna Said, Kuningan, Jakarta Selatan 12920, Indonesia. Tel: 5782723/5782752; Tlx: 62418 MEDIANETIA; Mata Graphic Design, Batujimbar, Sanur, Bali, Indonesia. Tel: (0361) 8073. (for Bali only)
Korea: Kaya Ad Inc., Rm. 402 Kunshin Annex B/D, 251-1 Dohwa Dong, Mapo-Ku, Seoul, Korea (121). Tel: (2) 7196906; Tlx: K 32144 KAYAAD; Fax: (2) 7199816.
Philippines: Torres Media Sales Inc., 21 Warbler St., Greenmeadows 1, Murphy, Quezon City, Metro Manila, Philippines. Tel: 722-02-43; Tlx: 23312 RHP PH.
Taiwan: Cheney Tan & Van Associates, 7th Floor, 10 Alley 4, Lane 545 Tun Hua South Road, Taipei, Taiwan. Tel: (2) 7002963; Tlx: 11491 FOROSAN; Fax: (2) 3821270.
Thailand: Cheney, Tan & Van Outrive, 17th Floor Rajapark Bldg., 163 Asoke Rd., Bangkok 10110, Thailand. Tel: 2583244/2583259; Tlx: 20666 RAJAPAK TH.
Singapore and Malaysia: Cheney Tan Associates, 1 Goldhill Plaza, #02-01, Newton Rd., Singapore 1130, Singapore. Tel: 2549522; Tlx: RS 35983 CTAL.
Sri Lanka: Spectrum Lanka Advertising Ltd., 56 1/2 Ward Place, Colombo 7, Sr Lanka. Tel: 5984648/596227; Tlx: 21439 SPECTRM CE.
U.K., Ireland and Europe: Brian Taplin Associates, 32 Fishery Road, Boxmoor, Hemel Hempstead, Herts HP 1ND, U.K. Tel: (2)215635; Tlx: 825454 CHARMAN.

APA PHOTO AGENCY PTE. LTD.

The Apa Photo Agency is S.E. Asia's leading stock photo archive, representing the work of professional photographers from all over the world. More than 150,000 original color transparencies are available for advertising, editorial and educational uses. We are linked with Tony Stone Worldwide, one of Europe's leading stock agencies, and their associate offices around the world:
Singapore: Apa Photo Agency Pte. Ltd., P.O. Box 219, Orchard Point Post Office, Singapore 9123, Singapore. **London:** Tony Stone Worldwide, 28 Finchley Rd., St. John's Wood, London NW8 6ES, England. **North America & Canada:** Masterfile Inc., 415 Yonge St., Suite 200, Toronto M5B 2E7, Canada. **Paris:** Fotogram-Stone Agence Photographique, 45 rue de Richelieu, 75001 Paris, France. **Barcelona:** Fototec Torre Dels Pardais, 7 Barcelona 08026, Spain. **Johannesburg:** Color Library (Pty.) Ltd., P.O. Box 1659, Johannesburg, SOuth Africa 2000. **Sydney:** The Photographic Library of Australia Pty. Ltd., 7 Ridge Street, North Sydney, New South Wales 2050, Australia. **Tokyo:** Orion Press, 55-1 Kanda Jimbocho, Chiyoda-ku, Tokyo 101, Japan.

This book had its genesis when **Brian Bell**, managing editor of the colour magazine published with *The Observer*, Britain's oldest Sunday newspaper, called at the Singapore headquarters of Apa Productions. His intention was to raid Apa's celebrated photographic library for material to accompany a series of features on Southeast Asian countries he was preparing for his magazine. Apa, he learned, was planning to extend its range of internationally acclaimed *Insight Guides* to cover Europe's leading travel destinations. He expressed the degree of polite interest which those familiar with British ways recognized as enthusiasm.

Hoefer

Bell

Two years later, at the beginning of 1985, those seeds of interest germinated when Apa Editor **Stuart Ridsdale** asked Bell to take on the project editorship of *Insight Guide: Ireland*.

Europe was the next natural area of interest for Apa Productions, which had already covered every major Southeast Asian destination and was undertaking an ambitious programme of guides to the United States. Europe was also the birthplace of the company's founder and Managing Director, **Hans Hoefer**, who came to Asia in the late 1960s from West Germany, where he had graduated in printing, book production, design and photography studies in Krefeld. Under his creative direction and reflecting his belief in the Bauhaus tradition of graphic arts, *Insight Guides* have pioneered a new kind of comprehensive and sensitive coverage of foreign cultures.

As editor of *Insight Guide: Ireland*, Bell readily responded to Apa's refusal to take societies at their face value. Ireland, he believed, is a misunderstood country; two countries, rather, because of the border that has divided the island since 1922. But the misunderstandings are understandable: the Irish manufacture myths about themselves the way some nations churn out microchips, and their habit of turning every conversation into a conjuring trick usually leaves departing visitors no wiser than when they arrived about what makes Ireland tick. It was agreed from the start that this book would cover both parts of

Ireland and would tackle head-on the controversial political issues that have moulded one of Europe's oldest societies.

Born and raised in British-run Northern Ireland, Bell has an insider's understanding of Ireland's obsession with nationality: he admits to feeling a little bit Irish but also a little bit British and, when labels have to be attached, will settle for being a hybrid Ulsterman. After graduating in psychology from Queen's University, Belfast, he began his journalistic career in that city, where he reported for Northern Ireland's leading newspaper, the *Belfast Telegraph*, the outbreak in 1968 of the "Troubles" that have violently divided the community ever since. Having lived in England since 1972, he now views with a journalist's detachment Ireland's attempts to work out its turbulent destiny, and is well used to explaining to the baffled English that, despite the headlines detailing the latest terrorist outrage, Ireland can still amply justify its former image as one of the world's most tranquil and hospitable countries.

As editor responsible for travel coverage on the *Observer Magazine*, Bell is well qualified to make such international comparisons. When not travelling, he divides his time between a weekday London apartment and a weekend retreat in rural Oxfordshire. As a warm-up to the Ireland project, he collaborated with his American-born wife, Diane Fisher, to write about England's north country for Apa's *Insight Guide: Great Britain*.

To convey Ireland's complexities to a worldwide readership, Bell began assembling a team of writers in three capital cities: Dublin, Belfast and London. His first call was on **Liam McAuley**, a friend and former colleague from *Belfast Telegraph* days. McAuley, now with the *Irish Times* in Dublin, had also moved to England, serving as deputy editor on *Campaign*, the weekly journal of Britain's advertising industry, and putting in two spells as an editor with London's *Sunday Times*. Between these stints, he spent a year in Amsterdam with *Holland Herald*, the in-flight magazine of KLM Airlines. As an Ulsterman living in Dublin, McAuley combines an outsider's and insider's knowledge of the city which he put to good use for this book. He also contributed the sections on the Midwest, the Midlands, Ireland's travelling people, a guide for would-be genealogists and—a particular labour of love—the chapter on the Irish enthusiasm for horses and horse-racing.

As if all this weren't enough, he collaborated with his wife, **Rosemary Head**, on compiling the "Guide in Brief." She juggled groundwork for the guide with tutorials at Dublin's University College and work on her philosophy doctorate.

The *Irish Times*, as Ireland's leading quality newspaper, provided several other talents for the book. **Seamus Martin**, a reporter and columnist, wrote the chapters on the Southeast and—a subject demanding lengthy research—pubs and drinking.

Belfast-born **Eugene McEldowney**, the paper's news editor, contributed the feature on "Song and Dance." He spent four years as a teacher before achieving his burning ambition to be a journalist. Not only does he have a deep interest in traditional Irish music, but he can also be persuaded, without very much encouragement or whiskey, to break into enthusiastic song.

Michael Foley, the paper's tourism correspondent, suggested the piece on Uninhabited Islands, magical places to which he escapes at every opportunity.

The *Irish Times's* cookery correspondent, **Theodora FitzGibbon**, came immediately to mind as the best person to write about food. She has already published 34 books on the subject, as well as two novels and two volumes of autobiography. Her life makes a war correspondent's seem dull by comparison: expelled from her convent school for gambling on horses, she travelled alone to Calcutta at the age of 16 to join her father, was friendly with Picasso in Paris in the 1930s, lived a bohemian life in London's Chelsea during World War Two, went to America as the GI bride of writer Constantine FitzGibbon, and, many adventures later, is now living in Dalkey, Co. Dublin, with her second husband, film archivist **George Morrison**, whose food photographs accompany her words in this book.

David Norris, a loquacious lecturer in English literature at Trinity College, Dublin, wrote the feature on "The Irish Way with Words." He is renowned in Dublin as an effective leader of pressure groups, especially in the conservation field, and his panel on "The Fight for Old Dublin" on page 104 is testament to his eloquence against the excesses of insensitive property developers.

For a portrait of Northern Ireland's capital, Bell turned to his own old paper, the *Belfast Telegraph*, and to one of its editorial-page writers, Derek Black. In his part-time role as the paper's motoring editor, Black travels the world testing new cars on behalf of his readers —and the area, having good roads, breeds motoring enthusiasts. In contrast to many people's perception of Ulster as verging on a war zone, he finds it a relaxing and beautiful place to come home to, and set

McAuley

May

Martin

Kellner

Stokes

Ó hEithir

Norris

out to portray honestly in this book the Belfast that seldom gets reported in the world's press.

For a candid view of a curious Ulster phenomenon, the summer "marching season," Bell called on a Scottish-born novelist and painter, **Naomi May**. Although she now lives in London, she travels to Northern Ireland each August with her Ulster-born accountant husband and her children to holiday in County Down, near the often serenaded Mountains of Mourne. One of her novels, *Troubles*, is a sensitive portrait of Ulster's Protestant Ascendancy in its last days of power.

The section on Sport, Fairies and Folklore, the Northwest and the Gaelic-speaking Far West were provided by **Breandán O hEithir**, (pronounced *Oh-heh-hir*). Schooled on the Aran Islands, he first worked as an itinerant bookseller and publisher's editor before becoming one of Ireland's best-known writers and broadcasters, both in Irish and in English. His books include *Over the Bar*, a history of rugby football in Ireland, and *Lead Us into Temptation*, a novel.

The Irish, valuing foreign coinage, will seldom have a bad word to say—in public, anyway—about tourism. So, for an impartial assessment of the Southwest tourist haunts of Kerry and Killarney, Bell turned to a leading English journalist, **Peter Kellner**, political editor of the *New Statesman*, an influential London weekly. Kellner goes to Ireland annually to visit his brother-in-law's family, who have set-

Kelly

Black

Purcell

FitzGibbon

McEldowney

Foley

tled in the Southwest: their respective children spend their summers playing, fighting and getting dirty together in West Cork.

Niall Stokes, who wrote on "The Youth Revolution," is founder and editor of *Hot Press*, a fort-

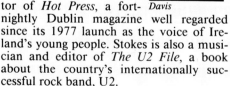
Davis

nightly Dublin magazine well regarded since its 1977 launch as the voice of Ireland's young people. Stokes is also a musician and editor of *The U2 File*, a book about the country's internationally successful rock band, U2.

Deirdre Purcell, who wrote the difficult chapter on the changing role of the Roman Catholic Church in Ireland, is chief feature writer on Dublin's *Sunday Tribune*. During a varied employment history, she has been an Aer Lingus reservations clerk in Dublin, a member of the Abbey Theatre's acclaimed acting company, a travel agent in Chicago, and a television newscaster in Dublin. She has also

published a book on Ethiopia's famine.

Derek Davis, who wrote about fishing, describes himself as an overweight angler who works as a TV presenter in Dublin to finance his angling habit and penchant for good food and drink. He has so far resisted job offers from America and Britain because "big money doesn't compensate for bad fishing."

To present a striking visual panorama of Ireland, Bell assembled the work of an international gallery of photographers, ranging from America's **Joe Viesti** and **Bruce Bernstein** to Germany's **G.P. Reichelt** and Italy's **Antonio Martinelli**. Not surprisingly, several *Observer* regulars featured strongly: **Peter Lavery**, **George Wright**, **Tony McGrath** and **Alain le Garsmeur**. But the biggest single contribution came from a distinctly Irish eye, belonging to **Thomas Kelly**. Limerick-born Kelly trained in London while doing "the usual Paddy stint" on a building site and has since photographed every continent except Australia.

Credit, too, goes to those ever-reliable photographic agencies **Tony Stone Worldwide**, **BBC Hulton Picture Library**, **Reflex**, **Network**, **Impact**, and **Frank Spooner Pictures**. Vital transparencies were provided by **Bord Fáilte** and the **Northern Ireland Tourist Board**.

We dedicate this book to all who decide to discover for themselves the secret of Ireland's endearing charms. And we dedicate it in particular to those visitors descended from the millions of Irish men and women who, over the centuries, have made their homes elsewhere in the world. In the United States, for example, Irish-Americans are even more vocally patriotic than Ireland's Irish, and Budweiser beer is dyed green to celebrate St. Patrick's Day. In the Caribbean, you can detect a distinct brogue in the accents of the Black inhabitants of Montserrat, originally settled by the Irish. Yet, curiously, there is no equivalent in the Irish language for the English word "emigrant." The nearest word is *deora,* which means "exile." And the host of exiles and descendants of exiles now far outnumbers the population of Ireland itself.

We would like to express our gratitude to **Jury's Hotel Group**, **Aer Lingus** and the Northern Ireland Tourist Board for their hospitality to our writers. To them and to the many others who proved that Irish generosity is everything it's cracked up to be, we raise our glass of Guinness and say, "*Sláinte.*"

— Apa Productions

TABLE OF CONTENTS

TABLE OF CONTENTS

Cartography
—by Nelles Verlag Gmbh, Munich

OTHER INSIGHT GUIDES TITLES

THE IRISH CHARACTER

"How do you recognize an Irishman in a car wash?"
"He's the one sitting on the motor bike."

The Irish take a perverse delight in the universal jokes made against them. Indeed, they even print selections on linen tea-towels, which they sell at fancy prices in souvenir shops. That explains the perverse delight, of course: there's money to be made in conforming to a stereotyped image and, by appearing to be dim, the Irishman can benefit from the dimness of others. Thus a guileful guide, deploying words like grapeshot, can charm the most sceptical travellers into paying good money to kiss the Blarney Stone in County Cork, at the same time reassuring them fulsomely that its promised ability to confer eloquence on all who kiss it is, in itself, just a bit of blarney.

Millions of visitors respond to this captivating charm by falling in love with Ireland at first sight. The national tourist slogan, *Céad Míle Fáilte*, fulfils its promise of "a hundred thousand welcomes" and the people's informal friendliness makes it exceptionally easy to take things easy. After achieving independence from Britain in 1921, an event accompanied by bloody internal strife, the new Republic signalled its priorities in its currency, with coins displaying images not of rulers or tyrants but of pigs, hens, hares and salmon.

But only the coins of *the Republic*, of course — for there are two Irelands. One consists of the 26 counties of the Republic, which evoke images of black beer and green shamrock, of still sunsets over Galway Bay and statues of the Virgin Mary that, according to thousands of eye-witnesses, miraculously move. Then there are the six counties of British-administered Northern Ireland, a harder place where terrorist outrages make headlines from Stockholm to Sydney, a wry place where a slogan daubed on the side of a derelict house asks: "Is there life *before* death?"

The paradoxes spawned by a series of

historical accidents multiply like Russian dolls. It doesn't take long for the enquiring visitor to begin pondering such puzzles as why a Dublin Roman Catholic will in all probability hate the British but respect the English, while a Belfast Protestant will badmouth the English yet swear eternal loyalty to the British. Non-residents should enter this debate only if they relish taking sides in marital conflicts.

Such stereotypes, naturally, soon turn into absurd oversimplifications. An English journalist, for instance, despatched to

Northern Ireland to seek out why its Protestant and Roman Catholic communities were at each other's throats, reported: "They are incomparably more pleasant to the outsider than any other people in the British Isles. Even the terrorists have excellent manners."

Yet, when dealing with each other, the inhabitants of the two Irelands—together adding up to just 5 million people—are in such a muddle that they can't even agree on the length of the border that divides them. The northern authorities claim it is 303 miles (485 km) long; the southern defence forces say it is 280 miles (448 km).

But nobody expresses concern about the discrepancy. It was the German writer,

Preceding pages, welcome at Ryan's Bar in Dublin; stablehands at Kildangan stud; schoolboys at Rockley College, Fermoy; fire station at Fethard, Co. Tipperary; girl at Mount Coole Stud, Co. Limerick. Left, football game at Croagh Park, Dublin. Right, Irish farmer.

Heinrich Böll, who identified the two turns of speech most characteristic of the Irish as "It could be worse" and "I shouldn't worry." In a world where worries proliferate daily, Ireland has more to offer than pigs, priests, potatoes and patriots: it has insane optimism.

Naturally the Irish have written down this philosophy on linen tea-towels, which they will sell to passers-through at a decent profit. It reads: "There are only two things to worry about: either you are well or you are sick. If you are well, then there is nothing to worry about. But if you are sick, there are two things to worry about: either you will get well or you will die. If you get well, then there is nothing to worry about. If you die there are only two things to worry about: either you will go to heaven or to hell. If you go to heaven, there is nothing to worry about. But if you go to hell, you'll be so damn busy shaking hands with friends, you won't have time to worry. Why worry!"

Never trust a clown: Not that the Irish won't give you cause enough for perplexity. Their character is as elusive as the fairy gold to be found at the end of Irish rainbows and their conversation as elliptical as an incomplete jigsaw puzzle. Hollywood, as so often, is partly to blame; it perpetuated the image of the stage Irishman, a clownish character with a liking for alcohol and argument, preferably indulged in simultaneously. But the Irish readily collaborated.

Unarguably, there is a strong theatricality about their character. There's a recklessness, a tendency towards exaggeration. There's a love of "codology," the Irish equivalent of "leg-pulling."

But there's an introversion, too, the proneness to melancholy captured by George Bernard Shaw in *John Bull's Other Island*, a play set in the land of his birth: "Your wits can't thicken in that soft moist air, on those white springy roads, in those misty rushes and brown bogs, on those hillsides of granite rocks and magenta heather. You've no such colours in the sky, no such lure in the distance, no such sadness in the evenings. Oh the dreaming! the dreaming! the torturing, heartscalding, never satisfying dreaming, dreaming, dreaming."

You can sometimes sense this aspect of the Irish character in a pub when, after the talk—once described as "a game with no rules"—has achieved an erratic brilliance, the convivial mood abruptly changes into one of wistfulness and self-absorption, and you know it's time to go. G.K. Chesterton

echoed the contradiction in his poem *Ballad of the White Horse:*

For the great Gaels of Ireland
Are the men that God made mad,
For all their wars are merry
And all their songs are sad.

This contradictory character led the 19th Century philosopher Søren Kierkegaard to muse that, if he hadn't been a Dane, he could well have been an Irishman: "For the Irish have not the heart to baptize their children completely, they want to preserve just a little paganism, and whereas a child is normally completely immersed, they keep his right arm out of the water so that in after life he can grasp a sword and hold a girl in his arm."

The Irish themselves have usually

looked less whimsically at their native land. The poet, Louis MacNeice, for example, described it as a nation "built upon violence and morose vendettas." Today, because of the guerrilla warfare that has been waged in the northeast of the island since 1969, this dark side of the Irish character is much more in evidence

Above, "marry a mountain woman," runs an Irish proverb, "and you'll marry the whole mountain." This couple married in Mayo, in the Far West, where Gaelic is still spoken.

than it was even 30 years ago, when John Wayne rollicked his way through the virulently green landscapes of *The Quiet Man*.

A hostile solitude: Perhaps the island's location has something to do with it. "With the exception it may be of Malta and of Iceland," wrote the actor and theatre director Micheál MacLiammóir, "no European island lies in so lamentable and hostile a solitude as Ireland, who has no neighbour on her right hand but her conqueror, and nothing at all on her left hand but the desolate ocean, not one dry step until you get to America."

This "wretched little clod, broken off a bigger clod, broken off the west end of Europe," as Shaw called it, has had a turbulent history, whose unfinished state is re-

flected in the island's partition. The current "Troubles" blighting Northern Ireland were at first seen by the world as a curious religious conflict, an inexplicable throwback to the Reformation. In reality, religious affiliation has been mostly a symbol. The conflict has had little to do with God but everything to do with nationalism. The doctrine of the Transubstantiation may be debated from the pulpits of fundamentalist preachers, but what everyone else is arguing about is the conflicting secular loyalties of 1 million Protestants,

who want to stay British, and half-a-million Roman Catholics, who feel a bond with the Republic. It's partly a question of insecure national identity, partly a realization that, in an area with too few jobs and not enough decent housing to go round, each tribe has to fight for its fair share.

What these divisions indicate is that there is more than one "Irish" character. The Northern Protestant is generally regarded as being more earnest, more unimaginative than the Northern Catholic, who is in turn seen as less outgoing, less impulsive than the Southern Catholic. The Irish refine these distinctions even further, giving the sense of place an importance seldom found elsewhere in the world. Two Irish people meeting for the first time will almost invariably try to ascertain precisely where the other comes from, down to the street name, and the family connections. Ireland is, in the end, a small place.

It proves too small for many. Patriots have gone overseas to escape imprisonment, writers to escape censorship, ambitious youngsters to escape the claustrophobia of the most conservative, church-influenced country in western Europe. In *Mother Ireland*, the novelist Edna O'Brien described the constricting parochialism and awful predictability that led her to emigrate to London: "Hour after hour I can think of Ireland, I can imagine without going too far wrong what is happening in any one of the little towns by day or by night... I can almost tell you what any one of my friends might be doing, so steadfast is the rhythm of life there."

But it is a rhythm well liked by many who follow it and by most visitors. It is an echo of an 18th Century pace of life that has not completely faded away, a psychological climate in which a racehorse attracts more admiring glances than a Rolls-Royce. It reflects the values of the railway guard answering a traveller who complained that the train was already half an hour late: "You must have a very narrow heart that you wouldn't go down to the town and stand your friends a few drinks instead of bothering me to get away."

It's this attitude to life, never far beneath the surface, that makes Ireland such a rewarding place to visit. As the novelist J.P. Donleavy, an exemplar of the less folksy style of Irish writing, expressed it winsomely in *The Ginger Man*: "When I die I want to decompose in a barrel of porter *(dark beer)* and have it served in all the pubs of Dublin. I wonder would they know it was me?"

IRLANDIÆ REGNUM.

21

Ireland, it is said, has no ancient annals: all its history is contemporary because yesterday's myths mould today's thought in an astonishingly direct way. In the words of the 19th Century historian, Thomas Babington Macaulay, dealing with Ireland is like stepping "on the thin crust of ashes beneath which the lava is still flowing."

It's an easy proposition to prove. Volunteer, at an Irish dinner party or in a bar, a statement about any aspect of the country's turbulent past, then sit back and listen as a catalogue of heroism and hatreds, claims and counter-claims, murderers and martyrs, decisive dates and disputed deeds pours out with vehemence and wit, populated with a cast of characters ranging from Brian Ború to Oliver Cromwell, from William of Orange to O'Connell the Liberator, from Henry VIII to Margaret Thatcher. In no other country in the world does the ordinary citizen delight in interpreting today's political deeds through such detailed and comprehensive reference to events that took place two, five, 10 centuries ago.

The reason for this lack of historical perspective lies in the extraordinary love-hate relationship that Ireland has had with its more powerful neighbouring island to the east. Ireland's history, in a nutshell, is its resistance to England. In this geographically forced marriage, the dominant partner sometimes deliberately abused the weaker, more often unthinkingly ignored her; yet the Irish, while hating the English for their arrogance and neglect, also admired them for their character and achievements and, until a surprisingly late stage, had no great wish for the marriage to be totally dissolved.

It is a tragic national drama, full of tantalising might-have-beens, and the English have long been resigned to the fact that they must play the villain. "Go into the length and breadth of the world," England's reforming prime minister William Ewart Gladstone told his parliament a century ago, "ransack the literature of all countries, find if you can a single voice, a single book... in which the conduct of

England towards Ireland is anywhere treated except with profound and bitter condemnation."

Magic and wizardry: Those seeking to understand rather than condemn must begin by travelling back several centuries before the birth of Christ. It was then that Ireland's first conquerors, the Celts (or Gaels), quick-tempered masters of horsemanship, came west from the mainland of Europe, mainly from France and Spain, to this wild, wet island at the continent's outermost fringes. They brought with them a

loose tribal structure, the blueprint for building a civilization, and had little trouble in overcoming the natives, an obscure, primitive people called the Firbolg (literally "Bag Men").

But old traditions of magic and wizardry survived so strongly that to this day you can find reverence for holy wells and for clumps of trees inhabited by "the fairies." Evidence of much earlier inhabitants survived, too, in the form of thousands of megalithic burial chambers. The Newgrange passage-grave in the Boyne valley, near Dublin, for example, is thought to be 5,000 years old. From the Bronze Age, when Ireland was one of the world's largest metal producers, beautifully crafted leaf-shaped

Preceding pages, girls at Ballina in Co. Mayo; how an Amsterdam atlas, the Mercador-Hondius, saw Ireland in 1606. Left, high cross at Monasterboice, Co. Meath. Right, detail from the *Book of Kells.*

Ireland and the English 23

swords and gold ornaments are preserved.

Europe's next conquerors did not get as far as Ireland. The Roman legions, hard pressed to hold southern Britain against incursions from the north by Picts and Scots, were disinclined to take on more trouble by adding the Gaels to their empire. Their inaction had far-reaching consequences: if Julius Caesar had successfully ventured west, it is unlikely that Ireland's character today would be so distinctly different from that of neighbouring Britain. Also, say cynics, the roads might have been better.

The divergences between the two cultures widened still further when the fall of the Roman empire plunged Europe into the Dark Ages. Ireland, in contrast, entered its Golden Age, becoming a lone

beacon of learning and civilization later dubbed the Land of Saints and Scholars.

Christianity had been brought to the island by an English-born rustic missionary, St. Patrick, who had been kidnapped as a youth and taken to Ireland to tend sheep. Later, he travelled widely in France and Italy, returning to Ireland in 432 to spread the word of Christ through the trackless forests. He found, in this land of which he was to become the patron saint, a largely peaceable people, though there was intermittent feuding between various provincial kings. Because kingship was elective, not hereditary, such power struggles were inevitable, especially since there were as many as 150 kings in a population of

500,000. They reigned, it was said, but didn't always rule.

In the absence of a Roman substructure of towns and cities, monasteries became centres of population. The kings kept their treasures there, which made the monasteries a target for plundering bands of Vikings, who sailed to Ireland in their high-prowed ships from northern Scandinavia. Tall round towers, many still standing, were built by the monasteries to serve as lookouts and refuges as well as belfries. Also surviving are some of the monks' exquisitely illuminated manuscripts, such as the *Book of Kells*, which the Vikings, being unable to read, ignored. Ireland's strong tradition of storytelling dates from this period. It can be seen on the many sandstone high crosses, designed to teach Bible stories by means of elaborate carvings.

The Norse tyranny was finally destroyed at the Battle of Clontarf in 1014 by the most celebrated of the High Kings, Brian Ború, who saw himself as Ireland's Charlemagne. But he himself died in the battle as he was praying for victory.

Salubrity and serenity: By the 12th Century, a traveller reported: "Bede states that Ireland is much superior to Britain both in the salubrity and serenity of the atmosphere. He is right as to its salubrity; but with due respect to his opinion, he is in error with regard to its serenity." The traveller had a point, for it was not just holy and learned men who found their way to this boggy, rainy island. Norman adventurers such as Strongbow came looking for land. His real name was Richard, second Earl of Pembroke, and he was answering a call for help from Dermot MacMurrough, a local chieftain. MacMurrough had outraged rivals by stealing another prince's wife—an offence which, not for the first time, was to change the course of history.

But the Norman lord's pedigrees were longer than their purses. Having gained a toehold, they began enriching themselves by building a power base, complete with fortified stone castles. This alarmed England's king, Henry II. He promptly paid a visit to Ireland, inaugurating an involvement between the two countries that was to last, with immeasurable bloodshed, for eight centuries and ensure that Henry would be remembered as Ireland's first of many absentee landlords.

Left, recalling ancient times, a stone pillar at Glencolumbkille, Co. Donegal. Right, Henry II makes the fateful decision to interfere in Ireland.

HENRY II. PRESENTING THE POPE'S BULL.
THE ARCHBISHOP OF CASHEL.

Over the next three centuries, the Normans, intermarrying with the natives, expanded their influence. Many of the country's elaborate castles, such as Blarney in County Cork and Bunratty in County Clare, date from this time. In 1429, Henry VI subsidized each new castle to the tune of £10, then a sizeable sum.

But, as the barons thrived, the English Crown's authority gradually shrank to an area around Dublin, known as "the Pale." It was Henry VIII, determined finally to break the local nobles' power, who proclaimed himself "King of this land of Ireland as united, annexed and knit for ever to the Imperial Crown of the Realm of England." Henry tried to make himself the source of all land ownership by demand-

Ulster. The new settlers were Protestants, firm believers in the Calvinist work ethic, and the racial mix that they created is still causing strife in Ulster today.

An early sign of the troubles ahead came in 1641, when Ulster Roman Catholics hoping to recover their confiscated lands rebelled at Portadown. The facts of the rebellion were rapidly overwhelmed by the legend as lurid tales spread of a drunken Catholic pogrom on the God-fearing settlers, with 12,000 Protestants knifed, shot and drowned, pregnant women raped, and infants roasted on spits. Whatever the death toll really was, the Protestants were never to forget the threat represented by 1641.

The Gaelic Irish had further cause to

ing that the lords surrender their lands to him, then have them "regranted by the grace of the king." When many refused, Henry seized their lands and resettled them with loyal "planters" from England and Scotland.

His daughter, Elizabeth I, fought four wars in Ireland. As well as trying to impose the Reformation on the country, she was determined to protect England's right flank against an invasion from her principal opponent, Spain.

Later, James I defeated a particularly powerful baron, Hugh O'Neill, Earl of Tyrone, at the Battle of Kinsale and planted new settlers on O'Neill's lands in six of the nine counties of the ancient province of

worry when, after Charles I was beheaded, the new Puritan Parliament in England began suppressing the Roman Catholic religion. Fanned by the flames of this resentment, a new Catholic revolt began to spread. This "Great Rebellion" was ruthlessly suppressed by the English Protector, Oliver Cromwell, whose 20,000 Ironside troops devastated the countryside. By 1652, about a third of the Catholic Irish had been killed. Much of their land was handed over to Protestants.

Left, William of Orange, victorious at the Battle of the Boyne. Right, a re-creation of the more elegant days at Casteltown, Co. Kildare.

When the monarchy was restored, Charles II disappointed Catholics by throwing his support behind the Protestants, on whom he depended for power. His successor, James II, himself a Roman Catholic, raised hopes by introducing an Act of Parliament that would have ousted the Protestant settlers; but, before it could be put into practice, James was defeated in 1690 at the Battle of the Boyne, near Dublin, by William of Orange. William had been called in by the English establishment to put a stop to James's "Popish ways" and his success in doing so at the Boyne is still commemorated annually by mammoth Protestant parades throughout Northern Ireland.

A persecuted minority: From that day in

and England. The country was left with only the land to rely on and the peasants put in the position of slaves. No hope of redemption was offered: if a tenant worked hard to improve his holding, the landlord responded by raising his rent. Even the king's representative, the Viceroy, reported in 1770 that the peasants were "amongst the most wretched people on earth."

Significantly, though, the king was not regarded as an enemy of the Irish people; it was the landlords who were the focus of hatred. Nor did the Catholic gentry resent the English monarchy's control; indeed, when the American colonies declared their independence in 1776, the Catholics reaffirmed their allegiance to George III. Also,

July 1690, Roman Catholics became a persecuted majority in Ireland. Their share of land ownership tumbled to just 15 per cent. New anti-Catholic legislation, the "penal laws," barred them from all public life and much social activity. They weren't allowed to buy land or rent it profitably. When a Catholic landowner died, his property was broken up between all his sons instead of passing to the eldest—unless one son turned Protestant, in which case he got the lot. By the middle of the 18th Century, only 7 per cent of land was in Catholic hands.

Any threat from the trading class was removed when swingeing restrictions were imposed on commerce between Ireland

many of the middle-class "Ascendancy" were prospering. Arthur Guinness, for instance, introduced his famous stout in the late 18th Century.

But trouble was inevitable and, gradually, violent groups of men began to ride out at night avenging themselves on their oppressors—maiming landlords' cattle, burning barns, firing shots through windows. These secret societies, with names such as the Whiteboys and the Ribbonmen, deflected much of the masses' energy from more political aims. Jonathan Swift, the Irish-born dean of St. Patrick's Protestant Cathedral in Dublin and the author of such incisive satires as *Gulliver's Travels*, had a more political sensibility: he endorsed the call to his fellow countrymen to burn everything English except their coal, and he advocated a separate parliament for Ireland. This parliament would still be loyal to the king—but in his role as king of Ireland rather than as king of England.

Pressure for political change was applied by Protestant patriots such as Henry Grattan. The threat of physical force was added in the shape of the Irish Volunteers, 80,000 strong by 1782. London caved in and agreed to a separate parliament in Dublin. At last Ireland was an independent nation—although only legislatively, since allegiance was still owed to the British Crown. Also a fatal flaw in the new arrangement was that the Catholic majority (three fourths of the population) were still denied any political role and the patronage at the disposal of the English parliament allowed it easily to manipulate policy in Dublin.

The echoes of the French Revolution were heard loudly in Ireland. For a time, fashionable Dubliners addressed each other as "Citizen," and demands grew for Catholic emancipation without delay. For its part, the government in London thought it had done rather well to pass two Catholic Relief Acts giving Roman Catholics limited voting rights and allowing them once more to own or lease land. As so often in Ireland, however, a well-meaning policy gave birth to anarchy. Catholics began buying land in Ulster, forcing up prices and alarming the Protestants, who formed a vigilante outfit, the Peep o' Day Boys, to burn out Catholics in dawn raids. In response, the Catholics set up their own vigilante force, the Defenders. The lines of a long conflict were drawn.

A secret society is born: Yet Ulster was the cradle in 1791 for a brave attempt by Protestants and Catholics to fight together for reform. Wolfe Tone, the son of a respectable Protestant coachbuilder, set up the first Society of United Irishmen club in Belfast and a second soon opened in Dublin. It began well, largely as an enlightened debating society, but was suppressed within three years when William Pitt, the British prime minister, feared an alliance between Ireland and France, with whom Britain was then at war. Tone, condemning England as "the never-failing source of all our political evils," fled to America. But the original Belfast club refused to accept defeat: it turned itself into a secret society, pledging itself to work for "a republican government and separation from England." It was a radical ambition for the time.

Government anxiety increased when the United Irishmen, largely a middle-class Protestant group, began forging links with the Defenders, who were mostly working-class Catholics. And soon an even more threatening alliance was being forged: the United Irishmen persuaded Tone, who had been thinking of settling down near Philadelphia as a farmer, to sail to France and rally support against Britain. Tone assured the French that their arrival in Ireland would trigger a national uprising, supported wholeheartedly by the Irish militia, and on Dec. 16, 1796, a French battle fleet of 43 ships set sail.

It was the weather that came to England's rescue. Severe storms first dispersed the fleet, then made an effective landing

impossible. In addition, the few troops who did land at Bantry Bay, on the rugged southwest coast, were greeted rather unenthusiastically by the Irish peasants, who believed that the French really had been sent by the northern Protestants to suppress them further.

In the end, it was the United Irishmen who were suppressed. Pitt, fearing a second French expedition, imposed harsh martial law in Ulster. The army, four-fifths of whom were themselves Catholic Irish peasants, began arresting the organization's outlawed leaders, identifying them as a result of information partly provided by informers, partly extracted through brutal beatings. Typically, a wooden triangle would be set up in a village street, victims would be spread-eagled naked on it and flogged until they betrayed their comrades. Soon Ulster was in the grip of terror and the stage was set for a significant new group to enter the Irish drama. These were the Orangemen, whose role in Ulster remains central today.

The movement began in 1795 after a bitter clash between Protestant Peep o' Day Boys and Catholic Defenders at the Battle of the Diamond, near Armagh, in which 30 men died. The Protestants, fearing worse was to come, reorganized as the Orange Society, named after their hero, William of Orange, and preyed as lawless bandits on Catholics. In defeating the United Irishmen, the government was glad to have

their vicious support.

The Great Rebellion: Disaffection with English rule climaxed in May 1798 in a major rebellion. But by then so many of the United Irishmen's leaders had been arrested that most of the risings throughout the country were too ill-organized to succeed. Also, the native yeomanry, revealing a disturbing aspect of the Irish character, reacted by torturing and shooting indiscriminately, often butchering the rebels after they had surrendered. Within six weeks, it was all over. Perhaps 50,000

How the Irish loyalists were massacred into martyrdom at Wexford Bridge during the unsuccessful Rising of 1798.

had died, giving birth in the process to countless ballads commemorating the heroism of a small nation's struggle for freedom. Slowly, the notion of an Irish patriotism independent of England's fortunes was taking root.

Napoleon Bonaparte, pressed by Wolfe Tone not to abandon French support for Ireland, belatedly agreed to another expedition, which set sail that August. But again the French had been misinformed. When one party landed at Killala, County Mayo, having been led to expect enthusiastic, disciplined battalions, they found instead supporters whom they could at best regard as rapacious simpletons. They issued rifles, only to find the Irish using them to take pot-shots at ravens. The more charitable French concluded that the harsh struggle for survival had turned the Irish into a nation of individualists rather than well-trained soldiers.

Tone landed with another party at Donegal, was captured and died in prison after an attempted suicide. His martyrdom was assured, but the French declaration of an Irish republic was as insubstantial as so many other Irish dreams before and since.

Pitt's exasperated response was to propose a full union between Britain and Ireland. The 300-seat Irish parliament in Dublin would be abolished and 100 seats for Irish representatives would be created within the Imperial Parliament in London. Englishman, Irishman, Welshman and Scot would therefore, in theory, be treated equally. Opinion in Ireland was split, less on any patriotic principles than on cool appraisals of individual self-interest and economic prospects. But London's mind was made up and soon those wavering found themselves offered peerages, offices of state and even outright bribes (of as much as £4,000, a scarcely resistible sum).

It was political wheeler-dealing on an ambitious scale, and it worked. Within a year a majority of five voting *against* the union had been turned into a majority of 46 voting *for* it. Ireland's parliament had abolished itself.

On Jan. 1, 1801, with all the pomp and circumstance that attend such occasions, Britain and Ireland entered, in Pitt's phrase, their "voluntary association" within the Empire with "equal laws, reciprocal affection, and inseparable interests." As with most marriages, the intentions were good. Certainly, no one present on that day early in a promising new century could have imagined the terrible suffering that lay ahead.

DANIEL O'CONNELL, ESQr.

"Painted by J Haverty, Esqr. for the late Catholic Association of Ireland."

Engraved by J.W. Cook.

None of Ireland's basic problems had been solved by the union. The peasants who worked the land still had no rights to it and no alternative employment had been created. They, therefore, did not applaud or even notice the new arrangement and agrarian disturbances continued, in the historian Lecky's phrase, "like the passing storms that sweep so rapidly over the inconstant Irish sky."

This was the situation that Robert Emmet found when he returned from France in 1802 after the Peace of Amiens had ended hostilities between Britain and France. Emmet, a Protestant doctor's son, had been much influenced by the United Irishmen and concocted a plan to seize Dublin Castle, the seat of Britain's administrative power in Ireland, in July 1803.

The rebellion, like so many others, misfired. For one thing, Emmet had kept it such a well-guarded secret that too few supporters knew it was happening; for another, the last-minute organization deteriorated into a comic opera of incompetence, with fuses for grenades being mislaid and only one scaling ladder being completed. Thirty people died in fitful rioting and Emmet, soon captured, was sentenced to be hanged, drawn and quartered.

It could have ended there, but for the condemned man's speech from the dock. "Let no man write my epitaph," said Emmet. "When my country takes her place among the nations of the earth, then and not till then let my epitaph be written." His last wish was granted more than a century later when Padraic Pearse, a leader of the 1916 Easter Rising that led to Ireland's eventual break with Britain, said of Emmet's death: "It is the memory of a sacrifice Christ-like in its perfection."

A more democratic approach was taken by Daniel O'Connell, a Catholic lawyer from a well-off Kerry family. Like many of his contemporaries, he had been educated in France and the ideals of the French Revolution had entered his thinking. He wanted no revolution in Ireland, though, not even a separation from the British

Crown. What he campaigned for, with powerful oratory, was the right of Catholics to become Members of Parliament. Soon landlords were alarmed by the success of O'Connell's Catholic Association, particularly when its leader, standing for parliament in 1828 as a "Man of the People", had an overwhelming victory. Sir Robert Peel, Britain's prime minister, was forced to introduce a Catholic Emancipation Bill, which was passed.

Once in the House of Commons, O'Connell, by now "the uncrowned king of Ire-

land," began to rally support for his next cause: a repeal of the union. When his appeals struck few chords in parliament, he took his arguments to his fellow countrymen, holding monster rallies throughout Ireland. At one meeting attended by 300,000 people at Tuam, a Union Jack flew from the cathedral spire to underline O'Connell's insistence that Ireland did not wish to relinquish its loyalty to either King or Empire but merely sought the right to run its own internal affairs.

There must be no violence, he told the crowds—and yet his vocabulary was so warlike that Peel's Conservative government might well have concluded that only O'Connell was preventing imminent civil

Left, Daniel O'Connell forcefully took the demand for Irish independence to Britain's parliament. Right, absentee landlords continued to evict the poor who didn't keep up with their rents.

war. Instead, believing he might be bluffing, they banned a rally at Clontarf, site of an ancient victory over the Danes by the warrior king Brian Ború. O'Connell backed down and was locked up for a short time on a sedition charge. Then, as he was regrouping his forces for another assault on the Union, fate intervened.

Ireland's greatest disaster: The Great Famine that began in 1845 wasn't a true famine at all; rather a failure of the potato crop. At its height, wheat and barley were being freely shipped to England, together with tens of thousands of cattle, sheep and pigs. But such produce was beyond the pockets of the peasants, whose every penny went towards paying rent to the series of middlemen—often as many as seven—

The crop failed again and a Mayo curate wrote of the people's plight: "They are to be found in thousands, young and old, male and female, crawling in the streets and on the highways, screaming for a morsel of food." Some ate seaweed. Instances were reported of mothers eating flesh from their dead babies. The *Mayo Constitution* reported: "The streets of every town in the country are overrun by stalking skeletons." And, all the while, food exports to England remained buoyant.

England's refusal to provide relief is regarded today as a horrifying failure of imagination, one of the worst in its colonial history. Even compassionate and otherwise enlightened men lacked the vision to question the wisdom of the pre-

who stood between them and their land's ultimate owner. All they could afford was the humble potato. When it was blighted, they starved.

Twenty years before the famine, the novelist Sir Walter Scott had written of the Irish peasantry: "Their poverty has not been exaggerated: it is on the extreme verge of human misery." And, as their numbers grew—the population doubled to 8 million between 1800 and 1840—so their misery deepened. Evictions began as the first potato crop's failure left tenants unable to pay their rents. An English MP described one large-scale eviction as "the chasing away of 700 human beings like crows out of a cornfield."

vailing economic orthodoxy, the rigid belief that it would make matters even worse to interfere with natural economic forces. The same principle was applied to the industrial working classes in England's factories, but their lot was less desperate than that of the Irish peasants.

A million people died in the Great Hunger and well over a million set off in squalid emigrant ships for a new life in America, where they would pass down to future generations a deep anti-British resentment. Around a third of the land in

Left, interior of a 19th Century peasant's cottage. Right, police open fire at Tallaght, near Dublin, during the Fenian insurrection.

Ireland changed hands as estates went bankrupt, but the new landlords, who were mostly Irish (of both religions, now that Catholics were allowed to buy land) were even harsher than their predecessors in increasing rents. O'Connell's talk of non-violent nationalism seemed quite irrelevant and a group of his middle-class supporters broke away to form the Young Ireland movement, which was prepared to use the threat of violence. O'Connell himself died in 1847, aged 71, his dreams shattered.

In 1848, a year which saw nationalist uprisings in several countries of Europe, an attempted rising in Kilkenny was easily put down; it was the usual bungled fiasco, with little support from a weakened popu-gle: "By consistent oppression they have been artificially converted into an utterly demoralized nation and now fulfil the notorious function of supplying England, America, Australia, etc with prostitutes, casual labourers, pimps, thieves, swindlers, beggars and other rabble."

That same year, James Stephens, a Kilkenny railway engineer, came home from France and took what he called his "3,000-mile walk" through south and west Ireland talking of an independent republic. But, failing to interest either the gentry or the tenant farmers, he concluded that perhaps only the labourers could be stirred to revolution. On St. Patrick's Day, March 17, 1858, Stephens founded a society which later came to be known as the Irish Repub-

lace and none at all from the influential priesthood. A few wild plans, like one to kidnap Queen Victoria during her visit to Dublin in 1849, didn't materialize. The Irish genius seemed to be for theatricality, not for effective action. As one disconsolate patriot put it: "God knows, if eloquence could free or save a people, we ought to be the freest and safest people on the face of the globe."

Revolution in the air: Tenant rights were talked about regularly by Irish MPs in the House of Commons, but a few good harvests after 1851 seemed to lessen the urgency. In a letter to Friedrich Engels in 1856, Karl Marx analysed Ireland's downtrodden populace in terms of a class strug-lican Brotherhood, dedicated to the idea of an independent democratic republic and branding its opponents as "ruthless tyrants" and "an alien aristocracy." An American branch was set up, called the Fenians after ancient Gaelic warriors. The American Civil War, Stephens noted, had given his supporters there valuable experience of battle. After a skirmish in Canada, Fenian participants were referred to as "The Irish Republican Army." It was the IRA's first appearance on the world stage.

Stephens was deposed as leader after his failure to organize an army of liberation from the United States, but by 1867 armed and well-drilled bands had been set up throughout Ireland. A rising was planned for that February. The idea was to capture supplies of arms and ammunition from Chester Castle in England and transport them by a hijacked train to a commandeered ferry and so to Ireland. Informers, seldom absent in any of Ireland's nationalist struggles, tipped off the authorities. The rising was aborted.

The next month, an attempted rising in Ireland collapsed after sporadic fighting; again, informers had put paid to its chances. During the fighting, some trains were derailed, marking the arrival in the country of a strategy that would shape Ireland's stuggles until the present day: guerrilla warfare. A ship, *Erin's Hope*, sailed from New York carrying much needed modern rifles and ammunition, but it

Londoners and maimed 30.

Ambition and arrogance: But it was not terrorism that was to further Ireland's cause most at this time. The two principal engines of change were driven by William Ewart Gladstone, who came to power as Britain's prime minister in 1868, and Charles Stewart Parnell, a tall, bearded, English-educated Protestant landowner from County Wicklow.

Gladstone's approach was far removed from the indifference of his predecessors. "My mission," he said, "is to pacify Ireland." He began in 1869 by removing one chronic grievance. Since the Reformation, the Protestant church had been the established church in Ireland, although it represented only a sixth of the popu-

reached Ireland too late and nobody could be found to receive the consignment. Yet another fiasco was chalked up, but yet another myth was made.

The same year, too, England learned for the first time what it meant to have Ireland's grievances brought to its own doorstep. A prison van carrying two captured revolutionary leaders was ambushed near Manchester, a police sergeant being shot dead in the raid. When three of the rescuers were caught and sentenced to death, an emotional appeal from the dock about the nobility of their cause transformed them into martyrs. Soon afterwards, an explosion meant to spring other Irishmen from Clerkenwell prison in London killed 12

lation. Gladstone abolished this privileged position. Next, he introduced a Land Bill designed to make it less easy for landlords to evict tenants. Sensing new hope, nationalists began to demand once more that Ireland should have its own parliament to administer Irish affairs, leaving international matters to the Imperial parliament in London. This aspiration became known as Home Rule.

Parnell, the product of an Irish father and an American mother, possessed an ar-

Above, two great opponents in the London parliament, William Ewart Gladstone (left) and Charles Stewart Parnell. Right, the Land League committee meets in Dublin.

rogant personality and a political pragmatism that enabled him to take on even Gladstone without the slightest sense of inferiority. Once in the House of Commons in 1875, he scorned its cozy, club-like conventions and perfected filibustering techniques for blocking parliamentary business: proposing endless amendments, for instance, and making speeches lasting several hours. In one case, he forced an infuriated House into a continuous 41-hour session. He had reason for concern about Ireland. After several relatively good harvests, 1877's summer was wet and a flood of cheap grain carried from America by the new fast steamships was lowering prices to a point where tenants could no longer afford their rents. A new wave of

were held. Funds from America flowed in to help the victims of oppression and threats of violence, frequently carried out, gave teeth to the Land League. In parliament, Parnell officially deplored the violence, and one Irish MP condemned the practice of shooting landlords because the gunmen often missed and hit the wrong person. At home the agitators gained some invaluable allies: the Catholic priesthood, which had previously stood aside from nationalist movements. Soon no-go areas were established within which justice was in the hands of the Land League. An effective technique was to ostracize anyone who took over an evicted man's land; it was applied so successfully to a Captain Boycott in County Mayo that his surname

evictions was threatened. With Michael Davitt, Parnell set up the National Land League of Ireland.

Davitt's parents, evicted from their Mayo landholding in 1852 when he was five, had emigrated to Lancashire in England, where Davitt lost an arm in a factory accident when he was 11. By the time he returned to Ireland, he had embraced Fenianism, completed a term of penal servitude, and was convinced that the only hope for tenants was to have rents reduced by law to a realistic level and then to devise a scheme enabling them gradually to own their own land.

The fate of Captain Boycott: Once again, across Ireland, massive demonstrations

entered the English language.

Gladstone's 1881 Land Act was regarded as revolutionary. It granted fixity of tenure to tenants who paid their rent; laid down that a tenant should be paid when he vacated a holding for improvements he had made; and decreed that fair rents should be defined not by the landlord but by a Land Court. Parnell didn't obstruct the Act since it was a lifeline to the peasantry; but, to placate those in Ireland and in America campaigning hard for independence, he felt compelled to denounce the government for the inadequacy of its measures. So forceful were his denunciations that the government responded by throwing him in jail and suppressing the Land League.

Even so, he might have negotiated useful progress with the government if Lord Frederick Cavendish, the new Chief Secretary for Ireland and Gladstone's nephew by marriage, hadn't been knifed to death in Dublin. Reform slid down the agenda.

When freed, Parnell founded the Irish National League to campaign uncompromisingly for Home Rule. A general election in 1885 gave him control of 85 of the 103 Irish seats in the House of Commons and ensured that he held the balance of power between Gladstone's Liberals and Lord Salisbury's Conservatives. Suddenly, Home Rule became the main issue in English politics.

The Conservatives found it hard to regard Home Rule as anything other than the

thin end of the wedge of full independence. After all, they argued, Home Rule would still leave the Imperial parliament controlling international affairs, war and peace, even customs and excise. How could any Irishman be satisfied with that? And yet the writings of the time show that most educated Irishmen, including nationalists, were happy to remain within the British Empire. All that self-respect required was that they should control their domestic affairs. Had Home Rule been granted in 1886, therefore, Ireland might well still be part of the United Kingdom, having "a distinct but not separate identity" rather like Wales and Scotland. It is one of the big "ifs" of Irish history.

Ulster goes on the alert: But one significant group would have hotly opposed such an outcome. A million Protestants still lived in Ireland, almost half of them in the northeast area of Ulster, and Home Rule would have severely limited the power of this influential minority. These Ulstermen saw themselves as different, as indeed they were. Their Presbyterian tradition had always been more radical than the loose Protestantism of their southern co-religionists and had given them a formidable self-reliance. Although security of tenure had always been greater for Ireland, the Protestant descendants of the 17th Century Scots settlers felt far from settled; they had retained an ineradicable tribal fear of being dispossessed of their lands by the Catholics.

What's more, they had a lot to lose. England's Industrial Revolution, which had been stopped from spreading to most of Ireland by trade restrictions, had taken root in Ulster. The linen industry, permitted to flourish because there was no equivalent industry for it to compete with in England, had brought prosperity to Belfast, whose population mushroomed from 20,000 to 100,000 between 1800 and 1850. Then, in the 1850s, shipbuilding became a major employer. In those few years, Belfast was permanently differentiated from Dublin. Some saw the city as a New Jerusalem created largely by jerry-builders; others regarded it as an outpost of industrial Britain. Not surprisingly, the northern Protestants saw their prosperity being threatened by anyone who wanted to weaken the link with England.

This uncertainty was a tonic to the Orange Order, whose belligerent cry of "No Popery, No Surrender" succinctly defined, and still defines, its attitude. Leaders such as the Earl of Enniskillen gave the movement a veneer of respectability, but signs of the Orangemen's violent origins weren't hard to find. Lord Randolph Churchill ringingly reassured the northern Protestants on behalf of the Conservatives that, if Home Rule were imposed, "Ulster would fight, and Ulster would be right." But the first Home Rule Bill was voted down in 1886.

England's values, so precious to the Orangemen, were being rejected in the south. A literary revival was growing, creating a

Left, Orangemen opposing Home Rule march to Belfast's City hall in 1886. Right, a cartoon for the humorous magazine _Punch_ pokes fun at the burgeoning arms trade.

YOUNG IRELAND IN BUSINESS FOR HIMSELF.

new appreciation of Celtic culture and myths and a new respect for the Irish language, hitherto regarded as a fast-dying vulgar tongue. W.B. Yeats, the son of a Protestant Irish artist, published collections of folk tales such as *The Celtic Twilight,* conferring a new dignity on the often ridiculed Irish peasantry. A Gaelic League was set up, declaring itself the archer that would slay the plundering crow of the English mind, its arrow being the Irish language. It was time, said the League, for the Irishman to stop being a "West Briton."

In the political arena, however, there were setbacks. Parnell lost political support when the scandal of his long-time affair with Kitty O'Shea, who had borne him three children, erupted in 1889. Her

husband, Captain Willie O'Shea, Home Rule MP for County Clare, finally sued for divorce and gave Gladstone the opportunity to force the Irish Party into rejecting Parnell as leader. Parnell died two years later, after being soaked with rain at a political rally in Galway. Gladstone himself retired from the scene in 1893, aged 84, having failed to get his second Home Rule Bill, which had been approved narrowly by the House of Commons, through the Upper Chamber, the House of Lords. It was time for the baton of the Irish cause to pass to a new generation.

New forces gather strength: As the 20th Century dawned, a Conservative government in England held out no hope of

Home Rule. Queen Victoria's visit to Dublin in 1900 and Edward VII's in 1903 were well received, but new forces of nationalism were being assembled by Arthur Griffith, a Dublin printer and journalist, and John McBride, a Mayo-born republican who had fought against the British in South Africa's Boer War. Griffith and McBride demanded not independence tied with some golden link to Britain but "an Irish Republic One and Indivisible."

Two general elections in Britain in 1910 left the Liberals and Conservatives almost equally split in parliament. Once again the Irish Party, now led by the moderate John Redmond, used its balance of power to press for a new Home Rule Bill. By this time the House of Lords had lost its power to veto any House of Commons business for more than two successive parliamentary sessions; therefore the Home Rule Bill introduced in 1912 by prime minister Herbert Asquith was bound to become law in time if passed by the Commons.

The Protestants in Ulster, realizing this real danger, began arming themselves. They found as leader a Dublin MP and brilliant lawyer, Sir Edward Carson, who had been Solicitor General in a Conservative government and who had earlier acted as prosecuting counsel against Oscar Wilde in the writer's celebrated homosexuality trial. What, asked Carson, was the point of Home Rule now that most Irishmen owned their farms, all major grievances had been removed, and even a Catholic university had been set up?

More than 440,000 Ulster men and women signed declarations, many in their own blood, that they would not recognize the authority of a Home Rule parliament. In 1913 recruiting started for a 100,000-strong Ulster Volunteer Force and large consignments of rifles began arriving in the country. "This place is an armed camp," said Carson. The southerners responded by setting up a counter-force, the Irish National Volunteers, whose badge carried the Letters "FF," for Fianna Fáil, a legendary band of warriors. The problem, then as now, could be simply stated. The Protestant majority in the northeast of Ireland wished to remain full British subjects and were prepared to fight Britain to retain that status. The Catholic minority in the area, like the Catholic majority in the rest

Left, Sir Edward Carson, a Dubliner, rallies Protestant Ulstermen against Home Rule. Right, British guard at an entrance to Dublin's Four Courts during the 1916 Easter Rising.

of the island, sought a more Irish identity. The two attitudes appeared irreconcilable.

Sir Winston Churchill, then a Liberal Minister, was first to voice publicly one possible solution. Six of the ancient province of Ulster's nine counties—those most heavily settled by Protestants during the early 1600s—might be excluded from any Home Rule settlement. Redmond, under pressure to get results, conceded that these six counties could *temporarily* be excluded for six years, after which time he hoped the Ulster Unionists would see the wisdom of rejoining their fellow Irishmen. From the nationalists' point of view, it was a fatal concession.

The Great War intervenes: Larger problems than Ireland loomed for Britain in 1914 with the outbreak of World War One. A deal was rapidly done under which a Home Rule Act was passed, together with an order suspending its operation for the duration of the war or until such time as an amendment could be added to take account of Ulster's concerns. Ireland was thus bought off, to the extent that a greater proportion of Irishmen volunteered for the British army than any other part of the United Kingdom's population. Irishmen won 17 Victoria Crosses in the first 13 months of the war. Surely, Redmond reasoned, such courage would eradicate even Ulster Unionist worries.

The reality was different. Carson, now a member of Britain's war Cabinet, saw the Ulster regiments' heavy losses in the war, particularly during the Battle of the Somme in 1916, as a subscription towards permanent membership of the United Kingdom. In Ireland, many still remembered the old adage that England's misfortune is Ireland's opportunity, and nationalists led by Arthur Griffith began grouping under the broad banner of Sinn Féin (pronounced *shin fayne* and meaning, self-reliantly, "We Ourselves").

James Connolly, a tough-minded labour organizer born into a poor Irish family in Scotland in 1868 and a soldier in the British army at the age of 14, had embraced socialist thinking, setting up an Irish Citizens Army to defend striking workers against brutal police suppression. Padraic Pearse, a shy and austere schoolmaster, had developed a mystical belief that bloodshed was necessary to cleanse Ireland, as Jesus Christ, by shedding his blood, had redeemed mankind. Philosophy and physical force came together on the sunny spring holiday morning of Monday, April 24, 1916.

As Pearse, commander of the patriots determined to liberate Ireland, set out to march down Dublin's Sackville Street, his sister pleaded with him to "Come home, Pat, and leave all this foolishness." Most Irish people would probably have echoed her sentiments if they'd had an inkling of the ambitions of the small band of unrepresentative middle-class intellectuals behind the Easter Rising. But Pearse proceeded and, with 150 others, armed with a variety of venerable rifles and agricultural implements, took over the city's General Post Office and solemnly read out, to the apathy of bystanders, the proclamation of the new Irish Republic.

Another 800 or so civilian soldiers took over a brewery, a biscuit factory, a lunatic

asylum and other key points. Eamon de Valera, a young mathematics teacher born in America of an Irish mother and a Spanish father, liberated a bakery against the wishes of its workers, who had felt that even in a republic people had to eat.

Bitter splits in the ranks: As usual in Irish politics, dissension among the rebel components was rife. The vigilante Irish Volunteers regarded the rival Irish Republican Brotherhood as Sunday soldiers. Yet it was a handful of men from the IRB military council who, usurping power from the majority, secretly planned the Easter Rising. Eoin MacNeill, president of the Irish Volunteers, vowed to do everything he could, short of informing the

British, to stop the revolt, considering it to be "rampant neurotic romanticism." He cancelled "manoeuvres" which Pearse had announced for the Easter Sunday and the Rising had to be postponed for a day until Pearse countermanded the instruction. The resulting chaos meant that only in Dublin was it possible to organize anything, and even there only 800 of a hoped-for 3,000 soldiers showed up.

Soon Dublin ground to a halt. Alarm and rumours spread. The poor looted stores and children ransacked sweetshops. A British gunboat on the River Liffey began to shell the rebel strongholds. It all seemed a bit unreal. On the Wednesday an inexperienced "soldier" asked for permission to leave the GPO because the Easter holidays were over and he wanted to get back to his regular job. The British were baffled, as were most Dubliners. A quarter of a million Irishmen were fighting in France at the time, and Dublin housewives, regarding the rebellion as treachery and madness, made tea for the troops sent in to quell it.

The inevitable end, when it came, was swift. The British set fire to the area around the GPO, burning out the rebels. By the time Pearse surrendered on the Saturday, 64 rebels, 134 police and soldiers and at least 220 civilians had been killed. The centre of Dublin lay in ruins. Martial law was imposed and 4,000 jailed.

"So far the feeling of the population in Dublin is against the Sinn Féiners," one leading Irish MP wrote to his party leader, Redmond. "But a reaction might very easily be created." He then added the prophetic words: "Do not fail to urge the government not to execute any of the prisoners." But Redmond's urgings went unheeded and on May 3 the first three leaders, including Pearse, were shot at dawn. The next day, four more were shot. On May 5, one more. On May 8, four more. On May 12, two more—including Connolly, who, because a bullet during the fighting had fractured his ankle, sat in a chair before the firing squad. Nobody knew how long the executions would go on. It was, someone said later, "like watching a stream of blood coming from beneath a closed door." Slowly, in Ireland, derision for the upstarts turned to sympathy, then support. As Yeats wrote in a famous poem, the rebels had been "changed, changed utterly. A terrible beauty is born."

That Christmas, as a goodwill gesture, David Lloyd George, the "Welsh wizard" who was now Britain's charismatic prime minister, released 560 Irish internees from prison in England. Among them were Arthur Griffith, Sinn Féin's founder, and a 27-year-old west Cork man, Michael Collins, formerly a clerk in London with the British civil service. Another batch of prisoners given an amnesty at Easter 1917 included Eamon de Valera, the sole surviving Easter Rising commandant. The cast was in place for the climactic act of Ireland's drama.

The hunger strikes begin: The new men wrote a script which was to be revived with uncanny fidelity in the 1970s and 1980s. They opposed Redmond's party at by-elections with Sinn Féin candidates, who began winning. Jailed supporters, on having their demand to be recognized as political prisoners turned down by the authorities, staged hunger strikes. When one striker died after being force-fed, Collins organized a show funeral, massively attended. Arms were stockpiled. Lawlessness reminiscent of the 18th Century started spreading in rural areas. By the time Redmond died (of natural causes) in March 1918, his hopes of achieving Ireland's independence peaceably had turned to dust.

The next month, panicked by a setback in the war in France, Britain finally extended conscription to Ireland, throwing in as a sop new Home Rule Legislation based on partitioning the island. It was a foolish move. The Catholic Church's hierarchy condemned conscription—which turned out to be unnecessary anyway, as the war was soon to end. The Irish Party walked out of the House of Commons, abandoning democratic attempts to achieve their cause. Sinn Féin had found a rallying cry, which it put to effective use, winning sweeping victories in the postwar general election of December 1918.

The new MPs boycotted the House of Commons forming their own parliament, Dáil Eireann, in Dublin's Mansion House. As president of their new "republic," they elected de Valera; the fact that he was in jail at the time was probably worth an extra vote or two.

Standing behind Sinn Féin were the Volunteers, known in the countryside as the Irish Republican Army, who increasingly saw violence as an effective weapon. They began killing anyone in uniform who stood in their way, then progressed to selective assassinations. Like so many Irish conflicts, this one rapidly took on some of the characteristics of a civil war. The corpses found labelled "Spy—Killed by IRA" were usually those of Irishmen. Women found wandering along a country road with their heads shaved were Irishwomen accused of consorting with policemen or soldiers. After an attempt was made in broad daylight on the life of the king's representative in Ireland, the Viceroy, England, perplexed as ever, suppressed Sinn Féin. "The English government in Ireland," jeered Arthur Griffith, "has now proclaimed the Irish nation, as it formerly proclaimed the Catholic Church, an illegal assembly." Undeterred, Sinn Féin did well in January 1920's municipal elections.

When some of the boycotted police force —about one in 10—resigned, they were replaced by recruits from England, many of them demobilized soldiers hardened to

laws. The government, with 10,000 police and 50,000 troops, was humiliated.

An eye for an eye: Before long, the police began fighting back, carrying out undisciplined reprisals after every IRA atrocity. On Nov. 21, 1920, "Bloody Sunday," Michael Collins had 12 British officers shot dead, mostly in their beds. That afternoon, at a Gaelic football match in Dublin's Croke Park, police shot dead 12 civilians. In the countryside, fearful families took to sleeping in hedgerows to escape the revenge killings. Guerrilla warfare spread, out of control.

In May 1921 Britain tried out a new idea, holding elections for two Irish parliaments, one in the North, one in the South. Sinn Féin swept the board in the South

killing on the battlefields of France. Because there weren't enough new uniforms to go round, some wore khaki trousers with their dark jackets, thus earning the nickname, soon to be feared, of "Black and Tans." Forming motorized anti-terrorist squads, they hit back quickly at any sign of trouble. But there were areas into which even they dared not go. In these, policing was taken over by the trench-coated Volunteers, who arrested and sentenced petty criminals such as house breakers and cattle stealers and enforced licensing

Ireland's independence did not end the bloodshed on the streets of Dublin but led instead to an all-out civil war.

and the Unionists dominated the North. Partition appeared inevitable. That October, a conference was called in London at which Britain and Ireland, faced with the prospect of declaring war on each other, sat down to thrash out a settlement. The compromises were agonizing. But on Dec. 5, 1921, at 2.20 in the morning, a deal was done, a document signed. It was the first fissure, signalling the eventual break-up of the British Empire.

To those present, however, the significance was somewhat narrower. Eight centuries of attempts by England's monarchs and ministers to rule their neighbouring island had, with surprising abruptness, come to an end.

LIVING WITH PARTITION

To David Lloyd George's dexterous political mind, the fact that the Anglo-Irish Treaty gave everyone *something* they wanted but nobody *everything* they wanted meant that it must stand some chance of success. This was the old mistake: the belief that the Irish were really Englishmen with brogues. In reality, the two peoples' expectations were quite different and, after eight centuries during which Irishman had fought Irishman over conflicting national allegiances, the first fruit of independence was true civil war.

The treaty gave the nationalists more than many had expected: an Irish Free State with a dominion status within the British Empire similar to Canada's. This was far greater freedom than Home Rule had ever promised. But one dark cloud cast a shadow over the deal. Six counties of Ulster—Antrim, Down, Tyrone, Fermanagh, Armagh and Derry—were retained within the United Kingdom, the British having recognized that even the deluge of a world war had not softened the resolution of the northern Protestants. Sir Winston Churchill expressed the dilemma graphically in the House of Commons: "As the deluge subsides and the waters fall short, we see the dreary steeples of Fermanagh and Tyrone emerging once again. The integrity of their quarrel is one of the few institutions that has been unaltered in the cataclysm which has swept the world."

To sell the long-resisted division of Ireland to nationalists, the government added a proviso: a Boundary Commission would decide which Roman Catholic-dominated areas of Northern Ireland would later be incorporated within the 26 counties of the Free State. Because of this stipulation, patriots such as Michael Collins had been prepared to swallow the bitter pill of partition: after the Catholic areas of Tyrone, Fermanagh and south Armagh had been removed, they reckoned, what would remain would not leave the new northeastern state a viable entity.

But Collins's hopes, faint though they were, were not universally held. Ferocious

arguments split the infant Free State, with long suppressed personal animosities coming out into the open. On the one side stood the pro-Treaty provisional government led by Arthur Griffith; on the other, the anti-Treaty forces massing behind Eamon de Valera. After a bitter 12-day parliamentary debate, the Treaty was carried by 64 votes to 57.

It was too narrow a margin to ensure peace, especially since the Irish Republican Army, mirroring the split in the country, was marching in opposite directions: about half with Collins, transforming itself into the regular army of the Free State, and the other half swearing its refusal to recognize the new government. Force had taken them to the conference table, the dissenting gunmen reasoned, and force would win them a free and united Ireland.

A fight to the death: By 1922 Dublin's O'Connell Street was in flames again, with 60 dying in eight days of savage fighting. The Free State government, in its first six months, executed 77 Republicans—far more than had been shot by the British in the preceding Anglo-Irish War. Northern Protestants, watching the struggle, vowed to have nothing to do with any redrawing of borders, declaring: "What we have, we

Left, Eamon de Valera, the Easter Rising revolutionary who was to become Ireland's leader of several decades. Right, the new nation looked to the Gaelic language in its search for a new identity.

hold." Fighting broke out in Northern Ireland, too, with the death toll rising to 264 within six months.

The new Ireland's first prime minister did not live to see the end of the struggle: in August 1922, heavily overworked, Griffith collapsed and died. Collins had a more violent end, being shot dead in an ambush on the Macroom to Bandon road in his native County Cork. He had been expecting just such an outcome: after putting his name to the Anglo-Irish Treaty, he had written to a friend: "Will anyone be satisfied with the bargain? Will anyone? I tell you this—early this morning I signed my death warrant."

When the Boundary Commission reported, it recommended only minor ad-

entered parliament (the Dáil) at the head of Fianna Fáil. He came to power in the 1933 election, ushering in a new era of pious respectability and vowing to reinstate the ancient Gaelic language and culture. "No longer," declared de Valera, "shall our children, like our cattle, be brought up for export." His vision was later spelt out in a famous St. Patrick's Day address, in which he described his ideal Ireland as "a land whose countryside would be bright with cozy homesteads, whose fields and villages would be joyous with the sounds of industry, with the rompings of sturdy children, the contests of athletic youths and the laughter of comely maidens, whose firesides would be forums for the wisdom of serene old age."

justments, and even these were never implemented. De Valera's view of the border as "an old fortress of crumbled masonry, held together with the plaster of fiction" had proved false. Permanent partition had arrived.

The civil war ended in 1923 with de Valera's effective surrender. But it was to dominate every aspect of political life in the Free State for the next half century. The country's two main political parties today, Fine Gael (meaning *Tribe of Ireland*) and Fianna Fáil (*Warriors of Ireland*) are direct descendants of the pro- and anti-Treaty forces.

In 1927, de Valera, seeing no further advantage in remaining outside the system,

It was a noble enough aim. It just didn't particularly belong to the 20th Century.

"Dev," as he became affectionately known, pursued a policy of economic nationalism, raising tariff barriers against England, which retaliated. A tax was even imposed on English newspapers. Yet not everyone was thrilled when, for example, Dev announced that Ireland was self-sufficient in shoelaces. Emigration, mainly to England and America, claimed yet another generation of younger sons unable to in-

Left, a man gathering turf in the agriculturally oriented Republic of Ireland. Right, Stormont, symbol of power in the new British-ruled Northern Ireland.

44

herit the family farm and younger daughters unable to find husbands. In the early 1920s, an astonishing 43 per cent of Irish-born men and women were living abroad. At the opposite end of the social scale from the farmhands, the once affluent Anglo-Irish—the Protestant "Ascendancy"—fell into decline and their "Big Houses" at the end of long, tree-lined avenues began to look dilapidated.

Treading a narrow path: Increasingly, southerners began to question the wisdom of following their leader's "Small is Beautiful" signposts. "It was indeed hard," one commentator recalled later, "to muster up enthusiasm for the cargeen moss industry, in the possible utilization of the various parts of the herring's anatomy,

by Catholic ideas and by Catholic ideas alone, you will never get the North," said Yeats. "You will put a wedge into the midst of this nation."

Thanks to the new constitution, a curious equilibrium was achieved. The priests in the South and the Orangemen in the North each exercised a sectarian and politically conservative pressure on their respective parliaments.

Although the Unionists would have been happy to remain an integral part of Britain, Lloyd George, emphasizing Ulster's "otherness," had given them their own parliament, Stormont—built on the outskirts of Belfast in the style of Buckingham Palace, only grander. And they had lost no time in making their makeshift

down to the tail and the fin, in portable, prefabricated factories themselves made of herringbone cement along the west coast." But what was the alternative?

Certainly not to imitate the United Kingdom, Dev insisted, and, to emphasize the point, he produced a constitution in 1937 which abolished the oath of allegiance to England's king and claimed sovereignty over all 32 counties of Ireland. But it also underlined the pervasive influence of the Roman Catholic Church, thus alienating northern Protestants for good. The poet Yeats, a member of the Irish Senate, had warned him of the dangers. "If you show that this country, Southern Ireland, is going to be governed

state impregnable. London, relieved to be rid of the perennial Irish problem, did nothing to stop them. Nor, fatally, did the Roman Catholics' elected representatives, who boycotted Stormont. The assembly, the Unionists boasted, was "a Protestant parliament for a Protestant people." The historic hatreds between Protestant and Catholic communities were left unhealed.

If anything, they were deepened. Taking advantage of the nationalists' boycott, the Unionists made sure that the plum jobs and the best housing went to their own supporters. Two distinct communities developed: Protestant dentists pulled Protestant teeth, Catholic plumbers mended Catholic pipes. When hunger marches by the unemployed during the 1930s Depression showed signs of uniting Protestant and Catholic workers, rabble-rousing leaders were quick to encourage them back towards sectarian strife. An all-Protestant part-time special constabulary (the "B" Specials) maintained close links with the Orange Order and helped the police keep dissension under control. The IRA, making little headway in Ulster, began a campaign in English cities in 1938, setting off suitcase bombs.

Neutrality at all costs: While Irish history was repeating itself, European history concocted another world war. The Unionists felt their self-interest had been justified when, as soon as Britain declared war on Germany in 1939, de Valera announced that Southern Ireland would remain neutral. Behind the scenes, Sir Winston Churchill, Britain's new wartime leader, offered de Valera a united Ireland at some point in the future if Ireland were to enter the war and allow the British navy to use its ports. But de Valera, convinced that neutrality would finally establish Ireland's identity as an independent nation, said no. All the same, 50,000 southern Irishmen volunteered to join the British forces.

Churchill's fears had not been unfounded. The Germans had been planning an invasion of Ireland, "Operation Green," as a springboard to an assault on Britain. In a handbook designed to brief their battalions, they noted that "the Irishman supports a community founded upon equality for all, but associates with this an extraordinary personal need for independence which easily leads to indiscipline and pugnacity."

Northern Ireland didn't escape German bombing. In one ferocious night raid on Belfast in April 1941, more than 700 people were killed. The Unionists claimed that the neutral South's lack of a blackout helped German bombers pinpoint their targets in the darkened North. Another grudge was chalked up on the blackboard of Irish history.

Over the years even the name of the Free State had been fiercely argued about. Both the English and the Irish seemed to find "Eire" (Gaelic for "Ireland") acceptable. But in 1948 a coalition government under J. A. Costello fixed the name of the country as the Republic of Ireland. Britain declared that, as a result, Ireland was no longer a member of the Commonwealth. At last, Ireland—or at least 26 counties of it—was truly free.

Politically free, at least. Economically

and culturally, Ireland remained chained. A commission set up in 1948 to investigate emigration, by now reaching epidemic proportions, reported: "We were impressed by the unanimity of the views presented to us in evidence on the relative loneliness, dullness and generally unattractive nature of life in many parts of rural Ireland at present." Censorship was alive and kicking, too. In 1954 a record 1,034 books were banned, and cinemagoers, if they wished to follow the plots of many films, had to travel to Northern Ireland to see the unscissored versions. London's more lurid Sunday newspapers published special Irish editions, substituting folksy local stories for tales of libidinous clergymen.

Northern Protestants looked askance at what they saw as the southern state's unacceptable intrusion into personal freedoms—its outlawing of divorce, for example, and its ban on the importation of contraceptives. Northern Ireland, Britain had pledged when the Republic left the Commonwealth, could remain part of the United Kingdom as long as a majority of its people wished. Since Protestants outnumbered Catholics by two to one in the Six Counties, that might mean forever.

Some Protestants were so fervently "loyalist" that they would never set foot in the alien republic. But others, suffering under Britain's postwar rationing, regularly caught a train across the border to buy coveted items such as bacon and new shoes. Before long, however, it was southerners who were climbing on board the "Smuggler's Express." As Britain rebuilt its economic strength in the 1950s, Northern Ireland began to feel the benefit of its welfare state and industrial incentives, while the Republic remained essentially a humdrum peasant economy.

The green consumers: In 1958, under the premiership of Sean Lemass, Ireland decided to rejoin the 20th Century. He set out vigorously to create new jobs by opening up the economy to foreign investment, attracting light engineering, pharmaceutical and electronics companies. The dream of Eamon de Valera—who was now president, a largely symbolic office—faded fast. Interest in Gaelic language and culture waned and the voice of management consultants was heard in the land. The Irish, embracing consumerism with unconcealed relish, seemed destined to become indis-

The Rev. Ian Paisley at a Protestant rally in the 1960s; over the next 20 years he was to become a leading political figure.

tinguishable from the English.

Even the IRA failed to command much support in its continuing fight for a united Ireland. A campaign of border raids between 1956 and 1962 netted a few arms hauls but gradually petered out. By 1965, it seemed the most natural thing in the world for Lemass to have a good-neighbourly meeting with Northern Ireland's premier, Captain Terence O'Neill. But it seemed shockingly unnatural to hardline Unionists. Uncompromising voices, including those of several Cabinet colleagues and a popular fundamentalist preacher, the Reverend Ian Paisley, reminded him that Lemass's Republic still claimed jurisdiction over the Six Counties.

O'Neill, with his upper-class back-

supporters of James II, thus cementing Protestant supremacy. (Nationalists, equally tutored in the city's history, reject its "English" name in favour of the original Derry.)

O'Neill's government, viewing the march not as a civil rights protest but as a nationalist conspiracy, banned it. Two thousand people marched anyway, and were met by the massed forces of the Royal Ulster Constabulary, complete with two mobile water cannon. Television viewers around the world were treated to the ensuing battle, as the RUC took their truncheons to the demonstrators with what looked suspiciously like enthusiasm. "It was as though they had been waiting to do it for 50 years," said a young civil rights

ground, was ill-equipped to cope with the Pandora's Box that was opened just three years later. It began innocently enough, when a Unionist-controlled council in Caledon, County Tyrone, where many Catholic families were badly in need of housing, allocated one of its dwellings to a young, single Protestant girl. Local nationalists, following the example of Blacks in the United States, first staged a sit-in, then a civil rights march. A second march was planned for October 1968, inside the walled city of Londonderry. This is a symbolic place for Unionists, who still commemorate the breaking of the city's siege in 1689 when Protestant supporters of William of Orange defeated Catholic

leader, Bernadette Devlin.

Younger Roman Catholics, better educated through the benefits of Britain's welfare state, were no longer prepared to accept the *status quo*. In January 1969, taking their cue from Martin Luther King, the protesters organized a 70-mile march from Belfast to Londonderry. Four miles from their destination, at Burntollet Bridge, they were ambushed and beaten by a Protestant mob. Later the RUC, a pre-

Above, Bernadette Devlin, a fiery Republican leader. Right: policeman on duty; and three prime ministers (Ulster's Brian Faulkner, Ireland's Jack Lynch and Britain's Edward Heath) stirring the pot in the early 1970s.

dominantly Protestant police force, ran riot in the Bogside, a Catholic housing estate in Londonderry. Residents erected barricades and announced the foundation of "Free Derry."

O'Neill, having seen his dreams for a civilized relationship between the two Irelands consumed by the fires of sectarian hatred, was forced out of office by militant Unionists. His successor, Major James Chichester-Clark, another scion of Ulster's aristocracy, was well-meaning but ineffectual, and the civil unrest worsened daily.

The troops march in: Almost inevitably, the Protestants' annual march through Londonderry in August sparked off violence. Petrol bombs were hurled, along with broken-up paving stones. The police

fearful resurrection: that of the IRA.

As a fighting force, the Irish Republican Army had virtually ceased to exist in 1962. By the late 1960s the declared aim of the small group of Marxists who constituted the rump of the IRA was to overthrow the conservative establishments in both parts of Ireland, then set up an ill-defined workers' republic. Lacking modern weaponry, they were acutely conscious of their failure to protect Catholic communities against Protestant mobs, a failure brought painfully home by graffiti which interpreted IRA as "I Ran Away." After a stormy meeting in the Republic, the movement split into two groups: the Official IRA, who remained committed to traditional nationalist ideals, and the Provisional

replied with CS gas. Fighting spread to the Catholic Falls Road and the Protestant Shankill Road. The RUC, hopelessly out of its depth, appealed for reinforcements and, on Aug. 16, 1969, a reluctant British government sent troops on to the streets of Londonderry and Belfast "in support of the civil power." The die had been cast.

At first the British soldiers were welcomed as saviours. Catholic housewives, many of whom had been preparing to take refuge in the Republic, plied them with endless cups of tea. Girls smiled sweetly at them. Perhaps, it seemed for a moment, all would be well. But it was already too late for such hopes, for this latest chapter of Ireland's Troubles had already caused a

wing, which put its faith in military might.

Recruitment to the Provisionals (or "Provos") soared when the British army embarked on late-night arms searches in Catholic areas. Guns and explosives were found, but the sympathy of moderate Catholics was lost. To keep the two communities from each other's throats, the troops hurriedly erected a ramshackle barrier of building blocks and corrugated iron, known as "the Peace Line." No one dreamed that, 15 years later, the line would have become a permanent concrete and steel fortification, a Berlin Wall within the United Kingdom.

Trust and understanding between nationalists and Unionists have always been difficult because the two cultural traditions have so few points of contact. Protestant children still attend Protestant schools supported entirely by the state, while Catholic children go to schools largely financed by the state but managed by their church. Catholic children are taught Gaelic games, Protestants play cricket. Catholics learn Irish, Protestants don't. Integrating the schools, a policy which might in the long term lessen the inheritance of hate, has proved an impossible nettle to grasp. The Roman Catholic church in particular argues strongly that Catholic children must have the spiritual nourishment of a Catholic education. And, in any case, so few communities remain in which Protestants and Catholics live side by side that in-

chester-Clark's. The last of Ulster's upper-class prime ministers was replaced in 1971 by a pragmatic middle-class politician, Brian Faulkner. By this time, the IRA's armed offensive was gathering pace, spreading terror by means of snipers' bullets, booby-trapped vehicles and bombs placed in crowded bars. In the Catholic ghettos, the initial songs of praise for the army had turned into a ghoulish refrain: "If you kill a British soldier, clap your hands." Protestant vigilante and terrorist groups such as the Ulster Defence Association and the Ulster Volunteer Force began to match violence with violence.

Faulkner, needing results, talked Britain's prime minister, Edward Heath, into introducing internment of suspected ter-

tegrated schools would mean bussing thousands of children back and forward from one area to another.

The Al Capone factor: In the anarchy of the early 1970s, relationships within Ulster were corroded further as shopkeepers in both Catholic and Protestant areas were visited regularly by vigilantes from their own communities demanding what amounted to protection money. Most paid; those who didn't frequently found their premises burned to the ground soon afterwards. Straightforward gangsterism, divorced from any political objective, was added to the witches' brew of Ulster violence.

A head had to roll and it was Major Chi-

rorists without trial—a drastic remedy, but one which had worked before. It didn't work this time. The Catholic community united against the policy, and soon stories of prisoners being tortured and beaten in the internment camps rallied international opposition too. The army, having arrived as mediator, was now in many areas the enemy.

The situation worsened dramatically when, on Jan. 30, 1972, shooting broke out at an anti-internment rally in London-

Left and right, British troops arrive incongruously on the streets of Ulster's cities in 1969 and a war-zone atmosphere descends which will last for at least a generation.

derry. At the end of it, 13 civilians lay dead, shot by paratroopers. The date, Bloody Sunday, became yet another Irish anniversary to be commemorated violently in the years ahead. The following month, as a reprisal, a bomb exploded at Aldershot Barracks in England, killing seven people. As in the 1850s and the 1930s, the Troubles had spread inexorably across the Irish Sea.

In the Republic of Ireland, which served as a refuge for IRA men on the run, leading politicians condemned the continuing violence in the North but were careful to ensure that the South would not easily be drawn into it. For, as bombs and bullets ripped Northern Ireland's economy to shreds, the Republic was enjoying

sunbelt of Europe."

Culturally, too, the climate was brightening. Writers and artists, once forced to emigrate in search of intellectual freedom, were exempted from paying income tax on their royalties. Some well-known names, such as thriller writer Frederick Forsyth, moved to Ireland to take advantage of the concession. But one or two more provocative authors found it peculiar that, while one arm of the government was allowing them to live free of income tax, another was banning their books.

Feminism reached Dublin, flourishing richly in a climate long hostile to female initiative. In one celebrated protest against the ban on importing contraceptives into the Republic, groups of women

unprecedented affluence. The inward investment policy had brought real, not fool's, gold to the end of the Irish rainbow. Large Mercedes and Toyotas sped German and Japanese industrialists through remote rural lanes, adding further unpredictability to Ireland's devil-may-care driving conditions.

After the country's entry into the European Economic Community at the beginning of 1972, financial subsidies descended, as seemingly inexhaustible as Ireland's rain. Former farm labourers, much to their delight, found themselves earning good money assembling electronics components, and one euphoric trade minister dared to describe Ireland as "the

staged well-publicized shopping trips by train to Belfast. On returning to Dublin, they made a point of declaring their unlawful purchases to Customs officers and, on being asked to hand them over, informed the embarrassed young men that they were wearing them.

London takes control: In the North, the sky was darkening further. Two months after Bloody Sunday, Edward Heath abolished the 50-year-old Stormont parliament, imposing direct rule from London, and began attempts to persuade Protestant and Catholic leaders to set up a power-sharing executive. To the English, power-sharing seemed a perfectly sensible compromise. But to both tribes in Ulster, it was anathema: the Protestant extremists saw it as the first step towards a united Ireland, and the IRA saw it as a permanent hindrance to such unity.

Small wonder, then, that the Executive which took office in January 1974 had so short a life. The first blow came when Heath called and lost a nationwide election, in which Ulster's Protestants voted overwhelmingly for anti-power-sharing candidates. The fatal blow followed three months later, in May, when Protestant workers, spurred on by the hellfire oratory of the Reverend Ian Paisley, staged a devastatingly successful strike, closing power stations and bringing Ulster to a standstill. The Executive, unable to govern, resigned. Direct rule was reimposed.

Under direct rule, discrimination in housing and in job allocation—the grievances that first ignited the violence—were all but eliminated. But the violence had gained a momentum of its own: too many people had a stake in its continuing and many of the jobless young who might otherwise have been in despair were given a vivid sense of purpose by this war of conflicting nationalisms. As atrocities multiplied, the death toll passed 2,500 and an entire generation reached adulthood without ever having known peace. Successive British governments suggested political formula after political formula; none were accepted. Even well-tried nationalist tactics were failing to work any more: a hun-

ger strike in an Ulster prison was ignored by Britain's prime minister, Margaret Thatcher, and 10 men starved to death.

British politicians sent across the Irish Sea had cause to remember the plea of one 19th Century predecessor who wrote to the then prime minister, Benjamin Disraeli: "Ireland is an infernal country to manage, statemanship wholly out of place. The only way to govern is the old plan (which I will not attempt) of taking up violently one faction or the other, putting them like fighting cocks, and then backing one. I wish you would send me to India. Ireland is the grave of every reputation."

The truth was that most people in Northern Ireland had adapted to the level of violence. As the estimated 300 to 400 gunmen of the IRA and the more left-wing Irish National Liberation Organization concentrated their fire on police and military targets, it was possible for the average citizen to live a relatively uneventful life. Indeed, it was reported that statistically the combined risk of being killed in the Troubles and on the roads was, at 22 per 100,000 population, much less than the combined risk of being murdered or of being killed on the roads in France (30) or the United States (32).

Economic recession, plus the understandable reluctance of industrialists to site factories in Northern Ireland, made unemployment seem a worse evil than terrorism. And in this respect the South was faring no better. By the early 1980s, the Common Market windfalls had been exhausted and the Republic was shouldering heavy foreign debts. The price of such essentials as petrol and whiskey rose alarmingly and the direction of the Smuggler's Express changed once again as Dubliners headed for Belfast's cheaper shopping.

A new initiative: In 1982 Dr. Garret FitzGerald, heading a Fine Gael/Labour coalition, took over the government from Charles Haughey's Fianna Fáil. FitzGerald's father, a Catholic revolutionary and poet, and his mother, a middle-class Ulster Protestant, had been in the Dublin GPO on the morning of the 1916 Easter Rising, thus giving their son nationalist credentials to add to his image as a genial, somewhat absent-minded academic. His personality inspired trust in Margaret Thatcher, and together they began trying to heal England's oldest political sore.

Their remedy, revealed late in 1985, was an Anglo-Irish Agreement giving the Republic a consultative role in Northern Ireland's affairs, yet reaffirming that the Six

Counties would stay an integral part of the United Kingdom as long as a majority of their people voted for that option.

Predictably, the Agreement pleased neither side. While the church bells were ringing in 1986, the IRA detonated a remote-controlled bomb in Armagh, killing two passing policemen; it was their way of saying their campaign for a united Ireland would continue. For their part, the 15 Unionist MPs elected to the London parliament resigned their seats, thus precipitating an election in Northern Ireland. All but one were decisively re-elected, presenting their victory as a vote by a majority of the population against the Agreement. Nothing new was proved. Opposition to the deal with Dublin grew fiercer. Protes-

chances of defeating the IRA's experienced guerrillas seemed slim. It could integrate the province completely with the rest of Great Britain; but that would mean being trapped in the quagmire for ever. It could press for a united Ireland; but a million Ulster Protestants would put up armed resistance. It could redraw the border; but that would create two new sets of embittered refugees. It could pull out the troops; but that might well provoke a bloody civil war which could spill over into English cities with large Irish populations. It could offer Northern Ireland independence; but that would simply re-create the pre-1969 conditions of a Protestant state discriminating against its Catholic minority.

tants even began to attack the RUC, which they had once regarded as "their own" police force. Yet another stalemate had been created.

If you think you understand the Irish question, someone once said, you've been misinformed. The average Englishman, who had never made much of an effort to understand it anyway, had now more reason than ever to be perplexed. What on earth could England do about Ulster?

It could continue direct rule; but the

Left, a Belfast loyalist states her opposition to closer links with the South. Right, Ulster's police come increasingly under attack from both sides of the community.

Both the British and the southern Irish have become impatient. As the writer Dervla Murphy put it: "They want the play to end—and who can blame them? It has gone on too long, the plot has become too confusing, it is very expensive to produce and the critics are not impressed." Overseas visitors are even more baffled. How can the Irish, North and South, be so charming as individuals, make strangers feel so welcome in their voluptuous country, yet carry on this interminable family squabble with such bitterness? Macaulay's answer remains as true today as ever: beneath the thin crust of the 20th Century, the hot lava of history, 800 years of it, refuses to stop flowing.

57

THE ROLE OF THE CHURCH

In 1985 there were two huge news stories in the Republic of Ireland, in each of which could be discerned the long arm of religion. The first, which ran from January to October, surrounded and perhaps spawned the second.

The first was the story of The Kerry Babies. A young unmarried mother gave birth to a child which died almost immediately and whose body she concealed in a ditch on her family farm. At about the same time, another dead baby, also a boy, like hers, was washed ashore on a remote beach in the same county of Kerry, but 43 miles away. This baby's body bore 28 stab wounds and had a broken neck. Two weeks later, the young woman, Joanne Hayes, was charged with the murder of this second infant, despite her protestations that her own baby was buried on her farm. And even when her own baby was found, the police persisted in pursuing the charge, despite forensic evidence arising from blood typing which showed that the second baby could not possibly be hers. The police advanced the theory that she had borne twins, conceived by different fathers within a 24-hour period. Their reasoning was that, since she had already had a child by her lover, she was an immoral woman.

The charges were eventually dropped, but public disquiet about police methods led to a lengthy Tribunal of Enquiry during which Joanne Hayes and her family were put on the witness stand. Joanne's mother was asked by Senior Counsel if she had confessed to her priest that a birth had taken place in her house. Joanne herself was subjected to five days of interrogation about her moral turpitude and physical appetites. This interrogation was conducted according to the prevailing ethos of the Roman Catholic Church in Ireland although the Church remained officially silent.

The Church remained silent, too, about the second big news story, although it might appear to be more directly involved. The Tribunal of Enquiry into the Kerry Babies' case had been sitting for about six weeks, when, also in County Kerry, a

group of schoolchildren reported that they had seen a plaster statue of the Blessed Virgin move its eyes and fingers in a tiny local church. For some, it was a sign that moral degeneracy, as personified by Joanne Hayes and the sympathy for her, stalked the land. They flocked in pilgrimage to the statue. Stewards had to be called in to control the traffic.

And then, in other parts of the country, notably in a little village called Ballinspittle in County Cork, other statues were seen to move, or heard to speak, or both.

In County Sligo, four schoolgirls saw bright visions in the sky. All over the country, by early summer, there were thousands and thousands of ordinary people, policemen, farmers, career women and even journalists, normally the most cynical of groups, bearing nightly witness to the phenomenon.

The newspapers were full of the stories—fervent in the local weeklies, slightly more analytical in the national dailies, which carried learned tracts by psychologists and even opticians in an effort to explain the mass sightings. The State radio station sent one of Ireland's leading intellectuals, Conor Cruise O'Brien, to Ballinspittle in the company of a reporter

Preceding pages, pilgrimage to Croagh Patrick mountain; church procession on Aran Island. Left, St. Patrick, patron saint of Ireland. Right, pilgrim on the misty slopes of Croagh Patrick.

with a tape recorder. Dr. O'Brien saw nothing. The statue looked to him like a perfectly ordinary one-ton concrete statue in a grotto and did not move so much as a little finger. By the end of the year, although there was still a hard core of devotees who maintained prayer vigils at the sites of the moving statues—over 30 in all—the fervour had largely abated. The church, which had cautiously welcomed the upsurge in piety and prayer, still refused to comment on whether the visions seen were genuine.

Disobedience rules: Taken together, these two stories graphically illustrate a fact not generally considered within the Republic of Ireland—that the Roman Catholic Church is, to a large extent, led from

behind. It is largely assumed by liberals and dissidents that the Church is an authoritarian one, imposing its undemocratic will on a servile people. But no bishop or parish priest rehearsed the senior counsel or police chiefs in the Kerry Babies' case. No curate hounded the people into the shrines and grottoes of the moving statues.

The Irish psyche is a complex one and attracted to disobedience. In fact, civil disobedience on relatively minor issues is common. There is widespread evasion of income tax within a flourishing black economy and the state television service has great difficulty in collecting the obligatory licence fees for its service. A successful strike against the hated ground rents (it is common for house owners in urban areas not to own the land on which their houses stand, having to pay an annual fee to an absentee landlord) has been organized by a coalition of housing organizations. People love to drink in public houses and lounge bars after the official licensed hours (and sometimes they are joined by their local policeman). A red light at a pedestrian crossing can be a challenge to a Dublin pedestrian.

Given all of that, it is difficult to see how an Irish Catholic can be led further than he wishes to go. Despite the Church's continuing ban on artificial contraception and even before the 1985 legislation which legalized it for people over 18 as far as the state was concerned, Irish women in great numbers had decided to follow their own consciences on the matter. It began to be known that growing numbers of priests were sympathetic to this view and would see no difficulty in granting absolution to practitioners of artificial contraception when they appeared in the Confession box. It is in this area of moral legislation that most controversy occurs about the Irish Catholic Church.

Until 1972, the Roman Catholic Church in the Republic of Ireland was guaranteed a "special" status under the country's written Constitution. Article 44 accorded "a special position to the Holy Catholic Apostolic and Roman Church as the guardian of the Faith professed by the great majority of the citizens." But Ireland was about to join the European Economic Community and the conflict in Northern Ireland had worsened. This Article was seen by many as being inflammatory to the Unionists in the North. Its removal, it was argued, would pave the way for more reasoned dialogue with them and might therefore contribute in some measure towards appeasement of their opposition to the Nationalists who, being Catholic themselves, identified with the Republic. So a public referendum was held. The Church itself had no objections to the proposed change, secure in its majority, and the referendum was carried by an overwhelming majority (84.4 per cent) of those who voted.

The issue of abortion: The Church continued its ecumenical dialogue with other Churches throughout the 1970s, turned a benevolent (although not official) blind eye to the tremendous social upheavals which were occurring, until another and deeply divisive Constitutional issue arose in the early 1980s.

There was never any question but that

the vast majority of Irish people abhor abortion and will abhor it for the foreseeable future. About 3,000 Irish women travel to Britain each year to obtain abortions, a situation deplored by the majority who see it as a breakdown in the "caring society" concept. It was forbidden by the Irish Constitution—but in terms which might not preclude some future decision in the courts to allow it. Consequently, a campaign began, backed stridently by the Church, to change the constitution to ensure that abortion was outlawed for ever.

The public debate which followed was deeply divisive. To the liberals, it flushed out the worst elements of the reactionary, right-wing factions in the Irish Catholic Church. At one point, mass-goers in

for that and for those agnostics, atheists and non-Catholics who may have voted, the result indicated that the proportion of Catholics who disobeyed the urgings of their Church was growing.

Two surveys, 10 years apart, showed this movement towards an independent line of thought among Catholics. One of the conclusions reached in the later one (1984) is that "there has been a movement over the past 10 years from full acceptance of various Church teachings to qualified acceptance or uncertainty—but not to outright rejection." By the end of 1985, for instance, opinion polls showed that there is now a majority (52 per cent) in favour of permitting divorce, also banned by the Constitution, where a marriage has irre-

a small town in Wexford were confronted with the sight of a living baby in a cot within the Sanctuary area of the altar. On the other hand, sincere Catholics were appalled by the very public stances taken by pro-abortion groups, mainly in urban areas.

In the end, the referendum result, always a foregone conclusion, favoured the Church position. What was significant was the majority. Despite the full weight of the Church, almost a third of those who voted, voted "No." There was a small turnout (53 per cent) at the polls, but even allowing

Left and right, Knock, a village in Co. Mayo, since 1879 regarded as the Lourdes of Ireland.

trievably broken down.

Marriages break down within the Republic of Ireland in the same way they do elsewhere in the world. In Ireland, however, there is no legal remedy, other than judicial separation, permitting no re-marriage. A tiny number of people go through the traumatic and very expensive remedy of State annulments, where a High Court accepts that the marriage was not valid in the first place. (It has been remarked that the courts are open to everyone—in the same way as a grand hotel!) The Church grants a small number of annulments, but in this case, although the parties may be free to marry again in Church, the State cannot recognise the validity of the marriage, because of the Constitutional ban. In the light of the limbo situation, another Constitutional referendum was inevitable.

Until recently, the Catholic Church in Ireland was served by a respectful media and an obedient legislature. But, said the Minister for Health: "Times have changed. People in general are much better educated and now speak and think for themselves. The Church no longer plays such a dominating role. Nevertheless, there are some within the Catholic Church and indeed within other denominations on this island who do not recognize that changed situation." This minister and many others are determined to begin the process of separation of Church and State.

The "other denominations" to which he referred include a tiny but very visible community (2,500) of Orthodox Jews, many of whom came to Ireland as a refuge from World War Two. Of the 166 members of the Dáil, the lower House of the legislature, two are Jewish. In this, they outnumber the Protestants, by two to one.

The Protestants—Church of Ireland, Methodists and Presbyterians—occupy a curious place in Irish society, at least in the Republic. There is a great affection towards them and great efforts are made to help them preserve their place. For instance, the state applies different and more liberal criteria to the Protestant pupils attending Protestant-run state schools in the granting of subsidized school transport. There are also more lenient standards applied to Protestant entrants to teacher training colleges with regard to proficiency in the Irish language. On the ground, particularly in rural areas where congregations have dwindled, Catholic neighbours rush to help with fund-raising if the roof of the local Protestant church needs repairs.

A better class of person: In a strange way, Irish Catholics place their Protestant neighbours on a moral pedestal. It is somehow assumed that they are more honest and upright, with a stricter moral code than their erratic selves. According to a Church of Ireland Bishop of the western diocese of Tuam, Killala and Achonry: "They like to see our presence there. They like to see the witness the parishioners give in their daily lives." Unlike the situation in Northern Ireland, where to be Protestant or Catholic is assumed to be wearing a badge of identification with a particular political cause, to be a Protestant in Dublin is not remarkable. "He's a Protestant, you know," is on the same conversational par as "he played minor football for Kildare in the early '50s."

All denominations are agreed on one issue at least. In January 1984, the Jews, Protestants and Catholics met for the first time since the establishment of the National (state) School system, 150 years ago, under which the huge majority of all Irish primary schoolchildren are educated. The hierarchies agreed that these schools should continue to be run along denominational lines. The State funds the system, giving free schooling, but the individual schools are run by boards of management, led almost always by a cleric. The parish priest would run the Catholic National school in his parish, the Protestant vicar would run his.

The Catholic Church now sees the school as its last line of total defence. In the face of increased liberalism, various organizations have sprung up within the Church, with its blessing. These have adopted a watchdog pose on the way Catholic children are being educated and have taken a combative approach to the Health Boards, for instance, which have sanctioned family planning clinics and sex education programmes. One of these groups, Family Solidarity, says sternly in its publicity leaflet that schools and parents "would be well advised to assess critically the roles of Health Boards" and that "the most suitable place for sex education is the religious class where it would be under the control of the churches."

Why nuns are needed: It must be said that the contribution of the Catholic Church to Irish society continues to be enormous. The religious orders of teaching nuns and brothers bolster the state educational system in a penurious economy, often by contributing their salaries as teachers to the running of the schools. Orders of nursing nuns run hospitals throughout the state and it is generally felt among the community that they give greater and more selfless service and care than is available in purely lay-run institutions.

The social services in the Republic are heavily reliant on the goodwill and vocational caring of priests and nuns, who run day-care centres for the homeless and elderly, work unstintingly with the "travellers" (itinerant families), and are in the forefront of all fund-raising, whether it is for their homes for the mentally handicapped or the rehabilitation of prisoners.

Most Irish homes contain symbols of Catholicism – one reason, say some, for the country's low appreciation of the visual arts.

Vocations to the priesthood and religious life have fallen in number in Ireland since the halcyon days when every Irish mother "gave" at least one son or daughter to the Church. But there has been a slight upturn in numbers. This could be as a result of unemployment, say the more cynical. It could be as a result of renewed idealism among youth, say the more charitable.

And the Irish are a very charitable people, at least when it comes to helping the less fortunate. Per capita, the Irish gave by far the most (IR£7 million—£2 for every man, woman and baby in the country) to Bob Geldof's Live Aid appeal for famine relief.

They are quite theatrical in the practice of piety. Every year, thousands climb

Croagh Patrick, a punishing, scree-covered mountain in County Mayo, many in bare feet, in atonement for their sins. They make pilgrimages to Lough Derg, a cold rocky island, where they deprive themselves of sleep and food for up to 48 hours, praying constantly, again in atonement, or to beg for special favours. And they donated £1.2 million to a charismatic parish priest, Monsignor Horan of Knock, County Mayo, so that he could realize his dream of an international airport to bring pilgrims to Knock Shrine, where the Blessed Virgin is said to have appeared. As in all things Irish, there is another dimension. The international airport, should it prove viable, will also help the trading position of the depressed West.

Death and damnation: There is one area in which the Church is involved unwillingly: the area north of the border between the two parts of Ireland's divided island. It is caught between the need to be unequivocal in its condemnation of violence and the leadership expected of it by members of the Nationalist community, a proportion of whom feel that violence is justified. In this dilemma, the Church is a victim of its own history. In the Penal Days, when the Catholic religion was proscribed by the occupying British, the priests were the focal point of information, education and morale. Local houses had "priest-holes" where priests on the run were hidden. Each parish had a Mass rock, usually a promontory around which lookouts could be posted, to watch for the enemy, while the forbidden Mass was being celebrated. As lately as 1916, the leaders of the Easter Rising went to confession and received absolution in a church in Dublin (Adam and Eve's on Merchants' Quay) on the night before they went out to fight against the British.

There are, inside and outside the Church, calls that is should be true to the cause of nationalism at all costs. A priest from County Fermanagh, Father Joe McVeigh, maintains that the Catholic Church has no right to condemn those who take up arms to "fight for freedom" in Northern Ireland "when they themselves remain unwilling to take on the British Establishment." At the same time, the Reverend Hamilton Skinner, president of the Methodist Church, finds it necessary to call on the Catholic Church to "distance itself from terrorism." It is assumed by a great number of Unionists that the Catholic Church is synonymous with support for the IRA.

The Catholic Church walks uneasily through this minefield in the North. In the South, for the first time in its history, its absolute authority on moral issues is being questioned. Sunday mass attendance has dropped to an all-time low of 87 per cent—still high, but worrying when set against the 95 per cent which one survey claimed only a few years ago. And many an Irishman will tell you that those figures, both of them, are too high.

At rock bottom, the position of the Church is secure. There is no questioning on matters of absolute faith, such as the Crucifixion of Christ or His Resurrection. Further up the mountain, the terrain is becoming slightly difficult.

YOUTH EXPLOSION

"*This is no country for old men.*" This dramatic assertion by the poet William Butler Yeats, framed in the opening lines of "Sailing to Byzantium" in 1926, would have seemed like a sad anachronism to the vast majority of young people reared in post-war Ireland. This was no country for *young* men and women in the 1950s, and the mail boat to England claimed some of the brightest talents of a generation.

Not that emigration was confined to the educated classes; it cut right to the core in a society which had been conned by the provincialism of the Republic's founder, Eamon de Valera, out of its colour, its vibrancy, its life force—and out of much of its potential. Socially, Ireland was a drab grey landscape, morose in its conservatism, backward-looking and defensive.

At the root of all this was fear. The architects of the Republic were resolutely and aggressively Roman Catholic in their aspirations, and their Catholicism was of a particularly lifeless hue. In the 1920s and 1930s, the Irish lived in a grim isolation, a claustrophobic community determined to turn creative individuals into drunkards and to drive underground or out of circulation those whose instincts were open or progressive.

The tunnel of grey: All the while, the country's lack of resources (and so of employment) ensured a constant seepage. Those who went, however, were to return, bringing with them intimations of other cultures, other influences, other possibilities.

By the 1960s the Irish reached the end of the long tunnel of grey. The driving force was money: it was an era of economic expansion and many in Ireland wanted a slice of the international cake. Legislators absorbed little of the prevailing liberalism; there was no evident drive to loosen the stranglehold of the Catholic church on education, for example. But Eamon de Valera had taken his long black coat and chillingly austere countenance with him to the presidential palace, leaving the helm of the state to a gregarious man, Sean Lemass.

It was a period of extraordinary excitement and helter-skelter change. Foreign capital was flowing in as investment. Export markets were opening up. Aerials sprouted on roofs as RTE television programmes began. They sprouted especially

high so that they could pick up TV programmes from Northern Ireland and Britain. New influences were afoot.

Emigration dwindled with the economic expansion, and the population began to expand. The Irish were producing children faster than anyone else in Europe and, as infant mortality fell, the children grew up to find jobs in the Republic and to procreate as well. The changes wrought were profound. Although legislatively backward, Ireland by the 1980s had become in most respects a modern, vibrant young society. International culture had made an impact, sometimes sitting uneasily alongside traditional values, sometimes embracing them.

In search of the grail: The effects were

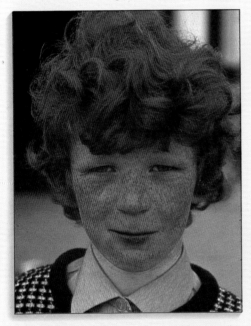

most tangible in the area of music, where there had been a rich folk tradition. Pop audiences' interest in folk music during the 1960s had brought new enthusiasts to traditional music sessions throughout the country. But while the wave peaked and faded elsewhere, interest continued in Ireland, not least because Irish traditional music is capable of attaining a transcendent magic uniquely its own yet monstrously infectious.

No wonder so many thousands of American, British and, above all, European young people take a boat or plane to Europe's most westerly point in search of the grail. To many, Ireland seems the last refuge of the irrational—and in many ways

it is. The dead hand of modern institutionalism hasn't penetrated too deeply into the countryside or psyche, and even Dublin retains a sense of community rare in cosmopolitan capitals. The characteristic Irish qualities of spontaneity and gregariousness have begun to reassert themselves. Visitors provoke inquisitiveness rather than paranoia.

With such a significant proportion of the population younger than 25—the figure is just below 50 per cent—the rate of change is accelerating. These children of the 1960s generation enter their teens with a totally different set of expectations. International pop culture vies with school and church and, in many cases, parents as the dominant influence in their lives. The new range of magazines, TV and radio programmes directed at the youth market has made young people more sophisticated, more cosmopolitan, more informed—and more demanding. It hasn't yet made them more radical politically, though that change may be just around the corner.

Young people are no longer prepared to sit around and wait for things to be done. The conspicuous success of the pop group U2 and the fund-raising for famine relief of Bob Geldof are mirrored in the energy being invested in music, film, video and radio by thousands of youngsters. If the Irish have special gifts and aptitudes, it's in the area of communications and music.

The pace of things: These qualities act as a magnet each year for thousands of curious young visitors. The grandeur of the west coast appeals to those who have searched in vain throughout civilized Europe for a taste of gritty authenticity. West Cork, Dingle in Kerry, the Burren in Clare, Connemara in Galway and Gweedore in Donegal—each has its special charm; but the secret of real satisfaction lies in stopping long enough in one spot to get the feel of the culture, to begin to understand the different, more restrained pace of things and to meet the people.

Despite the fresh air blown into the country in the past quarter of a century, Ireland is still a place for old men, with many lingering attitudes that Yeats would readily recognize. But the beauty of the new Ireland is that it is becoming increasingly a place for young people too.

Preceding page, Ireland's population explosion, which means high unemployment. Left and right, two faces of young Ireland, where half the population is under 25 and clearly tuned into international youth culture.

A stranger in Belfast on July 12, finding business at a standstill and the population waving British flags at an endless parade of marching men in orange sashes, asked what was going on. "Away home, man," he was angrily dismissed, "and read your Bible!"

But religion is only incidental. In the typical confusion of Northern Ireland's history, the Glorious Twelfth commemorates each year the victory in 1690 of a Dutchman, William III, Protestant Prince of Orange, over mainly French forces led by the Catholic James II. The battle took place at the River Boyne, in County Kildare, which is now in the Republic. But for Ulster's Orangemen, three centuries later, the issue is simple: they march, or "walk," to demonstrate their loyalty to their Protestant faith and the British monarch.

Preparations for the Twelfth go on for weeks. On calm summer evenings, backyards echo eerily to the sound of Lambeg drums, as the drummers practise until their wrists bleed. Sidewalk slabs all over the province are painted red, white and blue (the British colours); gardens are festive with the "loyal" flowers, orange lilies and sweet william; Union Jacks flutter from countless windows; and triumphal arches showing King Billy on his white charger soar proudly over bunting-festooned streets. On the eve of the great day, people sporting red, white and blue dresses, shirts, hats and umbrellas (the latter in deference to the climate) enjoy boisterous revels around bonfires fuelled with a year's accumulated garbage.

The Twelfth itself opens soberly. The largest march is in Belfast, where Orangemen start walking to various assembly points as early as 7 a.m., dressed in Orange sashes or collarettes, dark suits, bowler hats, white gloves and the inevitable umbrella. Bands form up, and large banners, which may need as many as four bearers, are raised, displaying the name and number of each Loyal Orange Lodge and emblazoned with emblems depicting King Billy's exploits, Ulster castles and

Preceding pages, a Lambeg drummer in Co. Antrim. Left, the Hibernians, and right, the Orangemen, the Roman Catholic and Protestant opposites in Ulster's long and colourful summers of marching.

churches, or Temperance slogans.

Drinking and smoking are strictly forbidden. So the respectable marchers are in stolid contrast to the exuberant spectators whose dry throats may need attention as they cheer the bands—brass, silver, flute, fife, accordion and, smartest of all, pipe bands with pipers in swinging kilts and the full plumage of a Scottish Highlander. (It is said that an Ulster Protestant is half-way between a Scotsman and a human being.)

The many Lodges converge around 10 a.m. at Carlisle Circus in Belfast, from

where they march round the City Hall, then up the Lisburn Road and out to the countryside and Finaghy Field, where there will be prayers, hymns, speeches—and refreshments. For many Protestants, the Twelfth is the most wonderful day of the year, and families picnicking with tea and sandwiches mingle in their thousands with heartier fellows intent on toasting Orangeism with crates of liquor.

Loyalists from Glasgow, Liverpool and faraway Canada, Australia and New Zealand walk, and later make merry, with the Orangemen. In Belfast, the Orange parades take up to four hours to pass any given point, and it is estimated that, throughout the province, around 100,000 Protestants annually turn out to "Remember 1690" and to remind all "holy Romans" that they will have "no Pope here."

The marching season: Northern Ireland is unique in its flourishing popular culture: there are bands in every village, every housing estate, and nowhere else in the United Kingdom do normally discreet citizens sing and dance in the streets. In the 1960s, when age-old tensions seemed on the wane, the parades were regarded as local pageantry, a potential tourist attraction.

Today spectators of the parades include thousands of police and British soldiers, while helicopters circle overhead on the look-out for trouble. There are many processions throughout the year, some quiet church parades, but during the July/August marching season the excitement can get out of hand.

On July 13, the Black Men dress up in period costume to re-enact King Billy's routing of the Catholic King James in the "Sham Fight" at Scarva, County Down. The Black Men (no women) are the élite of the Orange Order and their march on "Black Saturday," the last in August, usually passes without incident. More provocative is the march on August 12 of the Apprentice Boys through Londonderry in memory of 13 apprentices who, with a cry of "No Surrender!," closed the city's gates to prevent the Governor, "Traitor" Lundy, from handing over the city to "Popish" James. During the siege, relieved on August 12, 1690, the city's inhabitants came close to starvation.

Lady's Day, in honour of the Madonna, Mary Mother of God, is celebrated on August 15 by the Ancient Order of Hibernians, who are sometimes known as the Green Orangemen. (Green symbolizes Catholic Ireland, orange Protestant Ulster.) Like their Orange rivals, the Hibernians march with bands and banners, wearing sashes or collarettes (this time green with yellow fringes) to a country field where there are prayers and speeches, rounded off by festivities. Cynics say that, whereas the Orangeman starts off his big day sober and ends up drunk, the Hibernian sets off drunk and returns dead drunk.

Hierarchies and hooligans: There is, indeed, a similarity between the two Orders. Although the Orangemen admit only Protestants, the Hibernians only Catholics, both expect their members to uphold their faith and be of exemplary behaviour. Orangemen are grouped into a hierarchy of around 2,000 Lodges, Hibernians into 165 Divisions, which meet regularly in their own halls to pray, then to discuss their Order's business and affairs of the locality and to enjoy a social get-together.

The Hibernians date their origins to 1565 when Irish Catholics, persecuted after the Reformation, formed armed bands to protect their priests. The Defenders later combined with rustic saboteurs, the Whiteboys and the Ribbonmen, but it was not until 1838 that the various organizations expressing Catholic grievance were united as the Ancient Order of Hibernians, a title conferred on the brotherhood by Irish emigrants in America.

Marches are about territory, where people can and cannot walk, and the two

Orders came into being through peasant rivalry. The native Irish, dispossessed by their English rulers, savaged their Protestant landlords, while Protestant Peep o' Day Boys retaliated (usually at daybreak) with equal ferocity. In 1795, when the latter trounced their foes at "the Glorious Battle of the Diamond" in County Armagh, they regrouped as the Orange Order, a semi-secret society, borrowing Masonic symbols and ritual. The initiation ceremony is said to have inclu-

To an outsider's eye, it could be the same occasion. But the orange sashes on the left mean a Protestant parade, the green sashes on the right identify the Catholic Hibernians.

ded a ride on a billy goat.

When World War One was followed by the partition of Ireland, the Hibernians committed themselves to Irish reunification. But, by rejecting the use of force, they lost ground to extremists, and today the brethren number only 20,000. The Orange Order, by contrast, increased in influence and, through the Unionist Party, ensured that they retained "a Protestant parliament for a Protestant people" until its dissolution in 1972. Although middle-class support then fell away, Orange parades continue to provide a vent for Protestant working-class frustration, and membership is still reckoned to be 100,000.

The Orangemen's anti-Catholic prejudice, so bewildering to outsiders, is at

once religious, political and economic. Protestants, who see Jesus Christ as the only mediator between man and God, reject as heresy the honour given by Catholics to the Madonna and the saints. Where Catholics believe that, because their Pope is infallible, their church should influence every aspect of life, Protestants resent as authoritarian the Republic's banning of books and the illegality of birth control and divorce. And in the past they were convinced, too, that a land governed by priests was doomed to poverty. One version of the Orange Toast "to the Glorious, Pious and Immortal Memory of the Great and Good King William III" claims that he "saved us from knaves and

knavery, slaves and slavery, brass money and wooden shoes."

Catching them young: Children, who learn sectarian songs along with nursery rhymes, start marching at an early age. Little boys are lured into Junior Orange Lodges by the mystique of badges and passwords, the wearing of mini-collarettes, and the Worshipful Master's annual seaside outing. Twenty years ago a third of Ulster schoolboys were members; the figure now is less than 10 per cent. The Orange Order, with its moral pomp, seems dated to the young, vast numbers of whom are unemployed.

These workless youngsters, Protestant but no longer loyally British, parade in carnival spirit in more than 2,000 marches during the year, not as a display of religious or political allegiance but in search of cultural identity. Bowler hats are replaced by punk red, white and blue spikes, dark suits by denim and metal-studded leather. Marking out territory as always, "Kick The Pope Bands," the wilder of the Orange mods, confront Green or Irish mods in "shatter zones." On the whole, though, the young people stick peacefully to their own areas and the marches, where bacchic song and dance can be had for free, revive in a curious form the vivid ceremonials of Ulster popular culture.

Enthusiasm for bands and music remains as jubilant now as it ever was. Motorists in the Ulster countryside must beware columns of men in bowler hats solemnly drumming and tootling their way to a local contest. Scottish and Gaelic pipers compete with ecumenical harmony, at their own expense and "for the glory of it," in villages and small towns throughout summer. With a set of pipes costing around £1,500, that means £2.5 million worth of pipes keening at the average contest.

There are celebrated brass bands, like the Templemore and Britannia, while the world-famous flautist, James Galway, started his career in a Belfast band. Fife and drum, flute and even the tin whistle are favoured by the young, with accordians for girls. The musical range is colourful and varied: Irish or Scottish folk songs, "blood and thunder" party tunes (Orange or Green), military marches and, for Temperance bands, hymns.

The parades, while reflecting the profound divisions in Ulster's dual culture, may be enjoyed by the visitor simply as a spectacle. There are few places in the West where folk traditions have remained so central to everyday life, and Northern Ireland is worth a visit for this alone.

THE TRAVELLING PEOPLE

"When I was a child we were hunted from place to place and we could never have friends to be always going to school with. The little settled children would run past our camps—they were afeard of the travellers. Other people had a sort of romantic idea about us, because of the horses and the colourful wagons. They would ask us did we come from some place special like the gypsies that you see on the films. They thought that the travellers had no worries and that we didn't feel pain or hunger or cold. The truth is that we're people like everybody else but we're a different-speaking people with our own traditions and our own way of life and this is the way we should be treated, not like dirt..."

— from *Traveller*, an autobiography by Nan Joyce.

Among the ever increasing variety of vacations on offer to tourists in Ireland are trips in horse-drawn caravans. It is something of a bad joke that, while tourists trundle along the quiet backroads enjoying the freedom and leisure of a make-believe nomadic life, the country's real population of nomads subsist for the most part in poverty and squalor.

There are over 3,000 families of travelling people in Ireland, North and South, adding up to nearly 20,000 people. About 1,400 of these families are living in illegal campsites—by the roadsides, on waste ground, on land cleared for development. They are a tiny minority: 0.5 per cent of the population. But even the casual visitor is likely to see some of them: bedraggled women and children begging in the streets of Dublin—a rare sight in a modern European city—or a jumble of caravans, trailers, washing lines, dogs and children glimpsed by the roadside.

Many people still talk about "tinkers," a word deriving from the days of the travelling menders of tin kettles and pots. But no-one needs a tinsmith these days and, anyway, the word has become a term of abuse. Itinerants is another term, intended to be polite but smacking of condescension. The travelling people hate it. "Travellers" is the word they prefer.

Taking to the road: Their origins are uncertain. Some sociologists believe they are

descended from various groups who took to the roads in the past few hundred years: families dispossessed or evicted from their homes, tradesmen who had to travel to make a living, individuals or groups who "dropped out" from settled society, as some still do. It has also been suggested that today's travellers may be descended from the roving bards referred to in Irish literature or of a particular caste in ancient Gaelic society. They have no connection with the Romany gypsies of England and continental Europe. Although travellers' spokespersons (such as Nan Joyce, quoted above) sometimes describe them as a distinct ethnic group, they are ethnically indistinguishable from the rest of the Irish. Nevertheless, they are a distinct group, set

dealing in horses and donkeys, selling scrap, labouring on farms and playing music.

They became victims of the rapid changes in Irish society over the next two decades, as the country became more industrial and urban. The mechanization of farming and the decline in rural population destroyed their economic base. They drifted to the towns and cities, especially to Dublin. Their greater contact with town dwellers has led to increased friction. So has the sharp rise in the traveller population: over 150 per cent in the past two decades, compared with less than 25 per cent for the population as a whole. (The main reason for this is probably reduced emigration.)

apart from settled society, and are seen as such by themselves and by others.

The differences used to be more evident. Until the early 1960s, almost all travellers lived in brightly painted horse-drawn caravans or in tents. They dressed differently from other people—especially the women, with plaid shawls wrapped around their heads and shoulders. They had a secret language, known as *Shelta*, now used only by older travellers. It served as a defence, enabling them to converse without being understood by outsiders. They played a particular economic role for a society that was still predominantly rural: mending utensils, making baskets and sieves, peddling ornaments and knick-knacks,

Today, more than half Ireland's travellers live permanently in one place, whether it is a house, a shack, or an official caravan site. But occasional or seasonal travelling remains part of the lifestyle even of the "settled." The rest are nearly all in trailer caravans on unauthorized sites, the larger of which resemble Third World shanty towns. Those places have no water supply, electricity, sanitation or refuse collection. Inevitably, they are rat-infested.

Preceding pages, the travelling people park their caravans by the roadside at any convenient spot. Left and right, two faces of a people who make their living from scrap metal and horse dealing.

To make matters worse, the travellers are forced to move on frequently because of intimidation by nearby residents or eviction by local councils.

The question of drink: Like all minorities, they are the butt of prejudice. Travellers are said to be dishonest, drunken, lazy and dirty. The facts suggest otherwise. Police say their level of crime is no higher than among the settled population. As for drinking, a government review body reported in 1983 that "there is no evidence that excessive drinking is significantly worse than, or even as great as, among the general population." True travellers are sometimes seen drinking in public parks or in alleys, but nearly all bars deny them entry. As for laziness, traveller women

power, and prejudice remains the biggest bar to improving the travellers' lot.

Accommodation is the key issue. Most travellers would now prefer to live in a house, though a substantial minority want properly serviced caravan sites. But, with a shortage of public housing, travellers seem doomed to stay at the bottom of any waiting list. And, when they do get houses, they are rarely made welcome by their neighbours.

Opposition to providing serviced sites for travellers is even greater. Although Dublin County Council approved the building of 17 such sites in 1982 and 1983, work had not begun on any of them as 1986 dawned. In Belfast, a £200,000 site for 20 families was destroyed by local resi-

work hard to raise large families in brutal conditions and, while few of the men are in full-time work in a country of high unemployment, most keep busy mending and maintaining their caravans and cars and dealing in scrap. In this area, the travellers cannot win. Those who are poor are called lazy; those who manage to make some money are suspected of crime.

On cleanliness, the review body noted: "Contrary to what is frequently implied, travellers are, by nature, clean in their person and when given facilities they use them. This desired state of cleanliness is unobtainable for families encamped in surroundings of mud and scrap." But the irrationality of prejudice does not decrease its

dents before it was even completed.

There are some signs of hope. The travellers are acquiring lobbying and publicity skills, and some journalists are becoming more sympathetic to their cause. They are also finding allies among the rest of the community—as they indeed must, given their small numbers and lack of political clout.

The Irish, famous for their generosity, are also aware that homelessness shames those who have homes. Yet, although their contributions to suffering people in the Third World are unsurpassed, they seem to find it harder to love their neighbours in their own land. It's an old story, and a sorry one.

Digging Out Your Roots

The number of visitors to Ireland who want to uncover half-forgotten roots in the "ould sod" has mushroomed in recent years. And the trend has been given added impetus—especially among Americans—by the visit of President Reagan in 1984 to his ancestral home in County Tipperary.

The Hibernian Research Company, Ireland's largest genealogical agency, was responsible for identifying the grateful village of Ballyporeen as the home of the president's forebears. It has also traced the roots of mean, moody and magnificent John McEnroe to the counties of Cavan and Longford. According to its managing director, Tom Lindert, it receives 150 to 200 enquiries a week, and offers a twofold service. First, it gives free advice on how to go about tracing your own ancestry. "After all," says Mr Lindert, "one of the reasons genealogy is so popular is that people enjoy finding things out for themselves." Advice in writing costs IR£5.

However, the painstaking tracing and examination of old records is not to everyone's taste. More to the point, it is extremely time-consuming. This is where Hibernian's second, and more profitable service comes in. You can hire one of its panel of trained genealogists to research your ancestry, providing you with a presentation folder containing your family tree. There is no fixed charge—clients are paying for time, not results —but the average is IR£125.

Whether you intend to do your own research or hire a professional, it is important to gather as much information as possible in your home country. Try to find out the name of your emigrant ancestor; his or her place of origin in Ireland, as precisely as possible; approximate dates of birth, marriage and death; religion; occupation and social background; names of children. Ask older members of your family about their early memories. Look for old diaries, letters or family bibles.

In the US National Archives, Irish-Americans can often find their ancestor's date and port of arrival in the New World. Immigrant records and shipping lists show the country, age and trade of the immigrant and also the port of departure. Australian records are particularly useful because many immigrants arrived on state "assisted passage" schemes.

In Ireland, all centralized records for the 26 counties of the Republic are stored in Dublin. The main sources are as follows:

The National Library, Kildare Street, has an extensive collection of journals of local historical societies, trade directories, old newspapers, private papers and letters. The staff are patient and helpful.

The Public Record Office, in the Four Courts, was damaged badly in a fire in 1922 at the outbreak of the Civil War and many invaluable documents were lost (but, contrary to rumour, not all).

The General Register Office, Joyce House, Lombard Street, holds the civil registrations of all births, marriages and deaths since 1864.

The Register of Deeds, Henrietta Street, has deeds relating to property and marriage settlements dating from 1708. Most of these concern the gentry of the time.

The Genealogical Office, recently transferred to new offices in Kildare Street, includes the State Heraldic Museum. The office records and designs coats of arms and will carry out research for a fee.

The State Paper Office, Dublin Castle, is of special interest to Australians because it houses records of people sentenced to be transported there. There is no stigma attached to this, since the crime concerned was often petty or notional, or simply that of supporting the rebel cause.

For the six counties of Northern Ireland, records are held at the *Public Record Office*, 66 Balmoral Avenue, Belfast 9 (Tel: 661621). The Presbyterian Historical Society, Church House, Fisherwick Place, Belfast 1, has helpful papers.

In both North and South, records are often kept also at parish level, some going back over 200 years. If you know the parish your ancestor came from, you can write directly to the parish priest or minister.

Professional research agencies include: Hibernian Research Company, Windsor House, 22 Windsor Road, Dublin 6 (Tel: 966522); Heritage Research, 8 Powerscourt Townhouse, Dublin 2 (Tel: 712195) and 60 Howard Buildings, Howard Street, Belfast 1; Ulster Historical Foundation, 66 Balmoral Avenue, Belfast 9 (Tel: 661621).

Old family portraits can often provide a vital clue when tracing ancestors who emigrated from Ireland in the 19th Century.

Ireland

0   25   50 miles

0   40   80 km

Scotland

Coleraine

Letterkenny   Limavady   Antrim

Londonderry   Ballymena

Donegal   Derry   Larne

Donegal   Strabane

Tyrone   **Belfast**

Omagh

Ballyshannon   Northern Ireland   Down

Dungannon

Enniskillen   Armagh

Sligo   Fermanagh   Armagh

Ballina   Sligo   Newry

Leitrim   Monaghan   Monaghan

Mayo   Boyle   Cavan

Castlebar   Cavan   Dundalk

Westport   Carrick on   Louth

Shannon

Claremorris   Roscommon

Castlerea   Longford   Meath   Drogheda

Roscommon   Longford   Navan

Tuam   Westmeath   Mullingar   Trim

Galway   Athlone   Moate

Dublin

Galway   Ballinasloe   Offaly   **Dublin**

Loughrea   Tullamore   Kildare   Dun Laoghaire

Gort   Birr   Naas

Innis

Portlaoise

Ennis   Clare   Athy   Wicklow   Wicklow

Nenagh

Republic of Ireland

Carlow

Limerick   Thurles   Arklow

Tipperary   **Kilkenny**   Gorey

Limerick   Cashel   Kilkenny   Carlow

Tipperary   Wexford

Dingle   Tralee   New Ross   **Wexford**

Clonmel

Kerry   Mallow   Fermoy   Waterford   **Waterford**   Rosslare Harbour

Killarney   Cork   Youghal

Cork

Bantry   Bandon   Cobh

Atlantic

Ocean

Irish Sea

Celtic Sea

88

PLACES

What other city but Dublin, capital of the Republic of Ireland, could boast a General Post Office as a national shrine? Where else but Belfast, capital of Northern Ireland, could have endured nearly two decades of sporadic terrorist activity and remain so bustling, so commercially alive, so welcoming? Why does the South say that the border between the two states has 252 crossing points, while the North insists it has 287? How can a country apparently coming apart at the seams—with massive foreign debt, unemployment exceeding 17 per cent, and half the population younger than 25—still be one of the safest places in Europe?

"Sure," the Irishman will tell you, "it's only apathy that's saving the country from anarchy—but don't you worry your head at all about it now, the situation may be desperate, but sure it's not serious." Forget the statistics, therefore. Bring a raincoat, an umbrella and sturdy walking boots, but leave your preconceptions at home.

What you'll discover is a beguiling Irish stew of hidden loughs and ancient towns, prehistoric burial chambers and strange stone crosses, round towers and ruined castles, holy wells and high-spirited waterfalls. Racehorses are the local heroes and the villain is anyone too hurried to bid the time of day to a neighbour in a civilized manner. Kerry beckons with opulent valleys, nurturing arbutus, wild fuscia and scented orchids; Killarney, with jaunting cars and leprachaun lore designed to charm the punts from tourists' pockets; the remote Irish-speaking Gaeltacht in the far west, with its mile after mile of magnificent emptiness; Dublin, increasingly anglicized, americanized and hamburgerized, yet still the least lonely of cities; rivers like the Galway and the Shannon where you could knock a dozen salmon senseless with a single brick; Fermanagh's resplendent lakeland, where boats are still gloriously few and far between; and County Clare's bleak Burren, which Oliver Cromwell, one of the many invaders from across the Irish Sea, said had "not enough wood to hang a man, not enough water to drown him, not enough clay to cover his corpse."

It is a small country but, like vintage wine, should be savoured slowly. A signpost may present you with three ways of getting to a destination or it may show none. Ask a passer-by and, if he decides you look a bit tired after a hard day's sightseeing and comparing pints of Guinness, he'll probably assure you that it's "just a wee way ahead" because he doesn't wish to distress you by telling you it's really 40 miles by a narrow, twisting road.

Ireland, in the end, is less a place on a map than a state of mind, induced by exposure to its restful yet excitable people, who view life as a chaotic comedy. The inevitable, they promise, never happens in Ireland and the unexpected constantly occurs. Be prepared.

DUBLIN AND ITS ENVIRONS

"The only constants are the sea, the play of light and the same green curve of hills the Vikings saw when they arrived."

—Peter Somerville-Large

Dublin means many things to many people. For some, it is a city of writers, the city of Jonathan Swift, Oliver Goldsmith, James Joyce, William Butler Yeats, Sean O'Casey, Brendan Behan, and even Bram Stoker, creator of Dracula. For others, it is a shrine of Irish nationalism. For some, it is the gateway to the fabled Irish landscape. For others, it is a city of talkers, its pubs overflowing with Guinness and jokes. Some come to wander in its Georgian streets, squares and gardens. Others don't know what to expect. But the first thing that must strike nearly all visitors to Dublin—weather permitting—is its superb natural setting, on a wide plain bisected by the **River Liffey**, overlooked by hills and headlands and facing a broad, sweeping bay.

As for the city itself, they cannot help noticing that it looks, well, a bit dingy; for Dublin will not appeal greatly to those for whom cleanliness is next to godliness. It has an untidy, abstracted kind of elegance, as if its mind is on something more important than looking attractive. The once-fashionable clothes are now a little threadbare, but it can still sparkle when it tries.

Like the Irish weather and many Irish people, it has a repertoire of shifting moods, and sometimes seems to be in two moods at the same time. Its streets can be full of bustle and yet be places where people linger easily to look around them or to talk—there is always plenty of that. Clouds can glower over grey buildings as the wind whips rain in sheets along the sullen pavements; but within minutes, the city can shine again, with the redbrick Georgian terraces seeming to mellow in the sunshine.

Dear, dirty Dublin, someone once called it. The alliteration is infectious, and Dublin is certainly plural enough for that game: it is dignified and di-shevelled; decorous and demented; dismal and dazzling; decent and delinquent; debonair and decaying; diligent and dilatory; demure and degenerate; dependable and devious; distinguished and dejected; discreet and disputatious; devout and dissipated, full of churches and full of pubs.

It is also—throwing aside the whimsy and the dictionary—divided: by the River Liffey that flows through its centre and by the social differences which the river delineates. The writer Brendan Lehane has remarked that the development of Dublin over the past three centuries "has been rather like a fox-hunt, with the aristocracy and gentry for once becoming the prey and constantly striving to keep a safe distance between themselves and the deprived majority."

The chase began in the early 18th Century, when the rich moved north across the river from the old medieval city with its teeming slums to the fine new terraces and squares that were then springing up, such as **Henrietta Street** and **Mountjoy Square**. But within decades the fox was doubling back again to establish fashionable dens on

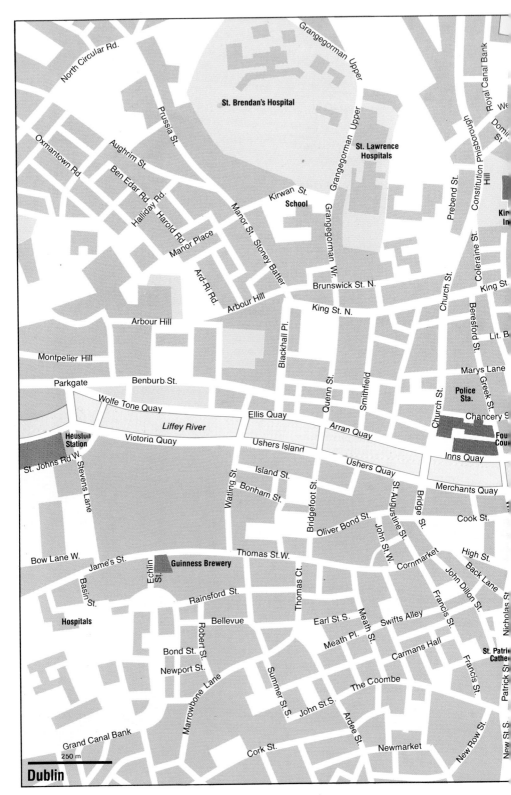

Dublin

250 m

94

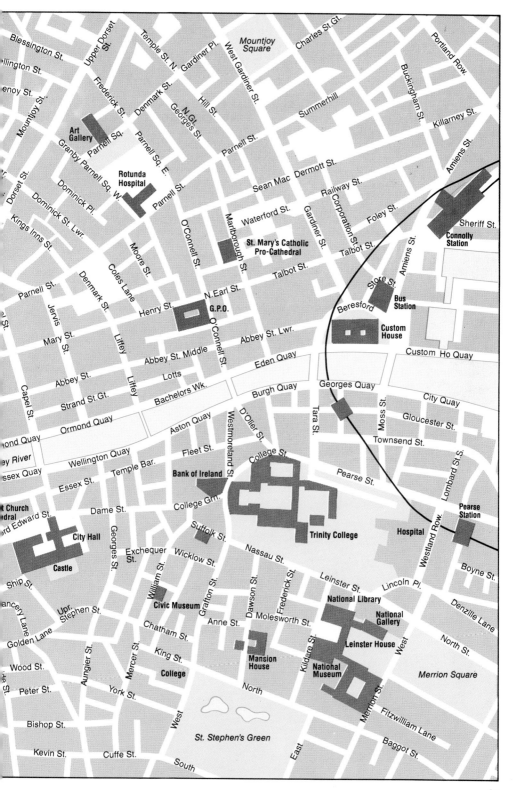

the southside in **Merrion Square** and **Fitzwilliam Square**, continuing in Victorian times through the suburbs of **Ballsbridge** and out along the coast to **Dun Laoghaire** and **Dalkey**. The chase goes on; but, as any fox knows, crossing the river is a great way of escaping the pack. There are still middle-class enclaves on the northside, but by and large southsiders are better-off, better-dressed and (to their own ears) better spoken. They are also determined and skilful in the preservation of their privilege. Like any snobbery, of course, the north-south chauvinism works both ways, and just as many southsiders "wouldn't be seen dead on the northside." Northsiders are inclined to judge that the southside is a wasteland of snobbery and pretension and that "them'uns are welcome to it."

Until recent times—and even now, to a small extent—it was a case of the Anglo-Irish fox versus the Irish hounds, for Ireland's divisions of class have long been complicated by those of culture. So, although the country has never had any capital but Dublin, the city has been an Irish capital only since 1921. A brief skip though its history will elucidate that apparent paradox.

It began by the banks of the Liffey, where there were Celtic settlements and churches at least from early Christian times, near a causeway crossing from which Dublin's Gaelic name, *Baile Atha Cliath*, "The Town of the Hurdle Ford," is derived. But towns as such did not figure in the old Celtic way of things, and it is generally accepted that Dublin was founded in the 9th Century not by the Irish, but by the Vikings, who were plundering and colonizing all the coasts of Northern Europe. They built a garrison port on the south bank of the river where its tributary, the **Poddle**, joined it to form the black pool, or *dubh-linn*, that gave the city its name. The Poddle, once a fair-sized river, is now an underground stream which trickles out through a grille in the south wall of the Liffey quay by **Grattan Bridge**—generally called **Capel Street Bridge** after the street that runs north from it.

Dublin was soon a lucrative base for both raiding and trading and the Danes hung on to it—despite persis-

Dublin's O'Connell Street Bridge, under an unusually clear sky.

tent attacks by local chieftains and a great defeat at the Battle of Clontarf in 1014—gradually intermarrying with the Irish and adopting Christianity.

The Anglo-Normans arrived in the 12th Century, but until Elizabethan times, direct English rule was restricted to a ribbon of land on the east coast known as **the Pale**, running roughly from Dundalk to the north to a little way south of Dublin.

The colonization by landlords from the neighbouring island in the 17th and 18th centuries, however, established a stability of Anglo-Irish rule under which the city started to flourish for the haves, if not the have-nots. The 18th Century was Dublin's "golden age," when many great buildings were erected and the city's social life was as fashionable as any in Europe. The spread of enlightened ideas—and the realization that England discriminated against Irish trade in her own interest—led to a demand for legislative independence, which was granted under the English Crown in 1783. But the Irish parliament in College Green was short-lived. After the rebellion of the United Irishmen in 1798, inspired by the ideals of the French and American revolutions, Britain passed the Act of Union which brought Ireland under direct control again and began a long period of decline in Dublin life.

At the turn of the present century, the city was at the heart of the political and cultural ferment that led to the Rising of 1916, the subsequent War of Independence and the establishment of the Free State in 1921. The next 40 years were a time of economic struggle as the emergent nation got to its feet—in an atmosphere that was often culturally and socially stifling because of the presence in Irish Catholicism of a particularly virulent strain of Victorian puritanism. (The city of Joyce was also the city where his works were banned long after his death.) That virus seemed to wane in the 1960s and 1970s, though there have been a few nasty outbreaks in the past few years.

Present-day Dublin has its problems, as many Dubliners are all too happy to tell you. It is growing too fast for comfort at a time of recession, and showing the strain in increased crime, drug abuse and pollution. Developers

Capturing attention in O'Connell Street; a lady preacher and a statue of pioneer labour leader Jim Larkin (1876-1947).

have spoiled some of its streets. But it still has grand public buildings, Georgian squares with gaily painted doors and graceful lamp standards, quiet galleries, green parks and gardens, a fascinating history, good bookshops and great pubs. Its people are still friendly; they still have time for you. And it can still feel like the greatest place on earth.

The southeast city: A good place to begin your walking tour of the city is **O'Connell Bridge**. Turn your back on the inviting breadth and bustle of O'Connell Street and instead walk down **Westmoreland Street** into **College Green**, which contains two of Dublin's most impressive and historic buildings: the **Bank of Ireland** and **Trinity College**. You might think that the bank, with its curving, columnar, windowless facade, seems to exude loftier ideals than those of commerce, and you would be right. It was begun in 1729 to house the Irish Parliament, whose builders could not have forseen how brief would be its age of glory.

The statue of Henry Grattan, the parliament's greatest orator, stands in the middle of College Green, frozen in mid-gesture, apparently delivering one of his ringing speeches. "Nations," he once said, "are governed not by interest only, but by passion also, and the passion of Ireland is freedom." The eastern front of the bank was added in 1785 by James Gandon, of whom more later. The building is open during normal banking hours and one of the liveried attendants will show you around. The modern sculpture near that of Grattan is a memorial by Edward Delaney to the 19th Century patriot, Thomas Davis.

Trinity College, whose sober grey facade is topped by a surprisingly bright blue clock, was founded in 1591 by Elizabeth I on the site of a confiscated monastery, but the frontage was built between 1755 and 1759. The porch inside the main gate leads to a spacious, cobbled quadrangle, on the right of which is the Theatre, or Examination Hall (1779-91), which contains a gilt oak chandelier from the old parliament and an organ said to have been taken from a Spanish ship at Vigo in 1702. On the left is the Chapel (1702) and beyond it the Dining Hall (1743), badly damaged by fire in 1984 but

Dublin's celebrated seat of learning and non-stop talk, Trinity College.

since restored. The 100-foot (30-metre) campanile which dominates the quadrangle was designed by Sir Charles Lanyon and erected in 1853 on a spot supposed to mark the centre of the medieval monastery church. To the right of the second quadrangle is the Old Library (1712-32), containing the *Book of Kells*, a magnificently ornate manuscript copy of the gospels, dating from the 9th Century, which must be seen by any visitor to Dublin. Also in the library are the *Book of Durrow* (7th Century), the *Book of Dimma* (8th Century) and the *Book of Armagh* (circa 807).

Leaving Trinity by the main gate and turning left, you face the mouth of **Grafton Street**, the southside's principal shopping thoroughfare, now pedestrianized. Its main department stores are Switzers and Brown Thomas, a near relative of London's Fortnum & Mason. Also worth a visit is **Bewley's Oriental Café**, one of a chain of large, old-fashioned coffee-shops/restaurants that has become a justly beloved Dublin institution. **Johnston's Court**, a narrow alley off Grafton Street to the right, leads to the rear entrance of the **Powerscourt Centre**, a collection of stylish shops and cafes under the roof of the former Powerscourt Townhouse, built in 1771-74 for Viscount Powerscourt.

On returning to Grafton Street, a right turn and a short walk take you to the corner of **St. Stephen's Green**, a delightful small park bordered by some fine houses, though there has also been some ruinous modern development—particularly on the west side, where the only surviving historic building is the neo-classical **Royal College of Surgeons** (1806). The green, formerly an open common, was enclosed in 1663, but it was not surrounded by buildings until the late 18th Century, when it became one of the most fashionable spots in Dublin. The gardens, laid out as a public park in 1880, are a relaxing refuge from the traffic and contain several interesting sculptures.

Turning left as you leave Grafton Street, and walking along the northern side of the Green, you come to the **Shelbourne Hotel**, built in its present splendid form in 1865. Dublin's hotels, it should be said, are much more

The city's streets are brightened by flower sellers but depressed by beggars.

than places to stay: they have an important role in the social life of the middle classes, being used as places to meet, eat and drink, exchange gossip and see whom you might see.

The best-known building on the southern side of the green is **Iveagh House** (numbers 80-81), now the Department of Foreign Affairs, but formerly the home of the Guinness family (recognize the name?). In **Earlsfort Terrace**, which branches from the southeastern corner of the green, is the **National Concert Hall**, formerly the headquarters of University College, Dublin—the university has now moved to a large modern campus in the southern suburbs at Belfield. The building, beautifully renovated, has first-rate acoustics.

Back on the north side of the Green, **Kildare Street** leads past the side of the Shelbourne Hotel and a block of modern state buildings to **Leinster House**, home of the national legislature, or *Oireachtas*, which is flanked by two nearly symmetrical edifices with columnar entrance rotundas. These are the **National Library** and **National Museum**, both built in 1890.

Apart from more than half-a-million books, the library has an extensive collection of old newspapers and periodicals. The large, musty reading-room, usually filled with sedulous students and researchers, can be seen by visitors and is well worth a look. Exhibits in the museum date from 6,000 BC to modern times.

Directly opposite Leinster House is **Molesworth Street**, and a few yards up it is **Buswell's Hotel**, a popular haunt among politicians and political journalists. At its far end the street meets **Dawson Street**, which contains several stylish shops. Turning left at the corner you find **St. Anne's Church** (1720), and a little further on, at number 19, the **Royal Irish Academy**, one of the learned societies of Europe. A few yards further up the street is the **Mansion House**, the residence since 1715 of the Lord Mayors of Dublin. A Queen Anne-style house, dating from 1705, it was decorated with stucco and cast iron in Victorian times. At the lower end of Dawson Street, you can turn right along **Nassau Street** and **Clare Street**, past the Kilkenny Design shop and Greene's fine old bookshop, into **Merrion Square**, one of Dublin's finest.

Laid out in 1762, it has had many distinguished inhabitants, Sir William and Lady "Speranza" Wilde, surgeon and poetess, and parents of Oscar, lived at number 1; Daniel O'Connell lived at number 58; W.B. Yeats, who was born in the seaside suburb of Sandymount but grew up mainly in London, lived at number 52 and later at number 82, after he had become a senator of the Irish Free State; Sheridan Le Fanu, author of the seminal vampire story, "Carmilla," lived at number 70. The Duke of Wellington, victor over Napoleon at the Battle of Waterloo, was born at number 24 Upper Merrion Street, which runs off the southwest corner of the square towards Merrion Row and St. Stephen's Green. The lush gardens in the square are open to the public.

Turning right from the end of Clare Street, along the western side of the square, you find on your left the **National Gallery of Ireland**. The statue on the lawn is of William Dargan, who organized the 1853 Dublin Exhibition on this site and used the profits to found the collection. To the

Left, the city's National Museum. Right, a lively market in Moore Street.

100

left of the entrance is a statue of George Bernard Shaw, who said he owed his education to the gallery and left it a third of his estate. Apart from a representative range of Irish work, the gallery contains a small collection of Dutch masters and fine examples of the 17th Century French, Italian and Spanish schools. Portraits of prominent Irish men and women line the winding staircase. There is a pleasant self-service restaurant.

Leaving the gallery and turning right up **Upper Merrion Street** past the lawns of Leinster House, there is a fine architectural view to your left along the south side of Merrion Square towards the distant cupola of St. Stephen's Church (1825). A left turn at the next intersection along Baggot Street, then a right up **Pembroke Street** leads to **Fitzwilliam Square**, the smallest, latest (1825) and best-preserved Georgian square in the city. Ireland's greatest modern painter, Jack B. Yeats (brother of the poet) lived on the far side of the square at number 18, on the corner of Fitzwilliam Street, the longest Georgian street in Dublin. In an infamous piece of state vandalism, 26 houses on its eastern side were demolished in 1965 to make way for a new Electricity Supply Board headquarters. We live and learn, perhaps. A left turn past the ESB brings you back to Baggot Street.

If you've still got the energy (remember, you have to come back again), you can turn right along **Baggott Street**, passing two notable modern edifices: on your left, the big, boxy, steel-and-glass administrative offices of the **Bank of Ireland** (including an exhibition hall used for contemporary art shows); and further along on your right, the headquarters of **Bord na Mona**, which oversees the extraction of peat from state-owned bogs. The bridge ahead offers a pleasant view along the **Grand Canal**, once an important commercial waterway connecting the capital with the River Shannon.

A granite-sided seat by the lock on the far side of the canal on **Mespil Road** commemorates the poet Patrick Kavanagh (1905-67); one of his poems, inscribed in the stone, describes the pleasures of the spot (less peaceful now than in his day). A few yards

Dublin's centre is small enough to stroll around easily.

away, on the corner of Baggot Street, is one of Kavanagh's favourite haunts: **Parson's bookshop**, a pearl of a place, run by three gentlewomen.

Wander back now to Trinity College, a good starting point to begin exploring the oldest part of the city.

Old Dublin: With your back to the facade of Trinity and the Bank of Ireland on your right, walk along **Dame Street**, passing on your right the imposing, layered structure of the modern **Central Bank**. The network of small streets between the bank and the river quays has become something of an artists' quarter in recent years, with studios, galleries, secondhand bookstores and craft-shops, though the area is threatened with demolition to make way for a bus depot. Later, perhaps, when you have acquainted yourself with the city's main landmarks, you might enjoy a browse here.

Shortly after passing the bank, you see on your right the ornate Victorian doorway of the **Olympia Theatre**. Despite its modest frontage, it is Dublin's largest; its programme consists of a mixture of straight plays, musicals, concerts and variety shows.

The street now rises towards the high ground on which the medieval city grew up around **Dublin Castle**. Just before reaching the castle, you see on your left the Corinthian domed exterior of **City Hall**, the headquarters of municipal administration. It was designed in 1769 as the Royal Exchange by the London architect Thomas Cooley (who won a £100 prize for the plan) and later served as a prison for rebels in 1798, as a military depot and as a corn exchange, before being taken over by the corporation in 1852.

Dublin Castle, built between 1208 and 1220 on the site of an earlier Danish fortress, was the bastion and symbol of English rule in Ireland for almost eight centuries. The building as it now stands is mainly 18th Century; the largest visible remain of the Norman structure is the **Record Tower**, in the lower Castle Yard, which contains the present-day State Paper Office. The **Bermingham Tower**, tallest in the castle, was originally early 15th Century, but was rebuilt after an explosion in 1775. Many rebels were imprisoned here, including Red Hugh O'Donnell and Henry and Art O'Neil, who es-

THE FIGHT FOR OLD DUBLIN

Dublin, in the 18th Century, was one of the ornaments of Europe, seat of an independent parliament, scene of the first performance of Handel's *Messiah* and cradle of some of the finest literary intellects of the time. It was an age of symmetry and decorum, a spirit that found physical expression in the distinctive graciousness of the capital's architecture.

The Georgian city was concentrated between its two artificial waterways, the Grand Canal on the south side with its series of delicate locks and bridges and the Royal Canal on the north, and was bisected by the River Liffey with its elegant quays. As the century progressed, so did the speed and splendour of the building programme. By an act of 1757, Dublin established the Wide Streets Commission, Europe's first town planning authority, which laid down practical and aesthetic guidelines for building development. Other bodies organized paving and lighting.

Great public buildings such as the Custom House, Four Courts and King's Inns rose at its centre. Elegant squares were laid out for a fastidious aristocracy, whose names they echo: Mountjoy and Rutland (now Parnell) squares to the north, neatly balancing Merrion and Fitzwilliam to the south. Simultaneously the upper reaches of the nobility vied with one another in the opulence of residences such as Leinster House (now Ireland's parliament) and Belvedere House (now a Jesuit school).

It was not an age of self-effacement. One of the princely developers, Henry Moore, Earl of Drogheda, even contrived to scrawl his signature vaingloriously over the map of central Dublin with a Henry Street, Moore Street, Earl Street and even Of Lane in close proximity.

After the Act of Union transferred political authority to London in 1800, the Wide Streets Commission was disbanded, property values plummeted and the great houses passed first into the hands of the professional middle classes, then became tenements housing Dublin's multitudinous poor. The seal was finally set upon the decay of the inner city when laws passed during World War One holding down rents made it uneconomic to maintain rented buildings properly. Conservation was far from a major issue after Ireland achieved independence in 1921, but at least the country's neutrality during World War Two ensured that Dublin was one of the few European capitals to escape major bombing.

The 1960s saw an unprecedented and unregulated explosion in property speculation. Whole streetscapes were depopulated, razed and replaced by often unsympathetic office development. Dublin businessmen collaborated greedily with offshore interests in the despoliation of the city, recalling James Joyce's words about those who would not only sell their country for four pence but get down on their bended knees to thank the Almighty Christ they had a country to sell. Those who raised objections were bewildered to find themselves reviled by politicians, who seemed to be wreaking vengeance on the bricks and mortar of historic buildings for the misdeeds of their long dead owners.

Many ordinary Dubliners were more farsighted. Architectural students were joined by priests and housewives in sit-ins, protests and demonstrations. These peaked in the late 1970s with a demonstration against the destruction of an archaeologically important Viking site at Wood Quay in order to build office blocks for city officials.

Even today, the preservation of historic buildings is sadly inadequate. In a city famous for the delicate beauty of its decorative plasterwork, not one interior has been listed. Unscrupulous developers still get away with murder.

But there are some signs of hope. Close to the tragically dismantled Mountjoy Square, tucked away behind O'Connell Street, lies North Great George's Street. Here, a group of pioneering restorationists have worked unofficially to preserve some of Dublin's heritage. Demolition has been halted. One great house, on the verge of being torn down, has been re-roofed and is being turned into a cultural centre. Here, delicate wrought ironwork and subtle variations in doorcases and fanlights reflect the genius of a vanished age, and the restorers hope that one day the street may become a national exhibition piece.

caped on Christmas Eve, 1591.

The most impressive part of the castle are the **State Apartments**—St. Patrick's Hall, 25 metres long and 12 metres wide, with a high panelled and decorated ceiling, is probably the grandest room in Ireland. It was used by the British for various state functions and since 1938 has been the scene of the inauguration of Irish presidents. The Gothic-style **Church of the Most Holy Trinity** was built as the Chapel Royal between 1807 and 1814 to a design by Francis Johnston; it was taken over by the Catholic Church in 1943. The exterior is decorated with more than 90 carved heads of English monarchs and other historical figures. The castle's history is both glamorous and grim: it was the centre of the glittering social life of the Ascendancy, but also of a repressive rule, brutally maintained. It has been remarked that the figure of Justice on Cork Hill faced the Viceroy and kept her back to the people.

Leaving the castle, retrace your steps a short way down Dame Street and turn right up busy **South Great George's Street**; on the left side is a Victorian shopping arcade containing many interesting and colourful shops and stalls. Continuing into **Aungier Street**, you see on your right the **Church of the Carmelite Fathers**, Dublin's largest church, and the only one to be re-established on its pre-Reformation site—the order had a church here in the 13th Century. Thomas Moore, the 19th Century poet and songwriter, was born at number 12 Aungier Street. John Field, Ireland's greatest composer and pianist, was born nearby in **Golden Lane** in 1782. He created the nocturne and originated the style of romantic pianism which culminated in Chopin's work. He spent nearly all his adult life in Russia, where he was lionized, dying in Moscow in 1837.

Continue now into **Wexford Street**, turn right, and cross **Heytesbury Street** into **Upper Kevin Street**, where you find **Marsh's Library** (1702), the oldest public library in Ireland, named after its founder, Archbishop Narcissus Marsh. Among countless interesting items there is Jonathan Swift's copy of Clarendon's *History of the Great Rebellion*, with

Merrion Square doorways; Georgian Dublin is still under threat.

Swift's pencilled notes.

The next junction marks the beginning of the **Liberties**, an area so named because it lay outside the jurisdiction of medieval Dublin. One of the city's oldest and most characterful working-class areas—most of its inhabitants have roots here going back many generations—it was also filled with some of the worst 19th Century slum tenements. The **Coombe**, which runs westward into the Liberties, was the "coomb" (river valley) of the Poddle.

Make a note to sample the character of the Liberties another time and turn right along Patrick Street to **St. Patrick's Cathedral**. Dedicated in 1192, it has been restored many times and, like Dublin's other cathedral, Christ Church, has belonged to the Church of Ireland since the Reformation. Swift, who was Dean of St. Patrick's from 1713 to 1745, is buried in it, near his beloved "Stella," Esther Johnson. He was infuriated by the poverty and inequality of Ireland, as he showed most savagely in his satire, *A Modest Proposal*, in which he bitterly suggested that the children of the Irish poor might be fattened and slaughtered as tasty joints for rich people's tables. His self-penned epitaph in Latin reads: "He is laid where bitter indignation can no longer lacerate his heart. Go, traveller, imitate if you can one who was, to the best of his powers, a defender of liberty."

Continue now along Patrick Street and Nicholas Street to **Christ Church Cathedral**, which was founded by Sitric, the Danish King of Dublin, about 1040, and greatly expanded from 1172 onwards under the aegis of Strongbow and St. Laurence O'Toole. The central tower was built about 1600 after storm and fire damage to the original steeples. Lambert Simnel, 10-year-old pretender to the English throne, was crowned here by his supporters in 1487. Christ Church became Protestant in 1551, though the Mass was restored for a short period under James II. The structure was greatly rebuilt in Gothic revival style in the 1870s. Two of the cathedral's many tombs are said to be those of Strongbow and his son, whom, according to legend, he killed for cowardice in battle.

Fishamble Street winds down to the river along the east side of the cathedral. The first performance of Handel's *Messiah*, attended by the composer, was given there in 1742 in the Charitable Musical Society's Hall, long demolished. **Wood Quay**, between Christ Church and the river, was the site of the original Viking town. During excavations in the 1970s for the building of new civic offices, the layout of the settlement was revealed and many valuable remains—of houses, walls, quays and artefacts—were found. Despite a vigorous public campaign for the preservation of Wood Quay as an historic site, building went ahead after excavation and removal of the remains. The office complex is, at the time of writing, only partly completed, because of a shortage of funds. You can form your own opinion about the squat, concrete towers with their slits of windows; most Dubliners find them hideous. Across the river to your left is the stately dome of the **Four Courts**; save it for a later tour.

High Street, which runs off the west side of **Christchurch Place**, was the backbone of medieval Dublin. Part of the old city wall and the only surviv-

St. Patrick's Cathedral, where Dean Jonathan Swift held office for 32 years.

ing city gate have been uncovered near the partially ruined **St. Audoen's Church**, which can be visited by arrangement. It was named by the Normans after St. Ouen of Rouen. Its aisle contains a font dating from 1194; the tower is 12th Century and three of its bells were cast in the early 15th Century, making them the country's oldest. On the other side of High Street, in **Back Lane**, is **Tailors' Hall**, the only surviving guild hall in Dublin, and now the offices of **An Taisce**, which works to preserve the country's natural and architectural heritage.

One part of the national heritage which seems well able to look after itself is enshrined about half-a-mile further west along Thomas Street: **Guinness's Brewery**, fount of the national beverage whose properties are often said (incorrectly) to derive from the waters of the Liffey. There is a visitor centre where you can watch an audio-visual show and enjoy a sample of the brew.

If you don't feel like walking quite so far for a drink, you may enjoy a visit to the **Brazen Head**, nearer at hand in Bridge Street. There is said to have been a tavern on this site since Viking times, though the present premises date from only 1688. It was a meeting place for the United Irishmen. As well as being old, it's odd. On your way back to O'Connell Street Bridge, you could cross over the narrow, arching footpath of the **"Halfpenny Bridge,"** from which there are fine views along the river, especially at sunset.

The north city: O'Connell Bridge is again your starting-point, but before acquainting yourself with the main features of O'Connell Street, stay a little longer on the south side, walking east along **Burgh Quay** and under the railway bridge for a view across the river to the **Custom House**, one of the masterpieces of James Gandon, the greatest architect of 18th Century Dublin. Although he was English, Gandon looked to the Continent for architectural models and it is easier to imagine the Custom House transposed to the banks of the Seine than to the Thames.

Finished in 1791, the building was extensively damaged in a fire started by Republicans to mark the Sinn Féin election victory in 1921 and has been largely rebuilt. The central copper dome, 120 feet (38 metres) high, is topped by a statue of Commerce, by Edward Smyth. The keystones over the arched doorways flanking the Doric portico represent the Atlantic Ocean and 13 principal rivers of Ireland. Gandon went on to design Carlisle Bridge (widened and rebuilt in 1880 and renamed **O'Connell Bridge**), the Four Courts, the eastern portico of Parliament House (Bank of Ireland) and the King's Inns.

The tall, 1960s edifice just upstream of the Custom House is **Liberty Hall**, headquarters of the country's largest trade union, the Irish Transport and General Workers Union. Its more modest predecessor was a nerve-centre of the labour struggle early in this century. It stands at one end of a crescent laid out by Gandon and named **Beresford Place** after his patron in the building of the Custom House, John Beresford, Chief Commissioner for the Irish Revenue. At the far end of the place is the **Busaras**, or central bus station, a daring work by Dublin standards when it went up in 1953. More recently it has been described, rather unfairly, as a "hideous edifice." Time may tell.

Walk towards O'Connell Bridge along the north bank and turn into **Marlborough Street**, where you find the **Abbey Theatre**, Ireland's national playhouse. The present building was erected in 1966 to replace a predecessor destroyed by fire. The Abbey, founded in 1904 by W.B. Yeats, Lady Gregory and their collaborators, played a vital role in the cultural renaissance of the time and quickly earned a world reputation through the great works of Synge and O'Casey and for its players' naturalistic acting style. Performances were often turbulent: the most celebrated uproar was that caused at a performance of Synge's *The Playboy of the Western World* by the use of the word "shift" (petticoat). Downstairs in the Abbey is its sister theatre, the **Peacock**, used for experimental work and for trial runs. Turn left now for O'Connell Street, passing on your right the Veritas bookshop, good for religious works.

O'Connell Street itself is not what it was, though the latter-day rash of fast-food joints, amusement arcades, ugly modern buildings, billboards and signs cannot quite obscure its inherent grandeur and elegance. It was planned (as Sackville Street) in the mid-18th Century by the first Viscount Mountjoy, Luke Gardiner, who widened the existing narrow roadway, Drogheda Street, and planted trees on a central mall. In 1794, the construction of Carlisle Bridge turned it from a fashionable residential promenade into the city's main north-south artery. A tall column surmounted by a statue of Nelson, like that still in Trafalgar Square, London, was erected in 1815 to mark the famous sea victory over Napoleon; republicans blew it up, neatly, by an explosion in 1966 to mark the 50th anniversary of the Easter Rising.

The **statues** still lining the centre of the street are (from the bridge end): Daniel O'Connell (1775-1847), a great leader of constitutional nationalism; William Smith O'Brien (1803-64), leader of the Young Ireland Party; Sir John Gay (1816-75), proprietor of the "Freeman's Journal" and organizer of the city's water supply; James Larkin (1876-1947), a great trade union leader; Father Theobald Mathew (1790-1856), the "Apostle of Temperance"; and Charles Stewart Parnell (1846-91), inspiration of the Home Rule movement and a tragic victim of intolerance whose career was ruined by the public outcry over his union with Kitty O'Shea, wife of another Irish politican.

Centrepiece of the street is the imposing Ionic portico of the **General Post Office** (1815), which was the headquarters of the 1916 Rising and the place where the rebels proclaimed the republic in ringing terms, to the initial bemusement of Dubliners—a reaction, in Yeats's words, "changed utterly" by the subsequent execution, one by one, of 15 captured insurgent leaders. The GPO's pillars are still pock-marked by bullets; although the building survived the fighting, much of the street was wrecked by British artillery and it suffered further ruin in 1922 in the Civil War.

But those stuggles are not the principal cause of O'Connell Street's fall from grace: it was rebuilt well enough in the 1920s but, as the journalist Frank McDonald wrote in his recent book, *The Destruction of Dublin,* "the dignified and noble facades... got

Bewley's Oriental Cafe, a chain of old-fashioned coffee shops that has become an institution.

scant attention from the developers who descended on the street during the late 1960s and early 1970s." In McDonald's angry words: "This magnificent thoroughfare could have become Dublin's answer to the Champs Elysées, lined with fashionable shops and terrace cafes where people could sit and watch the world go by. Instead, the capital's main street was transformed into a honky-tonk freeway, cluttered with fast-food joints, slot-machine casinos, ugly modern office blocks, vacant buildings and even the odd derelict site."

The Fine Gael party promised in an election manifesto to clean up O'Connell Street, providing for pavement cafes and stalls on its central promenade somewhat in the style of Barcelona's Las Ramblas. One lives in hope.

Turning off O'Connell Street just past the GPO, **Henry Street** is the northside's main shopping street. Its tributary, **Moore Street**, is filled with fruit and vegetable stalls staffed by colourful and vociferous women, and with a remarkable battery of butchers' shops. It is well worth visiting for a dose of down-to-earth Dublin. On the opposite side of O'Connell Street, walk down Earl Street and turn left into Marlborough Street to visit **St. Mary's Pro-Cathedral** (1816-25), the city's main Catholic Church. John Henry Newman first publicly professed Catholicism here in 1851. John McCormack, the great tenor (1884-1940) was a member of the church's Palestrina Choir. The area around the Pro-Cathedral was once a notorious red-light district, known as "Monto" (Joyce's "Nighttown").

At the north end of O'Connell Street are the late 18th Century **Rotunda Rooms**, now occupied by the Ambassador Cinema. The **Rotunda Hospital**, to the left (Europe's first maternity hospital) was financed by concerts in the Rooms. Behind the cinema, at the bottom of Parnell Square East, is the **Gate Theatre**, founded in 1928 by Micheál MacLiammóir and Hilton Edwards; it was here that the teenage Orson Welles made his first professional appearance.

A few yards past the Gate, the **Garden of Remembrance** (1966) commemorates those who died for Irish freedom. The sculpture by Oisin

When the feet get tired, the pubs seem especially welcoming.

Kelly, beyond the central lake, is based on the myth of the Children of Lir, who were changed to swans.

On the north side of Parnell Square is the **Municipal Gallery of Modern Art**. Its nucleus is formed by the mainly Impressionist collection of Sir Hugh Lane, who died when the liner Lusitania was torpedoed in 1915. Because of Dublin's tardiness in providing a suitable home for the paintings, he handed them over to the National Gallery in London and a codicil in his will bequeathing them to Dublin was held to be invalid. The dispute was resolved in 1959 by a compromise under which the collection was split in two; each part is alternated between Dublin and London at five-yearly intervals. The **National Wax Museum**, around the corner in Granby Row, is fun if you like that kind of thing.

Return to Parnell Square East, turn left and then right into Great Denmark Street, where on the left you find **Belvedere House**, a fine 18th Century mansion, which has been the Jesuit Belvedere College since 1841. James Joyce was a pupil here and describes its atmosphere in *Portrait of the Artist as a Young Man*. Straight ahead is **Mountjoy Square**, once one of the city's most stylish residences, now a sad testimony to official neglect and private "development."

Returning past the Municipal Gallery to Parnell Square West, turn right, then left into Bolton Street, then right again at **Henrietta Street**, the oldest and once, it is said, the finest of the city's Georgian streets, the home of archbishops, peers, and Members of Parliament. It is now mostly decrepit. At its far end are the **King's Inns**, the Dublin inns of court, where, in the English tradition, newly qualified barristers must eat a prescribed number of meals. The building was designed by Gandon and built at the turn of the 19th Century.

Continue now down Bolton Street, bearing left into **Capel Street**, which contains some interesting old shops. To the left in Mary Street is **St. Mary's Church**, built from 1697 by Thomas Burgh, architect of Trinity College library. Here, in 1747, John Wesley preached his first sermon in Ireland. Theobald Wolfe Tone (1763-98), founder of the United Irishmen and father of Irish republicanism, was born nearby in a street now named after him.

To the other side of Capel Street, Mary Street leads via Mary's Lane to Church Street, where you find **St. Michan's Church**, founded in 1095 as a Viking parish church. The present structure dates from the late 17th Century, but it was much restored in 1821 and again after the Civil War. Handel is said to have played on its organ. The vaults contain several mummified bodies from the 17th Century, preserved because the limestone walls absorb moisture from the air. Leaving the church, walk south to the quays and turn left to end this section of the tour as you began it: with a look at a Gandon masterpiece.

The **Four Courts** was built between 1786 and 1802, subsuming a building erected only a few years earlier by Thomas Cooley, architect of City Hall. The dominant lantern-dome is fronted by a six-columned Corinthian portico and flanked by two wings enclosing courtyards. In 1922, after the building was barricaded by anti-Treaty republicans, troops of Michael Collins's new government shelled it from

The Four Courts, a splendid pile which cost a quarter of a million pounds to build nearly 200 years ago.

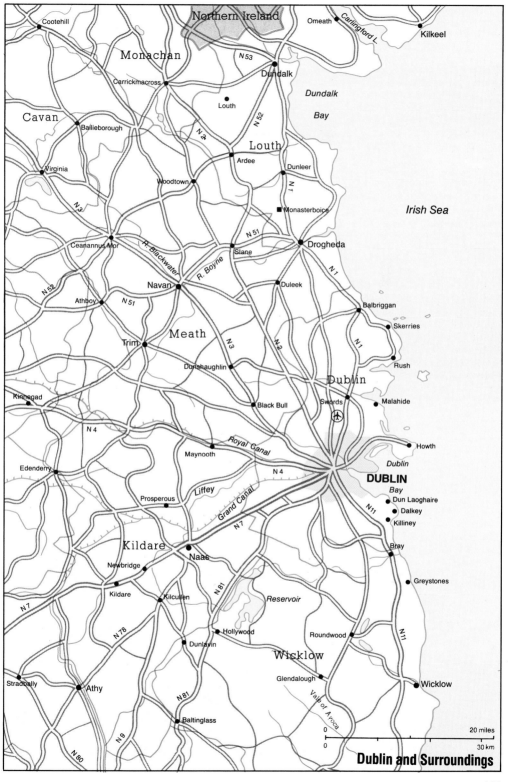

Dublin and Surroundings

111

across the river (so beginning the Civil War). In the ensuing fire, the Record Office was burnt and countless priceless documents went up in smoke.

Sean O'Casey described the rising cloud of paper: "all the records of the country, processes, cases, testimonies, bills of exchange and sales of properties to church and private persons, and all hereditaments chronicled since Strongbow came to Ireland, flying up... to come down scorched and tattered in every Dublin back yard and front garden." Restoration of the building was completed in 1932.

West Dublin: On the south bank of the river about 1.5 miles (2.5 km) west of O'Connell Bridge, and just past the Guinness Brewery, is **Kilmainham Jail** (1792), now disused and being restored as a museum. Its former inmates comprise an impressive roll-call of Irish patriotism. You can see the cells where they were locked and the yard where the 1916 leaders were shot.

To the east, across South Circular Road, stands **Kilmainham Royal Hospital**, (1680-84), founded by Charles II "for the reception and entertainment of antient *(sic)* maimed, and infirm officers and soldiers." The building has been painstakingly restored and is used for concerts and exhibitions.

You can now go down **Steeven's Lane** past Heuston Station and cross the river to visit the **Phoenix Park**, whose southern boundary extends west on the Liffey's north bank for about three miles (five km). At 712 hectares, it is more than five times as large as Hyde Park, London. Its name does not derive from the reincarnatory bird but is a corruption of the Gaelic *fionn uisce* ("clear water").

Among its features, all signposted, are: the **Wellington Monument**, an obelisk 60 metres high, erected after Waterloo; the **Zoological Gardens**, the third oldest public zoo in the world (1830), well known for the breeding of lions (it supplied the MGM announcer); the President's residence, **Aras an Vachtarain**, formerly the Viceregal Lodge (1751-54); the US Ambassador's residence, formerly the Chief Secretary's Lodge; and the "15 acres," an open space actually of 200 acres containing paths and playing fields, the duelling ground of 18th Century Dublin gentlemen. The **Phoenix Park racecourse**, a first-class track, is at the

113

northern end of the park.

Southside suburbs: Nearly all the places mentioned in this section are served by various buses departing from **Eden Quay**, beside O'Connell Bridge, and by the excellent DART suburban trains.

Travelling out through Merrion Square North, along Northumberland Road past the squat, circular block of the **American Embassy** (1964), you reach the prestigious suburb of **Ballsbridge**, named after the bridge over the River Dodder. The large greystone buildings to the right on Merrion Road, just past the bridge, are the headquarters of the **Royal Dublin Society** ("the RDS"), the traditional sponsor of improvements in agriculture and stock breeding. Its two great annual events are the Spring Show and the **Dublin Horse Show** (in August). The RDS's Simmonscourt Extension is used throughout the year for many exhibitions and concerts.

The **Chester Beatty Library and Gallery of Oriental Art** is a little further out, at number 20 Shrewsbury Road. Founded by an American mining tycoon, Sir Alfred Chester Beatty, it has a marvellous collection of Chinese, Japanese, Persian, Indian and Middle Eastern manuscripts, paintings and ornaments.

The main road south soon skirts the coast, affording fine views of the bay, and passes through **Blackrock**, where Eamon de Valera studied and later taught at the boys' college. A couple of miles further on is the large town and port of **Dun Laoghaire** (generally pronounced *Dunleary*), departure point for Sealink ferries to Britain. The harbour, with its long, granite piers reaching out to embrace the sea, was built between 1817 and 1859.

The next promontory, within easy walking distance, is that of **Sandycove**, with its **Martello tower** where Joyce lived for a short time in 1904. He used it as the setting for the opening scene of *Ulysses* and it is now a **Joyce Museum**. The nearby **Forty Foot** bathing place has been for generations a spartan haven of nude bathing for men, though feminists have made incursions in recent times.

About a mile further on is **Dalkey**, a meandering old village of great charm and some *cachet*; from nearby **Colie-**

Preceding page, faces at the races at Phoenix Park. Below, Dublin is still an important port.

more **Harbour** there are boat trips in summer to **Dalkey Island**, a stone's throw offshore, which contains another Martello tower and the ruins of a Benedictine church. The island is a bird sanctuary. From Vico Road, which continues along the coast, you can enter **Killiney Hill Park**; motorists should drive instead up Dalkey Avenue, to the public car-park.

At the summit of the park is a Victorian obelisk commanding splendid views of the broad sweep of **Killiney Bay** (often likened to the Bay of Naples), **Bray Head** (the hump-backed promontory at its far side) and the two **Sugar Loaf mountains**. DART travellers can easily continue on to **Bray**; as a seaside resort it has seen better days, but the seascapes *en route* are impressive and Bray Head offers bracing walks and fine views further southwards along the coast.

Northern suburbs: The attractions of the northside are somewhat more diffused, but it is worth making the trip to the north-central suburb of **Glasnevin** (buses 13 and 34) to see the beautifully arranged **Botanic Gardens**, which occupy the former demesne of

Howth, a picturesque village with a busy fishing harbour.

Joseph Addison, the English essayist and founder of *The Spectator* magazine, who lived in Dublin as secretary to the Earl of Sutherland.

The coastal route northeast by the Custom House leads past **Fairview Park** to the middle-class enclave of **Clontarf**, site of the battle in 1014 in which BrianBorú defeated the Danes. **Malahide Road** branches off to the left and to the left again is the recently restored **Casino**, once part of the seaside estate of Lord Charlemont, whose town house is now the Municipal Gallery. It is a small Palladian building, considered a gem of its kind, with several unusual features: the roof urns are actually chimneys and the columns are hollow, serving as drains.

Beyond **Clontarf** the coast road passes the **North Bull Island**, a huge sandbank growing from the North Wall of Dublin Port and containing two golf courses: **St Anne's** and the famous **Royal Dublin**. It is also an important sanctuary for winter migrant birds.

Carrying on via the isthmus at the suburb of **Sutton** you reach **Howth Head** (also accessible by DART and bus), whose rugged brow overlooks the

northern entrance to Dublin Bay. You can go directly to the village of **Howth** or start instead at The Summit and walk to the village around the nose of the promontory by a splendidly scenic cliff path, which descends steeply to the fishing harbour. The novelist H.G. Wells called the view from the head "one of the most beautiful in the world." The offshore island of **Ireland's Eye** was the site of a 6th Century monastery. Howth is the most fashionable place to live on the northside, and it is easy to see why. The gardens at nearby **Howth Castle** are beautiful, especially if you like rhododendrons.

Five miles (eight km) north of Howth lies the resort of **Portmarnock**, which has fine beaches and a championship golf course. From here, a turn west leads to **St. Doulagh's Church**, claimed to be the oldest still in use in Ireland; its high-pitched stone roof is 12th Century. **Doulagh Lodge**, nearby, was the home of the great landscape painter, Nathaniel Hone (1831-1917).

At **Malahide**, a pleasant resort and dormitory town seven miles (11 km)

north of Howth, is **Malahide Castle**, which was inhabited continuously by the Talbot family from 1185 until 1976, except for a short period when Cromwell was around. James Talbot, Earl of Tyrconnell, was Lord-deputy to James II; he fled after the Battle of the Boyne to France, where he died. The castle, now owned by Dublin County Council, houses many portraits from the collection of the National Gallery.

Excursions south: It is easy for Dublin dwellers to take for granted the wild beauty of the **Wicklow Mountains**, just a few miles to the south. As one writer has pointed out, it is, for a Londoner, as if the Lake District began at Golders Green. The so-called "hills" are great outcrops of granite thrown up by ancient earth movements. In the Ice Age, glaciers smoothed and rounded their peaks and carved deep, dark, steep-sided glens whose wide floors glitter with rivers and lakes. The region is sparsely inhabited—just a few villages, scattered farms and cottages, and the occasional great house.

The chief attractions of Wicklow are

An 11th Century round tower at Glendalough, Co. Wicklow.

well served by coach tours from Dublin. If you are driving, take the N8I southwest, through the bleak new suburb of **Tallaght**, to **Blessington**, a 17th Century village consisting mainly of one long, broad street. Just past the village, the large artificial lake of **Poulaphouca** lies to the left of the road. It supplies Dublin with its water supply and is part of the Liffey hydroelectric scheme. A popular scenic road encircles the lake.

Two miles (three km) on is **Russborough**, a Palladian house built in the 1740s by Richard Castle for the Earl of Miltown. Its 700-foot (210-metre) frontage is the longest in Ireland; inside is the Alfred Beit art collection, including works by Vermeer, Goya, Reubens and Velasquez.

Four miles (six km) south at Hollywood, a left turn leads into the wild heart of the mountains through the Wicklow Gap to **Glendalough**, a secluded, seductive valley, steep-sided and well-wooded, where in 545 St. Kevin founded a great monastic settlement between two lakes. The sight of the ruins—a cathedral and several churches, dominated by a 110-foot

(33-metre) round tower—evokes something of that deep longing for peace and solitude that was central to the monk's idea of sanctity. The sounds, too: of running water, wind in trees and birdsong. Given Ireland's richness of natural beauty, superlatives are a snare; but Glendalough is surely one of its loveliest retreats.

Driving south through **Rathdrum** you reach **Avondale**, the beautiful Georgian home of Charles Stuart Parnell, which is now a museum surrounded by public parklands. A couple of miles further south is the celebrated **Vale of Avoca**, where the Avonmore and Avonbeg rivers join, supposedly described in Thomas Moore's song, *The Meeting of the Waters*. At Avoca village you can turn northwards again and drive, via the unremarkable county town of **Wicklow**, to the village of **Ashford**, near which there are two spots of great beauty: to the south, the **Mount Usher Gardens**, a lush display of trees, subtropical plants and shrubs; to the northwest, the **Devil's Glen**, a deep chasm where there are spectacular walks above the rushing Vartry river.

Return to Dublin via **Roundwood** and **Enniskerry**, where you can divert to visit the magnificent landscaped gardens at **Powerscourt**, the 18th Century mansion there was destroyed by fire in 1974, and the nearby **Powerscourt Waterfall**, the highest in these islands (90 metres). You now drive directly back to Dublin or divert again through the magnificent valley of **Glencree**; the gaunt old military barracks there is now a "reconciliation centre" to promote understanding between the divided communities in Northern Ireland; nearby is a beautiful German cemetery for servicemen (mainly airmen and sailors) who died in or near Ireland in the past two world wars.

Excursions north: A half-hour's driving on the N2 road across the rolling fields of Meath takes you to the beautiful old village of **Slane**, built on a steep hill above a bridge on the **River Boyne**. The grounds of the nearby castle have been used to stage concerts by the Rolling Stones, Bob Dylan and Bruce Springsteen. The **Hill of Slane**, where St. Patrick proclaimed Christianity in Ireland by lighting a paschal fire in 433, is on the northern out-

skirts of the village. The ruins of a 16th Century church stand on the site of the church founded by Patrick. The view over the plain is striking.

A few miles east along the north bank of the Boyne is one of Europe's most remarkable prehistoric sites: the burial chamber of **Newgrange**, dating from the third millennium BC. It is a huge, circular, man-made mound of white and black boulders, largely covered with earth and grass, 240 feet across and 44 feet high (73 by 13 metres). An entrance, overlooking a broad bend in the river, leads by a narrow passage 20 metres into the interior to a central chamber containing decorated stones. A small aperture over the entrance is aligned so that the sun's rays penetrate to illuminate the chamber only at the winter solstice—a powerful symbol of rebirth and renewal. The road on to Drogheda, passes the site of the Battle of the Boyne.

Drogheda is a large town and port dating from Viking and Norman times and was a frontier outpost of the Pale. The name of Cromwell is still an accursed one here: during his campaign of suppression in 1649 he captured the town and slaughtered 2,000 of the garrison and inhabitants—"a righteous judgment of God upon those barbarous wretches."

The main features of the town are: the **Millmount**, a prehistoric mound surmounted by an 18th Century barracks, now including a museum; **St. Lawrence's Gate**, one of the best-preserved town gates in Ireland; the ruins of several medieval churches; the 18th Century **Tholsel**, or town hall, now a bank; and the 19th Century high Gothic **St. Peter's Church**, erected in memory of Oliver Plunkett, a Meath man who became Catholic Archbishop of Armagh. He was martyred in London at Tyburn (now Marble Arch) in 1681, and canonized in 1975. His head is preserved in a shrine at the church.

You have now crossed into **Louth**, Ireland's smallest county. Six miles (10 km) northwest of Drogheda, by the River Mattock, stand the ruins of **Mellifont Abbey** (1142), Ireland's first Cistercian foundation. The remains include those of a square tower, a large church, and a lavabo, an octagonal building where the monks used to wash. At **Monasterboice**, a few miles

northeast, are the remnants of a 5th Century monastic settlement founded by St. Buithe: a round tower, two churches, three sculptured crosses, two early grave-slabs and a sundial.

You can now join the main N1 route north to **Dundalk**, a busy border town and a good centre for exploring the picturesque **Cooley Peninsula**. This area features prominently in the great epic legends of ancient Ireland, particularly those concerning Cuchulainn, hero of the Red Branch Knights. At **Carlingford** village, a fine Norman castle commands the entrance to the sea inlet, Carlingford Lough. A corkscrew road through the nearby forest park climbs to a viewing point near the summit of **Carlingford Mountain**, providing splendid views of the Mournes to the north. **Greenore** and **Omeath** are small resorts.

The N52 road southwest from Dundalk leads to **Ardee**, or Irish *Baile Atha Fhirdiadh*, "The Town of Ferdia's Ford." It is here that Cuchulainn slew his friend Ferdia, the champion of Queen Maeve, in the great epic story of the Cattle Raid of Cooley. Continuing through Meath's county town of **Navan**, you reach **Kells**, where St. Colmcille founded a monastery in the 6th Century. The extant remains are more recent: a round tower and a high-roofed 9th Century building known as **St. Colmcille's house** are the most interesting. The traveller may by now be feeling rather antiquity-drunk, but **Trim**, another pleasant town 16 miles (26 km) further southwest, can claim the largest Anglo-Norman fortress in Ireland: its complex and well-preserved remains cover two acres and the surrounding moat could be filled from the River Boyne. A mega-ruin, you might call it. The ragged outline of the so-called **Yellow Steeple** (1358), part of a collapsed abbey, stands on a ridge opposite the castle.

Return now to Navan and take the main Dublin road, which passes near the **Hill of Tara**, the cultural and religious headquarters of ancient Ireland. A great assembly or *feis* was held there every three years to pass laws and settle disputes. By the 6th Century, when Niall of the Nine Hostages founded the house of O'Neill that was to rule Ulster until the Plantations, Tara had become preeminent among Ireland's five kingdoms, but its influence declined soon after as Christianity took root in the country.

It has remained a powerful symbol of Irish unity, expressed in Thomas Moore's song, *The harp that once through Tara's walls*, and Daniel O'Connell chose it in 1843 as the venue for one of his "monster meetings" to demand repeal of the Corn Laws. A million people attended, according to *The Times*. On top of the hill is a modern statue of St. Patrick and a pillar-stone said to have been used in the coronation of the ancient kings.

Excursions west: Kildare, the county to the west of Dublin, is the "horsiest" part of Ireland, but there are many charms even for those whose blood does not rise at the sound of hoofbeats. **Naas**, the county town, is a handy centre for touring the county. You can drive there quickly and directly over one of the Republic's few modern highways, or via **Celbridge**, an attractive village which was the home of Esther Vanhomrigh, the "Vanessa" who competed with "Stella" (Esther Johnson) for the affections of Jonathan Swift. He often came here to visit her and you can see the seat by the river where they sat and talked. Nearby is the magnificent Palladian mansion of **Castletown House** (1722), the largest private house in Ireland, now the headquarters of the Irish Georgian Society.

Drive west from Naas through Newbridge to reach the great expanses of the **Curragh**. Apart from the racecourse, scene of the Irish classics, and many training stables, it has contained an important military camp, established in 1646. This was the scene of the "Curragh Mutiny" of 1914, when British officers threatened to refuse orders to fire on Edward Carson's Ulster Volunteers, who had armed illegally to oppose Home Rule. Near the road south to Kilcullen is a depression known as **Donnelly's Hollow**, where a small obelisk commemorates an 1815 prize fight in which Dan Donnelly, the giant Irish champion, defeated George Cooper of England.

Kildare town, six miles (10 km) from Newbridge, was the site of a monastery founded by St. Brigid (circa 450-520), the most revered Irish saint after Patrick. Her attributes have been reinforced by others borrowed from the great goddess of the same name, who was venerated also in Britain and Europe. The **Cathedral of St. Brigid**, begun in 1229, has been rebuilt many times, most substantially in 1875. A mile from the town, at **Tully House**, is the **National Stud**.

At **Athy**, 16 miles (26 km) south of Kildare, a 16th Century tower, now a private house, overlooks a fine old bridge over the **River Barrow**, once an important commercial waterway to Dublin. But the town's main attraction is modern: the striking, fanshaped **Dominican Church** (1963-65). The painter George Campbell designed the stained glass and the stations of the cross.

Returning to Dublin from Naas, it is worth diverting via **Maynooth**, where Ireland's Catholic diocesan clergy are trained at **St. Patrick's College**. It was founded in 1795, when the British acknowledged that it was not in their interests that all Irish priests were trained abroad, and became a college of the National University in 1908. An ecclesiastical museum can be seen by arrangement. Beside the college gates is a massive, 13th Century Fitzgerald keep.

The neolithic passage grave at Newgrange, Co. Meath.

September

2 B. Ellena par. L. Joannis Tost & Catharina Burnck

2 B. Poorus S. Timotheus Fitzgerald & Margarita Mary

3 3 B. Michael fil. ... Thoma Regan & Margarita Murphy de
Eagles Y. Gulielmus Regan & Catharina Walsh

3 B. Petri ... fil. L. Thoma Sisk & Noricia Brien de
Curraghleagh Y. David & Maria Morley

1 4 B. Michael fil. L. Jacobi Beston & Maria Kenny de Gur
roe S David Casey & Juditha Casey Martinus Kam

4 B. Ellena fil. an L. Dionysii o Bruen & Ellena Barry
Kehenerinky S. Joannes Dunlay & Maria Fitz

5 B. Gulielmus fil. an L. Michaeli Murphy & Maria
de Coolzaname S. Joannes Shel & Ellena Moher

7 B. Maria fil. L. Valentini Wallez & Mary
Dunley de Gurteen M. Jacobi Dunley

11 B. Mariam w. L. Andri Vissy & Mary Lynch
Guthesdel S. ...

13 B. Margaritan fil. an L. Joannis o Brien & Maria S
Shea Knocknagopple S. Gulielmus Dunithoe

13 B. Michaelen fil. L. Edmundi Kent & Maria Moher de
Willia S. Michael Moher & Maria Henessey

15 B. Juditham fil. an L. Mauritii Mahony & Maria Sle
de Coolroe S. Morganus Dyer & Maria Slattery M.

25 B. Michaelen fil. an L. Joannis Keating & Ellena o Brien
de Foyle S. Thomas Keating & Maria Cahill M.

25 B. Edmundum fil. an L. Patricii Tobin & Ellena Kenny de
Sconson S. Joannes Murray & Juditha Mahony M.

30 B. Patriciam fil. an L. Patricii Culd & Catharina Rolly
Kehenerinky S. Cornelius Brien & Margarita

Octobris 5th — 1829

B. Saundum fil. L. Jacobi Cahill & Maria Hoar
Glenaun S. Richardus Moore & Maria Condon

6 B

3 Elizabetham Jacobi Joannis Burns Petri & ... Richardson de
Ballypoureen Sᵖ Gulielmus Gorman & Maria Richardson. 5B

5B Margaritam fⁱᵃ L. Dionysii Gorman & Catharina Keating
Jurteskall Sᵖ Thomas Grifitt & Catharina Mousey . M R

6B Gulielmum fⁱᵘ L. Jacobi McGrath & Margarita Walsh
de Ballywillie Sᵖ Gulielmus Murray & Maria Stoke... M R

10B Dionysium fⁱᵘ L. Edmundi Hally & Maria Connors de Dan-
gar Sᵖ Jacobus Sheehy & Margarita Hally Maito Red...

10B Gulielmum fⁱᵘ L. Gulielmi Walsh & Catharina Gorman de Glennacunna Sᵖ Michael Russell & Bridget Gorman M R

4B Julianam fⁱᵃ L. Mauritii Riach & Honora Condon de
... Sᵖ Joannes Casey & Ellen Williams. M R

7B Gulielmum fⁱᵘ David Keat & Honora Hine de Curra...
leigh Sᵖ Joannes & Maria Hennessy & M. Red...

8B Joannem fⁱᵘ L. Thoma Brien & Maria Sullivan De Highlanders
Sᵖ Michael Brien & Judith Collens & Martinus Redmond

5B Gulielmum fⁱᵘ L. Michaelis Cleary & Bridget & sculley de
Furtistall Sᵖ Gulielmus Gorman & Ellen Fitzgerald. M R

5B Mariam fⁱᵃ L. Jacobi Tunelors & Bridget Capli de ...
... apple Sᵖ Michael Fennessy & Elizabeth Ryan M Red...

8B Richardum fⁱᵘ L. Richardi Thornill & Bridget Ryan de
Coolbery Sᵖ Gulielmus Ryan & Elizabeth Mahony M R

25 Juditham fⁱᵃ L. Michaelis Brien & Juditha Brien De Shel-
binky Sᵖ Thomas Barry & Honora Hennessy M Red...

Novembris 1ᵐ 1829

1 Honoram fⁱᵃ L. Gulielmi Benan & Cath... ... Do
Coolpicuone & Joannes Walsh & Maria Collins. 6B

3B Bridgedam fⁱᵃ L. Jacobi Carew & Honora Hanlen de High-
... Hugo Hughes & Catharina Brunnock & M. Redmond

3 Joannem fⁱᵘ L. Mauricii ... & Margarita ... de
Anglin Sᵖ Thomas Casey & Judith ... Ryan & M. Edm...

Jacobum fⁱᵘ L. Timothei Dislane & Margarita ... de
Anglin Sᵖ Joannes ... & Bridget & Ellen ...

3B David... fⁱᵘ L. Edvardi Cued & Catharina Harri...
Brook... Sᵖ Michael Cull & Maria Walsh...

THE SOUTHEAST

The road from Dublin to **Cork** links the two poles of the Republic. Dubliners and Corkonians regard each other with greater envy and suspicion than do the people of Antrim and Kerry, who are much further apart geographically. The rivalry between the two cities is, in its small Irish way, similar to that between New York and Chicago.

Cork people, fired by a greater ambition than Dubliners, are proud that their **County Hall** is the tallest building in Ireland. Dubliners look more to tradition; they are not proud of the Trade Union headquarters, which is the second tallest in the land. They look on it, rightly, as an eyesore in a city whose centre is composed mainly of low-rise buildings constructed to a large extent in the elegant 1700s.

But when, in 1984, Cork decided to celebrate its 800th birthday, Dubliners were stung into action: 1987 was declared Dublin's 1,000th anniversary. It didn't matter that most people believed the city to have been founded in 841 by the Vikings. Cork's challenge had to be answered and, since 1,146 didn't sound a suitable number for a celebration, 146 years were lopped off the age of the ancient capital.

The people who live somewhere between the two cities don't have much time for the pretensions of either. Yet even the direct route between the cities became part of the big boys' rivalry: when the Anglo-Irish Treaty set up the Irish Free State in 1921, all the administrative functions of a national capital devolved to Dublin, thus creating a large number of new and powerful jobs in the public service. Much of the ambition to fill these jobs, naturally, had its base in Cork and the humorous magazine *Dublin Opinion*, in a celebrated cartoon titled "The night the treaty was signed," showed a mass of Corkmen trampling each other down in the rush to Dublin, ignoring in their haste even the most spectacular historical site on the way: the towering **Rock of Cashel** in County Tipperary.

If you choose to take the direct route from Dublin to Cork rather than meander through the scenic byways, the best bet is to make an early start before the army of articulated lorries gets under way. The N7 is a divided highway from the inner suburbs of Dublin as far as **Naas**, 20 miles (32 km) out. It then becomes a freeway (M7) for a short spell as part of the Naas bypass, then divided highway again until it reaches **Newbridge**, on the edge of the plains of the **Curragh**.

This town is a traffic bottleneck, so have patience. Sit in the inevitable jam and imagine the place as it used to be in the last century: a great military centre, with its own series of barracks, all now gone. Being the nearest town to the Curragh Camp, the major base of the British Army in Ireland, it gained the reputation of having more whores per head than anywhere else in the country—even more than Dublin, then so notorious that it merited a special entry under "prostitution" in the *Encyclopaedia Britannica*. Rumour has it that it was here that Edward VII lost his virginity. He never looked back.

The current Curragh Camp is the chief training and manoeuvres centre

for the Irish Army. To its right, on this flat plain, is the **Curragh Racecourse**, headquarters of Irish racing. It is here that the **Irish Derby** is held each June.

Star-studded stallions: A short stretch of divided highway on the Curragh can be used to overtake the procession of trucks and head on towards **Kildare**. This town is worth a short stop to see the ancient cathedral complex and the **National Stud**, one of Ireland's main racehorse breeding centres. Some of the most expensive stallions on earth are kept here. One of them, Shergar, was kidnapped from nearby Ballymany Stud and has never been found. In the Stud area is the **Museum of the Irish Horse** and the enchanting **Japanese Gardens**, laid out by Eida, a Japanese landscape artist invited over at the turn of the century. In the centre of Kildare stands the **Anglican Cathedral**, dating from the 13th Century, and its **round tower**, 300 years older still.

After Kildare, the road becomes undulating, narrow and winding for the next seven miles (11 km) until one reaches the small town of **Monasterevin**. To the left as one enters the town is the gate to **Moore Abbey**, a neo-Gothic mansion once the home of one of the greatest of Irish tenors, Count John McCormack. Having made a fortune through his concerts in the United States, he became a US citizen, but eventually moved back to Ireland where his love of the grand style of living and of not-so-fast horses ensured a considerable diminution of his wealth.

One story tells of the conversation between a leading bookmaker and one of his employees. The clerk asked the bookie if he was closing early. "Why should I?" replied the bookie. "Well, I thought you might be going to Dublin, John McCormack is singing at the Theatre Royal," said the clerk. "By the time we're finished with him, he'll be singing *outside* the Theatre Royal," replied the bookie.

The road goes on to **Portlaoise**, a fair-sized market town. Its best-known building is a major prison containing a great number of those convicted of terrorist offences on both sides of the border.

It is here that the road branches: to the left for Cork, to the right for Lim-

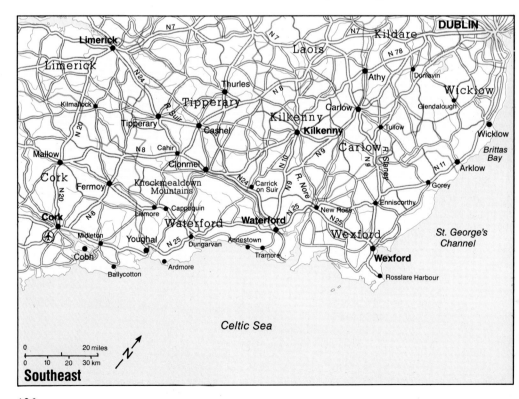

Southeast

Celtic Sea

St. George's Channel

erick. The Cork road leads through **Abbeyleix**, **Durrow** and **Urlingford** before entering County Tipperary near **Thurles**. A detour is recommended to **Holy Cross Abbey**, well signposted from the main road. The abbey, a medieval Cistercian foundation, has been superbly restored.

Ancient Cashel: A few miles on, the towering **Rock of Cashel**, where St. Patrick once preached, dominates the surrounding countryside. At its top, 300 feet (90 metres) high, is a splendid complex of 13th Century cathedral, 10th Century round tower and assorted monuments. By the base of the rock is a 13th Century Dominican friary. **Cashel town** has many fine shopfronts.

Eleven miles (18 km) on, **Cahir** has a massive **Norman castle**. Directly across the road from this considerably restored fortress is one of Ireland's smaller curiosities: **Keating's Draper's Shop**, which has steadfastly refused to introduce decimal currency. It gives good value, too. A serviceable raincoat costs from 69 shillings and 11 pence (which, in new-fangled money, is a fraction short of £3.50).

Mitchelstown is 17 miles (27 km) further on, at the foot of **Galtymore Mountain**. Just before the town, a signpost points to **Ballyporeen**, home village of Ronald Reagan's ancestors. It's a small, unremarkable place, but now has its **Ronald Reagan bar** and sells mementoes of the president's visit. Mitchelstown, a prosperous market town in the heart of the **Golden Vale**, Ireland's richest dairy-farming area, is the birthplace of the forebears of one of the American president's right-hand men, Donald Regan (whose family didn't change the spelling of their name when they arrived in the US). From here, it's a pleasant 32-mile (51-km) drive through the fine town of **Fermoy** (on the **Blackwater River**, good for salmon) and into Cork city.

Taking it quietly: You can drive those 160 miles (260 km) from Dublin to Cork in less than three hours. But, if you're not in that much of a hurry, a leisurely route off the main highway will take in the spectacular mountain scenery of **Wicklow**, the superb beaches of **Wexford**, the architectural gem of **Kilkenny** city, and the rugged coastline preceding **Youghal**, where

Sir Walter Raleigh had his home.

From Dublin, the mountains of Wicklow and the early Christian settlement of **Glendalough** can be seen in a day-trip, as suggested in the previous chapter. If you take in these beauties again you can then continue along the back roads through the lovely scenery of **Laragh**, **Avoca** and **Woodenbridge**. Alternatively, you can take the coast road via Wicklow town and on past the silver strand at **Brittas Bay** towards **Arklow**.

Arklow, another Viking settlement, is a town with a seafaring tradition, a former centre of industry—shipbuilding in the old days—and is now a popular seaside resort with good beaches to the north and south. It has a decent golf course, and a museum which concentrates on the town's maritime history.

Arklow is a short few miles from the county of Wexford, the part of Ireland nearest to mainland Europe, with ferry services to and from Le Havre and Cherbourg in France. This closeness to the continent and to Britain has shaped much of the county and the rest of southeast Ireland. It was here that the Norman invasion took place, and a local rhyme about the place where these warlike people first set foot on the island states: "At the creek of Baginbun, Ireland was lost and won."

Where Kennedy came from: Wexford is a county of seaside resorts and beaches, a favourite holiday place for Dubliners. It is also the county from which the forebears of President John F. Kennedy left for the United States. The Kennedy homestead is at **Dunganstown**, near **New Ross**. Nearby is Ireland's national memorial to the president: the **John F. Kennedy Park**, an arboretum containing thousands of trees, many donated from around the world.

To Irish people, Wexford is historically associated with the insurrection against British rule in 1798, and the battle sites are well signposted. **Wexford town** is a quaint place with a long maritime tradition. Its quay features a statue to another Wexford native with US connections, Commodore John Barry, the "father" of the American Navy.

Like most of the coastal towns in

The ancestral home of former US President John F. Kennedy at Dunganstown.

the southeast, it was founded by the Vikings and developed by the Normans, English and Anglo-Irish. Its centre, the **Bull Ring**, reminds one of the cruel medieval pastime of bull-baiting. Nowadays the town's pleasures are more refined, and a highlight of each fall is the **Wexford Opera Festival**, which features some of the lesser-known works of the greatest operatic composers.

Almost in the centre of County Wexford, on the main inland road from Arklow to Wexford town, is **Enniscorthy**, a major centre of the 1798 insurrection. On **Vinegar Hill**, the rebels suffered their great defeat at the hands of the Crown forces under General Lake. The overall command of the British army was in the hands of Lord Cornwallis, who had led the British to defeat in the American War of Independence. This time, though, he was successful. Enniscorthy, a hilly town, boasts that the mother of Giuseppe Marconi, the inventor of radio, was one of its daughters.

Kilkenny's treasure trove: Twenty-seven miles (43 km) to the northwest of New Ross is **Kilkenny**, once the capital of Ireland and still, despite its size, insisting on being called a city rather than a town. The Confederate Parliament sat here for six years from 1642 to 1648. When Oliver Cromwell, England's Protector, arrived in 1650, he treated Kilkenny's architectural glories with disdain, stabling his horses in the great cathedral of **St. Canice** and smashing its stained-glass windows. In the **Dominican Black Abbey**, every sacred image was destroyed.

But it is a measure of the people's pride in their city that most of the great buildings have now been restored, making the city one of Ireland's jewels, a mini-Edinburgh with the main thoroughfare starting at the massive **Castle of the Butlers** at one end of the city and ending at **St. Canice's Cathedral** at the other.

In between lies a treasury of medieval buildings such as **Shee's Almshouse** dating from 1581; the house of the Rothe family, cousins to the Shees, with its double courtyard (1594); and religious foundations such as **St. Mary's Church** and the **Black Abbey**. It was in the Black Abbey, still used

Old straw-thatched windmill at Tacumshane village, Co. Wexford.

for worship, that Friar Clyn recorded the ravages of the Black Death that raged from 1348 to 1349: "I leave Parchment to carry out the work if perchance any man survives..." At that point, another hand records the death of Friar Clyn.

Nowhere in Ireland are there so many visible connections with the Middle Ages. Dublin was a larger medieval centre, but its houses were of wood and didn't survive. Only Galway in the far west, with its houses of stone, can rival Kilkenny for ambience and style. Of the two, though, Kilkenny is more complete and most resembles the kind of small, historically redolent city often found in Europe.

And it is in Europe that most of Kilkenny's history began. The first Butler was Theobald Fitzwalter, whose family came from Caen in Normandy. He was appointed Chief Butler of Ireland in 1177. Because the family astutely ensured that it was represented on all sides of the political and religious struggles that have tormented Ireland, there were both Catholic and Protestant Butlers. Anne Boleyn was the grand-daughter of Thomas Butler, the Earl of Ormonde, and her marriage to Henry VIII strengthened the family's ties with the seat of power in London. But there was also a tradition of loyalty to the Stuarts, strengthened by the marriage of Piers Butler to Harriet, the illegitimate daughter of James II by Arabella Churchill.

The Butlers lived in **Kilkenny Castle** until 1935. Since 1967 the castle has been in public ownership and the present head of the Butler family lives in Chicago. The castle is open to visitors and its most spectacular attribute is the long gallery adorned with portraits of the Butlers since the 14th Century.

Directly opposite the castle's entrance, in what used to be its stables, is the **Kilkenny Design Centre**, founded as the state's centre of design. Its shops here and in Dublin provide the biggest range of high-quality Irish products.

A short stroll towards the **High Street** and a step or two left at the traffic-lights brings you to the **Shee Alms House**, now a tourist office. Walking tours, indisputably the best way to see the city, start from here.

Passing the 13th Century St. Mary's Church, the tour reaches the **Tholsel**, or town hall, built in 1761 but modern by Kilkenny standards. It then passes down **Butter Slip**, one of the myriad medieval "slips" or lanes. It was here that an ancient public relations man coined the rhyme: "If ever you go to Kilkenny, look out for the Hole-in-the-Wall; You'll get twenty-four eggs for a penny and butter for nothing at all." There's no truth in the rhyme today.

The Butter Slip leads to **St. Kieran's Street** and the colourful and historic **Kyteler's Inn**. This old coaching inn, built of local limestone, is structurally much the same as it was in 1324 when owned by Dame Alice Kyteler. She was charged with witchcraft by Bishop de Ledrede; but, being a sharp operator who had outlived four wealthy husbands, she quickly skipped overseas, leaving her maidservant Petronella to be burned at the stake in her place. Her inn still serves food and drink.

More ancient atmosphere fills the **Rothe House**, across the High Street from the 1794 **Court House**. The **Below, Kilkenny Castle. Right, an approach to Kilkenny, once the capital of Ireland.**

130

Rothe House, now used to exhibit the work of local artists, is 200 years older than that and is Ireland's only extant example of a wealthy Tudor merchant's town house. Its double courtyard indicates that several generations of the family lived in the same building.

Also on the High Street are the remnants of the **Franciscan Friary** built in 1232. A more substantial part of the site is the **St. Francis's Brewery**, from which Smithwicks Kilkenny Ale is despatched through Ireland and abroad. To the irritation of locals, it is possible to buy a six-pack of the brew in a Monoprix supermarket in Paris for less than half its price in Kilkenny. Tourists are invited to taste.

The ancient Black Abbey, still in the hands of the Dominican friars, is noted for its stained glass. St. Canice's, the Anglican cathedral, has Ireland's second longest nave (the longest is in St. Patrick's Cathedral in Dublin). And, as if all this weren't enough, there's **St. John's Church** with a window dating from 1250 and **Kilkenny College** dating from 1660. This boarding school's alumni include Jonathan Swift, William Congreve and Bishop George Berkeley, the philosopher after whom the University of California at Berkeley is named.

Kilkenny, with three quite good hotels, is a neat touring base. The great **Norman Abbey of Jerpoint,** now in ruins, is close by in the beautiful old world village of **Thomastown** at the head of the **Nore Valley**. The **Dunmore Cave**—once described as having "a dreadful romantic appearance, as if one stood in the mouth of a huge wild beast"—is within easy driving distance, as are a host of attractive old villages.

Carlow, the second smallest of Irish counties, boasts **Rathvilly**, one of the country's tidiest communities, and the county town of Carlow, a modern market town rather than a great tourist draw. It does, however, have a very fine golf course—one of the best parkland layouts in a country where linksland golf is more prevalent. Also in Carlow is the charming village of **St. Mullins** on the **River Barrow**, one of Ireland's most spectacular navigable waterways. Now a sleepy village, St. Mullins was a great ecclesi-

A time not to be drinking and driving in Kilkenny town.

astical centre and there are ruins of several churches and abbeys. For the serious visitor, Patrick Mackey's *A City and County Guide to Kilkenny* is invaluable.

Crystal and quays: Thirty miles to the southeast is **Waterford city**, home of Waterford crystal glass. The city, on the south bank of the **River Suir**, is a Norman foundation. **Reginald's Tower**, at the end of the quay, dates from 1003, taking its name from Ragnvald, son of Sigtrig the Viking, and qualifies as an ancient monument even by the most demanding European standards. The Viking connection is retained in the name of **St. Olaf's Church**, founded in 870, rebuilt in Norman times and restored in 1734.

Waterford's history is a proud one, and its proximity to England gave it a major role in Ireland's history in the days of Norman and, later, English rule. It had strong connections with continental Europe, too, some of which are maintained through its thriving container port. Others are maintained through its glass factory, which still has links with the great crystal craftsmen of Bohemia. The fac-

tory can be visited, and **Waterford Glass** is abundant in local shops.

From here the N25 to Cork goes through **Tramore**, a modern seaside resort with a fine beach; through the lovely village of **Annestown**; and along a superb coastline to **Dungarvan**. One can then detour to the **Comeragh** and **Knockmealdown Mountains**; to **Lismore**, Irish seat of the Dukes of Devonshire; and to **Mount Mellary**, a Cistercian monastery which still functions and where one can observe the almost medieval life of monks insulated from the pressures of the 20th Century.

Lismore, incidentally, was the site of one of the great cathedrals of Ireland in the Middle Ages, but it was almost totally destroyed by Elizabethan forces at the end of the 16th Century. The **Anglican Cathedral**, a graceful building in beautiful surroundings, was built on the site in 1663.

The more direct route from Dungarvan passes close to **Ring**, a remarkable village where Gaelic has survived in a pocket entirely cut off from the major Irish language centres further west in Cork, Kerry, Galway and Mayo.

Waterford's crystal-glass factory, open to visitors.

Crossing the **River Blackwater**, one arrives in County Cork at the quaint town of **Youghal** (pronounced *yawl*). This ancient place, with its narrow main street and clock tower, was used as the home port of Captain Ahab in the movie version of **Moby Dick**. The town has associations with Sir Walter Raleigh, who lived on his estates here and is believed to have introduced the potato to Ireland.

Next stop is **Midleton**, the new home of all the Irish whiskies except Bushmills and Coleraine. Nowadays Jameson and Powers and Hewitts and all the others are produced in a modern distillery which also makes gin and vodka. The newly marketed 20-year-old Midleton Very Rare has its origins here and, if you have over £40 to spare, you might buy a bottle before making the 21-mile run into the very proud city of Cork.

Cork's continental air: If you want a reasoned, unprejudiced view of **Cork**, the Republic's second city, don't ask a Corkonian. A strong characteristic of the inhabitants of the "city by the Lee" is their inordinate pride in their home town. The city's two great comic characters Cha' and Miah (short for Charles and Jeremiah) once exemplified this on Irish television. "I read in the paper the other day that Cork is being described as the Paris of Ireland," said Cha'. To which Miah replied tetchily: "Is that so? And why are they not calling Paris the Cork of France?"

Cork, whose population of just over 130,000 hardly rivals Paris, does have a continental air. There are waterways all around, an abundance of French-style mansard windows on its older houses, and a leaning towards pastel shades in the painting of private residences. There are also, particularly in the north inner city, warrens of narrow hilly streets reminiscent of the older towns of Provence.

This continental influence seems to affect even the names of its inhabitants. Nowhere else in Ireland will you find large numbers of men called Florence (usually shortened to Flor or Florry) or Cornelius (usually abbreviated to Con or Neilly).

Local chauvinism has had good and bad consequences. It's usual to hear Cork unfavourably compared to Dub-

Cobh Harbour, where countless emigrants embarked for America.

134

lin. But local pride has seen to it that the city is tidier and far less ravaged by property developers than Dublin.

The old city of Cork was founded by St. Finbar in the 6th Century. The present city centre is situated on an island between two branches of the **River Lee**. Most of its medieval buildings have long since disappeared and the fabric of today's Cork dates mainly from the 18th and 19th centuries.

The centre, perfectly level, is known to locals as "the flat of the city." To the north, however, a steep escarpment tumbles spectacularly down to the river. This aspect is seen at its most dramatic from the end of **Patrick Street**, Cork's most important thoroughfare, looking northwards to **St. Patrick's Hill** which, lined on both sides by fine houses, reaches for the sky like an architectural Jacob's ladder.

At one time Cork was a city of some wealth, particularly in its days as a major base for the British navy and in its pre-eminent position as butter capital of the world. From here, the fresh butters of Cork and Kerry were salted and exported to the best tables of Europe. More recently, heavy industry made Cork prosperous. In the past few years, though, the pendulum has swung again: Ford closed its car plant (its oldest outside the United States), Dunlop shut its tyre factory, and Verolme Shipyards closed their gates.

Perhaps the jaunty city's most important asset in building a new future is tourism. It has sparky inhabitants, is linked by sea and air to Britain and the European mainland, and is just 50 miles (80 km) from Killarney and the wonderful attractions of Kerry. Its restaurants are outstanding, too. The **Arbutus Lodge**, on the city's north side, caters for the gastronome, and the nearby seaside village of **Kinsale** has quite a few first-rate restaurants. In this respect at least, Cork can claim to be the Paris of Ireland.

The city centre offers many pubs of character; and there are elegant walks in the parks by the river or down the **South Mall**, the most stylish street in the south of Ireland. The sights to see include the tower of **St. Anne's Shandon**, the "English" market full of bustling stalls, **the Church of Ireland (Anglican) Cathedral of St. Finne Barre**, the university, and the city hall. Corkonians are proud of all of them. A good "What's on" guide can be found in the *Cork Examiner*, known to the locals with characteristic lack of humility as "The Paper."

Trips out of the city are particularly rewarding. Cork has a spectacular harbour and its outport of **Cobh** was the departure point in the last century for countless famine-stricken emigrants to America. The forebears of many US mayors, congressmen, senators and governors passed through here on the way to the land of opportunity. Several hundred of the 1,198 victims of the liner Lusitania, sunk without warning off the coast in 1915 by a German submarine, are buried in Cobh's old church cemetery.

There is a wildlife park, arboretum and good collection of Irish landscape paintings on **Fota Island**, six miles (10 kms) east of Cork. First-class cultural entertainment can be found at the **Cork Opera House**, and, for the more outdoor-minded, there is hurling, the city's favourite sport and a few-holds-barred game said to be the fastest played on dry land.

The Grand Parade in Cork City.

THE SOUTHWEST

Cork and **Kerry** are Ireland's wettest and greenest counties. They are where the Atlantic first touches Europe—and, as a corollary, where Dublin (and, historically, London) last touch the Irish. Both climatically and politically, the location of Cork and Kerry governs their character.

The saying goes that there is a lot of weather but not much climate in the southwest. It is far from unusual for the same day to present blazing sunshine and driving rain, and for prudent tourists to take both swimming trunks and umbrellas everywhere they go. But from month to month the climate varies less than almost anywhere else in Europe. The reason is the Gulf Stream, whose full force is felt by the Cork and Kerry peninsulas that stick out into the Atlantic. The currents of warm water that flow from Florida across the ocean prevent frost in winter and excessive heat in summer. The mean temperature on the west coast is contained within the range of 8°C (46°F) in January to 16°C (61°F) in July.

The vegetation is the clearest product of this climate. Too cool to be tropical, Cork and Kerry nevertheless display a richness of trees and fields and hedgerows and flowers that alone almost justify a visit. From April to October, bloated bushes of flowering fuscias, heavy with their scarlet offerings, dominate many country lanes. No frost contains their growth, no drought shrivels their leaves.

Starting from Cork City, the greatest of these delights lie some way to the west—an hour's drive if you hurry. But why hurry? After all, a favourite Irish road sign reads: SLOW VILLAGE AHEAD. The unintended (or maybe intended) ambiguity of that statement says much about the rural southwest. There is no such thing as a fast village in Cork and Kerry. Drivers who zap through at 50 miles an hour not only threaten the lives of the locals but ruin their own enjoyment.

A load of Blarney: If there is one village whose vulgar commercialism appears at first sight to invite a burst on the gas pedal, it is **Blarney**,

five miles (eight km) to the northwest of Cork city. The sight of tourist shops and parked coaches will repel all except those whose idea of foreign travel is to remain as close as possible to tourist shops and parked coaches. Do not be put off by Blarney's first impressions. Its castle is set back from the village, and is protected by grounds that conceal the castle and the village from each other. The castle itself is not vast—it is a keep rather than a palace—but it is better preserved than most buildings of its age. It was built in 1446 by Cormac Mac-Carthy as part of the MacCarthy family's intermittently successful attempts to rule West Cork as the Kings of South Munster. (Their main enemies were the English, until the Battle of the Boyne brought all such contests to a conclusion.)

At the top of the castle is the Blarney stone. Its preposterous legend still excites people to perform the strangest contortions. To kiss the stone, and so acquire "the touch of the Blarney" (the gift of eloquence), you have to lie back with your head lower than the rest of your body

Preceding pages, Co. Kerry's enchanting lakes; west coast vista near Caherdaniel. Left, Slea Head on the Dingle Peninsula. Right, Killarney signposts its attractions.

rather as if you were about to descend a helter-skelter backwards. You must then raise your head to kiss the stone. For decades, queues of tourists have lined up to endure this ritual. But such is its pulling power, and such was the fear among the residents of Blarney that people would stop doing it, that considerable efforts have been undertaken to persuade visitors that you cannot contract AIDS by kissing the stone.

For anyone willing to be persuaded by rational medical arguments, these reassurances ought to be sufficient. But then, if science is allowed to supersede superstition, why kiss the stone in the first place? There are various accounts of how Blarney became synonymous with eloquence. One story holds that Queen Elizabeth I complained that the Lord of Blarney procrastinated with "fair words and soft speech," without making any firm deals, until the Queen exploded, saying: "This is all Blarney." A different story, more directly related to the stone itself, tells of an old woman who rewarded a king of Munster who had saved her from drowning. She prom-

ised him that if he kissed the stone at the top of the castle he would acquire a gift of speech that would persuade everyone to do as he wished.

The moving madonnas: A more recent superstition concerns **Ballinspittle**, 24 miles (38 km) to the south of Cork. During the summer of 1985 it became Ireland's most famous small village, when thousands travelled to witness its "rocking Madonna." Like many other Irish villages, Ballinspittle has a grotto containing a stone statue of the Virgin Mary. One evening in July 1985 a local girl, Clare Mahony, was passing the statue at dusk. She looked up at it—the statue is set about 30 metres back from the road and overlooks it from the rocky hillside—and saw it rocking back and forward. Other villagers heard what Clare had seen, and they saw the same thing. The *Cork Examiner*, the area's local newspaper, reported what was happening, and within days hundreds—and soon thousands—of people travelled to Ballinspittle nightly to see for themselves.

Various scientists, starting with a team of psychologists from Cork Uni-

Ballinspittle's Madonna; did it move or didn't it?

142

versity, pointed out that it is difficult to stare for any length of time at an illuminated object set against a dark background 30 metres away at twilight without the light playing tricks on the eyes. But not only was Ballinspittle reluctant to surrender special place in Mary's affections; other villages started competing for that place, as they claimed supernatural properties for their madonnas.

Tiptoeing carefully away from Ballinspittle, we find ourselves at a good place to start the drive along County Cork's south coast. The road itself touches the coast at only a few points; but it provides the base for some magnificent walks—out to the **Old Head of Kinsale**, for example: a promontory with the remains of an old castle and, more recently, of one of Ireland's earliest lighthouses.

Clonakilty is one of many local touring centres. It contains West Cork's regional museum, and is near one of southwest Ireland's relatively few good beaches on Inchadony "island," now permanently linked to the mainland by a causeway. At **Templebryan**, north of Clonakilty, is the site of one of the larger early Celtic churches; within the enclosure is the smaller site of the later medieval church.

West from Clonakilty are reminders of Ireland's literary past. Drive through **Ross Carbery** and a mile past it on the left is the shell of **Derry House**. At the turn of the century it was the home of Charlotte Payne-Townshend, who married Bernard Shaw. Shaw first visited Derry House in 1905, during which visit he revised *Captain Brassbound's Conversion.* (Derry House was burned out in 1921.)

Further on, away from the main road and down by the sea, is the site of a less elevated but more specifically local memorial to Irish writing: the village of **Castletownshend**, home of Edith Somerville and Martin Ross, and inspiration of their stories of *The Irish RM* (resident magistrate). Castletownshend has a single street, sloping steeply down to the sea. Their hero, the magistrate, was an Englishman whose job was to uphold the law, but who in practice found himself constantly outwitted by the wily locals. Until a recent Anglo-Irish TV series based on the books revived the popu-

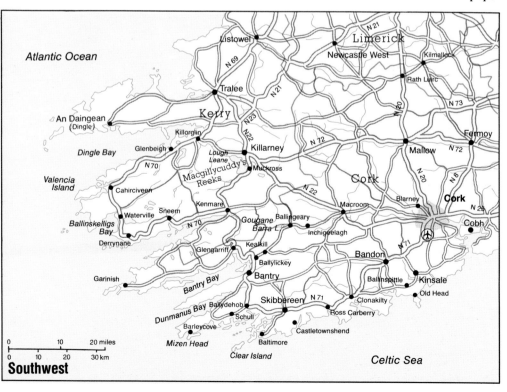

Southwest

larity of the stories in Ireland, they were rather frowned on by all self-respecting Irish people, as they failed to portray the Irish as possessing sufficient nobility or patriotism. Since the TV series, and on the basis that the English emerge as more ridiculous than the Irish, the books have been discreetly rehabilitated.

The Eagle has died: The gateway to the most southerly of the Cork and Kerry peninsulas is **Skibbereen**. As a town, it has little to commend it except some good shops and a modest slice of history. As the self-proclaimed centre of West Cork, it has traditionally provided the area's weekly newspapers. At the end of the 19th Century there were two: the pro-British, and hence pro-Imperial, *Skibbereen Eagle*, and its nationalist rival, the *Southern Star* (one of whose shareholders was the patriot, Michael Collins). The *Eagle* is most notorious for the wonderful pomposity of its leading articles. One, at the turn of the century warned Moscow's rulers: "The *Skibbereen Eagle* has its eye on the Czar of Russia." Today the *Eagle* has gone the same way as the Czar; weekly news and comment is the monopoly of the *Star*.

South and west of Skibbereen lie a number of coastal villages, all claiming their share of local glory. In **Baltimore** was built the *Saoirse* (meaning "Freedom"), the first Irish ship to sail round the world. This venture, in the 1920s, helped the village to recover from the shame of having been the victim in 1631 of a raid by, of all people, some Algerians, who massacred local inhabitants and removed others as white slaves to Africa.

From Baltimore a boat sails daily to **Clear Island**, the most southerly place in Ireland. It is arguably the most Irish place in Ireland; most of the remaining inhabitants speak Irish, and they resent Dublin's attempts to "modernize" the country. The story is told of the woman who had to interview some of Clear Island's inhabitants for an opinion poll in the early 1970s on whether Ireland should join the European Economic Community. She came across an elderly man a good walk from the nearest road and asked him whether he supported Irish entry. "Good lord, no," he replied;

Kissing the Blarney Stone gives eloquence, not elegance.

"have those continental juggernauts thundering past my house day and night? No, thanks."

One of the joys of Clear Island is the **Cape Clear Bird Observatory**, one of the places that has pioneered sea-bird watching in Britain and Ireland. Apart from familiar gulls, cormorants, puffins and kittiwakes, other, rarer species can be seen, including the black-bowed albatross. Keen ornithologists intent on staying at the observatory should be prepared for the most basic of amenities: bunk beds, rough blankets and an invitation outside the privy for gentlemen to use the bushes at the east end of the house.

Back on the mainland, the road to Mizen Head takes travellers through **Ballydehob** and **Schull** and past **Barley Cove** which, on a warm day, boasts the best beach in West Cork. Unlike most others it is flat and sandy. Not that anyone with any sense would travel to West Cork to lie on a beach; the weather is too unreliable. But if you are in the area and it is hotter than usual, then Barley Cove is the place to head for.

Fog warnings: Mizen Head provides as dramatic a spectacle as anyone could wish for. At its southwest tip, Ireland comes to a full stop, as near-vertical cliffs of layered sandstone rock plunge into the sea. In thick fog the signal station fires flares to warn ships off the rocks; over the years many ships have been wrecked here.

The contrast between the appeal of the Mizen peninsula to the visitor and its harshness to the smallholder could scarcely be greater. The road back along the North coast of the peninsular, behind **Mount Gabriel** and over-looking **Dunmanus Bay**, is exceedingly beautiful; but the land is exceedingly barren. Depopulation occurred here well before the great famine; it was triggered by the Napoleonic wars, which screwed up the opportunities for locals to sell locally caught fish in continental Europe. Today ruins remind the observant visitor of the time when people were driven back from the peninsula towards the (relatively) more fertile land round Bantry.

According to the owner of the **Anchor Inn**, the key to **Bantry**, a fishing port and market town, is that it is farther from Dublin than any other

The lure of the Atlantic on the Ring of Kerry.

town of any size in the country. It is 180 miles (290 km) away as the crow flies—twice as far as from Dublin to Belfast. As a general rule, the farther you go from Dublin, the poorer and more pious are the people, the more genteel are the landowners, and the slower is the way of life. Like all generalizations, it is a peg on which exceptions may be hung; but it is a useful peg nonetheless.

The Anchor Inn itself, on the corner of the large town square, is *the* place where people in Bantry meet. On the first Friday of each month the square is largely taken over by people from the countryside around selling their home-grown vegetables and home-made handicrafts (even if, just occasionally, the "home-made" activity consists of little more than peeling off the "made in Hong Kong" labels). On these Fridays, the Anchor Inn fills up in late morning; but even so nobody hurries. If the (genuinely) home-cured smoked mackerel is available, it is a treat. Given the difficulty in finding good restaurants outside the main Irish cities, prudent visitors either lower their sights or accept gratefully what above-average dishes they can find.

Unlike some towns (Skibbereen, for example), Bantry *breathes*. It is not contained by oppressively narrow roads. Stand in the square with the bay at your back and the hills above Bantry ahead of you, and you see a friendly, comfortably proportioned town. Tourists have been coming here since at least the early 19th Century. According to Thackeray, "Were such a bay lying upon English shore, it would be the world's wonder."

On the edge of the town, **Bantry House** offers one of the best views over the bay. First built in 1765 by Richard White, the first Earl of Bantry, it has a collection of tapestries, carpets and furniture on display to the public, and the grounds are laid out in formal Italian style. The library is one of the finest rooms of any building in the area: large and beautifully proportioned. When local musicians gathered for a concert to raise money for Live Aid, it was in the library that they entertained their audience.

Diving inland: On any roughly clockwise tour of Ireland, the natural next

Digging for sea urchins at Bantry Bay.

stop after Bantry is **Glengarriff**. But the pull of Cork's coastline is inclined to overpower anything inland. So Glengarriff will have to wait just a little while we dart inland at **Ballylicky**, drive through **Kealkil** and head for the hills.

There are two main reasons for this. First, from the Ballylicky/Inchigeelagh road it is possible to see some of the best on-site handicrafts in the region being made. Just a mile east of Kealkil a road sign points up a track towards **Teadagh Candles**, where waxen shapes of wondrous varieties, colours and fragrances are moulded by Mark O'Hora. Further east, three miles (five km) beyond **Ballingeary**, another road sign to the left takes you first to Alan and Rosemary Taylor's leather-work studio (for wallets, belts, handbags etc) and, above them, to Bob Pinker's Woodery (for boxes, table lamps, chopping boards and salad bowls). Not only do these places sell their products more cheaply than the tourist shops they supply; there is an extra pleasure from seeing how and where they are made and the people who make them.

The second reason for taking this road is **Gougane Barra**. It consists of a lake surrounded by one of Ireland's finest forest parks with well-prepared walks, nature trails and places to park and picnic. On an island in the lake, legend has it, St. Finbar first arrived, founded an oratory and finished off one or two jobs that St. Patrick had missed, like drowning a local monster. More recently, Father Denis Mahoney, a Carmelite recluse, settled here in the 18th Century. The modern romanesque chapel post-dates both St. Finbar and Father Mahoney. But when the weather closes in from the **Shehy Mountains** round Gougane Barra, it is not hard to understand how the story of the lake is one of saints, monsters and recluses. A magical place.

Tracking back to the coast and resuming our leisurely journey towards Kerry, we come to **Glengarriff**. This is a sheltered resort at the end of an inlet off Bantry Bay. In summer, at the eastern entrance to the town, are invariably men waving cars down to offer a trip in a boat. This is one occasion when one of the offers is worth accepting.

A few minutes' sail from Glengarriff lies **Garnish Island**. This used to be a barren rock, but during the early years of the 20th Century soil was carted to the Island so that its owner, John Allen Bryce, could turn it into a miniature botanical paradise. The sheltered site of the island provides ideal conditions for growing trees, shrubs and flowers from all over the world. It contains an especially beautiful formal Italian garden. Try and see Gougane Barra and Garnish Island on the same day: the wild and the tame of southwest Ireland, both at their best.

To the west of Glengarriff lies the **Beara Peninsula**, which offers outstanding hill walks—notably to **Sugarloaf Mountain**, just west of the town. The alternative to touring the peninsula is to take the direct hill road north towards **Kenmare** and into County Kerry. Stop at the highest point of the road, the county border: the view back over Bantry Bay is truly majestic.

Then into Kerry: Kerry folk are to the rest of the Irish what the Irish are to the British: the butt of "stupid" jokes. Thus: "What do you find on the bot-

On the road in a self-drive caravan at Dingle.

tom of a Guinness bottle destined for Kerry?" "Open other end."

Why Kerry jokes rather than, say, ones about people in Cork or Donegal? Kerry is no further away from Dublin; but it has historically looked west across the 'Atlantic rather than east across the hills for much of its trade and human contact. Perhaps this has created a psychological rather than geographical distance that has made Kerry seem somehow different.

Driving north from Glengarriff, the first town you reach is **Kenmare**. Where most towns in County Cork are marked by narrow streets and frequent traffic congestion, Kenmare's two main roads are wide and spacious. This is because Kenmare was designed as a landlord's town. In 1775 the Marquess of Lansdowne decided what he wanted, the planning was done and the town was built. This gives the centre of Kenmare a pleasing architectural harmony, with its rows of substantial limestone houses.

That is the visible face of Kenmare's history. Its less visible face is its claim to fame as the place where one of the least probable solutions to Anglo-Irish relations was first mooted. In around 1670 Sir William Petty, who developed the ironworks, lead-mines and sea-fishing on which the area's economy was initially based, proposed shipping 20,000 Irish girls to England, and bringing the same number of girls back from Britain— so that succeeding generations of local children would be reared as loyal "English" boys and girls.

Kenmare is one of the starting points for one of Ireland's justly famous tourist itineraries: the **Ring of Kerry**. Taking first the inland section, head north from Kenmare towards Killarney. The road climbs towards **Moll's Gap**, from which the first sight of the lakes to the west of Killarney is obtained. It is tempting to stop here and admire the view; but a little further on, **Ladies' View** provides a more stunning spectacle across **Upper Lake**, **Muckross Lake** and the largest of them all, **Lough Leane**.

Pictures of Ladies' View tend to show it bathed in sunshine, interrupted by just a few wispy white clouds. Sadly the reality is less certain. If you are lucky you get an unbroken view of miles of lakes; if you are unlucky,

an unbroken view of miles of clouds. As with much else in this part of the country, Ladies' View is designed for the visitor with an entrepreneurial temperament—that is, one who takes risks.

Down the hill, the road to Killarney passes the edge first of the Upper Lake and then Muckross Lake. Red deer still roam the woods by the lakes; one of the pastimes of 18th Century British settlers was to chase them down the hills and into the lakes, and then take to their boats to continue the pursuit.

Past Muckross Lake and to the left is **Muckross House** and its gardens. The house has a Tudor appearance but was built in 1843. Both the house and gardens now belong to the National Parks and Monuments Service; the house serves as a local folk museum and the 10,000-acre (4,000-hectare) grounds as spacious, beautifully kept, lakeside gardens from which a variety of well-signposted walks can be undertaken.

The tourist trap: Four miles (6.5 km) north of Muckross House is **Killarney.** You can tell you are getting close by the number of tourist pony-and-trap riders you have to overtake along the tree-lined road. For this reason, many people don't like Killarney, dismissing it as expensive and pretentious. The two buildings of note in the town are neo-Gothic churches, both built in the 19th Century: the **Catholic Cathedral** and the (Anglican) **St. Mary's Church.**

Killarney's value is not *what* it is but *where* it is. Even that can be something of a nuisance; Killarney's roads are narrow and there is no by-pass. Unless you have a compelling reason to stop, its most memorable characteristic is likely to be its capacity to create the greatest traffic jams in southwest Ireland outside Cork city.

There is an alternative way round the ring of Kerry on leaving Kenmare. Take the coast road west out of the town and head towards **Sneem.** This is a bright, open village which looks like an adult version of a set of dolls' houses. The front of each house is freshly painted each year in pastel shades. Even the petrol stations manage to retain a pristine appearance, as if forever freed from the grime of oil and axle grease. Sneem has a proud,

Preceding page, the landscape deep in agricultural Ireland near Kenmare. These pages, left, and right, scenic vistas like these lure people into circling the Ring of Kerry.

quiet way of attracting tourists; some of its prices may not be much lower than Killarney's, but you don't resent paying them so much here.

Continuing the Ring of Kerry to the west of Sneem, we come to one of the loveliest and historically most evocative places in the area, **Derrynane**. The house and grounds, which run down to the ocean, provided for centuries the home of one of Ireland's most distinguished families, the O'Connells. Today the house has become a museum—although that word has too musty a flavour for such a moving collection of artefacts—that celebrates the family, and in particular "The Liberator": Daniel O'Connell, one of the greatest of 19th Century Irish nationalists.

Continuing round the Ring of Kerry from Derrynane, we come to **Waterville** and **Ballinskelligs Bay**. This is the site of one of Ireland's legends, demonstrating what many visitors suspect: that the more precise the story, the less plausible it is. Noah's son Bith and grand-daughter Cessair, so the legend runs, arrived here 5,000 years ago after being excluded from the Ark. With them were two other men and 49 women. The women were shared among the three men, who soon found they couldn't cope with the excessive demands made on their masculinity. The pilot of their ship, Ladra, a lad of 16, soon died, and Bith expired a little later. The third man, Fintan, was Cessair's favourite all along, but faced with the prospect of 50 women to himself, he fled. At which point Cessair died of a broken heart. Fintan survived to pass on the story, going through various transformations in the process: at one point he turned into a one-eyed salmon.

Lords of the Ring: Back to reality and the Ring; north to **Cahirciveen**, whose wide main road looks like a botched Irish attempt to imitate an American cowboys-and-injuns frontier town. In the early part of the 19th Century Cahirciveen was so cut off from the rest of the country that it had greater contacts with America than with Dublin; letters and newspapers from the Irish capital even arrived via New York. The town's links with America were strengthened by the fact that the European terminal of the first trans-

atlantic telegraph cable was **Valentia Island**, just to the west. After a number of false starts—broken cables, water penetrating the insulation—contact was first established in August 1857. By 1866 an intermittent service was replaced by a new, stronger and permanent cable link.

This cable was to have played a role in what might have become Cahirciveen's moment of Irish glory. Just off the town's main street, down by Valentia river, are the ruins of some magnificent police barracks. (Actually, they were never meant to be so magnificent: they were designed for India's northwest frontier, but the plans were mixed up.) In 1867, during one of the nationalist uprisings, the plan was to occupy the barracks, then contact the telegraph station at Valentia Island and from there inform the world via the newly installed cable that a free Irish republic had been proclaimed. This is almost certainly the first occasion when anyone used the now well-known first commandment of anyone planning a *coup d'état*: make sure you command the means of communication.

Eastwards, the road makes its way towards **Dingle Bay**, with fine views of the Dingle peninsula to the left and, a little later, of the highest mountains in Ireland, the **Macgillycuddy Reeks**, to the right. Not that Himalayan landscapes should be expected: the highest peak, **Carranntoohill**, is just 3,414 feet (1,040 metres) high.

One of the finest views over Dingle Bay can be had from a ruin just above the road near **Glenbeigh**. At first sight it looks like one of many old castle ruins that can be found in Cork and Kerry, but on closer examination, Glenbeigh's "castle" is different. It was, in fact, built just over 100 years ago by an eccentric nobleman, Lord Headley. He wanted a castle of his own and commissioned an equally odd architect, E.W. Godwin, to design it. Godwin's mind, however, wandered from the task in hand—among other things he was occupied with winning and keeping the affections of the actress Ellen Terry—and Headley's castle ended up with leaking roofs and walls. The castle, or **Glenbeigh Towers** as it is now known, was reduced to ruins during the 1922 Trou-

Horse for sale at Killorglin's Puck's Fair.

bles. This was, perhaps, one of the few destructive acts for which the perpetrators might be wholly forgiven.

Puck's luck: Killorglin, six miles (10 km) east of Glenbeigh, almost completes the Ring of Kerry. A prettier village than many, Killorglin stands on the banks of the **River Laune**, by which the waters from Killarney's lakes reach the sea. Every August 10-12, Killorglin celebrates **Puck's Fair**. This probably has its roots in a pagan harvest festival, although, if you prefer to believe it, the fair is also said to commemorate the occasion when goats saved Killorglin from Cromwell's army. According to this version, goats ran into Killorglin's streets, warning the locals that the English army was heading their way, and giving them time to defend the town. During Puck's Fair a wild goat is brought down from the hills and "enthroned" as King Puck in the town square. Its horns are adorned with ribbons and rosettes, upon which event everyone celebrates with what one official Irish guide describes as "unrestricted merrymaking."

Fresh seafood dominates the southwest's menus.

From Killorglin, you can either fork right and complete the Ring of Kerry by heading back to Killarney, or turn left towards **Castlemaine** and the Dingle peninsula. Dingle and the hills behind it are well worth the detour. **Dingle** itself is a lively fishing town and is one of the few places where it is easy to eat well, with its variety of restaurants serving fresh fish. Like Killarney, Dingle's economy also depends on the tourist trade; unlike Killarney, Dingle has not been spoiled excessively by this fact.

This is partly a matter of Dingle's intrinsic geography: hemmed in by the sea on one side, the hills on the other, Dingle cannot sprawl (although a plethora of recently built bed-and-breakfast homes along the road to the east and west make it hard to see where the town begins and ends). Back from the harbour, the town's streets climb steeply.

Just look anywhere: North from Dingle, the road over **Connor Pass** provides one of the most exhilarating drives, even by local standards. At the top of the pass, where a car park allows plenty of time to stop and enjoy the views, the scenery is remarkable in every direction. Behind, Dingle Bay and Kerry's hills. Ahead, **Brandon Bay** and the **Maagharee Islands**. To the left, **Brandon Mountain**, Ireland's highest peak outside the Macgillycuddy Reeks. To the right, more hills and lakes. If the wind is not too strong, make time to stop here to walk around and slowly absorb the views.

The road then heads down towards Brandon Bay and Tralee Bay, before arriving at **Tralee**. Much of the town is eminently forgettable: it is Kerry's largest town and its industrial centre. But in the centre is some splendid 18th Century architecture, particularly **Denny Street** where the houses are majestic and the street wide enough to do them full justice. And for anyone who wishes to absorb Irish culture in a serious manner, Tralee contains the **Siamsa Tire** theatre, the National Folk Theatre of Ireland. After a hard day's immersion in the history, legend and scenery of Kerry— and very possibly its wind and rain— the theatre provides a wholly amenable way to spend the evening, before heading on for Limerick and Clare.

THE MIDWEST

The mid-western counties of **Tipperary**, **Limerick** and **Clare** contain a rich-textured variety of landscape, from the barren hills and jagged coastline of north Clare to the soft mountains, rolling pastures and winding river valleys of Limerick and Tipperary. The region is rich also in historic relics. Hundreds of castles, mostly ruined, remind you that this was the land of the great Gaelic chieftains of Munster, such as the O'Briens, and of Norman-Irish warlords with names like de Burgo, Butler and FitzGerald (still a name to be reckoned with).

Ireland now is again part of the wider world, and **Shannon International Airport**, where many overseas visitors first touch its soil, is more than a point of arrival: it is the key to the modern-day development of the mid-western region. Opened in 1945 as the first Customs-free airport in the world, it has attracted many foreign-based companies to its surrounding industrial estates, providing the region with jobs, greater prosperity and a new feeling of confidence. It has also been the impetus for the development of many tourist centres highlighting Ireland's past. At the same time, of course, it has accelerated the disappearance of the old ways that many tourists come to see—an irony common to tourism anywhere.

That point is well illustrated at the first—and the premier—stop for many tourists: **Bunratty Castle and Folk Park**, which stand beside the main road between Shannon and Limerick city.

The folk part is a gem, as absorbing for an Irish visitor as for an American or Japanese. It contains more than 20 replicas of rural and urban houses as they would have appeared to a visitor to mid-western Ireland in the late 19th Century. There is a grey limestone cottage from north Clare; a whitewashed mountain farmhouse from west Limerick; the comfortable, though far from opulent, home of a well-to-do farmer in Tipperary's Golden Vale; nearby, the hovel inhabited by his hired hand; and so on. One of the houses on display actually stood on what is now a runway at Shannon Airport.

There is something of a "Marie Celeste" feeling about the place: a turf fire smoulders in each hearth, farm implements lie around, as though casually put aside a few moments before. In one cottage, an old pair of socks is drying by the fire. There is even a village street, with pawnbroker, pub, drapery, printworks, grocery and post office. "Stepping into the past" has become a tourist cliché, but at Bunratty the idea really works.

Corny banquets: Bunratty Castle, which dates in its present form from about 1450, became a stronghold in the 16th and 17th centuries for the O'Briens, earls of Thomond, as this part of Munster was then known. It was restored in the 1960s and fitted with an impressive collection of 15th- and 16th-Century furnishings. "Medieval banquets," at which guests are served and serenaded by beguiling medieval colleens, are held in the castle twice nightly all the year round. It sounds corny—it *is* corny—but most visitors love it.

About eight miles (13 km) northwest, near the village of **Quin**, is **Craggaunowen Castle** (1550), which was restored in 1975. In its grounds are a reconstructed *crannog*, or bronze-age lake dwelling, a ring fort and a *souterrain*, or underground chamber. Also on display is **the "Brendan"**, a leather boat in which the adventurer and writer, Tim Severin, sailed from Ireland to Newfoundland in 1976-77 to prove that St. Brendan the Navigator could have made such a voyage in the 6th Century, as ancient chronicles relate. Nearby **Knappogue Castle**, of similar vintage to Bunratty, is another venue for banqueting and balladry.

Those who seek more authentic, living traditional music should note that Clare is celebrated for its musicians, particularly concertina players and pipers. You should find good "sessions," especially in summertime, in the pubs of almost any of the coastal towns and villages, such as **Kilrush, Kilkee, Milltown Malbay, Ennistymon, Lahinch, Liscannor** or **Doolin**. If you feel like a break from the drink, the music and the chat, take a drive or a stroll and view the bleak, rocky landscape spilling out to the Atlantic. The most spectacular feature along this coast are the **Cliffs of Moher**, between Loscannor and Doolin, which stretch for about five miles (eight km), towering sheer above the sea to nearly 700 feet (200 metres).

In north Clare lies the strangest landscape in Ireland: **the Burren**, a bare, hilly area of about 100 sq miles (260 sq km), devoid of trees and surface water, which is often likened to the surface of the moon. This type of landscape, composed of highly porous, carboniferous limestone, is called *karst* by geologists, after a region of Yugoslavia.

Beneath the Burren's eerie surface is a labyrinth of pot-holes, caves, streams and lakes, but only one small stretch of it, **Aillwee Cave**, is accessible to visitors without special training and equipment. A local herdsman, Jacko McGann, discovered this cave in the 1940s and explored much of it, but it has been open to the public only since 1978. Its entrance, two miles (three km) from **Ballyvaughan** (and signposted much further afield), includes a

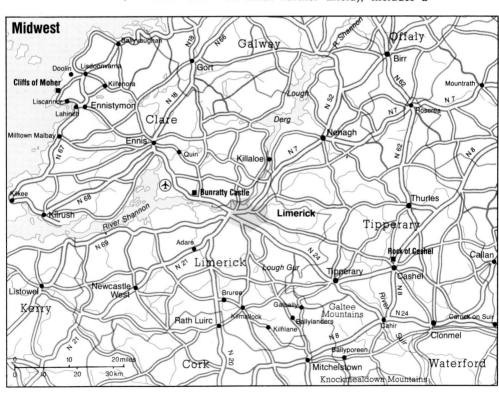

craft shop, snack bar and information bureau, but it blends so well into the hillside as to be almost invisible; not surprisingly, it has won several architectural awards, including the EEC's Europa Nostra prize. The cave itself, several hundred metres long, contains many strange rock formations, as well as the bones of a brown bear, lying in the hollow where he died snoozing the winter away thousands of years ago.

The **Burren Display Centre**, at **Kilfenora**, explains the geology and rare flora of the area with a variety of visual aids. The town of **Lisdoonvarna**, Ireland's only active spa, is a popular resort, especially in September, when a match-making festival is held.

Ennis, the county town, stands on the main road to Limerick. It has a Franciscan abbey (1250); a neo-classical statue of Daniel O'Connell, the great 19th Century leader of constitutional nationalism, who was MP for Clare from 1828 to 1831; and a locomotive that ran on the West Clare Railway (1887-1961), which was immortalized in Percy French's comic song, "Are you right, there, Michael, are you right?"

Unliked Limerick: And so to **Limerick**, Ireland's fourth largest city (60,000 people), and a place which many Irish people, and not just Dubliners, claim to detest. On a casual acquaintance, it's hard to see why. It has many fine Georgian houses, wide bridges over the Shannon, interesting old quays and a lively arts centre (the **Belltable**, in O'Connell Street). Its busy shopping streets, thronged with young people, give it a lively air. Perhaps one has to learn to hate it.

King John's Castle (*circa* 1200), at the east end of **Thomond Bridge**, is an imposing Norman fortress. It bears the marks of a bombardment in 1691 during the Williamite-Jacobite war, in which Limerick played a critical part. **St. Mary's Cathedral** (1172), now used by the Church of Ireland, is noted for its black oak misericords (elaborate carvings on the undersides of the choir stalls) which are unique in Ireland. **St. John's Cathedral** is a gloomy, grandiose piece of 19th Century Catholic triumphalism. Its 280-foot (85-metre) spire is said to be the tallest in Ireland. The city's 17th Century **Granary** has been nicely modernized to house the main tourist office for the region.

If you feel like a break from the city's bustle, take a trip to the **Clare Glens**, a few miles east of Limerick, where scenic walks are signposted along a wooded gorge by the cascading **Clare River**.

An orderly place: 10 miles (16 km) southwest of Limerick, on the N21 road to Killarney, is **Adare**, often described as the most beautiful village in Ireland. It is certainly picturesque, highly atypical in its rather English orderliness, and well worth an afternoon's browsing. On the outskirts of the village, in a leafy setting by the **River Maigue**, are the ruins of the 13th Century **Desmond Castle** and a 15th Century **Franciscan friary**, as well as a 14th Century **Augustinian abbey**, restored for use by the Church of Ireland.

The village itself, with its wide main street and quaint cottages, is largely the creation of the third Earl of Dunraven (1812-71), who was converted to Catholicism in the 19th Century Oxford Movement. The **Trinitarian Abbey** (*circa* 1230), at the northern end of the main street, was restored in

Memorial in Limerick city commemorates the 1916 Easter Rising.

1811 by the first Earl of Dunraven and given to the Catholics of Adare as their parish church.

Driving south from Limerick city through rolling pastures and woodland, you are likely enough, in autumn or winter, to encounter a party of men and women in fancy dress mounted on horses, perpetuating one of the chief pastimes of the Anglo-Irish Ascendancy: fox-hunting. Twelve miles (19 km) from the city, around the shores of **Lough Gur**, are a series of remnants of much older ascendancies, starting with the neolithic. They include stone circles, forts, dolmens, standing stones and the sites of prehistoric houses. Two simulated stone-age dwellings house an "interpretative centre."

Further south, the **Galtee mountains** are seen rising steeply from the plain like folds of dark green velvet. By the town of **Kilmallock** stand the graceful ruins of a 13th Century **Dominican priory**, reached by a footbridge across the **River Loobagh**. **Blossom Gate**, one of four which once guarded the town walls, straddles one of the main streets. Kilmallock also boasts a Norman castle and the 13th to 15th Century **Church of Saints Peter and Paul.**

In **Bruree** village, four miles (six km) to the northwest, is a museum named after Eamon de Valera, the former Prime Minister and President of the Irish Republic, and the author of its Constitution. It is housed in the school he attended as a boy. The western approach to the village, dominated by an old water-mill by a bridge on the River Maigue, is most attractive.

Six miles southeast of **Kilmallock** is the pleasant town of **Kilfinane**; its main feature is the **Kilfinane Moat**, a tall, flat-topped mound encircled by three ramparts, which may have been a place of inauguration for local chieftains. Seven miles further east is the village of **Ballylanders**, which has a circular, modern Catholic church; its corrida-like interior is striking.

The road from Ballylanders through **Galbally** village leads into County Tipperary through the glorious scenery of the **Glen of Aherlow**, which spreads between the Galtee Mountains and the **Slievenamuck** range. For more on County Limerick, an excellent book is Mainchín Seoighe's

Slowly through the lanes of Limerick.

160

Portrait of Limerick, which vividly details its history and topography.

Long way to Tipperary: The Glen of Aherlow is a fine gateway to Ireland's largest inland county. There is great variety of scenery in Tipperary's mountains, pastures and river valleys, but the abiding impression is of lushness. In the slanting sun of a summer, the **Golden Vale** seems well named indeed. The dominant features of Tipperary are the Galtee and Knockmealdown Mountains and the lonely height of **Slievenamon**, all in the south of the county, and the broad, central plain, watered by the winding **River Suir**.

It is the Suir that gives the towns of south Tipperary their charm. **Cahir** has a fine central square and a splendid castle commanding a bridge and a V-shaped weir. There was a fortress on the spot as early as the 3rd Century, but the castle, begun in 1142, is largely 15th Century. It is fully restored and houses an interpretative centre for the area. **St. Paul's Church** was built to an 1820 design by John Nash, architect of London's Regent Street.

Tipperary's largest town, **Clonmel**

Small-town Ireland as seen in Nenagh, Co. Tipperary.

(12,500 inhabitants), is 10 miles (16 km) to the east. It enjoys a lovely riverside setting, looking across at the **Comeragh Mountains** of County Waterford. A surviving portion of its old town wall girds **St. Mary's Protestant Church**, which has an octagonal tower, and the old **West Gate** still arches over a main street. The **Main Guard**, a large garrison house, bears the town's arms on its front wall. The civic regalia in the **Town Hall** include the mayor's gold chain, to which each holder of the office must add a link. **St. Mary's Catholic Church** is a spacious, 19th Century neo-classical structure with an ornate gilt ceiling. A former mayor of Clonmel, the Italian Charles Bianconi, gave Ireland its first public transport service, the "Bianconi cars," which began by running between Clonmel and Cahir in 1815. Laurence Sterne, author of the novel *Tristram Shandy*, was born in Clonmel in 1713.

Carrick-on-Suir, 13 miles (21 km) further east, is a good base for exploring the **Comeragh Mountains**. **Carrick Castle** is a well-preserved Elizabethan fortified mansion.

THE MIDLANDS

Since the time of the Gaelic revival at the turn of the century, it has been a received wisdom that the "real" Ireland is to be found in the west, in the Irish-speaking areas of Kerry, Connemara and Donegal. For many people, in Ireland and abroad, this seemed a forgotten land—a land of stony fields, rocky coasts, bare mountains, thatched cottages, donkeys, old storytellers and travelling musicians. It is an Ireland that still, just, exists. Undeniably, it is real. Whether or not it is *the* real Ireland is another question, a question that the Irish, in their obsessive grappling with self-identity, will doubtless debate for years to come. But certainly the Ireland of the Midlands is the forgotten Ireland of today.

When we think of Ireland we think easily of Dublin, or of Cork and Kerry, or of the bleak, beautiful west, or of the troubled North. The Midlands come to mind less readily. But, like "Middle America," (often forgotten in the clamour from New York and California) the middle of Ireland has much, and maybe more, to tell a visitor about the country and its people.

This is a mundane Ireland—though not without its magic—and a mundane image is apt for its landscape. Irish schoolchildren used to be taught that Ireland could be thought of as a saucer, the raised rim standing for the mostly mountainous coastal regions and the flat base representing the lowlying midlands. Imagine that the user of the saucer has spilt his tea and you have the additional truth that the midlands are largely liquid. The tract of country running north from County **Laois** through **Offaly**, **Westmeath**, **Longford** and **Roscommon** consists of bog, pasture and water, water, water: old canals, scores of rivers, hundreds of lakes and streams, thousands of ditches, gullies and backwaters—and all of them pouring or percolating, in unending aqueous abandon, into old man **Shannon**, who just keeps rolling into the Atlantic.

Occasionally, the skies of Ireland weep too much for even the Shannon's swollen arteries, and the brown waters spill out over the bogs, the pastures and the farmland. Not surpisingly, fishing and boating dominate the region's attractions, but there are many pleasures also for those who prefer dry(ish) land: quiet, seductive landscapes, absorbing antiquities, and the accidental delights of the country towns.

The visitor will also be struck, as elsewhere in Ireland, by the less attractive features of modern Ireland: the shameful littering of the countryside with domestic refuse and rusting cars; the uncontrolled spread of roadside hoardings and garish shop signs; the disappearance of hedges and stone walls in favour of corral-style fences and concrete walls; above all, perhaps, the proliferation of tasteless and ostentatious new bungalows and houses, which often manage to combine, say, *ersatz* Georgian pillared doorways with hacienda-style arches and mock-Tudor latticed window. God save Ireland. It is all part, one supposes, of grappling with self-identity.

Ruins and forests: Maybe it's best to begin our meandering progress safely

Preceding pages, the Midlands in its magical, rather than mundane, mood. Right, travelling circuses are still popular.

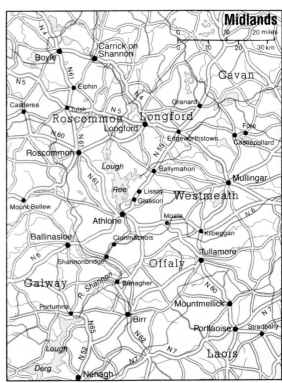

in the distant past: at the splendid ruins of the 12th Century Cistercian abbey at **Boyle**, County Roscommon. Boyle is a pleasant, raggedy town standing in a bend of the river of the same name, overlooked by the beautifully named **Curlew Hills**. Its main street was once the avenue to the stately home of the local landowners, the King family. The abbey, founded in 1161, is a mixture of the Romanesque and Gothic styles.

Two miles to the northeast lies **Lough Key**, which is bordered by a large, State-owned forest park with caravan, picnic and camping sites, a shop and a restaurant. On one of several wooded islands in the lake is a ruined abbey. The lake and its environs were once the property of the MacDermotts, princes of Moylurg, but in the early 17th Century they were seized, in the fashion of the day, and granted to one Sir John King, in whose family they remained until 1959. The forest park is a fine spot for walking, fishing and boating. A modern viewing tower stands on the site of an earlier structure by the Regency architect, Sir John Nash. It is

connected by tunnels to the lakeshore and estate—a *jeu d'esprit* by one of the King family.

On the N61 road south to the county town of **Roscommon**, a striking sculpture dominates the skyline at a crossroads near the village of **Elphin**. It is a memorial to the men of the Roscommon IRA killed in the War of Independence. Its combination of military pride and simple piety is typical of the ethos of rural Irish republicanism.

Roscommon town contains a ruined 13th Century Dominican priory and a Norman castle. The fine **Bank of Ireland** building in the wide main street was once the courthouse and later served as the Catholic church. The adjacent old county jail once had a female hangman, "Lady Betty," a murderer who was spared the noose on condition that she carried out the executioner's job without a fee.

But one of the best things in Roscommon is the Victorian shop premises of **James J. Harlow, "Funeral Requisites and Furniture Stores."** The left-hand side of the emporium is a hardware shop with a bar at the

Come and buy; an Athlone trader.

rear. The shop is crammed with a cornucopia of household implements; the bar is practically a museum of advertising, except that it is all very much alive. Both evince a highly individual sense of display and are clearly the work of a talented collector. No visitor to Roscommon should pass by.

Longford, chief town of the neighbouring county, lies 22 miles (35 km) to the east on the far side of the Shannon. It is an unremarkable place, dominated by **St. Mel's Cathedral**, a grey, 19th Century edifice in Renaissance style. The saint's 5th Century crozier is preserved in a museum at the rear. The village of **Edgeworthstown**, eight miles (13 km) further east, has a long association with the Edgeworth family, whose best-known member was Maria (1767-1849), author of the novel, *Castle Rackrent*. Another Edgeworth, the Abbe Edgeworth de Firmont, was confessor to Louis XVI of France, and attended him on the scaffold.

Salmon and saddles: Eight miles north, **Granard** is an angling and riding centre. The imposing hill rising behind the church at the southwest end of the town is the **Motte of Granard**, an ancient redoubt fortified by the Normans. Edward Bruce sacked and burned the town in 1315 after being refused winter quarters.

Twelve miles (19 km) southeast is the attractive village of **Castlepollard**, County Westmeath, which is laid out, English-style, around a green. It is a good base for fishing or for touring this picturesque region of low hills, lakes and small woods. Three miles east, in a secluded hollow, is the tiny village of **Fore**, standing amid a group of ecclesiastical ruins. A graveyard beside the road from Castlepollard contains the 7th Century **St. Fechin's church**. In the sloping field above is an ancient tower, once inhabited by a hermit, and an adjoining mausoleum erected in the last century by the Greville-Nugent family. In the middle of the valley stands a 13th Century **Benedictine abbey** in the style of a Norman castle. The ruins and their sleepy setting have great charm.

Mullingar, Westmeath's bustling county town, is about 10 miles (16 km) to the south, in the centre of a great cattle-raising area. ("Beef to the

Below, ruins at Clonmacnois. Far right, spuds for sale by the roadside.

167

heels, like a Mullingar heifer" was a phrase once used to celebrate a woman of ampler charms.) The town's dominant structure is a large, Renaissance-style cathedral, built in 1939.

Athlone, the county's largest town, bestrides the Shannon 30 miles to the west at the southern end of **Lough Ree**, one of its three major lakes. Here you can fish, sail, row, cruise, swim or water-ski. **Athlone Castle**, at the western end of the Shannon bridge, has been a strategic military post since the 13th Century. The town was the birthplace of the tenor John McCormack (1884-1945), the first great star of the gramophone. A plaque marks his house in The Bawn, off **Mardyke Street**, and a bust of him stands on the riverside promenade.

The N55 road leads north from Athlone through the so-called **"Goldsmith Country"**, which lies between the villages of **Glasson** and **Ballymahon**. Oliver Goldsmith, author of *The Vicar of Wakefield* and *She Stoops to Conquer*, is believed to have been born at **Pallas**, County Longford, three miles east of Ballymahon, in 1729. He went to school at **Lissoy**,

near Glasson, and the district may have inspired his poem, *The Deserted Village*. Places supposedly described in it are now signposted.

Going south from Athlone on the N62 road into County Offaly, you come upon the remains of the greatest of all the monastic cities of Ireland, **Clonmacnois**. Founded by St. Ciaran in 548, it flourished for several centuries and was the burial place of the last High King, Rory O'Conor, in 1198.

A place of repose: Clonmacnois stands on a rise overlooking a broad, reedy bend in the Shannon. At the small jetty below, tourists now moor their cabin-cruisers where pilgrims from all over Europe once arrived to study and pray. The site contains a cathedral, eight churches, two round towers, three sculptured high crosses and parts of two others, and the remains of a castle. There are also over 200 ancient inscribed sepulchral stone slabs, dating from the 6th to the 12th centuries. Especially in early morning or at dusk, Clonmacnois is a place of ethereal repose.

At the village of **Shannonbridge**, a few miles south on the river, a grim,

The steam museum at Stradbally, Co. Offaly.

grey Napoleonic fort and a 16-arch bridge loom over a sheltered jetty. **Banagher**, the next crossing-point downstream, is a popular base for cruising and fishing and an attractive town in its own right. Some of its stores are unchanged since the 1940s and earlier. Others are well-stocked with wines, spices and exotic vegetables to cater for Continental holidaymakers. *Bienvenue à Banagher.*

Eight miles (13 km) further south, by the **River Brosna**, is **Birr**, Offaly's elegant Georgian county town. **Birr Castle**, home of the Earl and Countess of Rosse, is not open to the public, but you can stroll in its extensive gardens and pleasure grounds, where over 1,000 trees provide fine sprays of colour in spring and autumn. The box hedges are the tallest in the world, according to that bible of useless facts, *The Guinness Book of Records.*

East of Birr, the heathery ridge of the **Slieve Bloom** mountains marks the borders of County Laois. Because of their solitary interruption of the low horizon, they can seem quite grand, but they rise only to about 1,700 feet (520 metres). The "Blooms" are intersected by 24 tranquil glens and many places of particular charm are signposted. **Mountmellick**, at the northeast end of the range, is a 17th Century Quaker town almost encircled by the Owneass river. At **Rosenallis**, four miles (six km) northwest, is the oldest Quaker cemetery in Ireland.

One of the country's most historic fortifications, the **Rock of Dunamase**, rises by the roadside four miles east of the county town, **Portlaoise**. Originally a Celtic stronghold, it was plundered by the Vikings and later became part of the dowry of Aoife, daughter of the King of Leinster, when she was married to the Norman lord, Strongbow. In 1650, when it was a stronghold of Irish resistance, it was blown apart by Cromwellian artillery. There is a fine view from the top. If you continue east through **Stradbally** and take the road for Carlow, you can enjoy another panorama—this time including the **Barrow Valley** as well as the central plain—where there is a car park and picnic site for the purpose.

Casual cruising: One of the best ways to see the Midlands is from the waters of the **Grand Canal**. Once a busy, vital, commercial link between Dublin and the Shannon, the canal is now a peaceful retreat for angling and boating. A holiday on its waters is strictly for those who like a quiet time—during a week's cruising on it in June you might see only one other boating party. You can hire an old-fashioned narrowboat near **Tullamore**, itself a pleasant, lively town with many fine old houses—and your only worries then are coping with the locks (easy when you get the hang of it) and deciding whether to head west towards the Shannon or east towards the smaller and quieter **Barrow**.

The still stretches of the canal are lined by grassy banks lush with yellow irises, dogdaisies and orchids; trees and bushes sometimes form a green tunnel that screens you entirely from the world. Where the vegetation is sparser, there are broad vistas over undulating pastureland dotted with trees and scrub, or across the vast, brown bogs. Excitement is provided by the occasional blue flash of a kingfisher, the soft splash of an otter, or a family of ducks crossing your path with reckless decorum. If peace is what you seek, you'll find it here.

Horse-made Ireland still needs blacksmiths.

THE FAR WEST

Galway city stands at the mouth of the salmon-filled river that flows between **Lough Corrib** and the sea. It began as a fishing village, but by the 13th Century had become a walled and fortified town in the most sheltered corner of **Galway Bay**. The fishing village survived until the mid-1930s as a neat collection of picturesque thatched cottages. They were demolished, for sanitary reasons, and replaced by the present-day **Claddagh**; a cluster of grey, slated cottages. The place has given its name to the distinctive Claddagh finger-ring, carrying a crowned heart motif between two hands.

The city developed as a Norman-English settlement surrounded by hostile natives. Its governors were very loyal to the English crown and the city gained its Royal Charter, as an independent city state, from Richard III in 1484. This led to a long period of political stability, material prosperity and increased trade with England and the Continent. During this period the city was ruled by the representatives of the 14 most prominent families, or Tribes, and Galway is still known as the City of the Tribes.

The style in which they lived can be judged by what remains of their architecture. The **Church of St. Nicholas**, on the market place, is the largest parish church of the medieval period in Ireland and has been the Anglican Cathedral since the Reformation. **Lynch's Castle**, town house of the premier Tribe, is now a bank on the main street, and **Browne's Gateway**, which was the entrance to the town house of another great merchant family, has been erected at **Eyre Square**, near the **John F. Kennedy Memorial Garden**.

The city's relationship with the "mere Irish," outside the walls, can be established from the old ordinances which set down the hours during which they could remain inside the gates, the prescribed way of wearing their hair, and even the games they were allowed to play. At no time were they supposed to indulge in "the hurling of the little ball" but only the playing of "the great football." For their part, various native Irish tribes regularly assaulted the city from their mountain retreats to the west, and not without results. Over the west gate of the city was inscribed the motto: "From the fury of the O'Flahertys, good Lord deliver us." The O'Flahertys came from the Irish-speaking area of Connemara.

Myth makers: In a country where myth is often as potent as history, and in a city much given to creative folklore, the visitor will hear much that must be taken with a grain of salt. One of the main tourist "sights" in Galway is **Lynch's Window** where, in 1493, Walter Lynch, mayor of the city, hanged his own son for the murder of a Spanish guest. It was a crime of passion and such was the son's popularity with the people that the mayor feared a mob would release him from jail. He then decided to perform the hangman's task himself.

Some writers have speculated that this event originated the term Lynch Law. However, historians have found no basis for the story in any of the contemporary records. But the win-

dow is worth seeing and is only around the corner from the Church of St. Nicholas, where Christopher Columbus is reputed to have heard Mass before leaving to discover America. The "evidence" for this is that one of his crew was known as William of Galway.

Much more of the architectural excellence of this period in Galway's history would have survived had the city fathers not backed the wrong political horse in the middle of the 17th Century. But they staunchly backed England's Royalist forces against Cromwell's invading army and paid the price. When the city was forced to surrender in 1652, the Roundheads pillaged, plundered and burnt, destroying many of the finest stately homes. One can see the mutilated and defaced statues in the church of St. Nicholas where the Cromwellians stabled their horses. But 14 other churches and their towers were obliterated forever. All that remains of the elaborate city walls is the portion known as the **Spanish Arch** across the river from Claddagh.

Although this military defeat result-ed in the decline of Galway as a major port and commercial centre, it also began a new relationship between the city and its hinterland. Today, Galway is the only city or town in Ireland where two languages, English and Irish, can be heard spoken daily in the streets. In summer many other languages can be heard as the city has become one of the country's major tourist centres: the gateway to the Aran Islands, Connemara and Mayo.

Most travellers who have written about Galway agree that it possesses in abundance two attributes which are very difficult to define: atmosphere and character. Seán O'Faoláin, novelist and historian and himself a Corkman, once wrote: "No man who wants his daughter to learn the truth about life could do better than send her for six months to Galway. With the relief of the actor whipping off a wig, they will tell you story after story, in gushing delight at the vagaries of human nature.... Yet, I think my daughter might well return from Galway and say to me, in an awed voice, 'My father, *is* that the truth?' I should have to say, 'My child, of

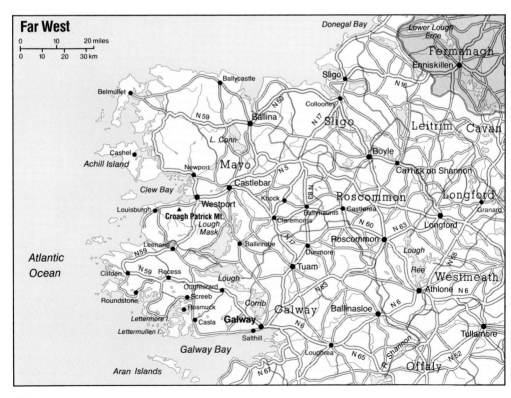

course it is not the truth. But it *is* life!' Galway is and lives a folk-tale."

Galway's gatherings: Galway today is a prosperous place. In 1986 it became Ireland's first newly created borough, since independence was achieved with a population of over 50,000. Alone among Irish cities it has managed to retain, virtually intact, the maze of narrow, winding streets that comprise its commercial centre. This extends from **Eyre Square**, through **Williamsgate Street**, **Shop Street** and **Mainguard Street** as far as **O'Brien's Bridge**; including the many streets that meander away toward the Corrib and the docks.

Saturday is a great day to be in the city. The streets teem with masses of people, in from the country to the east and west, doing their weekly shopping. Itinerant musicians play along the streets and farmers and their wives sell their produce in the marketplace.

Although busier in summer than in winter, because of the influx of tourists, Galway is always a bustling place. It has a growing university (the original limestone building and quadrangle dates from 1849) as well as a College of Technology, two large hospitals, docks and a thriving industrial complex on the outskirts of the city. All this contributes to creating a large stable, as well as transitory, population. Most of the hotels are busy all year round and the guest houses and bed and breakfast establishments that cater for tourists in summer open their doors to students in autumn.

These facts explain the presence of a great variety of eating-places that serve food at almost all hours of the day and the fact that Galway boasts of two theatres: **An Taibhdhearc**, which stages plays in the Irish language; and the **Druid Theatre**, which in a decade has created a reputation that extends to the West End of London.

The highlight of the year is the summer **Race Week**, held during the last week in July. The racecourse is situated on the slope of a hill at **Ballybrit**, about four miles (six km) from the city centre and overlooking Galway Bay and the Aran Islands. It is as much a carnival as a race meeting and, although over £1 million is wagered daily, many of those attending remain in the popular enclosure and rarely see a horse, such is the variety of sideshows: hawkers, musicians, fortune-tellers, beer-tents, three-card-trick operators and travelling people who converge on Galway from all parts of Ireland. Perhaps the greatest tribute to the fun that is to be had at Ballybrit is that the city closes down every afternoon to enable everyone to get there.

To recover from the excesses of a day at the races—not to mention the hectic nightlife that follows—victims would be well advised to head for the nearby seaside resort of **Salthill**. It is within pleasant walking distance from the city centre, and although it is not a particularly beautiful place—consisting mainly of functional tourist hotels, pubs, clubs and casinos—it has a magnificent two-mile (three km) stretch of promenade that skirts the sea, with an uninterrupted view of the bay and the Burren beyond. It is said locally that an early morning walk from one end of it to the other has the curative powers of two gins and tonics.

But gentler pleasures are also to hand. One could stand for hours on the **Salmon Weir Bridge**, which spans the river at the point where it flows out of Lough Corrib. Here the salmon

Wild Connemara, a challenge for walkers.

lie in ever-shifting ranks waiting to assault the weir on their way upstream.

The bridge leads to what was once Galway Jail, now the site of Ireland's newest cathedral. This is the **Catholic Cathedral of St. Nicholas and Our Lady Assumed into Heaven.** It was consecrated in 1965 and is constructed in an amazing variety of architectural styles in local limestone and Connemara marble. It also contains some unusual mosaics in its side-chapels; particularly the mortuary chapel where the lately-departed are presided over by John F. Kennedy and Pádraic Pearse.

Stars and stripes: President Reagan visited Galway during its quincentennial celebrations in 1984 and, like President Kennedy, who visited the city in 1963, is enrolled as a Freeman. The Kennedy visit is marked by a stone tablet in the garden named in his honour at Eyre Square.

At one of its corners stands a beautiful limestone statue of the writer, Pádraic O'Conaire. Although born in the city he was reared in Connemara and wrote exclusively in Irish until his death at an early age in 1927. As he was as famous for his nomadic life-style as he was for his writings and was very partial to the bottle when he had the price of it, some of the more respectable citizens were scandalized when it was proposed to erect this statue in his honour. It has long since become one of the country's showpieces, as most of the country's recently erected statuary is quite hideous, and Galway has the distinction of being the first town in Ireland to erect a memorial to a contemporary artist.

The striking fountain, with its triangular brown centrepieces, which stands behind **Brown's Gateway**, was erected to commemorate the city's quincentennial. The motif are the sails used on the traditional Claddagh fishing boats, known as hookers. They no longer exist in Claddagh but in recent years many of the surviving boats have been restored along the Connemara coast for use as pleasure craft.

Before venturing west from Galway it is necessary to know that without benefit of a car (or a conducted coach tour) it is difficult, if not impossible, to explore Connemara and Mayo with the aid of public transport. Railways have almost vanished from this part of Ireland and buses are few and far between. But the main roads are good and the secondary ones reasonably so, if only because most people who use them also travel by car.

Aran adventure: Before moving out of the city, though, it is worth casting an eye at the three **Aran Islands** that straddle the mouth of the bay, like three limestone whales at rest on the surface of the Atlantic. Without the benefit of this natural breakwater, Galway Bay would be a very exposed harbour and it is from Galway that the regular ferry boats to Aran sail all through the year. There is also a daily plane service to the three islands, run by Aer Arann (Aran Air) from **Carnmore Airport** near the Racecourse. The air-journey takes only 15 minutes; the sea-journey three hours. However, the air-journey is much more expensive. During the summer months (June to September) many small ferries run between **Ros a' Mhíl (Rosaveel)** on the Connemara coast and Inishmore. This journey takes about an hour.

The three Aran Islands, **Inishmore,**

A sharp eye for a piece of pork in Belmullet.

Inishmaan and **Inisheer**, have been inhabited long before recorded history and contain many pre-Christian and early-Christian remains. Most noteworthy of these is **Dún Aengus** stone fort on Inishmore, one of Europe's finest prehistoric monuments. It is perched on the edge of a vertical 200-foot (60-metre) cliff over the sea and consists of four semicircular defensive walls. Outside these there is an additional barrier of thousands of upright limestone pillars placed at various angles, like modern tank-traps.

The experts have failed to date Dún Aengus with any degree of accuracy: some say 4,000 BC and others 1,000 BC. But apart from its striking aspect and historic interest, the view from its ramparts is one of the most striking imaginable. On a clear day one can follow the sweep of coastline from Kerry and Clare to the south, as well as the length of Galway to the western extremity of Connemara.

The islands have long attracted artists writers, philologists, antiquarians and film makers. Robert Flaherty's film *Man of Aran* (1934) made the islands known to a worldwide audience. Playwright John Millington Synge wrote his book *The Aran Islands* while living on Inishmaan, where he also heard the plot of his most famous play, *The Playboy of the Western World*. Inishmore has produced one internationally known writer, Liam O'Flaherty. Born in the shadow of Dún Aengus, he is famous for his nature stories and as author of the novel *The Informer*.

Irish is the daily language of the people of Aran, but the majority of them are equally fluent in English. This is also true of the people who live on the southern shore of the Connemara coast, across the bay. Both areas are part of what is known as the Gaeltacht. The latest census shows that there are about 65,000 native speakers of Irish living in areas of varying sizes in Waterford, Cork, Kerry, Galway, Mayo and Donegal.

Language barriers: The Connemara Gaeltacht begins on the outskirts of Galway, on the coast road through **An Spidéal (Spiddal)**. This is obvious to the tourist for, suddenly, the signposts are in Irish only instead of being bilin-

Wind-breaking patterns on the Aran Islands.

gual. This is a recent innovation, brought about by public agitation in the 1970s as part of an effort to strengthen the role of Irish in everyday life. It also resulted in the setting-up of a special radio service for all the Gaeltacht areas with its headquarters in Connemara. (Because most of the existing road-maps still carry the anglicized forms of the place-names, these forms are also given in brackets here.)

Connemara is one of the most beautiful regions in Ireland and also one of the most barren. To travel through it is to understand why so many of its people are to be found in Boston, Birmingham and London. The amazing thing is that so many remained to eke out a precarious existence on the rugged, marshy land and on the sea. They are a hardy and resourceful people and one of the ways by which they supplement their income is through the illegal distillation of a white spirit called poteen: from the Irish *poitín,* a little pot.

The tourist is bound to hear of it, and may even be offered some to drink or to buy, as it is now made in even greater quantities among the hills

and on the remote lake and sea islands that abound in Connemara. It is made from a mixture of barley, sugar, yeast and water. The resulting liquid, or "wash," is then boiled over a constant flame and the steam run through a home-made still: usually a coil of narrow copper piping in a barrel through which cold water flows.

In the days before the invention of bottled gas the police were always on the look-out for the constant spiral of peat-smoke in isolated places. The pungent smell of the boiling "wash" made isolation necessary and the penalty for being caught in the act meant a heavy fine and the confiscation of the equipment as well as the poteen. Now the odds are very much in favour of the makers, and poteen is available at about half the price of legal whiskey. If the liquid is run through the still three times the poteen is perfectly safe, if exceedingly fiery, to drink. One-run poteen, or poteen to which some unscrupulous distillers add commercial alcohol, is dangerous and the uninitiated should exercise caution.

The tourist would also be well advised to remember that the penalty for possession is also severe; although the law usually deals leniently with those who plead that the spirit was not intended for personal consumption but to loosen the limbs of a rheumatic greyhound! But for the benefit of those who like to live dangerously, the greatest centres of poteen-making in Connemara are **Leitir Móir (Lettermore), Leitir Mealláin (Lettermullen)** and **Ros Muc (Rosmuck)**.

Bays and hills: By following the coast road to **Casla (Costello)**, then turning right to **Scríb (Screeb)** and then left again along the much-indented coast road through **Cill Chiaráin (Kilkieran)**, **Caiseal (Cashel)**, **Roundstone**—where one re-enters the non-Gaeltacht part of Connemara—and on to **Clifden**, one sees all that typifies coastal Connemara. The land is painfully poor, with great tracts of lake, mountain and moorland stretching as far as the eye can see to the north. To the south lie the deep, curling bays filled with islands and fringed by black, red and orange seaweed. Along the road, and away in the hills, are clusters and villages of whitewashed cottages and modern bungalows. The village of Roundstone is outstanding among them.

Clifden is the region's principal town and one of the best places to buy traditional tweed. If time permits it would be worth doubling back towards Galway, through **Recess**, **Maam Cross** and **Oughterard**. This road affords a fine view of the **Twelve Pins** mountain range and the islands on Lough Corrib. Those who come to Ireland with a view to fishing for salmon, trout, and a variety of coarse fish would find an agreeable and rewarding base in any of the many hotels and guest-houses along this road.

From Clifden one can also enter **Mayo** by a most pleasant route. It goes by **Kylemore Abbey**, one of the country's most-photographed buildings, which looks even better in reality. It is a late 19th Century limestone and granite building erected by a Liverpool merchant, as a gift to his son, and is now run by the Benedictine nuns as a boarding-school for girls.

Mayo is Ireland's third largest county but most of its interesting features are in the western half, particularly along its varied coastline.

The road from Kylemore Abbey leads to **Leenane** and **Killary Harbour**, Ireland's only fiord—so deep and sheltered that it could accommodate the entire navy of any world power—and a left turn takes you to **Louisbourg**, a small town at the back of **Croagh Patrick**, Ireland's holy mountain. It is a place of pilgrimage for thousands on the last Sunday of July, but a climb to its summit, on a clear day, is rewarding for even greatest unbeliever.

It affords one of the finest panoramic views in Ireland: out over the Atlantic and the offshore islands, to the west; south over the mountain fastnesses of Mayo and Connemara; the rolling plains of central Mayo to the east; the island-studded **Clew Bay** to the north with **Achill Island** looming in the distance. The English writer William Thackeray, who visited the west in 1842, described the scenery around Clew Bay as the "most beautiful in the world."

Westport lies on an arm of Clew Bay and is unique among Irish towns in that it was designed to the plan of the well-known architect of the Georgian period, William Wyatt. The Mall, with

There are hundreds of main streets just like it: this one is Castlebar, Co. Mayo.

its lime trees lining both sides of the **Carrowbeg River**, is one of the country's most charming thoroughfares.

On the way from Westport to Achill Island the huge disused, arched railway bridge that dominates the little town of **Newport** is a sad comment on the social life of this area, and particularly Achill Island. It is all that now remains of the railway that once linked the island and Westport. It was built as a result of an outcry, in the mid-19th Century, when a boat carrying migrant workers from Achill to Westport foundered in Clew bay with heavy loss of life. They were on their way to Scotland to harvest potatoes.

Because of the outcry the railway was built to link with the Westport-Dublin line, but by 1936 it was deemed uneconomic and was closed. However, some days before the official closure, a party of boys and girls from Achill were smothered by fire in a cottage on a farm in Scotland, where they were harvesting potatoes. The last train from Westport to Achill carried the coffins containing their charred remains.

Although Achill has been connected by a bridge to the mainland since 1888, it still retains many of the characteristics of an island. It is dominated by two mountains, skirted by wild moorland. The rest of the land is a dazzling combination of magnificent cliffs, golden strands, purple heather and scattered cottages that look even whiter than they are because of the dark background.

Knock's miracle: To the north lies one of the most desolate and depopulated areas in Ireland, the boglands of **Erris** that lead to the Erris Peninsula, where **Belmullet** is the principal town. The coast road from Belmullet to **Ballina**, through **Killala** (where the French forces landed during the Rising of 1798) overlooks some fine cliffs. On the way south again, to the county's principal town of **Castlebar**, it is worth making a diversion to the village of **Knock**.

Here, on a wet evening in 1879, several local people saw the Blessed Virgin silhouetted on the gable of the local church. Now a basilica that seats 15,000 dominates the village, and although no great miracles have been claimed or verified by Catholic authorities, hundreds of thousands of pilgrims, many of them invalids, journey to Knock annually. It was to celebrate the shrine's centenary that the Pope came to Ireland in 1979 at the invitation of the local parish priest, Monsignor James Horan.

Since then, on the top of the nearby mountain of **Barrnacuige**, the main runway of what is hoped will be an international airport has been laid down. The airport was the brainchild of Mgr Horan, who maintained that the west needed a major airport to attract industry and to bring in pilgrims to the shrine. At first, he was regarded as a crackpot, but he succeeded in getting £8 million out of one vote-conscious government. That was enough to lay the main runway on the mountain and complete the terminal building.

Unfortunately for him, the government that came to power in 1983 regarded the venture as a "foggy, boggy white elephant" and stopped further finance. In the west of Ireland, however, most people think that Mgr Horan, the Pope's friend, will prevail and that Knock will achieve its technological miracle on a mountaintop.

Miracles are what Knock is all about.

THE NORTHWEST

One of Ireland's most enigmatic counties is **Sligo**. It contains everything necessary to become a major tourist centre; in many ways it rivals Killarney in its beauty and in the variety of its natural attractions, with the Atlantic on its doorstep as a bonus. Apart from that, the county holds such a concentration of antiquities that it might be considered one of the oldest parts of the world; and also one of the youngest, for **Lake Achree**, in the north of the county, was formed by a volcano as late as 1490.

When one adds the fact that Nobel prize-winning poet, William Butler Yeats, named most of its beauty-spots in his poems and plays—and that his brother, Jack B. Yeats, painted pictures of local races, fairs and carnivals—the question is, "Why did Sligo choose to hide its many lights under a bushel for so long?"

Part of the answer may be found in the staid county town of **Sligo**, the principal commercial centre of the northwest region. It was always regarded as a prosperous town, its commercial life presided over by the conservative heirs to long-established family businesses. When Irish tourism was organized nationally in the 1950s and 1960s, other areas rushed to the forefront; Sligo seemed either reluctant or indifferent. All that has changed during the past decades. Sligo is making up for lost time and the area now has the advantage of a perceptible freshness which one misses in some of the well-used tourist centres.

To explore the county in any direction the ideal base is Sligo town. Situated on the **Garavouge river**, which flows from Lough Gill to the sea, it is surrounded on three sides by distinctive mountains. The most spectacular is **Benbulben**, to the north, in the shadow of which the Poet Yeats is buried, in **Drumcliff Churchyard**, a few miles from the town.

Yeats has become something of a growth industry in the Sligo area in recent years. The **Yeats Summer School**, held annually in August, attracts scholars and students from as far afield as Japan and Australia. Indeed, Sligo abounds in hotels, pubs, lounges and tea-rooms named after the poet. Some say that this commercial activity, battening on his reputation, has the poet whirling in his grave, for which he composed the epitaph carved on the tombstone: "Cast a cold eye on life, on death. Horseman pass by!" They forget the poet's own acute commercial instinct. When the editor of the *Irish Times,* R. M. Smyllie, rang him with the news that he had been awarded the Nobel Prize for Literature, Yeats's first words were, "How much, Bertie, how much?"

Not far from Drumcliff is the seaside resort and excellent golf-links of **Rosses Point**, and across Sligo Bay, to the south, the quaintly old-fashioned resort of **Strandhill**, nestling between Knocknarea and the sea.

An ancient place: Knocknarea is another of the area's dramatic mountains. Although its chopped-off cone is only 1,000 feet (300 metres) high, it dominates the countryside in an eerie way. It is crowned by an immense cairn, comprising about 40,000 tons of loose rock, constructed in such a way that the removal of those at the base

Northwest

0 10 20 miles
0 10 20 30 km

Malin Head

Tory Island

Lough Swilly

Creeslough

Gweedore

Milford

Ramelton

Buncrana

Arranmore Island

Burtonport

Dungloe

Grianan of Aileach

Londonderry

Letterkenny

Donegal

Glenties

Strabane

Ardara

Glencolumbkille

Malinmore

Killybegs

Donegal

Lough Derg

Tyrone

Kilcar

N 56

Pettigo

Omagh

Donegal Bay

Ballyshannon

Inishmurray Island

Mullaghmore

Bundoran

Lower Lough Erne

Fermanagh

Benbulben Mt.

Enniskillen

Rosses Point

Sligo

Lough Gill

Source of River Shannon

Upper Lough Erne

Strandhill

Sligo

Garrowmore

Tubbercurry

Ballymote

Lough Allen

Drumshanbo

Belturbet

Cavan

Lough Arrow

Leitrim

Boyle

Cavan

Northwest 185

would lead to a gigantic avalanche of stone. It is said that this is the burial-place of Maeve, Queen of Connacht, the first truly liberated woman in Irish mythology. Her pursuit of the Brown Bull of Cooley and the bloody war that resulted from it between the armies of Ulster and Connacht is the subject of one of Ireland's best-known sagas, *The Táin* (available in an excellent English version by the poet, Thomas Kinsella).

Knocknarea, which means "Hill of Executions" in Irish, falls away in a series of steep slopes and acute preci-pices. To the west is **Carrowmore**, site of one of the biggest megalithic tombs in Europe. To the east, is a perfect view of one of the country's most beautiful lakes, **Lough Gill**. The lake may be explored by boat and you may land on the island that inspired Yeats's best-known lyric, *The Lake Isle of Inishfree*.

A little to the north of Sligo town, on the road to Bundoran, is the site of a battle which sounds like a myth but happens to be historically accur-ate. The "Battle of the Books," in which 4,000 men were killed, took place in Cuildrevne in 561, between the followers of St. Columba and St. Finian over the unlikely issue of copyright. Finian lent a rare psalter to Columba who copied it surrepti-tiously. When Finian found out he de-manded the copy and, when Columba refused, asked the High King of Ireland to give a judgement. This he did in the famous sentence: "To every cow its calf and to every book its copy." But the hotheaded Columba defied the judgement and both sides went to war. Columba's army won but he was then overcome by remorse and decided to make reparation by leaving Ireland forever. After building a monastery at Drumcliff, fragments of which still survive, he sailed to Iona in Scotland and spent the rest of his life as a missionary.

Uninhabited island: Further north, at the little harbour of **Mullaghmore**, boats may be hired for the trip to **Inishmurray Island**, about four miles (six km) out to sea. The last inhabi-tants left for the mainland in 1947 but the island contains a very interesting collection of antiquities; including one of the country's earliest Christian churches. There is also a most unchris-

tian collection of Cursing Stones. These rounded stones are the subject of a legend which claims that nobody has ever succeeded in counting them correctly twice in succession, though they number only about 40.

Ballymote, in the south of the county, takes special pride in the vast 14th Century **de Burgo Castle** with its six towers, and the **Franciscan friary** where *The Book of Ballymote*, key to the ancient Ogham characters, was written in 1390.

Here again the prehistoric is much in evidence and at nearby **Karrowkeel**, on a hilltop in the **Bricklieve Mountains**, there is an impressive collection of passage graves. Excavations on the site have revealed pottery and other articles from the late Stone Age.

For those who can take antiquities, or leave them alone, the circular drive around nearby **Lough Arrow**, with its tree-laden islands, will provide a relaxing feast for the eyes. But even here the past provides another imposing relic. **Ballinafad Castle** was built in the late 16th Century to defend a pass in the **Curlew Mountains;** a mere Johnny-come-lately in Sligo terms.

Before moving east towards Leitrim a nearby lake is worth a visit. **Lough Nasool** (The Lake of the Eye) disappears through a hole in its bed, every so often, only to fill up again just as suddenly and inexplicably. And, like everything else in Sligo, thereby hangs a tale.....

Ireland's Cinderella: County Leitrim has very little going for it, particularly in the matter of travel-writing. William Thackeray ignored it in his *Irish Sketch Book*, as did most other writers. Leitrim people are understandably sensitive about being the Cinderella of the 32 counties. It is a narrow county, only 46 miles (74 km) in length, with a maximum breadth of 18 miles (29 km). Of coastline it can only boast a mere two miles, wedged between the golden beaches of Sligo and Donegal. Most of the county is hilly, some reaching rounded peaks of 2,000 feet (600 metres). But because of the composition of the soil—shale, sandstone and millstone grit—the countryside is moorish and undulating, with few dramatic features.

To compound its problems, Leitrim lacks both industry and natural re-

Tranquillity in the lanes of Leitrim.

sources, apart from an uneconomic coalmine at **Arigna**. It is constantly drained by heavy emigration, to Dublin as well as to the United States and Britain. Alone among the counties of Ireland, it failed to show any increase in population since emigration was stemmed in the 1960s. The population is still in decline, with a high percentage of elderly people.

If Sligo was late entering the tourist scene it can be said that Leitrim is still trying to make an entrance. Its greatest assets, in that respect, are the **River Shannon**, a mass of lakes and an expanse of totally unspoiled countryside for those who would relish an unconventional holiday.

Lough Allen, six miles long and three miles broad (10 by five km), is one of the three great Shannon lakes. It is surrounded on all sides by bleak mountains. But it is a paradise for coarse fishermen, most of whom come from the English Midlands in search of pike, perch, rudd and bream. The nearby town of **Drumshanbo** specializes in catering for anglers, and it is also a great centre of Irish music.

With the growth in popularity of cruising holidays on the Shannon, the county town of **Carrick-on-Shannon**, has become the main centre of this activity, which is particularly popular with continentals. By comparison with the overcrowded and much-polluted European waterways, the Shannon is a virtual ocean. Cabin cruisers may be hired at Carrick-on-Shannon. The river and its many lakes are navigable as far south as Killaloe, 14 miles (22 km) from Limerick. For anyone wishing to get "lost" in the most leisurely way possible, a cruise on the Shannon, with its many islands and secluded harbours, would be difficult to beat.

Deserted Donegal: The best way into **County Donegal** is by the coast road through **Bundoran**. This is a well-established resort of the old school, much favoured by visitors from Northern Ireland. It is also a centre for surfers as the Atlantic thunders onto the broad beach in a series of rolling breakers. To the north, the town of **Ballyshannon** rises on the steep banks of the **River Erne**, with **Assaroe Falls** nearby. A right turn here leads to the village of **Pettigo**, one half of which is in the Republic and the other in Northern Ireland.

About five miles (eight km) from Pettigo is the strange penitential island in **Lough Derg**, still visited by thousands of pilgrims each year. The lake is isolated and surrounded by moorland and heathery hills, and is known as St. Patrick's Purgatory. Legend has it that St. Patrick spent 40 days fasting and praying in a cavern on an island, called **Station Island**, about half a mile from the shore. It has been a place of pilgrimage for centuries, even when such practices were forbidden under the Penal Laws.

The Lough Derg pilgrimage is a very serious matter. From June 1, when the pilgrimage season begins, until August 15, only genuine pilgrims are allowed on the island. It is less than an acre in extent and almost completely covered by a basilica and a church as well as hospices for the pilgrims.

The penitential exercise takes three full days, on each of which only one meal (of dry bread and black tea) is allowed. Water may be taken at other times. Pilgrims must go barefoot during their time on the island, and the exercises include the saying of prescribed prayers at St. Patrick's and

Gossip is the stuff of life in a Donegal village.

188

St. Brigid's crosses, and while making the circuit of the basilica and of each penitential bed: these are the remains of the stone cells of the early Christian monks. And as if all that is not enough, the first night on the island is spent in a vigil in the basilica and most pilgrims do not eat a full meal until they arrive home from the island.

Border problems: Donegal Town is an excellent centre for touring the southern side of the mountainous county. Donegal was the county most affected by the partition of Ireland. The eastern part of the county, where the land is good and the landscape dull, has a high proportion of Protestant farmers and shopkeepers, who look towards Northern Ireland.

For the people of the north Donegal area, many of whom are Irish-speakers, **Derry** (Londonderry to the English) was their regional capital. It was the port from which they sailed to Scotland, for seasonal work in the fields, or more permanent work tunnelling and building roads. The local paper most of them read—and still read—was published in Derry. For these people, Derry and Glasgow were homely places, rooted in their oral traditions. Glasgow Celtic was the soccer team they followed, and during the years when Derry City soccer team disappeared, as a result of the violence, a new team called Finn Harps was set up in **Ballybofey**.

The people of south Donegal did not feel so isolated by the border. They turned naturally to Sligo. To the people of Donegal Town, and its hinterland, Dublin did not seem as dimly distant as it did to the people of Inishowen Peninsula.

Seventeen miles (27 km) west of Donegal Town is the town of **Killibegs**, the major fishing-port on the west coast. The arrival of the fishing-fleet, festooned by flocks of sea gulls, is a sight not to be missed as the pier is right in the centre of the town.

Kilcar, a little further west, is the centre of the Donegal tweed industry, and beyond it, the village of **Carrick** is the starting-place for the ascent of **Slieve League** (1,972 feet, or 600 metres). It must be emphasized that this climb, rewarding though it is, is not for anyone suffering from even

A village bar in Dunfanaghy, Co. Donegal.

mild vertigo, or who is not fully fit. It is scarcely worth while setting out for the summit if the day is not reasonably clear. When the summit is reached, after a hair-raising walk along a narrow ledge—with a drop of 1,800 feet (550 metres) into the sea on one side, and an equally steep escarpment on the other—one can rest and enjoy a view ranging over five counties and a large expanse of ocean.

A visit to the village of **Glencolumbkille** is recommended. It is at the end of a long valley rich in monuments dating back to pre-Christian times. But the place gets its name from the fiery patron of Donegal and Derry City, St. Columba or Columkille (Dove of the Church). A **folkvillage,** consisting of four cottages representing different periods of Irish life and containing furniture and utensils of the period, is well worth a visit, as is the craft centre run by the local co-operative.

A tidy town: For the traveller heading north, the most interesting route is through **Ardara** and **Glenties.** Glenties has won the annual award for Ireland's tidiest town, sponsored by Bord Fáilte, many times. It is picturesquely set where two glens converge and is a thriving place with a knitwear and hosiery industry.

From here the road leads to an area of more than 60,000 acres of rock-strewn land, intersected by streams and dotted with many lakes, merging with a coastline dotted with islands. It is known as the **Rosses,** meaning a place of many islands, and the village of **Dungloe** is its "capital."

Nearby **Burtonport** is another busy fishing-port, where more salmon and lobster are landed than at any other port in Ireland or Britain. From here a regular ferry-service runs to **Arranmore Island,** three miles (five km) off shore.

The area between here and **Fál Carrach (Falcarragh)** to the north is another Gaeltacht with its heartland in the parish of **Gaoth Dobhair (Gweedore).** It is a place renowned for the industry and good husbandry of its people, many of whom spend part of the year working in Scotland. When viewed from the road that skirts the verge of **Bloody Foreland** (so called because of the colour its stone assumes in the setting sun) the

Tory Island hangs on, off the coast of Donegal.

Gweedore area looks like a large town, particularly at night, so dense is the mass of houses. In an attempt to provide employment for the people in their homeland, the organization for the development of the Gaeltacht regions has created an industrial estate in the middle of the parish. It includes a theatre and the regional studios for the Gaeltacht radio service.

Tory Island, which looms large to the north of Bloody Foreland, is nine miles (14 km) away. It has a population of about 200, who are holding out against a movement to have them relocated on the mainland. It is a unique community and boasts a school of primitive painters.

Visitors to Tory must be prepared for adventure, as it is not easy to cross the turbulent sound, even in summer. But for anyone interested in seeing an isolated community struggle to retain its identity and traditions, in the face of bureaucratic resistance, a trip to Tory Island could be the most rewarding experience during an Irish holiday. At the moment the people of Tory seem to be winning. The island's first legal pub opened at the end of

1985 and an occasional helicopter service runs during the winter months.

Even a cursory look at the map will indicate a wealth of scenic beauty along the heavily indented coastline between **Horn Head** and the **Inishowen Peninsula**. The **Fanad Peninsula**, from **Milford** to **Fanad Head** and back to **Rathmelton** is skirted by a newly-constructed scenic road over 45 miles (72 km) long. It has some of the most striking cliff scenery in Ireland.

Letterkenny, the county town, is the best centre for touring north Donegal, but, apart from having one of the longest main streets in the country, has little else to recommend it.

Rocks and wells: Seven miles (11 km) west of the town, a little off the main road at **Kilmacrenan**, is **Doon Rock**. This was the inaugural place of the O'Donnell's, chieftains of Donegal up to the beginning of the 17th Century. Although the flat rock at the summit is only a short climb, because of the lie of the land it was possible for the chieftain to see the borders of his kingdom from this spot.

Nearby is what is known in Ireland as a "Blessed Well"; **Doon Well**. It is believed to have certain curative powers and the simple exercise performed by pilgrims consists of attaching a piece of personal clothing to a bush near the well, so that it always looks like a strange sort of totem pole. A steady flow of pilgrims still attend Doon Well.

The Inishowen Peninsula is a mountainous region leading to **Malin Head**, the most northerly point in Ireland and one of the most desolate. A 100-mile (160-km) circular scenic drive is well-signposted around the wild and beautiful landscape. The main town is **Buncrana**, much-favoured by visitors from Derry City, but **Malin** village (another winner of the Tidy Towns competition) is typical of Donegal villages and towns: neat, clean and somewhat austere.

About 10 miles (16 km) south of Buncrana is the most interesting relic of antiquity in Ulster, the **Grianán of Aileach** (Grianán means a sun-palace), which is a unique circular stone fort on the top of an 800-foot (240-metre) mountain. It was built about 1700 BC, was at one time the residence of the kings of Ulster, the O'Neills, and is not to be missed.

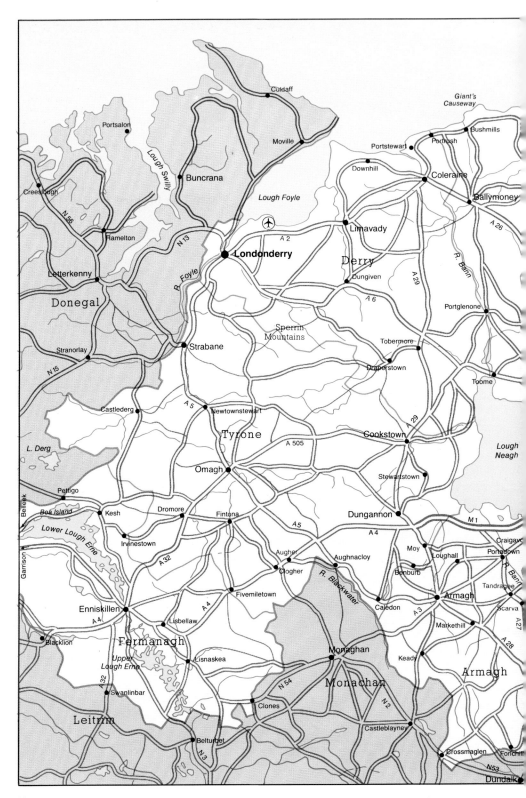

0   20 miles

0   30 km

and

Murlough Bay

lycastle

Cushendun

North Channel

Cushendall   Red Bay

Waterfoot

Carnlough

trim   Glenarm

Brougshane   Ballygalley

Larne

llymena

A 36

A 8

Island Magee

stown   Ballyclare

Antrim   Carrickfergus

Templepatrick   M 2

A 52   Bangor

Donaghadee

Holywood

Belfast   Newtownards

A 20

A 7

A 26   Comber   Ballywalter

Lisburn   Greyabbey

Strangford

Moira   Hillsborough   Saintfield   *Lough*

an

Dromore   A 7

Ballynahinch   Portaferry

anbridge   Strangford

Downpatrick

Down

A 24   Ardglass

Castlewellan

Newcastle   *Dundrum Bay*

Slieve Donard
Mt.

Mourne Mts.   Silent
Valley

Warrenpoint

Irish Sea

Carlingford L.

Kilkeel

THE TWO ULSTERS

Twenty years ago it was often hard to tell when you had crossed the border from the Republic into Northern Ireland. Perhaps you noticed that the post boxes and telephone booths were no longer green but red. Perhaps you became aware that the road surface had suddenly improved and deduced that British rather than Irish taxes had financed it. But that was about all. No passports were required. A few of the major crossings had Customs posts, but most people were casually waved through.

Today the differences are more marked. Passports are still not required, but many lanes which used to weave across the border and back again, as unpredictably as a St. Patrick's Day drunk, have been blocked by wedges of reinforced concrete a metre thick. On authorized roads, the visitor's first glimpse of Northern Ireland is of a British Army checkpoint, a concrete bunker with bullet-proof glass and silver anti-sniper screens, manned by a soldier wearing a flak jacket and carrying an automatic rifle. It can be an unsettling sight. At some crossings, as one soldier asks you for some means of identification, an unseen colleague inside the bunker taps your car registration number into a terminal linked to a computer at police headquarters. This is programmed with details of all suspect vehicles and within seconds you are cleared—or arrested.

Further along the road you may come across a footpatrol of soldiers, rifles at the ready and faces smeared with camouflage paint. Hedge-hopping Army helicopters pick them up and set them down, in order to make terrorist ambushes less likely. As you reach each village, you can readily identify the police station: it is the fortress protected by sandbags, barbed wire and anti-rocket screens, from the top of whose thick concrete walls video cameras scan all who approach. These outward and visible signs of Ulster's inheritance of hatred do little to prepare the stranger for the warmth and hospitality that the people extend to visitors—or at least to those visitors who avoid expressing strong opinions about the province's sectarian squabble.

One reason it is so difficult to be sure of the border's exact location is that it snakes its way along 18th Century county boundaries through farming land that is sometimes bleak, more often breathtakingly beautiful. It takes little account of natural boundaries, such as rivers, or of the cultural differences that separate Republican-minded Roman Catholics and British-oriented Protestants. A priest may find part of his parish on one side of the border, the rest on the other. Houses straddle the border so that, as the joke has it, a man may sleep with his head in the United Kingdom and his heart in the Republic of Ireland.

Political expediency accounts for the absurdities. It had been intended to redraw the border rationally after partition in 1922, and a Boundary Commission was set up to advise. But in the end the British government, hoping to avoid further disturbances, suppressed the commission's report and left things as they were. Had they decided differently, there might be no need today for army patrols and fortified police stations.

Many confusions were created. Whereas the ancient Irish province of Ulster consisted of nine counties, the new state of Northern Ireland, popularly known as Ulster, consisted of only six: **Antrim**, **Down**, **Armagh**, **Derry**, **Fermanagh** and **Tyrone**. Yet the three counties which went to the Republic—**Donegal**, **Cavan** and **Monaghan**—are still cemented to the other six by firm family and trading ties. To many local inhabitants, therefore, the border is something of an abstraction. And indeed it is difficult to take it wholly seriously when the states it divides cannot even agree about its length, the Republic claiming it is 280 miles (448 km) long and the Northern Ireland authorities adamant that it is 303 miles (485 km).

Since this book's concern is for the convenience of travellers rather than with tribal loyalties, we have included Donegal in the previous chapter and will here roam freely within the remaining eight counties of ancient Ulster. And, despite the war-torn image of northeastern Ireland, it *is* possible

Preceding pages, the Giant's Causeway in Co. Antrim; the nearby Dunluce Castle. Below, a border road block in Co. Fermanagh.

to roam freely, for there are other realities besides conflict. As the Northern Ireland Tourist Board—a body never short on optimism—has pointed out, its bailiwick really consists of 1,200 golf holes with a number of towns and villages scattered among them.

The Board's views are always worth listening to. Shortly before the present Troubles began, it put out a booklet stating: "Shooting is a popular sport in the countryside. Unlike many other countries, the outstanding characteristic of the sport has been that it is not confined to any one class."

Mild Monaghan: Some of the sadder consequences of partitioning a small island can be seen in **Clones** (pronounced *Clone-ess*), a small agricultural town in County Monaghan. Its most famous son is Barry McGuigan, the "Clones cyclone" who became world featherweight boxing champion in 1985. This turned him into an industry in his home town, unleashing Barry McGuigan tee-shirts, Barry McGuigan crisps and Barry McGuigan peanuts. The Catholic champ now lives with his Protestant wife in a small white bungalow a few hundred yards outside the town. This places him across the border in County Fermanagh—one reason, perhaps, for his popularity with both of Northern Ireland's feuding factions.

Clones's commercial centre is Fermanagh Street, signalling the town's former significance for the farmers of south Fermanagh. But, just as partition destroyed its role as an important railway hub, so the recent Troubles have hit trade as northerners have become more reluctant to cross the army-infested border. Also, the two tills on most shop counters hint at the effect of two different currencies. Since the Irish pound (or *punt*) broke its long-standing link with the British pound in the 1970s, it has usually been the weaker of the two, making prices in the South uncompetitively high compared to those in the North.

Clones has an ancient lineage. The remains of a 12th Century Augustinian abbey (known as "**the Wee Abbey**") can be seen in Abbey Street. An ancient cross in the marketplace shows scenes from the Bible, such as the Fall of Adam and Eve and the

Border checkpoint manned by the Irish police and army.

Adoration of the Magi. The cemetery has an early **round tower**, 75 feet (23 metres) high and rather dilapidated, and an early Christian carved **sarcophagus**, the key to which can be òbtained from nearby Patton's pub. Several Georgian houses are a reminder of the town's greatest period of prosperity, in the 18th Century. Another sign of the vanished "Ascendancy" era are the "big houses" dotted around the countryside. Once the homes of the well-to-do Anglo-Irish, many have now fallen into disrepair.

Monaghan is a quiet, trim county of snug farmhouses and tranquil market towns, and lakes and rivers that draw fishermen. Its administrative centre, **Monaghan**, 12 miles (19 km) northeast of Clones, has a **Market House** dating from 1792, an imposing 19th Century Gothic Revival cathedral (**St. Macartan's**) and an attractive **museum** highlighting prehistoric relics and local arts and crafts.

To the south, **Ballybay** and **Castleblayney** are unremarkable except for their proximity to **Lough Major** and **Lake Muckno**, both filled with a variety of coarse fish and surrounded by nature trails and picnic sites. Further south, **Carrickmacross** has fine displays of lacemaking and, just outside it, some interesting limestone caves.

Cavan's cruising: Landlocked County Cavan bridges the two Irelands by providing the source of two great rivers: the **Shannon**, which flows south to the Atlantic, and the **Erne**, which flows north into Fermanagh's magnificent lakes. Both rivers are ideal for cruising. Most of the county's scattered towns and villages have small hotels to cater for visiting fishermen.

Cavan town is the site of a 14th Century Franciscan friary, of which only a belfry tower remains. The Roman Catholic Cathedral, in contrast, dates from 1942. The Cavan Crystal factory offers glassblowing displays.

A tour of the county going west and north from Cavan would take in **Arvagh**, a peaceful village by Lough Garty; **Cornafean**, where Corr House has a fascinating collection of curios such as three-legged pots and cow bells housed in a converted pighouse; **Killeshandra**, by Lough Oughter; **Dowra**, near the Black Pig's Dyke, thought to

The red telephone booth tells you that you've crossed the border into Northern Ireland.

be an ancient frontier earthwork; **Blacklion**, a hamlet surrounded by many prehistoric ringforts and cairns including a beehive-shaped sweat house, an original form of Turkish bath; and **Butlersbridge**, where Ballyhaise House, now an agricultural college, has a rare 1733 oval saloon and two storeys vaulted over in brick.

A tour going east and south would cover: **Cootehill**, which has a splendid Palladian house built for the Coote family in 1730 in Bellamont Forest; **Shercock**, where the playwright Richard Brinsley Sheridan once lived; **Kingscourt**, whose Catholic church has some renowned stained glass; **Bailieborough**, which has a fine main street; **Virginia**, planned as a garrison town in 1610 and now a handsome, peaceful place; and **Ballyjamesduff**, with a well-designed market house.

The area is rich in folk traditions. In the late 1960s, for example, thousands of people from all over Ireland flocked each week to **Lough Gowna**, a remote hamlet where a 17-year-old boy was reputed to have great powers of healing through being "the seventh son of a seventh son" and could supposedly cure even serious ailments by laying his hand on the afflicted person.

Across the border: Fermanagh, adjacent to Monaghan and Cavan, has many things in common with them, particularly its tempo. Politically it is part of Northern Ireland and is the province's lakeland playground: a third of it is under water.

The county town, **Enniskillen**, a Protestant stronghold since Tudor times, is built on an island between two channels of the River Erne as it flows from **Upper** to **Lower Lough Erne**. In summer, pleasure boats sail from a central pier. The town's strategic importance is shown by **Enniskillen Castle**, the earliest parts dating from the 15th Century and an imposing water gate from the late 16th Century. The castle houses two museums, one specializing in prehistory, the other in military relics.

Like many cozy Ulster market towns, Enniskillen is rich in small bakeries and butcher's shops, and there's a gossipy atmosphere as farmers mix with townsfolk. A secret is soon shared in such a place. As elsewhere in Ulster, two similar looking variety

Cruising is the main attraction around Lough Erne.

stores, F.W. Woolworth and F.A. Wellworth, challenge each other across the main street—which changes its name six times between the bridges at either end. Equally familiar are the patrols of armed security forces and the injunction (common since the advent of car bombs) not to leave vehicles unattended in certain streets.

A true taste of the region's flavour can be gained by circling Lower Lough Erne. Three miles (five km) northwest of Enniskillen is **Devenish Island**, accessible by boat from the town. It is the best known of the lough's 97 islands because of its elaborate and exceedingly well-preserved round tower, which you can climb by internal ladders. Close by are the decorative ruins of the 12th Century Augustinian Abbey of St. Mary. A few miles further along the lough's north shore, **White Island** has a 12th Century church along one wall of which are lined up eight mysterious pagan statues, discovered only this century. Their origins continue to fox experts; some speculate that seven may represent the deadly sins.

A few miles further, past the village of **Kesh**, with its modern sailing

school and fortified police station, is the strangest of all the ancient stone figures: the two-faced Janus statue on **Boa Island**, which is joined to the mainland by a bridge at each end. In most countries, such a find would have been turned into a major tourist attraction. Here, you have to watch for an easily missable road sign pointing to "Caldragh Cemetery," then tramp through cowpats down a farm lane until you come across a field full of overgrown, moss-covered gravestones, in the middle of which lurks the inscrutable Celtic figure. The lack of refurbishment makes the place feel splendidly eerie; you look at the hollow in the figure's head and wonder whether it may have held sacrificial blood.

A second Janus figure was discovered on the little island of **Lustybeg**, near Kesh. There are holiday chalets for hire on this island.

Pilgrims and picnics: Following the lough's shoreline, you reach **Pettigo**, an old plantation town which was once the railhead for pilgrims visiting the holy sites at Lough Derg, just across the border in County Donegal. The River Termon, running through Pettigo, now marks the border and is said to be stuffed full of bilingual trout. It is also said that when a man had his skull fatally cracked during a fist fight in the middle of the bridge a surveyor had to be called to determine whether he had died within the jurisdiction of the Northern police or the Southern police. An oak tree on one side of the bridge was planted in 1853 to celebrate the British victory at Sebastopol. A statue on the other side commemorates four IRA men who died fighting the British in 1922.

A bizarre two-till economy copes with the fact that, thanks to Ireland's two currencies, stamps, gasoline and whiskey can cost 50 per cent more on one side of the river than on the other. The only reason the more expensive gas station doesn't go out of business is that the Republic's police and Customs officers feel obliged to patronize it rather than the cheaper British station. The same patriotism doesn't always extend to drink and it's not unknown for cars to be driven very gingerly out of Northern Ireland, their engine compartments packed full of whiskey bottles.

Depths of time: an ancient Janus figure on Boa Island.

Castle Caldwell, a ruined 16th Century castle by the loughside nearby, has become the centrepiece of a forest park, popular with picnickers and bird watchers. Worth seeing is a "Fermanagh cot," a 30-foot (10-metre) wooden barge used for transporting cattle and sheep to and from the islands of Upper and Lower Lough Erne. A fiddler who, the worse for drink, fell off a barge and drowned is remembered on a fiddle-shaped monument with a cautionary verse that ends:

On firm land only exercise your skill.
There you may play and safely drink
your fill.

The border touches the River Erne again at **Belleek**, where anglers assure you that you can hook a salmon in the Republic and land it in Northern Ireland. You can sense how tightly knit the town is by reading the advertisements on table-mats in the restaurant of the Hotel Carlton. On one, a local businessman offers to provide you with souvenirs, confectionery, Sindy dolls, cigarettes and his personal services, day and night, as a funeral director.

The village is famous for its **Belleek** pottery, manufactured from felspar imported from Norway. For 50p, you can take a half-hour tour of the factory, watching piece-workers put together the lustrous ornaments, surrounded by statuettes of Jesus Christ and posters proclaiming: "We support the hunger strikers." You can never quite escape from politics in the border country.

You can take the scenic drive back to Enniskillen along the south side of the lough, stopping at **Lough Navan Forest**, where a lookout point offers a panorama of five counties. At **Monea**, four miles (six km) off the main road is a well preserved 17th Century fortress.

"Over 300 million years of history" —impressive even by Irish standards—is the slogan used to promote **Marble Arch Caves**, an extensive network of limestone chambers containing remarkable stalactites. A 75-minute tour includes an underground boat journey. The "Moses Walk" is so called because the dammed walkway has been created through a lake, with more than three feet of water on either side. The caves are open from March

through October and can be reached by following the A4 southwest from Enniskillen for three miles (five km), then branching off on the A32 in the direction of Swanlinbar.

Two miles (three km) southeast of Enniskillen on the A4 is Ireland's finest classical mansion, **Castlecoole**. Begun in 1790, it is now owned by the National Trust and has been undergoing major renovation. The park lake's flock of graylag geese was established here 300 years ago.

Unknown Tyrone: As you drive into **Omagh**, the county town of Tyrone, 27 miles (43 km) along the A32 from Enniskillen, the religious fragmentation of Northern Ireland is immediately apparent. On the right is the Presbyterian Church (Trinity); on the left, the Methodist Church; next, St. Columba's Church of Ireland; then the Gothic spires of the Roman Catholic Church of the Sacred Heart, a poor man's Chartres Cathedral. There are many more. The joining of the Rivers Camowen and Drumragh to form the Strule make the location pleasant enough, but Omagh is more a town for living (and praying) in than for visiting.

In its shops, alongside the usual Irish linen souvenirs, can be found plaques and statuettes made of local turf (or peat). This is cut from the **Black Bog** between Omagh and Cookstown, 27 miles (43 km) to the east.

Cookstown, the exact middle of Northern Ireland, is renowned for its main street, two miles (three km) long and 160 feet (50 metres) wide, and can be located from miles away by the 200-foot (61-metre) spire of the Gothic-style Catholic church. The town (population 6,700) has a strong tradition of nationalism, often refined in its many old-fashioned pubs. Local livestock sales give a good insight into the rough amiability of the rural Ulster character. An 18-hole golf course occupies the grounds of **Killymoon Castle**, whose towers and battlements were designed in 1803 by John Nash, architect of London's Regent Street. Some years ago, a farmer bought the castle, then derelict, for £100.

Around both towns are sprinkled many Neolithic graves and stone circles, preserved under peat for millennia, and villages such as **Clogher** and **Coagh**, **Moneymore** and **Pomeroy**, noted

Yesterday rebuilt today; the Mellon homestead at the Ulster-American Folk Park.

for fine traditional musicians and a variety of ecclesiastical architecture. There's a run-down air about some, the result of chronic unemployment. But it's as well to remember writer John Broderick's advice in *The Pilgrimage*: "The city dweller who passes through a country town and imagines it sleepy and apathetic is very far from the truth: it is watchful as the jungle."

In late 1985 a Klondike-style boom threatened to awaken any slumberers in **Gortin**, a wide-streeted village 10 miles (16 km) north of Omagh, when geologists announced that they could be sitting on top of one of Europe's richest gold finds. Further bore holes were needed to determine whether the metal was worth mining commercially.

American dreams: During tough economic periods in the 19th Century, the area's strong Scots-Presbyterian work ethic spurred many to seek their fortune in the original Klondike—or indeed anywhere in the United States. The results were remarkable and Northern Ireland claims that 11 **American presidents** have had roots in the province: Andrew Jackson, James Knox Polk, James Buchanan, Andrew

Johnson, Ulysses S. Grant, Chester Alan Arthur, Grover Cleveland, Benjamin Harrison, William McKinley, Theodore Roosevelt and Woodrow Wilson. Genealogists are continuing to pore over old documents, hoping to add a few more names, and many ordinary Americans visit each year to seek out their own ancestral homes.

The Mellon banking family of Pittsburgh, having traced their roots to **Camphill**, four miles (six km) north of Omagh, endowed the **Ulster-American Folk Park** on the site. To illuminate the transition made by the original emigrants, craftsmen's cottages, a schoolhouse, a blacksmith's forge and a Presbyterian meeting-house from the Old World have been rebuilt on a peat bog alongside log cabins, a Pennsylvania farmstead and a covered wagon from the New World. Peat is kept burning in the cottages, adding to the authenticity, and there are regular demonstrations of candle-making, fish-salting and horse-shoeing. An indoor exhibit recreates the main street of an Ulster town at the turn of the century, its hardware shop displaying foot warmers and lamp wicks, its medical

Ancestral home of US president Woodrow Wilson at Dergalt, Co. Tyrone.

hall containing Bishop's Granular Effervescent Citrate of Magnesia and Belladonna breast plasters. It could all have turned out terribly twee, yet there's not a whiff of Disney in this "museum of emigration," thanks to a scrupulous attention to detail and a refusal to make the past appear cleaner and tidier than it really was.

With the eclipse of Ulster's once-flourishing textile industry, hard times have again come to villages such as **Draperstown** (built in 1818 by the London Company of Drapers) in the archaeologically rich, blue-tinged **Sperrin Mountains**. The fortunes of towns like **Dungannon**, 13 miles (21 km) south of Cookstown and once the seat of the great O'Neill clan, have faltered too. Three miles (five km) to the northeast, **Coalisland's** name and clay-heaps are the main reminders of a coalfield that never fulfilled its enormous promise.

Sion Mills, 17 miles (27 km) northwest of Omagh, is another village whose name betrays its origins. The linen-workers' old cottages are charming. The Parish Church of the Good Shepherd is a striking Italian-style edifice, contrasting sharply with the modern architecture of St. Teresa's Catholic Church, whose facade displays a large image on slate of the Last Supper.

Three miles (five km) further along the A5 is **Strabane,** a border town paired with Lifford on the Donegal side. It was here in Gray's Printing Press, preserved by the National Trust, that John Dunlap, printer of America's Declaration of Independence, learned his trade. It's a friendly town, despite its many terrorist bombings and an unemployment rate approaching 50 per cent. Two miles to the southeast, at **Dergalt,** is the ancestral home, a whitewashed cottage, of America's President Woodrow Wilson.

Old Derry's walls: Fifteen miles (24 km) to the north, **Londonderry** is also famously friendly; even in its sectarian squabbles, it is noticeably less implacable than Belfast. If the 19th Century Scottish historian Thomas Carlyle came back today, he might no longer call it "the prettiest looking town I have seen in Ireland"; the doorways of many derelict houses have been bricked up and security screens protect shop windows. Nor do the sprawling housing estates (coloured green for Catholic or orange for Protestant on the British Army's tribal map) do much to enhance the city's visual appeal. But Londonderry, though finely situated on the **River Foyle,** doesn't set out to be a calendar girl; it prefers to provide exhilarating company, and it succeeds.

The city's growth was financed by London guilds, which in 1614 created the last walled city in Europe. Londonderry's purpose was mercantile success and you can still see traces of its former economic confidence in the ornamental facades of the old shirt-making factories, which provided the city with its livelihood for may generations. In a pointed rejection of Londonderry's imperial links, local nationalists always shorten its name to "Derry." The walls themselves, 20 feet (six metres) thick and complete with watch-towers and cannon such as the 18-pounder **Roaring Meg** (dating from 1642), are still marvellously intact. You used to be able to walk right round the inner city on top of the walls, but security precautions these days don't permit the entire circle to be made.

206

Two 17th Century sieges failed to breach the walls, earning the sobriquet "maiden city." Some say the city still has a siege mentality, a theory reinforced by the IRA's daubed slogan "You are now entering Free Derry." This was the name given to the **Bogside**, a densely populated Roman Catholic housing estate, when its inhabitants barricaded it against the police after the present Troubles began in 1969. Before partition, Londonderry's natural hinterland was Donegal—still a popular haven for gunmen on the run and drinkers escaping from Northern Ireland's "dry" Sundays. After partition, the governing Unionists fixed constituency boundaries to ensure a permanent majority for themselves in what was a mainly nationalist area. Feeling isolated from the prosperous eastern counties, Derry's citizens built up both a resentment that finally boiled over and a wonderful community spirit.

The most famous siege—which is still commemorated by Protestant marches today—took place in 1689, when the Catholic forces of James II, the last of England's Stuart kings, blockaded the Protestant supporters of William of Orange for 15 weeks, almost forcing them into submission. About 7,000 of the 30,000 people packed within the city's walls died of disease or starvation. One member of the besieged garrison chillingly recorded the selling prices of horse flesh, dogs' heads, cats, and rats "fattened by eating the bodies of the slain Irish."

The city's eventual relief is depicted on the siege memorial window of **St. Columb's Cathedral**, a graceful 17th Century Anglican church built in "Planters' Gothic" style. The chapter house contains relics of the siege. Outside the walls, **St. Columb's**, built in 1784 and known as the Long Tower Church, has a lavish interior.

Streets from the city's original four gates (Shipquay, Ferryquay, Bishop's and Butcher's) converge on **the Diamond**, a perversely square-shaped marketplace which stands at the top of Shipquay Street, the steepest main thoroughfare in Ireland. Contrasting with the street's predominantly Georgian character is a gleamingly new American-style shopping mall (less

gleaming, perhaps, since a car bomb exploded close by). At the bottom of Shipquay Street, the **Guildhall**, one of those Tudor-Gothic structures popular throughout Northern Ireland, clearly shows the influence of the London merchants. Its grandeur has been stained by the Troubles too. In one typically bizarre episode, a Republican entering the building as a newly elected councillor turned out to be the same man who had blown part of it up 13 years previously. He had been making a political statement by carrying in the bomb, he explained, and he was making the same political statement now.

Behind the Guildhall is **Derry Quay**, celebrated in song by the hundreds of thousands of emigrants who sailed down the Foyle from here, bound for a new life in America. As a reaction, perhaps, to the hard economic times that have again returned, there has been a renaissance in community activity, especially in the arts. Local enthusiasts will tell you that Londonderry is the first city in Western Europe to be facing up to the realities of the post-industrial age.

Causeway coast: The A2 out of Londonderry along Lough Foyle passes through **Ballykelly**, originally built by the London Company of Fishmongers and now patronized by a nearby army base. It has some handsome churches. **Limavady**, the district town, recalls Georgian Ireland, with fine old doorways and yard entrance arches. Its six-arch Roe Bridge dates to 1700, and the Monday cattle market, established in the early 1600s, is still held in Main Street. The famous *Londonderry Air* was noted down here in 1851 by a Miss Jane Ross from a tune played by an itinerant fiddler.

Ignoring the direct route to Coleraine, take the A2's 20-mile (32-km) loop via **Magilligan Strand**, Ireland's longest beach. Along its magnificent seven miles (12 km) of sand dunes can be found teal, tern, mallard, snipe, wild geese, and 120 different kinds of seashells. At the beginning of the strand is a **Martello Tower** with walls 10 feet (three metres) thick, built during the Napoleonic wars. The barbed wire and watchtowers of Magilligan prison camp, now empty but used during the 1970s to intern suspected terrorists, is a reminder of

The restrained resort of Portstewart.

the province's more recent troubles.

Further along the A2, on a windswept headland, the massive roofless ruin of **Downhill Castle** (1780) dominates the skyline. The **Mussenden Temple**, perched precariously near a 60-metre cliff, once housed an eccentric bishop's library and possibly his mistress; it was inspired by the temples of Vesta at Tivoli and Rome. **Downhill Forest** has lovely walks, a fishpond and waterfalls.

Coleraine, a dullish market town on the wide River Bann, houses the New University of Ulster, set up in 1968. More life can be found in Portstewart and Portrush, two seaside resorts close by. **Portstewart** is the quieter, a tidy Victorian town with safe beaches and good facilities for big-game anglers. **Portrush** is brasher, offering amusement arcades, souvenir shops, guesthouses, a children's adventure play park and two championship golf courses. Long-distance walkers can pick up the **North Antrim Coast Path** at Portstewart Strand; it forms part of the Ulster Way and extends eastwards for 40 miles (64 km) to **Murlough Bay**.

About three miles (five km) from

Portrush along the coast road are the romantic remains of **Dunluce Castle**. Poised on a rocky headland beside sheer cliffs, the 14th Century stronghold is immense and dramatic. The novelist William Makepeace Thackeray wrote of "those grey towers of Dunluce standing upon a leaden rock and looking as if some old old princess of old old fairy times were dragon guarded within." It was abandoned in 1641, two years after part of the kitchen collapsed into the sea during a storm, carrying many of the servants to their death. In the graveyard of the adjacent ruined church are buried sailors from the Spanish Armada galleass *Girona*, wrecked on nearby rocks in 1588 with 1,300 men on board and located on the seabed as recently as 1967.

The hard stuff: The distillery at **Bushmills**, a couple of miles away, boasts the world's oldest whiskey-making licence, granted in 1609. Old Bushmills, Black Bush and Bushmills Malt, made from local barley and the water that flows by in St. Columb's Rill, can be tasted after a tour.

When the winds blow in from the Atlantic, a drop of the hard stuff fortifies one wonderfully for a visit to the **Giant's Causeway**, two miles outside the village. Dr. Samuel Johnson, when asked by his biographer James Boswell whether this wonder of the world was worth seeing, gave the immortal reply: "Worth seeing? yes; but not worth going to see." It was a shrewd judgment in the 1770s when roads in the region were primitive enough to turn a journey into an expedition; indeed, the existence of the Causeway's astonishing 37,000 basalt columns, mostly perfect hexagonals formed by the cooling of molten lava, hadn't been known at all to the outside world until a gadabout Bishop of Derry stumbled upon them in 1692. Today this geological curiosity is easily accessible to the most monstrous tourist coaches, but it can still disappoint some visitors, who expect the columns to be bigger (the tallest, in the **Giant's Organ**, are about 12 metres) or who find that their very regularity serves only to diminish their magnificence. It remains worth seeing, though.

At the Causeway's eastern end is **Dunseverick Castle**, the slight remains of a 6th Century fortress perched on a high crag overlooking a picturesque fishing harbour. After **Whitepark Bay**, a very fine moon-shaped beach, and **Ballintoy Harbour**, popular with artists, the road passes **Carrick-a-rede Rope Bridge**. Assembled each May and dismantled each September, it swings its 65-foot (20-metre) way over a chasm to an island salmon fishery. The views are memorable, but it's not for anyone prone to vertigo.

The best time to visit nearby **Ballycastle** is during the **Ould Lammas Fair**, held on the last Monday and Tuesday of August. Then this unspoiled town turns into one throbbing marketplace as farmers with impenetrable accents bring their livestock in from the glens and hundreds of stalls sell souvenirs, bric-à-brac, dulse (dried, edible seaweed) and yellowman (a sweet confectionery). The big attraction is "the crack" (the talk, enlivened by a glass or two of Bushmills). It's great fun—an authentic folk event that owes nothing to the manipulations of tourist boards.

A seafront memorial marks the spot where, in 1898, Marconi first seriously tested wireless telegraphy. He made his historic transmission between here and **Rathlin Island**, eight miles (13 km) off the coast towards Scotland's Mull of Kintyre. The boomerang-shaped island, whose population has slumped from 1,000 to 100 over the past 130 years, makes its living from farming and fishing and attracts geologists, botanists and especially bird-watchers (there are an estimated 20,000 birds of 175 species, 79 of them breeding). The daily crossings by small boat depend on the weather, and high seas can strand you on Rathlin for days on end. There is one pub and one hotel. But there's no policeman, and no need for one.

Just east of Ballycastle lie the ruins of **Bonamargy Friary**, founded around 1500. A vault contains the massive coffins of several MacDonnell chieftains who stood out successfully against the forces of England's Queen Elizabeth I. Nearby, **Corrymeela Community House** is an inter-denominational conference and holiday centre, whose idealism shines out amid Northern Ireland's prevailing political cynicism.

Down the coast: After Ballycastle, one can either carry on down the coast, alongside the Irish Sea, or dive deep into the heartland of Antrim.

The rewards of the first route are spectacular views of brown moorlands, white limestone, black basalt, red sandstone and blue sea along the **Antrim Coast Road**. A notable engineering achievement, it was designed in 1834 by Sir Charles Lanyon as a work of famine relief and opened up an area whose inhabitants had previously found it easier to travel by sea to Scotland than overland to the rest of Ireland.

At various points along the road, you can turn into one or other of Antrim's celebrated nine glens—**Glenarm, Glencloy, Glenariff, Glenballyeamon, Glenaan, Glencorp, Glendun, Glenshesk** and **Glentaisie**—and into another world. It's a world of weather-beaten farmers in tweeds and baggy trousers; a world of sheep sales solemnly conducted by auctioneers who talk like machineguns; a world with a baffling dialect that turns a ewe into *a yow* and "six" into *sex*; a world where poteen, the "mountain dew," is distilled in lonely places. If you don't look like the police, it's not hard to track down this illicit (and potentially

Eating seaweed, a delicacy at Ballycastle's Ould Lammas Fair.

210

lethal) alcohol. "It's floating about," they'll tell you. "In fact it's practically running down the streets."

The famous coastal scenic drive starts at **Cushendun**, 12 miles (19 km) from Ballycastle along the A2, just after the towering **Glendun Viaduct** (1839)—or a bit longer via the winding coastal lane past the lonely **Torr Head**. Cushendun, a village of charming Cornish-style white cottages, graceful old houses and friendly pubs, has been captured on countless canvases and the entire place is protected by the National Trust.

Five miles (eight km) to the south, **Cushendall**, "capital of the glens," was created largely by a wealthy 19th Century landowner, Francis Turnly. His most striking structure was the four-storey red sandstone **Curfew Tower**, built as "a place of confinement for idlers and rioters." The village has a good beach and is a popular sailing centre. Just to the north is **Layde Old Church**, dating back to the 13th Century and containing some ancient vaults.

Past the curving sandstone beach of **Red Bay** stands the village of **Water-foot**, where an Irish song-and-dance festival is held each July. It is also the entrance to **Glenariff Glen**, a deep wooded gorge dubbed by Thackeray "Switzerland in miniature." Wild flowers carpet the upper glen in spring and early summer, and slippery rustic footbridges carry walkers over the Glenariff River, past postcard-pretty waterfalls.

Carnlough, to the south, has a fine harbour and, running over its main street, a white bridge built in 1854 to carry limestone from the quarries to waiting boats. The Londonderry Arms hotel (also 1854) retains the charms of an old coaching inn. **Glenarm** has a beautiful park adjoining a fussy castle, home of the Earls of Antrim. **White Bay** is a picnic area around which small fossils can be found. **Ballygalley** has a 1625 fortified manor house (now a hotel) and, inland from the coast road, a well-preserved old mill and pottery.

From here, the road runs into **Larne**, a port with frequent daily ferries to and from Stranraer in Scotland (only 70 minutes away). The old town hall in Cross Street has an historical centre featuring turn-of-the-century utensils and photographs.

Antrim's obsessions: Travel inland from Ballycastle and you pass through relatively prosperous farming country "east of the **Bann**." This long, underused river, which flows from the southeast of the province through Lough Neagh and into the Atlantic near Portstewart, is a rough and ready political dividing line between the western counties of Derry and Tyrone, with their preponderance of nationalists and Roman Catholics, and the eastern counties of Antrim and Down, with their Unionist/Protestant majority. In a thriving market town like **Ballymoney**, 17 miles (27 km) southwest of Ballycastle, archaic words that would have been familiar to Shakespeare crop up naturally in everyday conversation—a legacy of the Scots Presbyterians planted here as settlers in the 17th Century.

As elsewhere in Ulster, churches loom large. There's one on each of the four roads leading into a small village like **Dervock**, for instance, four miles (six km) north of Ballymoney and ancestral home of America's President McKinley (assassinated in

1901). Legend says that this strategic siting of churches keeps the Devil out. Locals suggest it probably keeps him in. The people in these parts are honest and decent (pronounced *day-sent*), and are courteous, if a mite wary, towards strangers. But political open-mindedness isn't one of their virtues. If stuck for a topic of conversation, therefore, you'd be best advised to try the weather.

Ballymena, 19 miles (30 km) southeast of Ballymoney, is the staunchly Protestant business centre of Antrim and, as a result perhaps of the strong Scottish influence, has been called the meanest town in Ireland. **Antrim**, the county town, 11 miles (18 km) to the southeast, has more to see. There's an almost perfectly preserved round tower, more than 1,000 years old, on Steeple Road, and the **Antrim Castle Demesne** is laid out like a mini-Versailles. Its gardens run down to the shore of **Lough Neagh**, whose 17-mile length and 11-mile breadth (27 by 18 km) make it the largest inland sheet of water in the British Isles.

Because of the lough's marshy edges, it has surprisingly few access points. But recreational facilities for sailing and water-skiing are at last being developed, with marinas at **Oxford Island** (south shore) and **Ballyronan** (west shore). A large eel fishing industry is based at **Toome**, employing 400. Until it was restructured as a fishermen's cooperative, feuding over fishing rights was bitter; indeed, before the current Troubles, the most frequent gun battles in Northern Ireland used to take place on Lough Neagh between police patrol boats and the vessels of organized poachers.

A less fraught view of the lough can be had from the steam locomotives on **Shanes Castle Railway**, a narrow-gauge track on a private estate on the north shore near **Randalstown**. There's a deer park and nature reserve here too.

Bandit country: To the southwest of the lough is **Dungannon**, a quiet market and textile manufacturing town. To the south is County Armagh, traditionally known as the Apple Orchard of Ireland, and more recently, thanks to terrorist activity near its border with the Republic, by the less-inviting sobriquet of Bandit Country.

On the right track at Shanes Castle Railway.

212

Its county town of **Armagh** (always called a city despite a population of just 12,000) symbolizes many of Northern Ireland's problems. Its two striking cathedrals—one Protestant, one Catholic, both called **St. Patrick's**—sit on opposite hills like, someone once said, the horns of a dilemma. The two communities reside in separate parts of the city, behaving for the most part as if they were living on different planets. Car bombs have badly scarred what used to be some of Ireland's most dignified Georgian architecture.

There's still much to see. At one end of an oval **Mall**—where cricket is played in summer, rugby football in winter—is a classical Courthouse, at the other a jailhouse. A small Ionic-pillared museum on the Mall contains many local artefacts, as well as records of Ireland's worst railway disaster, which happened in 1889 just outside Armagh; 80 Sunday School excursionists died when 10 uncoupled carriages ran down a steep incline into the path of an oncoming train. Nearby is the museum of the Royal Irish Fusiliers, exhibiting a variety of regimental uniforms, medals and flags.

Adjacent to the **Observatory** on College Hill is Ireland's only **planetarium**, featuring daily "star shows." Just to the west of the city is **Navan Fort**, said to have been built in 300 BC and to have been the most important place in Ireland. All that can be seen now is a grassy mound, badly signposted, and a limestone quarry has been threatening to encroach on what little remains of this neglected antiquity.

The city is surrounded by neat villages, reached through a network of pleasant lanes. Each May, the countryside around **Loughgall** is radiant with apple blossom. Near **Markethill**, in **Gosford Forest Park**, Gosford Castle is a large turreted mock-Norman edifice built of local granite. **Bessbrook** is a model linen-making town, created by a Quaker and therefore lacking a pub. **Crossmaglen** has a remarkably large market square, containing a bronze monument to the IRA; this village is in the front line of the battle between the IRA and the security forces—as its police station, heavily fortified against rocket attacks, shows. **Tynan** has a 10th Century sculptured stone cross,

13 feet (four metres) high.

Between Armagh and Belfast is a chain of towns built on commerce. **Portadown**, 10 miles (16 km) to the northeast, has found its role scaled down from that of a major railway junction to a prosperous market town noted for rose growing and coarse fishing. Linen manufacturing has lessened in importance, too, as it has in **Lurgan**, six miles (10 km) further along the A3. In the 1960s it was decided to link the two towns to form the "lineal city" of **Craigavon**, thereby reducing congestion in Belfast; but a mixture of civic pride and a downturn in the economy has kept the separate identities of Portadown and Lurgan very much alive despite the mushrooming between them of housing estates, schools and countless traffic circles.

Frontier town: Twenty miles (32 km) southeast of Armagh, **Newry** is a bustling border town, disfigured by the Troubles but, thanks to the resilience of the Northern Irish, a cheery enough place. Its mercantile history is recalled by a canal, one of Britain's oldest.

The atmosphere lightens as you travel southwest to **Slieve Gullion** (where a forest drive winds up to two mountain-top Stone Age cairns) or southeast to the respectable little resorts of **Warrenpoint** and **Rostrevor**, overlooking Carlingford Lough. Warrenpoint has two piers (good for fishing), a spacious square and a half-mile promenade lined with trees. Rostrevor, a favoured retirement spot sheltered by high hills, has more of a Victorian atmosphere. A steep half-mile walk up the slopes of **Slievemartin** brings you to **Cloghmore**, a "Big Stone" supposedly hurled by the Irish giant Finn MacCool at a rival Scot. The geological explanation for this misplaced piece of granite is more mundane, having to do with glacial drift.

Skirting round the **Mourne Mountains** takes you to the active fishing village of **Kilkeel**, capital of the so-called "Kingdom of Mourne." Its winding streets, stepped footpaths and old houses are alluring. There's a choice here: you can proceed along the coast via **Annalong**, a smaller fishing village with old cottages and a cornmill with waterwheel, or you can turn inland to climb into the

The rolling downs of Co. Down and the Mountains of Mourne.

Mournes themselves.

Meandering in the Mournes: They're "young" mountains (like the Alps) and their chameleon qualities attract walkers. At one moment the granite is grey, then it changes to pink. You walk by a bleakly located farmhouse, and within moments you find yourself in the middle of a wilderness. One minute, the Mournes justify all the songs written about them; the next, they become plain scrubland and unexceptional hills. The weather has a lot to do with it. The remote **Silent Valley** cradles a large dam. **Slieve Donard**, the highest peak at 2,796 feet (850 metres) offers exhilarating views.

As you reach the foothills of the Mournes, turn right just before Hilltown towards **Newcastle**. This is east Down's main resort, with a fine, sandy beach and the celebrated Royal County Down Golf Club. Several forest parks—**Donard, Tollymore, Castlewellan**—are good for riding (by pony or bicycle) or walking. This is unquestionably an area that invites you to unwind, that doesn't understand people who are in a hurry.

Five miles (eight km) inland from

A game of cricket, English style, on Armagh's Mall.

Newcastle, **Castlewellan** is a picturesque village with a wide main street. Nine miles (14 km) to the west, **Rathfriland** is a steep-streeted plantation town with lively livestock sales and, as elsewhere in Ulster, kerbstones painted red, white and blue to indicate the place's political allegiance. Between here and Banbridge to the north is **"Brontë Country"**, a confusingly signposted trail invented by the tourist authorities to capitalize on the fact that Patrick Brontë (or Brunty), father of the novelists Charlotte, Emily and Ann, was born in a cottage at **Emdale**, three miles (five km) southeast of Loughbrickland. The family's fame was cemented in Yorkshire, not in Emdale, and there's nothing here to conjure up the claustrophobia of *Wuthering Heights* or *Jane Eyre*. But the drive through country lanes so narrow that the hedges almost meet is well worth taking and, if you lose track of Patrick Brontë's trail on Ballynaskeagh Road, or Ballynafern or Lisnacroppin, it doesn't much matter.

Banbridge, where the River Bann makes another appearance, has a peculiar main street, bisected by an underpass taking through traffic, with sections of road on either side serving a varied collection of small shops.

St. Patrick's place: As an alternative to heading into the Mournes from Newcastle, one can continue round the coast to **Ardglass**, where several small, ruined castles hint at its strategic importance in the Middle Ages to unwelcome kings visiting from Britain. It is an important herring fishing centre.

Seven miles (11 km) inland to the northwest is **Downpatrick**, which has a Georgian air and a cathedral supposedly built on the site of St. Patrick's first stone church. The saint himself is said to be buried here. The **Struell Wells** to the east of the town are evidence of pagan worshippers long before the dawn of Christianity.

North of the town there begins a prosperous commuter belt, populated by well-spoken professional people who tut-tut about the Troubles and put their money into making their homes ever more comfortable. The source of their prosperity and the commercial magnet to which they are drawn each working day lies to the north: **Belfast**.

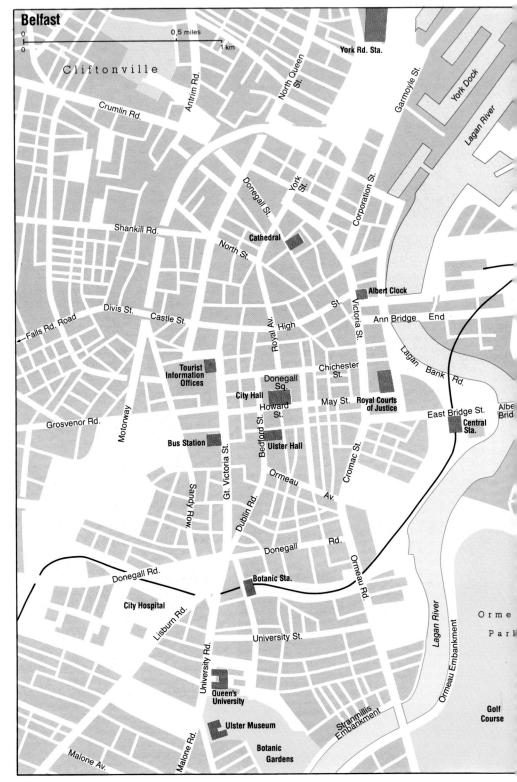

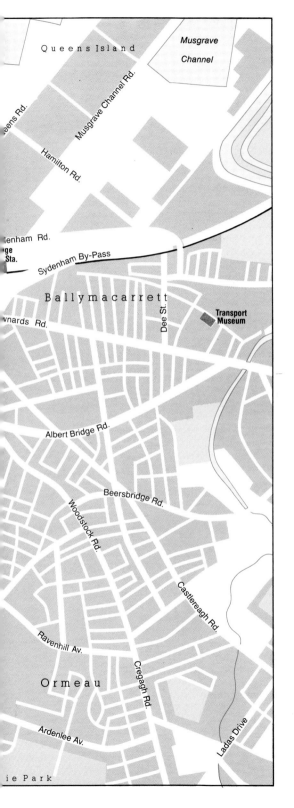

BELFAST AND ITS ENVIRONS

Belfast has become a buzz-word for trouble, a place of bigotry, bombs and barricades. But there is another Belfast, home to 400,000 hospitable people. The first-time visitor, therefore, may well travel from Aldergrove international airport, 15 miles (25 km) to the northwest of the city, with a mixture of curiosity and foreboding. At the probable army or police checkpoint, armed officers heighten the expectation of a war zone.

As the M2 motorway dips towards the sea, the first sudden vista is reassuring. The setting looks so peaceful. There are green hills on either side, with the city nestling at the head of a sheltered lough. A pristine 10-lane freeway and an aura of normality defy the darker images.

But the threat of violence is always lurking in the shadows. A suspicous parcel or a car parked in the wrong place can trigger off a well-practised routine by the security forces. Streets are rapidly sealed off and robot bomb defusers are despatched to investigate. In this city, the visitor must pick his parking spot with care. Yet, a few streets away, life proceeds as normal. Office workers battle with boredom, shoppers peruse possible purchases, hairdressers snip away and pavements bustle with activity. The sound of an explosion will no more than momentarily disturb the routine.

The visitor will find it strange to be frisked as he or she enters a shop, bizarre to see steel gates sealing off shopping streets, and unsettling to see signs warning of a **Control Zone** where an unoccupied car will attract the instant attention of the police and soldiers. This is Belfast, a city which has adapted itself to what others would regard as unreal.

In recent years, however, such inconveniences have become rarer. Security has become more discreet in response to a falling graph of violence. Statistically, Belfast is still a much safer place to be than most American cities. Confidence is returning, and with it a resurgence of commercial and social life. First-time visitors are fascinated at the way the city continues about its everyday business, and by the warmth of the ordinary citizen, who will go out of his way to assist the stranger. Whether Protestant or Roman Catholic, they unite in universal hospitality to the outsider.

A turbulent past: Belfast evolved as Ulster's dominant city because of its strategic position at the mouth of the **River Lagan**. Nearby towns such as Carrickfergus and Holywood (the difference is more than just the spelling) were originally more significant settlements, but the city later outstripped them as a port and an industrial centre. The city's name may well be a corruption of *Fearsat*, the ancient word for a ford or river crossing. Past hostilities over its control make today's look tame. Danes and Norwegian voyagers were among the first to be attracted to the river mouth as a trading post.

There are records of a battle of the Fearsat in AD 666. The Anglo-Norman invasion came in 1171 and John de Courcy was set up as Earl of Ulster by King Henry II of England. Names like **Castle Street** and **Castle Place** give clues to the site of his fortress. Edward Bruce destroyed this castle in the 14th Century, and the city later passed into the possession of the O'Neills, the Earls of Tyrone, who were based in what is now the suburb of **Castlereagh**, on rising ground to the east of the city centre.

Much blood was spilled in the Lagan Valley during medieval times, as control of Belfast was continually in dispute. After the assassination of Brian O'Neill, in 1571, the town passed to Sir Thomas Smith, and then to Sir Arthur Chichester, whose name graces another downtown street. Belfast was granted its first charter from James I in 1631, and grew as a trading centre to eclipse Carrickfergus, the former Norman stronghold with its splendid castle on the north shores of the lough. But it was still far from peaceful: a rebellion flared up in 1641.

More turbulent centuries followed with a later "owner" of the city, the Earl of Donegall, killed by the Duke of Marlborough's army. Henry Joy McCracken, a Protestant idealist, was hanged as a rebel at the corner of **High Street** and **Cornmarket**, not far from the site of today's Woolworth store. To walk the streets of downtown Belfast today takes one through the corridors of a savage history, with street names signposting the city's long-gone warrior masters. But, despite the agony and the gore, the place managed to become one of the most fascinating successes of Britain's Industrial Revolution.

Mud and money: Establishing a city on the soft, blue-grey muds of an estuary was always a challenge. But a blind engineering genius, Alexander Mitchell, devised a method of screw piling used in other soggy cities. Then came the early elements of Belfast's commercial success: rope-making and linen (hence **Linenhall Street**). The city was home to pioneers of printing in the late 17th Century. In 1737 the *Belfast Newsletter* was born, and is believed to be the world's oldest daily newspaper. High Street was the main artery of early Belfast, and had a river, now culverted, running down its length. Ferries from Liverpool came up the River Lagan and disembarked their passengers in small boats in the days before the docks were built.

Little shipyards sprang up at the mouth of the Lagan. The most famous of them all, Harland and Wolff, was established in 1859. Many of the great passenger liners of that era, including the ill-fated "unsinkable" *Titanic*, were built here. Harland and Wolff remained one of the world's largest yards until as recently as the 1950s. Its wartime significance made Belfast a target for German air raids, with tremendous loss of civilian life. More recent successes include aircraft carriers like HMS *Eagle*, and the cruise ship *Canberra*.

The modern Belfast skyline is dominated by the shipyard's two huge, yellow-painted cranes, affectionately known as Samson and Goliath and towering to 315 and 348 feet (96 and 106 metres). Today, Harland and Wolff uses computer technology to build mainly oil tankers and bulk carriers. The yard symbolizes the proud industrial spirit of Belfast, combining ingenuity with grit.

The other bulwark is the aircraft factory of Shorts, which adjoins the shipyard. Set up by two brothers, this company has a record of innovation, although it has not enjoyed commercial success until more recent years. It is here that the wartime

Belfast, Ireland's only industrial city: in the foreground is the City Hall.

218

Sunderland flying boats were made. Shorts also conceived the Belfast freighter, one of the world's largest cargo carriers. The world's first turbo-jet vertical take-off and landing aircraft, "the flying bedstead," was developed here for the British Ministry of Defence. But the money-spinners have proved to be the economical and practical Skyvan freight carrier and the 330/360 passenger planes, the "flying shoebox" now in regular service worldwide. These squat and square planes are a frequent sight in the skies over Belfast.

The largest private employer in Northern Ireland is the tobacco industry. Gallaher's, now part of an American-owned multinational, was set up in 1857 by Tom Gallaher, a Derry man. Now one of the UK's most successful marketing companies, it has one of its two major manufacturing plants in Belfast. Half of the pipe tobacco smoked in the UK is made in Gallaher's York Street factory.

The business zeal and worldwide connections of men like Harland, Wolff, the Short brothers and Gallaher were quite amazing, and overcame the geographic disadvantages of Belfast, which had no indigenous raw materials, to establish industry there. Other engineering companies include Davidson's Sirocco works, which makes huge ventilation fans for mining countries, and the Hughes Tool Company. Ford and General Motors have car component plants supplying their assembly plants in Europe and the US.

Linen and garment making were the other major activities of yesteryear, and though they have suffered from the emergence of synthetic materials and cheap Eastern competition, they are still around on a smaller scale. The Ulster Weaving Company specializes in decorated tea towels which are exported worldwide.

Empty factories in and around Belfast indicate the industrial decline of recent years—as much due to the world recession as the Troubles. Worst-hit have been man-made fibre plants in towns like Antrim and Carrickfergus. Successive British governments have made job promotion a priority, with mixed results. Spectacular crashes of public-funded ventures like the De Lorean gull-wing sports car and Lear Fan carbon-fibre-aircraft projects have overshadowed the gains, and the unemployment rate is the highest in the UK: almost half of the male adults in some west Belfast housing estates.

Much of the past commercial success of Belfast can be attributed to the work ethic of its inhabitants. Their skills and diligence have been compared to the Japanese. Industrial relations and productivity are above the British norm. It is part of Ulster's tragedy that its traditional industries were dominated by the Protestant community, and that Roman Catholics have not participated so much in the prosperity. Despite more enlightened recruiting policies in recent years, the lack of growth has ensured that the historic imbalance has continued.

But one thing that both communities share is the hard Belfast accent, sometimes mistaken by strangers as Scottish because of the close historic connections. At its best, it has launched a small army of television reporters, said to speak English more clearly than the English. At its worst, it can verge on the unintelligible.

Belfast's housewives are famously house-proud.

War and peace: The Troubles, as they are known locally, have separated the working classes into modern ghettos. The **"Peace Line"**, a fortified wall separating the Protestant **Shankill Road** area from the Catholic **Falls Road**, is one of the city's less happy sights. Its construction was ordered by an army general in the days when street rioting was widespread. The city is divided into Orange (Protestant) and Green (Catholic) zones, though in middle-class areas the religions are mixed.

West Belfast is the Catholic stronghold though there has been some spillover into the north of the city. The east is overwhelmingly Protestant. But the Shankill remains a loyalist bastion in the west.

The Belfast character tends to be tough on the outside and soft within. In public utterances, the politicians are hardline and uncompromising with each other. But everyday life sees an informal tolerance, which is in direct contradiction to the purveyed image—provided, of course, the conversation is steered away from religion or politics.

Normally, the soft heart of Belfast shines through to the visitor. Ask for directions and most likely you will be taken personally to the place you seek. At a social event, you will be overwhelmed by the hospitality. Charity collections have a field day in this city.

Sport often brings people together. Returning champions are paraded along the main street, **Royal Avenue**, through a sea of cheering citizens. Olympic gold medal pentathlete Mary Peters still remembers the ecstasy of her reception. Such is the dichotomy of the Belfast, and indeed the Ulster, character: people unwilling to "give an inch" on the political front pour out their hearts to a local winner.

Informality, humour and friendliness are all part of the Belfast personality. Jokes flow freely and the welcome for strangers is almost surreal, a mixture of pleasure that you have come to their town, and relief that you are someone who can be spoken to with lowered defences. In a curious way, many Belfast people feel comfortable in their prejudices. There is almost a smugness, shared by both communities, that comes from a

Republican mural hails Irish revolutionary leader James Connolly.

THE GREAT ONLY APPEAR GREAT BECAUSE WE ARE ON OUR KNEES

LET US RISE

SPONSORED BY TRADE UNION GROUP

belief that they are right and the other guy is wrong.

Jewels and thorns: Despite its over-hasty industrial growth, Belfast's curious patchwork does contain some fine examples of architecture. The late Sir John Betjeman, Britain's poet laureate, surprised locals by finding much to praise. One building which cannot be missed is the **City Hall** (1903), a great white block of Portland limestone, designed by Brumwell Thomas in Renaissance style. Its green domes are actually corroded copper and, inside, there is Italian marble and stained glass. Sheer splendour beside many more mundane neighbours. Betjeman was much taken by the City Hall, which he described as having a "swagger" and "a gratifying lack of austerity."

Other treasures take a little finding. The Corinthian **Customs House** (1857) down by the waterfront was the work of Sir Charles Lanyon. Not far away is the **Albert Clock**, a leaning tower that is Belfast's answer to London's Big Ben. Churches and banks also vie for interest. The **Bank of Ireland** in High Street (1897) has copper domes; the **Ulster Bank** around the corner in Waring Street has an interior like a Venetian palace; and the nearby **Northern Bank** (1769) was originally a markethouse.

They started building **St. Anne's Cathedral** in 1899 and bits were added at later dates. It is still aspiring to a spire, but is otherwise magnificent. Inside are mosaics by Gertrude Stein and carvings by Morris Harding. St. Anne's holds the tomb of Unionist leader Lord Carson, but has more recently been the venue for ecumenical services.

The old **Presbyterian oval church** (1783) in Rosemary Street is worth a peep for its curved interior. More sumptuous is **St. Malachy's Roman Catholic Church** (1848), in Alfred Street, with its turretted exterior. Georgian elegance is appropriately found in **St. George's Church of Ireland** (1819) in High Street.

To find a more modern and uniquely Ulster church, you have to travel across the Albert Bridge and a mile along the Ravenhill Road to the **Martyrs Memorial Free Presbyterian Church**. There, the church's founder, the Reverend Ian Paisley, Ulster's

222

fire-breathing fundamentalist preacher and leading Protestant politician, holds court. His oratory each Sunday is inimitable, denouncing Rome and calling for a silent collection (no coins). His uncompromising tones are echoed in his prospering churches throughout Ulster, and he has established a few outposts in the Irish Republic.

Homes, great and small: Moving to the north of the city centre, the **Old Charitable Institute** (1771), set in gardens at Clifton Street, is described as Irish Georgian. Further out, on the Antrim Road, is **Belfast Castle** (1870), another Lanyon creation of interest, but hardly a castle in its dimensions.

To the south, the area surrounding **Queen's University** is one of the most attractive in the city. Stylish terraces lift the surrounding streets above the rest of the city. And the main university building (1849), again by Lanyon, is a redbrick replica of Magdalen College at Oxford.

Parliament Buildings at Stormont, the seat of the now-disbanded Northern Ireland Government, looks splendid in 300 acres of lawns and trees six miles (10 km) to the east of the city centre along the Newtownards Road. The front drive is a mile long and the imposing Palladian building is constructed from Portland stone and local Mourne granite. In the grounds is the smaller, baronial **Stormont Castle**, where the Ulster prime minister lived. Stormont, now mostly government offices, has recently been the home of various failed attempts to establish a cross-community local administration. Its upper and lower chambers are now the mere trappings of power as the province is run by a Secretary of State and junior ministers from the British Government.

The more humble residents of Belfast used to live in monotonous brick terraces of houses, affectionately regarded as "wee palaces." These are disappearing as the city is redeveloped on a massive scale. (Building sites are often thought by visitors to be the results of bombing.) High-rise housing is limited, having proved unacceptable to people who prefer to keep their feet on the ground. Vivid contrasts are to be found in the pattern of housing. Smart new enclaves of surprisingly

stylish dwellings are popping up to replace the terraces. But there are still some hideous examples of post-war folly, and some parts of Belfast have housing conditions among the worst in Europe.

Over the past decade pristine **leisure centres** have sprung up all over Belfast as part of a government plan to counter social deprivation. They are surprisingly well equipped, usually with swimming pools and indoor sports facilities; some even run to saunas and solariums. All of them are open to the public for modest entrance fees.

Business as usual: Newtownards Road is one of the few remaining examples of shopping as it was. Scores of little merchants used to line the radiating commuter roads out of the city centre. They provided the daily needs of generations, along with a measure of friendly chatter. But these easy-going havens of commercial humanity are dying out—to the chagrin of many. American-style shopping centres are taking over. Faceless automation means keener prices, but is diluting the flavour of Belfast life.

After many lean years, the centre of Belfast is making a come-back. Most of the old-style department stores have gone, but Anderson & McAuley's and the Belfast Co-operative Society survive, managing somehow to combine modern marketing with a whiff of more leisurely days. Major UK stores such as Marks and Spencer, British Home Stores, Boots, and Littlewoods are the magnets for the modern shopper. They seem to do particularly well in Belfast, at the expense of making its city centre look remarkably similar to that of many provincial towns in Britain.

One bonus of the security situation is that a number of central streets are pedestrianized. The **Ann Street** area is the hub, and **Fountain Street** is another trendy plaza. Late-night shopping on Thursdays, complete with buskers, has a carnival atmosphere.

There are some relics of former times, such as **Queen's Arcade**, where expensive jewellery and fashion can be bought. At the other end of the scale, street trading from barrows is enjoying a revival in **Castle Street**. And there is a variety market in **May Street**

Grand Opera House, popular with artists and audiences alike.

each Tuesday and Friday which has atmosphere but little of quality.

Stage and screen: Performer after performer has been impressed by the enthusiasm of Belfast audiences. "They'll clap at anything," observed one local cynic, but after years as an entertainment ghost town, the applause is sincere. The auditorium beloved by artists and their customers is the **Grand Opera House**. Described as a gem of a Victorian theatre, it was painstakingly restored to its original splendour after a fire some years ago. Its international repertoire of opera, ballet, theatre and pantomime is impressive by any standards.

A few streets away, the **Ulster Hall** is a more sombre venue for events from boxing to orchestral concerts. It is the home of the Ulster Orchestra, an impressive troupe and well worth hearing. Adjoining the big hall is the tiny **Group Theatre**, the home of Ulster comedy and local artists.

Nearer Queen's University is the **Arts Theatre**, a larger but fairly uninspiring auditorium which exists on the vitality of its performances. The home of more high-brow acting is the **Lyric Theatre**, in Ridgeway Street, an attractive modern building where they like to stage Irish work.

Cinemas are a dying breed in Belfast, as elsewhere. Next door to the Opera House, the **ABC** is a three-screen job; and the **New Vic**, across the street, switches between films, pantomime and pop concerts. Another multi-screen cinema is the **Curzon** on Ormeau Road, about two miles (three km) out of the centre. The small **Queen's Film Theatre**, near the university, specializes in uncommonly good cinema.

Culture vultures should visit Belfast in November when it is festival time around Queen's University. It is a quite remarkable beanfeast which can offer anything from the Royal Shakespeare Company or Russian ballet to pop music or lessons in Chinese cookery. More than 100 events are packed into two weeks, from early in the morning until early the next morning, forcing agonizing choices. Critics rate **Belfast Festival** as one of the best in the UK, almost as good as Edinburgh.

To entertain the populace for the rest of the year, a **"Golden Mile"** of

The Crown, Ulster's only pub preserved by the National Trust.

pubs and restaurants has sprung up on the south side of the city centre, running from the Opera House to the University area. The choice of cuisine is becoming cosmopolitan, with French, Indian, Chinese, German, Italian and Greek food on offer as well as more staple fare such as steaks, ham and salmon from local sources. Fast food follows the global pattern with hamburger parlours, Chinese takeaways and Kentucky Fried Chicken joints peppered among the more traditional fish-and-chip shops.

Pubs are also moving in on the food scene and the better ones offer home cooking. But even the most humble have an intimacy and a speakeasy atmosphere. The **Crown Bar** in Great Victoria Street, recently restored, is an authentic Victorian bar with elaborate tiling and stained glass. Nearby is **Robinsons**, another old-world place with carved wooden fixtures.

The city centre, particularly the south side, has inviting hostelries with names such as **The Elbow**, the **Crow's Nest**, **Kelly's Cellars**, the **Linenhall**, and the **Duke of York**. All fine places to sup, and while away an

Victorian values powered Belfast's growth as well as its architecture.

hour or two simply listening to the inimitable chatter of the locals. **Harper's Bar**, in the Forum hotel—named after a former manager in the times when it had the dubious distinction of being Europe's most-bombed hotel—offers folk music and exaggerated tales from visiting pressmen.

As in Wales, if you want a drink on Sunday you will have to wait until Monday. Licensing laws differ from England in that pubs close on Sundays—but, as compensation, they stay open all afternoon on the other six days. You can, however, get a drink on the Seventh Day in hotels, restaurants and, if you are the guest of a friendly native, in the myriad of social clubs dotted around the city. These also offer cabaret.

Those who enjoy the seamy side of life will be disappointed. The occasional (and rather jaded) lady of the night can still be found in the docks area. But Belfast's only strip club was an early victim of a bomb—perhaps the terrorists have a puritanical streak? Good clean fun is more the order of the day. Disco pubs are major boy-meets-girl venues and conven-

tional dance halls are a thing of the past. The latest trend are late-night clubs, where you bring your own bottles to get around the licensing laws. It 's all very Irish.

A city once described as a cultural Sahara is awakening to the arts, and to the art of good living. Each year sees more places open as entrepreneurs join the bandwagon. Belfast is slowly discovering that, despite its warts, it can become an international city, too.

Beauty and blemishes: It may surprise the stranger to learn that Belfast won a UK award as a "City in Bloom." There are leafy suburbs draped in cherry blossom each spring, and crowned in golden splendour each autumn. And an inspired programme by the council has seen flowers sprout in the most unexpected places. But there are also plenty of examples of neglect and vandalism as in most British inner cities. Litter often spoils the appearance of an attractive location.

There is a plethora of parks. One of the most interesting is **Botanic Gardens** beside Queen's University, which boasts a 130-year-old Palm House, another Lanyon creation with tropical plants almost as old as the building. It also has a Tropical Ravine where bananas are grown.

Dixon Park, in Upper Malone, is the scene of annual rose trials—Ulster's damp climate favours the queen of flowers. Thousands of blooms are on show and nearby is the **Barnett's Demesne** with acres of woodland and lawns rolling down to the River Lagan at **Shaw's Bridge** where there is a canoe run. The **Lagan Valley Park** takes in nine scenic miles (14 km) of river along the former canal towpath. Also in this area is the **Giant's Ring**, a neolithic tomb.

At the other side of the city, the **Belfast Zoo** occupies the steep lower slopes of the Cavehill. A tour leaves the unfit a little breathless, but it is worth it for the flamingoes and a fine collection of monkeys. If you have any energy left, you can walk up through the **Hazelwood Park** to the caves themselves only to find that the panoramic view of the city and the lough is more enticing.

Belfast is above par for **golf courses**, with eight examples within its boundary. There are also a number of soccer

Ulster's peaceful face: the River Lagan at Shaw's Bridge.

stadiums, the most notable being **Windsor Park**, where international matches are played in an atmosphere akin to a bullfight.

Those interested in perusing the history of the city in more detail can visit the main **Belfast Library** in Royal Avenue which has old photographs and literature on the city. The **Linenhall Library**, opposite the City Hall, specializes in old newspaper files, and has an absorbing collection of Irish literature.

The **Kings Hall** at Balmoral, cream painted and with a curved roof, is Belfast's major exhibition venue. Its grounds include lawns and show-jumping arenas which form the setting for the large agricultural show in the spring and the **Harberton Theatre** is nearby. Another highlight here is the Ulster Motor Show in February, a highly professional offering reflecting local enthusiasm for the motor car.

The **Ulster Museum** at Stranmillis Road, near Queen's University, has a collection of Irish art, furniture and costumes. It also specializes in industrial archaeology with displays showing the inventiveness of the Ulsterman

through the ages. It houses a prized collection of gold and silver recovered from the wreck of the Spanish armada ship, the *Girona*, which was wrecked off the north Antrim coast in 1588. But the exhibit which has most fascinated generations of children is the mummy.

Belfast has seven art galleries, mostly small except for the one at the museum. The **Magee Gallery** concentrates on established painters, with the **Tom Caldwell** and **Malone** galleries focusing on Irish artists and painters. The **Octagon Gallery** is run by artists and displays the work of young local artists.

Tales of transport: A unique aspect of the Troubles in Belfast is its "Black Taxi" system. It emerged, under paramilitary control, at a time when public transport was often disrupted by no-go areas. Now legitimized, the service plies the commuter routes in both loyalist and nationalist areas using second-hand London cabs. But these black taxis cannot be hailed; instead they "poach" from the major bus service by stopping at regular points. Belfast also has a plethora of private

The Royal Belfast, one of Northern Ireland's many golf courses.

hire taxi fleets, some of which are illegal. But the legitimate operators do offer a very competitive service and many of them are identifiable by rooftop signs. An unmarked "taxi" could be a pirate operator.

The red **Citybuses** form the regular city public transport system. They have survived some difficult times, thanks to the Troubles and vandalism, and so offer hard plastic seats and screened-off drivers. Service is limited to civilized hours; night-owls need to make other arrangments. Both City bus and **Ulsterbus** (covering rural areas with its blue buses which don't pick up passengers in the city except from the terminus) are run by a flamboyant German immigrant, Werner Heubeck, who specializes in removing suspect parcels personally.

Rail services in Northern Ireland are limited, and Belfast's **Central Station** is known by cynics as the "not so central station" because of its location on the Albert Bridge some distance from the city centre. But there is a bus link to the main shopping area. The busiest service is the Bangor line, which services the south shore of Belfast Lough. Of interest to the enthusiast are the steam train runs during the summer months from York Road Station.

Getting out fast: Belfast is an easy city to escape from. That girdle of green hills has restricted overspill to along the loughshore and to the Lagan Valley. A few minutes drive in most directions brings a sharp transition from urban to rural. The tranquillity of country life has acted as a magnet over the troubled years. Nearby market and seaside towns have become swollen dormitories for the socially mobile. During the 1970s, the population of Belfast shrank by 100,000 in a middle-class exodus.

Just a few miles from the city, commuter traffic can be held up while a farmer herds his cattle across the road for milking. Habits from past generations fade slowly, and in any case, the pace of life rarely gets beyond a trot.

The A2 southeast from Belfast to Bangor runs through what locals enviously describe as the **"Gold Coast."** This is stockbroker country, where lush lawns meet mature woodland. Hillside sites, overlooking the shipping lanes, **Band concert at Bangor, Co. Down.**

have traditionally lured the well-heeled. **Holywood**, an ancient religious settlement five miles (eight km) from Belfast, enjoys a quiet prosperity since it was by-passed. Nothing much happens here, apart from the odd dance around the Maypole, but it has pleasant little shops, and good pubs and restaurants. **Cultra**, two miles (three km) further on, has leafy lanes, splendid houses, and the resplendent **Culloden Hotel**. They go in for yachting, golf and horse riding around here. Nowhere is more removed from the television image of Northern Ireland.

Nearby is the award-wining **Ulster Folk and Transport Museum**, which brings social history to life. Farmhouses, cottages, churches and mills have been painstakingly reconstructed—often brick by brick from their original locations. Freshly made soda bread, a local speciality, is sometimes baked over a traditional peat fire. On another part of the site the Transport Museum has its own fascination; exhibits range from the horse-drawn chariots right up to a prototype of the ill-fated De Lorean sports car. Brilliant Ulster engineer Harry Ferguson, a pioneer of flying, tractors and four-wheel-drive cars, is the prize example of the remarkable local contribution to air, sea and land transport. (Trams and trains are exhibited in another section of the museum located at Whitla Street in east Belfast.)

Before reaching Bangor, a signposted detour to the left will take in the beaches of **Helen's Bay**, the wooded **Crawfordsburn Country Park**, and the picturesque village of **Crawfordsburn** with its charming **Old Inn**. Such havens are unusual so close to a city.

Bangor itself was orginally a small seaside resort, noted for its Abbey. The seafront is somewhat faded today with a collection of fast-food bars and souvenir shops. Rowing around the bay in hired punts is an evergreen attraction, as is swimming in the open-air **Pickie Pool** when the weather permits. When it doesn't the town has a leisure centre with heated swimming and diving pools. For some reason, perhaps the bracing sea air, the town is favoured by evangelists who trawl for souls along the sea wall by the little harbour.

The old Bangor has been overgrown by acres of new housing developments, many of them inhabited by people who work in Belfast. It is a busy shopping town with a weekly open-air market, plenty of pubs and eating places, and parkland. The best beach is nearby **Ballyholme Bay**, a sandy arc which is invaded when the sun shines.

Down by the sea: Beyond Bangor there are a string of smaller seaside towns, popular with day trippers. **Donaghadee**, six miles (10 km) to the south, is notable for its much-painted harbour and lighthouse, and the promise of summer boat trips to the **Copeland Islands** (a bird sanctuary), which are just offshore. The twisting road passes quieter beaches at **Ballywalter** and **Ballyhalbert**, and the fishing port of **Portavogie**, which has occasional evening quayside fish auctions.

At the tip of the **Ards Peninsula**, a 23-mile (37-km) long finger dotted with villages and beaches, is **Portaferry**, where the tides boil in and out of **Strangford Lough** and a regular car ferry chugs a slanted course over to its twin town of **Strangford** on the other side. Sunset here is as fine a sight as anywhere in the world. The local lobster should not be missed.

The Vikings are said to have had a trading post at Strangford in the 9th Century. Nearby is **Castleward House**, an 18th Century Georgian mansion, once the home of the lord of Bangor. Overlooking the lough, the house has two "fronts" in differing styles because the Lord and his Lady had diverging tastes. Wildfowl are to be found in the grounds and there is a Victorian laundry, an 18th Century summer house and two small castles dating back to the 15th Century. A dream home by any standards.

Nine miles (14 km) north of Portaferry along the A20 is the one-street town of **Kircubbin**, a boating centre with a small pier jutting into Strangford Lough. Two miles (three km) inland takes you to the **Kirkistown circuit**, a wartime airport and the home of car racing in Northern Ireland. Race meetings are held monthly over the summer season. Motor sport has a keen following in Northern Ireland, particularly motorcycle racing and rallying—the latter can take place on public roads closed by Act of Parliament for the events.

Four miles (six km) further north on the A20 is the pretty village of **Greyabbey**, site of a Cistercian abbey dated 1193, and one of the most complete of its type in Ireland. Two miles north of the village is **Mountstewart**, another National Trust treasure, an 18th Century house which has several fine gardens and a mild microclimate which fosters delicate plants untypical of the area. The **Temple of the Winds** in the grounds is modelled on another in Athens, and overlooks the lough.

Strangford Lough is a watersport centre and noted for its myriad of islands, most of which are sunken drumlins, the smooth glacial hillocks which characterize the County Down rolling landscape. Narrow roads lead down to its eastern waterside from the A22 south of Comber. There are rocky shores on this side of the lough at places like **Whiterock Bay**, which rejoices in a restaurant called Daft Eddy's. **Mahee Island**, accessible by a bridge, has a golf course and the remains of **Nendrum Abbey**, an early monastery.

Newtownards, a sprawling commuter town at the head of Strangford Lough, belies its name; it's an old town, dating back to the 17th Century. It was an old market town and still is a bustling shopping centre with a blend of traditional shops and a covered shopping centre. There is a fine sandstone town hall and other buildings of historical interest include **Movilla Abbey** on the site of a 6th Century monastery about one mile to the east of the town. The airfield, a centre for amateur fliers, stages a spectacular annual display of aerobatics. Overlooking the town is **Scrabo Tower**, a 19th Century memorial to the third Marquess of Londonderry, offering splendid vistas of the lough and the soft-hilled country side and walks in the nearby **Killynether wood**.

Comber, also at the head of Strangford Lough, was a linen town and still has an operational mill. The centre of the town retains its old character, despite efforts of the developers, with single-storey cottage shops and a central square.

Castle by the sea: Striking out along the north shore of Belfast Lough takes one through the suburbs of **Whiteabbey** and **Greenisland**, with some opulent

Donaghadee, where day trippers go.

housing mirroring Cultra on the other side.

Carrickfergus, 12 miles (19 km) north from Belfast along the A2, is yet another market and dormitory town. Its big synthetic-fibre plants are empty now—a contemporary monument to its industrial past. The imposing **Norman Castle** beside the harbour, scene of gun-running exploits early this century, still attracts justifiable attention for its authenticity. It is a real castle in every sense with a portcullis, ramparts looking out over the sea, chilling dungeons, cannons and a regimental museum in the keep. Looking to the new age of leisure, the town's **marina** has 300 berths, with full back-up services. The parish church of St. Nicholas in the town dates back to the 12th Century. A mile to the east, in the townland of **Boneybefore**, is the reconstructed thatched cottage home of Andrew Jackson, the seventh President of the United States.

The countryside north of Carrickfergus becomes rich meadow land, with the sleepy seaside town of **Whitehead** nestling at the mouth of the lough, with a seashore walk to the

Blackhead lighthouse. Beyond this begins the peninsula of **Islandmagee**, with unspoilt beaches and caves, which wraps around Larne Lough. Across the mudflats is **Magheramorne** and **Glenoe**, the first of the Glens of Antrim.

South and west: Due south of Belfast, along the M1 motorway and connected by continuous conurbation, is **Lisburn**, another clamouring commercial centre with little to detain the traveller heading towards the halcyon countryside beyond. **Hillsborough** is a plantation town with its Government House set in parkland which also contains a massive fort. This was the home of the former Governor of Northern Ireland, and is a safe retreat for visiting Royalty or politicians. Sadly, security precludes the public from seeing more than a glimpse through the railings. The town, with its 18th Century courthouse, retains its Georgian character remarkably well and has been described as the most English of Ulster towns.

Guarding Belfast to the west are the twin summits of the **Black Mountain** and **Divis Mountain** (with its identifying television masts). Their bracken-covered slopes lead down to a rather blighted side of Belfast. Views from the **Horseshoe Bend** on the A52 are even more commanding than from the County Down side, but the area has not been so popular with the prestige developers.

Over the hills takes the visitor through somewhat bleaker countryside before descending to green farmland, and the famous **Dundrod Circuit**, one of the few remaining venues in the world for motorcycle road racing. The Ulster Grand Prix in August brings tens of thousands of spectators for the amazing sight of daredevil riding at speeds of up to 170 miles (273 km) an hour on narrow and twisting country roads.

Templepatrick, a trim town on the route from Belfast to the airport at Aldergrove, leaves the departing visitor with a final image of tranquillity. Medieval remains lie undisturbed in the stone-walled grounds of **Upton Castle** on the right. A restaurant on the left could be a roadhouse in Oxfordshire or Connecticut. This is the other, and rarely seen, side of Northern Ireland.

UNINHABITED ISLANDS

As the motor launch rounds Bray Head, off the Kerry coast, the island of **Skellig Michael** towers above like a cathedral. The sea is alive with birds diving for fish, and a school of porpoise swims round the boat. Thousands of gannets glide off the face of **Little Skellig**, leaving their nesting place on the guano-covered rock to dive like stones into the sea. Fulmers, shearwaters, petrels and gulls screech, then one of the boat's passengers points to the clown-like face of a puffin looking down curiously at them. As the boat approaches the landing place, a seal cub swims frantically away into a cave.

Skellig Michael encourages an air of pilgrimage: the 90-minute sea journey, the climb from the landing area to the monastic settlement 500 feet (150 metres) above by way of 600 steps carved into the rock a thousand years ago by Anchorite monks. Instead of prayer books, scapulars and rosary beads, today's pilgrims carry video cameras, binoculars and guidebooks.

From the settlement, an enclosure encompassing dry-stone beehive dwellings, the remains of a church and a boat-shaped dry-stone oratory, the Kerry coast looks much as it must have done to St. Brendan when he sailed for America from up the coast, from the Dingle peninsula. View the Atlantic from the summit 200 feet (61 metres) further up the rock and you can imagine the isolation of the monks who scratched out a living on this rock at the edge of the known world. Vikings attacked four times during the 9th Century, but it was the Church of Rome, preferring the monastic reforms of the 12th and 13th centuries to the practice of piety, which finally closed the island monastery.

According to legend, St. Patrick, aided by St. Michael, fought venomous serpents in a battle that helped rid Ireland of snakes. The island is the most isolated of Europe's mounds associated with St. Michael, such as St. Michael's Mount off the English coast and Mont St. Michel off the Brittany coast. The Skellig is a magical place.

"The dead man," one of the Blasket Islands off Slea Head.

234

Legends claim 365 islands off the Irish coast; one for every day of the year. In reality, there are many, many more, ranging from the **Aran Islands** off Galway and **Tory Island** off Donegal to outcrops of rock. Some are joined to the mainland by a bridge or causeway and have lost their island atmosphere; others were the homes of once thriving communities which have evacuated the islands, leaving behind forts, churches, houses, pathways and field systems long since reclaimed by nature.

North of the Skellig is the six-island group of the **Blaskets**, off the Dingle peninsula. These are some of Ireland's most famous uninhabited islands, thanks to a unique literature produced on the **Great Blasket** during the early years of this century, before the final evacuation of the island in 1953. Generations of Irish schoolchildren were reared on the works of this strange island community as they learned the Irish language. The Blasket islanders, never more than 200-strong, produced three writers: Tomas O Cromthain, who wrote *The Islandman*; Peig Sawyers, who wrote *Peig*; and Maurice O'Sullivan, who wrote *Twenty Years A-Growing*, a wonderful account of growing up on the Blaskets. Two English observers, Robin Flower and George Thompson, provided a sympathetic account of island life.

Only one of the six islands can be visited. A daily ferry service operates, weather permitting, between Dunquin and the Great Blasket during the summer. You don't even need a map of the Blaskets since one is thoughtfully provided by the Irish Central Bank on the back of their £20 note. One island, however, is missing from the note: it is **Inishvickillaune**, which is no longer uninhabited, having been bought as a holiday home by an Irish prime minister, Charles Haughey.

Near the landing area on the Great Blasket are the remains of a village, the ruins of the traditional cottages sheltered against the winds. Above are houses built by the government for the rural poor, one operating intermittently as a guest house or cafe. A lovely beach faces the mainland and the island's paths are still clear. Many dry-stone walls survive. Great Blasket, about four miles long and two miles wide (six by three km), rises to nearly 1,000 feet (300 metres). It is a wild, beautiful place, with steep cliffs and spectacular views and the most wonderfully shaggy sheep munching their way freely across the island. Visitors tend to return.

Until the 1950s, many conventions of 18th Century Gaelic culture were preserved and the hard life of the islanders, who scraped a living by fishing from canvas-covered *curraghs*, has since gained a heroic stature. The neglect of the islands contrasts with the growing interest in their literature—a state of affairs that proves to many people the lack of interest in Gaelic culture shown by successive governments.

On Ireland's east coast are the two islands of the **Saltees**, reached from the lovely Wexford village of Kilmore Quay. The only inhabitants today are an estimated 3 million birds, from 47 species—a big attraction. The islands have some associations with the Wexford Rising of 1798 and are today owned by a Mr. Michael Neales, who has proclaimed himself "Prince Michael the First of the Saltees." His by-laws welcome all to the island but he asks that it be left as found.

Also on the east coast, close to Dublin, **Dalkey Island** to the south and **Ireland's Eye** to the north are easily accessible.

A lesser known gem is **MacDara's Island**, lying a few miles off Connemara's coast near Roundstone. Although only 60 acres (24 hectares), it has an exquisite 6th Century oratory, recently restored. It was named after St. MacDara, the first recorded Irish saint to have a surname; he was a protector of sailors and, until recently, of the Galway Hookers, sailing vessels which dipped their sails in acknowledgement as they passed the island.

There is no regular ferry service to the island, but local fishermen will transport visitors for a small fee. The problem, of course, is the unpredictable weather.

Today ferries operate to the Skelligs from Cahirciveen, Derrynane, Portmagee and Valentia. But the winds and the tides still make getting to any island destination uncertain. That, after all, is part of the allure and adventure of the islands of Ireland.

SONG AND DANCE

An English traveller, writing from Ireland in the 17th Century, had this to say of rural diversions on a Sunday afternoon: "In every field a fiddle, and the lasses footing it till they are all of a foam." No doubt the writer exaggerated slightly, for if a fiddle was to be provided for every field in the country, it would have kept several factories operating around the clock. But his comment echoes the experience of thousands of visitors to Ireland in the intervening years and bears out the general view that the Irish are a remarkably musical people. Time after time, in letters and reminiscences, we keep coming across references to music, dance and song.

Today's traveller will still find in every town and hamlet, particularly at weekends, a traditional music session taking place in some pub or other. And it won't be something laid on for tourists; it will reflect an authentic musical tradition going back hundreds of years, mixing haunting airs, lively jigs and soul-stirring ballads, and revealing the influences of classical, Italian and even Spanish music.

A minor miracle: While other countries have seen their traditional music wither under the assault of mass-produced pop music, Ireland has witnessed a minor miracle: thousands of youngsters all over the country have been picking up the old tunes and songs and carrying them forward into the 21st Century. With the international success of such groups as the Chieftains, Clannad, and the Furey Brothers, Irish music has taken on a new lease of life at home and abroad. The Chieftains even toured China.

But what exactly *is* Irish traditional music? The Irish being a disputatious people, there is no single answer. True *aficionados* would probably frown on songs such as "Galway Bay" and "Danny Boy," songs regarded internationally as typically Irish. Although "Danny Boy" undoubtedly has deep roots, the folk music purist would argue that such songs, pleasant as they might be, are too modern in composition.

Preceding pages, traditional embroidery; decorative hotel front in Listowel, Co. Kerry; travelling musicians draw crowds in Listowel. Left, street musicians are tolerated in the capital too. Right, Irish dancing at the Galway Oyster Festival.

He would insist that material can be properly classified as traditional only if it is several hundred years old and fits a closely defined style of playing or singing.

Yet, in fairness, it is common at traditional music sessions to hear people singing songs of quite modern vintage, such as emigrant songs or patriotic songs of the past hundred years, or even songs composed in recent times such as the haunting anti-war song "The Band Played Waltzing Matilda." This song, by the Scottish singer Eric Bogle, recalls the terrible slaughter

of Australian troops in the Dardanelles during World War One. What this proves, perhaps, is that the Irish have a catholic taste and, providing the words or tunes are interesting, they'll sit back and enjoy them.

Indisputably, the instrument most associated with Ireland is the harp. As the national emblem, it even appears on the coinage. References to the harp can be found in documents dating back to the 11th Century, when it was used to accompany the poetry of the Irish bards at the courts of the Gaelic kings and princes. However, as the ancient Gaelic civilization began to break down under increasing English pressure in the 17th Century, harpists had to find a new role. Many, taking to the

roads, travelled the country, entertaining the aristocracy in the "Big Houses" of the time.

Other instruments used by the ancient Irish for making music include the bagpipes, which were similar to the modern Scottish equivalent. The country's literature contains many references to them, especially to their use by soldiers marching into battle, and also at funerals and sporting events. In time, though, these gave way to a uniquely Irish instrument, the uillean or union pipes. These are played by using a bellows rather than blowing to inflate the bag. They are regarded as outstanding among the pipes of the world for their sweetness of tone, and are one of the principal instruments used by today's leading traditional musicians. Others include the fiddle, concertina, flute, tin whistle, guitar and bodhran (a round goatskin tambourine or drum played with a small stick).

Pipers call the tune: Closely allied to the playing of traditional music was Irish dance, which seems to have come into its own in the second half of the 18th Century. Travellers of the period have remarked that dancing was so widespread among the poor that dancing masters would tour the countryside from cabin to cabin, accompanied by a piper or fiddler, and would be paid by the peasants to teach their children to dance. Such men, by all accounts, were a cut above the rest of the population, dressing themselves neatly and considering themselves gentlemen.

Each master had a defined territory and would settle into a district for up to six weeks, ensuring that there would be a festival of music and dancing for the duration. Stories are told of rivalry between various dancing masters for control of certain districts, and at fairs and sporting events they would often hold solo exhibitions of their prowess to decide who was best. A visitor to a town in County Kilkenny recounts seeing a large crowd gathered around two dancers who were taking it in turns to perform on the soaped head of an upturned barrel. They were, he was informed, dancing masters contesting which of them should "own" the parish.

The main occasions for dancing appear to have been Sundays, fair days, at sporting events—and, of course, at weddings, where the musician would be paid for his performance. For many of them, indeed, it was their only means of livelihood. The dances themselves involved communal and group dancing between the sexes to a variety of tunes and tempos which are known today as jigs, reels and hornpipes. There was also great interest in individual prowess, such as dancing within a confined patch of ground. When it was raining, the events were held in barns. In fine weather, they would take place in level fields, or very often at a crossroads.

Many of the tunes and songs heard on these occasions had been handed down from one musician to another. A lot would have been lost to modern ears, though, if it hadn't been for the work of several great music collectors who began to travel the country in the early 19th Century annotating and writing down the tunes.

Spurred on by nationalism: Another boost to tradition came at the end of that century from the growth of nationalism and a

revival of interest in the Irish language and culture generally. After the founding of the Republic, a great deal of emphasis was put on the teaching of folk music and traditional dancing in schools. The new state's broadcasting station, Radio Eireann, devoted a great deal of airtime to the native culture. More recently, interest has been stimulated by respected composers such as the late Seán O'Riada and his group Ceoltoírí Chualann, the forerunner of the Chieftains. The Clancy Brothers were a great popularizing influence.

But perhaps the greatest credit should go to the Comhaltas Ceoltoírí Eireann, the body which looks after traditional music and song. It has hundreds of branches, in every county of Ireland and abroad, and organizes regular festivals which culminate in an annual three-day event called the All-Ireland Fleadh Ceoil. This joyous festival, held each summer, usually in a town in the west of the country, can attract more than 100,000 people and answers the wildest prayers of local publicans. Information about these events can be had from the Comhaltas Ceoltoírí Eireann at Belgrave Square, Monkstown, County Dublin.

Major centres such as Dublin, Belfast and Cork hold their own festivals. In addition, there are specialist festivals such as the one devoted to uillean piping. This event, held in Milltown Malbay in County Clare each July, is named after a famous Clare piper, Willie Clancy. (For further information, telephone Dublin 744447.)

In the tourist season, many hotels lay on after-dinner dancers and traditional musicians. Medieval castles do the same sort of thing in grander style: near Shannon airport in the west of the country, for example, you can find Knappogue Castle, Quin, County Clare; Dunguaire Castle, Kinvara, County Galway; and Bunratty Castle, Bunratty, County Clare. But for authenticity you can't beat the musicians who sing and play primarily for their own pleasure rather than for the tourist coach parties—and you'll mostly find them in plain, unadorned pubs.

Small back rooms: Dublin alone has dozens of regular events, most held in the backrooms of pubs. In the city centre, pubs such as O'Donoghue's in Merrion Row have long been a magnet for lovers of traditional music. It was from O'Donoghue's that the world-famous Dubliners were launched in the early 1960s, and most nights of the week a lively session gets under way in the same back room. Other reliable venues include the Brazen Head, one of the city's oldest pubs, located in Lower Bridge Street; Slattery's of Capel Street; and the International Bar in Wicklow Street.

To the north of the city, out in the picturesque fishing village of Howth, the Abbey Tavern has an international reputation for traditional music and song. There's a small fee for entry to the sessions, held in the authentic old stone bar room. Dinner is also available. On the south side of the city, the headquarters of the Comhaltas in Monkstown hosts regular events.

Preceding page, blowing the bagpipes at Enniscorthy, Co. Wexford. Left and right, modern music draws young people in Dublin.

THE IRISH WAY WITH WORDS

The Irish are noted for their ability to perform remarkable conjuring tricks with the English language, written and spoken. This gift ranges from the calculated blarney of the professional tourist guide or the frothy whimsicalities of a Dublin pub through masters of conversation like Oscar Wilde and Sir John Mahaffy to some of the greatest names in world literature, from Jonathan Swift to George Bernard Shaw, Edmund Burke to Samuel Beckett.

And yet James Joyce, the ultimate virtuoso of the English language, noted wryly in *A Portrait of the Artist as a Young Man* the sense of cultural alienation that underlies its use by an Irishman. In this novel, Joyce's *alter ego*, Stephen Dedalus, uses a word unfamiliar to the Dean of Studies at his university. The Dean, Father Darlington, an Englishman, suspects wrongly that the word is Irish in origin, which prompts Stephen to reflect: "The language in which we are speaking is his before it is mine. How different are the words *home*, *Christ*, *ale*, *master*, on his lips and on mine! I cannot speak or write these words without unrest of spirit. His language, so familiar and so foreign, will always be for me an acquired speech. I have not made or accepted its words. My voice holds them at bay. My soul frets in the shadow of his language."

Indeed, few visitors today realize how recent is the general use of English in Ireland. Few know that Irish, not English, is still the official first language of the state and that, in matters of law, the Irish-language version of the constitution holds superior authority.

A minority language: In 1835 the number of Irish speakers was estimated at 4 million. This number consisted almost entirely of a deprived rural class which was devastated by the great famine of the 1840s and subsequent mass emigration. By 1891 the number of Irish speakers had tumbled to 680,245. Today, the everyday use of Irish is confined almost exclusively to the officially designated Gaeltacht areas along the western seaboard, whose combined population is around 75,000. Yet

over a million people claim some knowledge of the language, thanks to the government's policy of compulsory instruction.

The ancient Irish language survived repeated waves of invasion by Vikings, Normans and English planters. In 1366, so many of the Anglo-Irish settlers had "gone native" that the Statutes of Kilkenny forbade the use of Irish in a vain attempt to stem the encroachment of Celtic customs and language among the colonizers.

The decisive abandonment of Irish in the 19th Century was brought about not just

by the impact of the famine but by the introduction of the National School System in 1831. This system decreed that English would be the proper language of instruction, and children who spoke the native tongue were beaten or gagged. The situation was made worse when national leaders such as Daniel O'Connell recognized that English was the language of political effectiveness. O'Connell, though a native Irish speaker himself, declared that he was "sufficiently utilitarian not to regret its gradual abandonment."

Far different was the attitude of the 20th Century leader Eamon de Valera, who somewhat surprisingly said that "Ireland with its language and without freedom is

Preceding pages, a performance in Dublin's Abbey Theatre of Sean O'Casey's classic play Shadow of a Gunman. Left, Oscar Wilde and, right, George Bernard Shaw, two celebrated Irish-born playwrights.

preferable to Ireland with its freedom and without its language." The virtual extinction of Irish as a living language was certainly a tragedy. *Gan teanga, gan tír* was the slogan of the revivalists — "No language, no country" — and a certain element of the Irish identity withered as English took over. Irish had a venerable tradition, being the earliest variant of the Celtic languages and the earliest language north of the Alps in which extensive writings are still extant. It had a special alphabet of distinctive and beautiful characters. This script was, in a strange quirk of history, carried over into print by order of England's Queen Elizabeth I, who ordered a fount to be cut in 1571 for an Irish version of the Protestant catechism.

Unfortunately this elegant script was officially superseded by Roman script in the 1960s in an attempt to make the language more "modern" and accessible, and the use of Irish script is now rare. Outstanding examples can be seen in the Book of Kells or the Book of Armagh, kept in Dublin's Trinity College library, or in the Book of the Dun Cow in the Royal Irish Academy. A section of this last book appears on the back of the new Irish pound note.

Sure it's only talk: The 19th Century shift from Irish to English was so sudden and so resented that the mark of the earlier language was imprinted on its successor. There is an intriguing anecdote in *Mo Scéal Féin* ("My Own Story") by Ant-Athair Peadar O Laoghaire (Father Peter O'Leary), which tells of two West Cork children during the famine period:

"Con," said she,
"Coming Sheila," said he,
"I have no talk now," said she.
"Why, what else have you, Sheila?"
said he.
"I have English," said she,
"And sure English is talk Sheila,"
said he.
"English, talk?" said she, amazed, "Sure if it was, people would understand it."

Irish is seen here as "talk," the language of communication and imagination, whereas English is not "talk" but a necessary and utilitarian, though not fully understood, vehicle.

During the 19th Century it became commonplace for many people to think in Irish, then translate their thoughts into English. This process led to the development of the so-called Hiberno-English dialect, and sometimes produced effects of great beauty and elegance, even in the simplest phrases. Thus the bald statement in English "that is true" becomes either " 'Tis true for you" (Hiberno-English) from *Is fíor é sin* (Irish) or "There's not a word of a lie in it" from *Níl aon focal bréige ann*.

What's more, received standard English is a language that is imperial and rational, its preoccupations administrative and its social tone most characteristically represented by the genius of Jane Austen. No Irish hand could have written the celebrated opening line of *Pride and Prejudice:* "It is a truth universally acknowledged that a single man in possession of good fortune must be in want of a wife." For all its wit and elegance, it is too precise, too exact, too conscious, and, above all, too lacking in the essentially subversive irreverence of the Irish way of thought. Anglo-Saxon pre-

cision is alien to the Irish mind, which would be more at home with Humpty-Dumpty's dictum: "When I use a word it means just what I choose it to mean—neither more nor less."

A classic illustration of this is the story of Daniel O'Connell's battle of words with an old Dublin fishwife, reported to have the most virulent flow of invective in Ireland. A colleague bet O'Connell that even he could not best this woman in dispute. He accepted the challenge and, on

Two of Ireland's greatest 20th Century writers: above, James Joyce, who arm-wrestled English into new forms; right, Sean O'Casey, who dramatized Ireland's political anguish.

the appointed day, a quarrel was deliberately engineered. The old harridan attacked O'Connell with all the considerable verbal venom at her disposal. He bided his time and, when she was finally exhausted, let fly at her, eschewing vulgar obscenity and profanity, employing instead only the terms of Euclidian geometry. When he reached a climax of mathematical abuse, describing her as a shameless parallelogram, an inveterate isosceles triangle and an unregenerate hypotenuse, she collapsed in tears, protesting her virtue. O'Connell was the victor.

It is no accident that it was an Irishman, the 18th Century playwright Richard Brinsley Sheridan, who gave the world the immortal Mrs. Malaprop in his comedy

The Rivals. She resents "an aspersion to my parts of speech" and avers that "if I reprehend anything in the world it is the use of my oracular tongue and a nice derangement of epitaphs."

A politician, Sir Boyle Roche, did similar violence to English in real life, once informing the Irish House of Commons: "Mr Speaker, I smell a rat; I see him forming in the air and darkening the sky, but I shall nip him in the bud." It was Roche who disdained the future with the memorable phrase: "Posterity be damned. What has posterity done for us?"

But of course such innocent buffoonery, acceptable as a joke within the family, could make the Irish look ridiculous to outsiders. In the 20th Century, a new generation of writers rediscovered the collision of sensibility between the Irish mind and the English language, and set out to explore its literary potential. William Butler Yeats and Lady Gregory, instrumental in founding Dublin's Abbey Theatre, decided that the Irish peasant was a noble creature, and they determined to correct the balance of earlier representations by giving him a speech that was real and melodic rather than phonetic and contrived.

John Millington Synge (pronounced *sing*) had the added benefit of being fluent in Irish, and carried the experiment even further, although his lilting stage speech was sometimes dismissed as "Synge-song." In the preface to his controversial play *The Playboy of the Western World*, he wrote: "Anyone who has lived in real intimacy with the Irish peasantry will know that the wildest sayings and ideas in this play are tame indeed when compared with the fancies one may hear in any little hillside cabin in Geesala or Carraroe or Dingle Bay."

A web of lyricism: Synge, in fact, manufactured a convincing theatrical language from a small number of Irish-derived constructions: ending a phrase with *surely* as in "It's destroyed he'll be surely"; using *do be* in the sense of a continuous present, as in "In the big world the old people do be leaving things after them for their sons and children"; and inserting the adverbial *and*, as in "There were two men and they rowing." Synge had the technical command to use these apparently simple devices as a frame over which he stretched the web of a remarkable new lyricism.

When one considers the contribution of Irish writers to literature in this century, even an incomplete list astonishes: Yeats with his poetry of the Celtic Twilight and beyond; Sean O'Casey with his miraculous ear for the cadences of the Dublin slums; Frank O'Connor's powerfully humorous but unsentimental stories of childhood in Cork; the plays of Beckett and Shaw; Somerville and Ross's world of the Irish RM (resident magistrate), in which tweedy English officialdom gets its come-uppance from the brilliant improvisations on language of the Irish peasantry; the poetry of Patrick Kavanagh, Brendan Kennelly and Seamus Heaney.

Although very different in their genius, they all share one thing in common: an almost physical delight in words that springs from a sharpened sensitivity to a language that is never entirely their own.

FAIRIES AND FOLKLORE

During the summer of 1985 thousands of people began to go on pilgrimages to Marian shrines, in various parts of the country, because people claimed to have seen them move. After a time the phenomenon became a national and international news story; much to the indignation of the country's advanced liberals who saw these pilgrimages as a further manifestation of national obscurantism. The Catholic Church authorities, in the areas where pilgrims collected, counselled caution. They advised people to seek physical and rational explanations for what was happening rather than supernatural ones. But still the thousands travelled until the strange happenings ceased just as suddenly as they had commenced.

By then a book had been produced, in which, tucked away among the eyewitness accounts from the contemporary pilgrims and descriptions of apparitions from the past, there was a contribution by a lecturer in the Department of Folklore in University College, Dublin. This erudite essay showed that the phenomenon of moving statues originated in the early Middle Ages, was well-known in Ireland and was the subject of many tales and legends.

This is just one manifestation of Irish folklore, as well as being an example of the past returning to embarrass the present. Other forms of folklore have been used to good effect by Irish writers, particularly those who were instrumental in launching the Irish Literary Revival at the turn of the century. W. B. Yeats, Lady Gregory, John M. Synge, Padraig Colum and James Stephens drew on the vast number of myths and legends which were beginning to emerge out of the Celtic Twilight in translations from the Irish language.

There were the heroic tales concerning Fionn MacCool, leader of Fianna Eireann, and his band of warriors. They defended Ireland against invaders, hunted and indulged in feats of strength between May and November. Then, for six months, they retired to the winter quarters where they feasted, told tales, listened to music on harps and played chess. The ancient Irish had only two seasons, summer and winter, and in rural Ireland May Day and Hallowe'en are still the days that mark the beginning and the end of the agricultural year. For instance, potatoes that

have not been dug before Hallowe'en will remain in the ground, and children will not pick blackberries after that date.

There were many other series, or cycles, of tales concerning the same characters. One of the most famous is the series on the Red Branch Knights and Cuchulainn, the Hound of Ulster, a mythical hero whose statue in Dublin's General Post Office commemorates the Rising of 1916. Here again, myth and stark reality meet.

Leprechaun lore: Other writers drew inspiration from tales of spirits, benign and malign, and the little people, sometimes called leprechauns, who guarded hidden treasure and had a thousand tricks to distract the greedy mortals who sought it. They also indulged in games of hurl-

changing a word or an emphasis. Some of these tales, concerning personages such as "The King of Ireland's Son" and his adventures in Spain and Africa, could take more than two hours in the telling. About eight really top-class storytellers still survive and their art has now been preserved on film for posterity.

One of the principal reasons why so much of Ireland's past lives on today is to be found in the method St. Patrick used to propagate the Christian message when he arrived in 432. He found a people immersed in pagan beliefs and rituals. His debates with the Druids (the pagan priests) enliven much of early Irish literature. He even confronted Oisín, son of Fionn MacCool, who had unwisely returned from

ing, sometimes borrowing a champion from the world of mortals to assist them. If they won, he was suitably rewarded. It was believed in Sligo that the great traditional fiddle player, Michael Coleman, who recorded all his music in New York, had learned his flawless bowing technique from a band of little folk whom he had befriended.

The storytellers who preserved most of these tales, before the scholars came to write and record them, were custodians of a very ancient oral tradition. They were called *seanachaithe* from the Irish *seanachas* meaning lore. Some could relate more than 300 tales, learned by rote from their elders, and could recite them without

the Land of Eternal Youth only to become an old man as soon as he touched the soil of Ireland.

St. Patrick helped preserve Ireland's social structure and many of her customs even as he changed fundamental beliefs. He clearly did not believe in the politics of confrontation—which is as good a proof as any, some say, that he was not an Irishman. When he ascended Croagh Patrick, Ireland's holy mountain in County Mayo,

Preceding page, Irish illustrator Jim Fitzpatrick's drawing of an early Norse invader from "The Silver Arm." Left, a fairy ring, said to have magic powers. Right, holy well, keeping alive ancient superstitions.

the peak was sacred to the pagan God Crom. When he descended, after battling for 40 days and nights with a legion of evil spirits, including the Devil's mother, he declared the summit sacred to the Christian God. The people were to continue paying homage, but in a new form. So it came about that every year tens of thousands of pilgrims, from all parts of the country and beyond, converge on Croagh Patrick on the last Sunday in July (still called Black Crom's Sunday in the Irish language). They climb at dawn, many of them barefoot, to the oratory on the summit.

Where paganism lives on: Most of the holy wells, where people come to pray and perform intricate patterns of prayer and

tale merely serves to strengthen laudable reverence for the dead.

Another form of folklore, now getting a new lease of life due to the increased interest in herbs and alternative medicine, is the area of folk cures and folk medicine. It is an area in which one finds received wisdom and superstition inextricably mixed.

How is it that only a member of the Doogan clan can guarantee that earth from Tory Island, off the Donegal coast, will banish all rodents from your home by handing it to you? Why is the seventh son of a seventh son capable of curing certain ills and ailments, depending on which family he comes from? If he is a Shanaghan, for instance, he has the cure for whooping cough. Why is it that direct

mortification of the flesh, were also deemed holy in pre-Christian times. The famous Puck's Fair, in Kerry, is also a continuation of a pagan fertility rite.

What is sometimes regarded as mere superstition is very often based on something very different. Visitors to Ireland often ask for an explanation for a piece of land, frequently with a white thorn bush growing on it, untouched by the farmer who has sown the field of wheat or barley. They are informed that it is a fairy tree and that bad luck will quickly follow the person who disturbs it. It is a good story to brighten an uneventful journey, but the truth of the matter is that what people call "fairy forts" are old burial places and the picturesque

acceptance of financial reward will remove the capacity to cure, while indirect payment, or payment in kind, will not?

Of course, folklore never ceases to evolve in an island the size of Ireland, in which traditions linger on and emerge in new guises when least expected. Television may have hastened the death of the gatherings around the storyteller at the fireside, but it has not yet fully demolished the delight Irish people take in listening to a tall tale well told. The moving statues of 1985 have already created enough stories to ensure that another generation will have another folk-memory passed on to them orally. That is how it all begins; and that is how it all began.

BARS AND BOOZING

A common stereotype of the Irishman abroad is that of a maudlin drinker seated at a bar in London or New York or Chicago, gazing dolefully into his glass and mouthing inanities to himself about the green fields and the clear mountain streams of his native land. An ill-chosen word from a stranger will quickly rouse his anger and, in the twinkling of an eye, a rip-roaring riot is in progress.

This image of the Irish exile, conveyed principally by movies of a certain vintage, has a strong element of truth in it—and so too has the stereotype of the Irish when they are at home. The same movies portray the home-based Irish as jovial, garrulous, welcoming in the extreme and brilliant at the art of conversation. A more realistic view is that the Irish are sad abroad and happy at home because of the drink. And is it any wonder? The *Esquire Drink Book's* expert on alcohol gets it absolutely right: "Ireland is a country where, except for a species of moonshine called poteen, there isn't any bad liquor. The general level strikes me as positively Himalayan."

From tap to throat: But what makes the Irishman surly in foreign climes is, usually, the lack of quality in, or the total absence of, a pint of Guinness. This brew, a strongish black beer with a creamy white head, is, even more than Irish whiskey, the country's national beverage. Brewed in Dublin since 1759, it is a temperamental drink, needing great care in pouring from the tap to the glass. Constant temperature in the cellars, the distance from cask to tap and the frequency of the flow are all considered important factors in the art known as "the pulling of a good pint."

If the pint isn't good, it is sent straight back. Experts embark on long discussions on the pint's quality in different bars throughout the country. Dubliners, who travel frequently inside Ireland, make lists of the provincial pubs which have the best pints. The visitor's best criterion is this: if the place is crowded with locals, then the pint is probably good. And you'll know a good pint when you get one. It won't taste like what passes for Guinness in Britain, where the beer is sloshed into the glass by

The welcoming facade of one of Dublin's thousands of pubs.

insensitive barmen, or like the Guinness in America, where the long sea journey from Dublin does nothing for the quality. It will taste, in a good pub in Ireland, as smooth as velvet.

There are other Irish beers, too. Harp, brewed in Dundalk, sells well internationally, particularly in Britain. Smithwick's Ale, lighter than Guinness and darker than Harp, is very popular in Ireland and has made strong inroads into the specialist beer market in France, especially around Paris.

As far as spirits are concerned, the Irish rank highly as connoisseurs. One French Cognac house was surprised to discover that some of the highest sales per head for its premium brandies were in a less than affluent Dublin suburb. But it is Irish whiskey (note the extra "e") which reigns supreme on its home territory. Triple-distilled for purity and lightness, Irish whiskey was overtaken by Scotch on the world market during World War Two. One main reason was selfishness on the part of the Irish.

It was an Irishman, Aeneas Coffey, who invented the patent still in the 1830s. This permitted the mass production of blended whiskies. Scottish distillers, in the main, switched to the new method. The Irish and the smaller Scottish malt-whisky producers stuck with the old tried and tested "pot still" method, which involved a single whiskey acquiring its mellowness through long ageing. In the 1940s, the Scots diverted their production to export and rationed the sale of their whiskies at home. The Irish did the opposite, keeping their whiskies to themselves. The result was disastrous. GIs from all over America acquired their taste for Scotch in the European theatre of war and, when they got back home, brought the taste with them. Irish, whose popularity in the royal courts of Europe had led Russia's Peter the Great to describe it as "the best of all the wines," went into a decline from which it has only recently begun to recover.

Maturing the malts: The comparative affluence and sophisticated tastes of the 1980s have stimulated the demand for Ireland's more traditional whiskies as well as Scotland's rarer malts. There are 15 or so different whiskies on sale in Ireland. John Power's Gold Label is by far the most popular. Next come Jameson, Bushmills, Coleraine (which sells in Northern Ireland), Paddy, Hewitt's and Dunphy's. Murphy's sells mainly in the United States, and Tullamore Dew, a particularly light brand, does well in Europe.

Two popular premium brands are Black Bush (from Bushmills in County Antrim, the world's oldest distillery) and Crested Ten, matured for 10 years in the Jameson stable. At the top of the range are liqueur whiskies, among the most exceptional drinks on earth. Bushmills Malt is a single 10-year-old; Jameson 1780 is aged for 12 years; and Redbreast, also 12 years old, is matured in wood by the house of Gilbey, renowned for its wines, ports and sherries. To put ice in these last three whiskies

that's important in Ireland: it's where you drink it. Here there are no dainty pubs like those that dot the English countryside. Ireland's rural bars are usually functional in design; nothing to look at from the outside, but warm, cozy and well filled inside. They have other advantages over their English equivalents: they don't shut for the whole afternoon and, outside Dublin, what licensing laws there are tend not to be strictly enforced.

Picture a bar in a small village on the Atlantic coast. It is two o'clock in the morning, long after the official closing time. There is a rap on the door, sharp enough to suggest authority. A local police sergeant enters, in full uniform, torchlight in hand. Yet no-one present

would be an act of sacrilege to an Irishman. They should be sipped neat like the finest of Cognacs or Armagnacs, although the foreigner is permitted to add a dash of pure Irish water.

While all the major international brands of gin, vodka and other spirits are readily available, the Irish are inclined to stick to the home products. Thus Cork Dry Gin far outsells the more famous British gins. One often-mentioned drink, poteen, isn't on sale anywhere legally. Some of it, like Schnapps in Germany, can be quite good; but, if carelessly prepared, this secretly distilled drink can seriously damage your health.

But it's not only the drink itself

interrupts the conversation—except for a few visiting English and Americans. Half an hour later, the scene has changed entirely. Not a murmur of conversation is to be heard. The sergeant, his cap placed on the bar in front of him, is clasping a pint of Guinness in his right hand and, with his eyes closed in the prescribed manner, is singing the old lament "The Blackbird of Sweet Avondale."

This sort of scene can be found easily

Left, singing and supping at Megaw's pub in Brookeborough, Co. Fermanagh. Right, Irish pubs, such as this one at Buttevant, Co. Cork, are owned by publicans rather than breweries and so have great individuality.

enough anywhere on the west coast, where the summer tourist season is short and the after-hours trade compensates for the meagre takings in the desolate winter months. In Dublin, Belfast, Cork and Limerick, however, this laxity does not exist. Last drinks are served at 11 p.m. in winter and 11.30 in summer, and the law is .strictly enforced. Well, fairly strictly.

City pubs are different, too. In Dublin some bars are richly caparisoned in.brass and mahogany, with antique mirrors proclaiming the merits of whiskies long since defunct. Some such pubs, particularly the most popular, are virtually unchanged in decor since the middle of the last century.

Women who tippled: To experience the value placed on the traditional, visit public servants, prominent journalists and a group of economists known informally as "the Doheny and Nesbitt School."

Nesbitt's, as it's known for short, fulfills the function that private clubs would play in most capital cities, with the distinct advantage that any member of the decent Irish drinking public is free to walk in from the street and join the company.

Inspect Nesbitt's lavatories, however, and you may decide that they don't measure up to the highest international standards of pristine cleanliness. It is still true that, if you enquire in most Irish bars "Where's the toilet?," the barman will suggest you "follow your nose." There are, of course, squeaky-clean, plush plastic lounges in the major hotels,

Doheny and Nesbitt's in Dublin's Baggot Street. This is an old-fashioned pub, long and narrow with a "snug" at each end. A snug is a small area partitioned off from the rest of the bar in which up to 10 people can drink in almost complete privacy. It even has its own private service hatch, and is a hangover from the days when women who fancied a tipple didn't want to be seen consuming it. The atmosphere is one of talk and more talk, for if there is one thing that is as important as the drink in a Dublin pub it is the conversation. The general appearance is dowdy enough, with hard bar stools and not the slightest attempt at plushness. Yet this bar is the haunt of government ministers, senior

but these tend to be inhabited by squeaky-clean, plush plastic lounging people.

An exception is the Horseshoe Bar of the Shelbourne Hotel on St. Stephen's Green. It has retained its intimate character despite the overweening renovations carried out under the ownership of international hotel operator Lord Forte.

Other Dublin pubs with good character and conversation include Mulligan's of Poolbeg Street, Neary's of Chatham Street and Ryan's of Parkgate Street. Mulligan's, which welcomed its first customer in 1782, is also divided into sections.The entrance to the left of the building leads into the older part of the pub. Here one finds students, the occasional retired docker and photographers from the *Irish Press,* whose head office is nearby. The door to the right of the building admits the client to the first of two bars in the slightly more modern section. The first is occupied by newspaper and television people. Go straight through to the far bar and you are in left-wing territory, where the clientele ranges from moderate trade unionists to militant Trotskyists.

Neary's is a beautifully furnished old-style pub which attracts permanently posing actors from the Gaiety Theatre. Ryan's, situated in an area a little distance from the centre of Dublin's action, is a real gem: its clients are those who appreciate good conversation, good atmosphere and the traditions of Dublin pub life. They are prepared to travel a bit from the city centre to enjoy the place. So should the visitor.

But traditional decor and character don't always combine with good atmosphere. The Long Hall in George's Street is a case in point: it is a showpiece pub, well worth a visit, but it's a bit like drinking in a museum—there's just no pizzazz. The same can be said for the most gloriously baroque pub in Ireland, the Crown in Belfast's Great Victoria Street. This place looks so truly Victorian that it has been bought by the National Trust and declared a national monument. But, for warmth and friendliness, try Robinson's, just next door, or nearby Kelly's Cellars.

Pubs outside the immediate city centre are, like most things in Belfast, divided on a politico-religious basis. Visitors are best advised to stick to the beaten path and, unless they are accompanied by a local they can totally trust, not to try to gain entry to any of the after-hours or Sunday drinking clubs or illegal *shebeens* operated by some rather suspect organizations.

A witch's brew: In Cork, the Oyster Tavern is a fine place to eat and drink, if a trifle on the snobbish side, but its chauvinism is an almost endearing characteristic of Ireland's third city. Kyteler's Inn in Kilkenny, once owned by a woman burnt as a witch, is a bit touristy these days; but Bollard's, a couple of doors down, has a good atmosphere where the talk is of greyhounds and the game of hurling.

Galway has a host of excellent pubs, almost all worth a visit. One curiosity is Mick Taylor's in Dominick Street, a bar which supplies reading matter to those not wishing to join in the conversation or an occasional song. You can stumble across a variety of material, from *Chums,* a turn-of-the-century magazine for upper-class schoolboys, through Churchill's *History of the English-speaking Peoples* to the day's morning and evening newspapers.

Not far from Galway city, on the road to Gort, lies Kilcolgan. Take a right turn here and follow the signs for Moran's of the Weir, a traditional country pub with a difference. The thatched roof gives the place a quaintness that can be equalled by other Irish bars, but what Moran's promises to provide, if there's an R in the month, are the best oysters in Ireland. The oyster beds are just outside the front door, and their contents are begging to be consumed with Guinness, their perfect partner, in one of Moran's little alcoves or private rooms.

Salmon and singing: Along the Atlantic coast is a tremendous selection of fine pubs, but none better than those in north and west Clare, not far from Galway. In the spa town of Lisdoonvarna, Curtin's "Roadside" tavern smokes its own salmon and has fresh shellfish in season. At night, there are traditional fiddlers, pipers and flute players.

Down the road at Doolin, in Gus O'Connor's, music is played at any hour by some of Ireland's most renowned traditional musicians, who live in the area. On past the spectacular Cliffs of Moher, at Liscannor, home of lobster fishermen, the action is at Joe McHugh's bar, which resembles a dark alleyway, regardless of whether the sun is shining outside or not. In this pub, as in many others in Ireland, you can buy almost anything. Call for a pair of Wellington boots, a pound of pork sausages, some barley sugar sticks from the jar on the counter, a mousetrap, a pint of stout, a large Jack Daniels on the rocks, a gin and tonic, or some freshly sliced rashers of bacon—and your wish will be granted.

Just three miles south of McHugh's lies Lahinch, the St. Andrew's of Ireland. In this little village, everyone knows everything about golf. The talk centres in Donal Kenny's in the village street, especially in August during the local club's open week.

There are about 12,000 pubs in the island, and in them visitors can experience something of the real Ireland. Drinkers will usually respect a stranger's privacy, talking only when a willingness to talk is shown. Those who join in, however, will seldom forget the experience: the talk is even better than the scenery.

It may not be great art, but the message on this Donegal pub door is crystal clear.

263

FOOD IN IRELAND

Irish people abroad can be surrounded by exotic fruits and vegetables, yet think longingly of Irish soda bread and potato cakes. For the brown soda bread made from stone-ground wheaten flour is baked in countless homes and farmhouses all over the country. It is crusty, yet soft inside and is the perfect accompaniment for the excellent smoked salmon and shellfish such as mussels, crabs, lobster, scallops and oysters to be found around the coast. Galway is considered the best place for salmon and in the season, the large fat fish can be seen, packed like sardines, lying in the shallows under Salmon Weir Bridge, right in Galway town. The Galway oyster beds are famous, too, and at the opening of the season on September 1 an oyster festival is held where every pub for miles around serves fresh oysters with brown soda bread, butter and pints of Guinness.

Later in September is the Kenmare fish festival in County Kerry, when prodigious amounts of delicious scallops, prawns, lobsters and sole are consumed. The mussels, particularly at Wexford and St. Castlemaine Harbour in West Cork, are of astonishing size and succulence, and are served in many imaginative ways. Fine mackerel are smoked like trout and sometimes the "silver of the sea," herrings, are for sale.

Getting into a stew: The rich, grazing land nurtures fine cattle, the purplish slopes of the hills of Kerry and Wicklow provide superb mutton and lamb. As Thackeray wrote in his book about Ireland: "We can feel the beauty of a magnificent landscape perhaps: but we can describe a leg of mutton and turnips better." Irish stew is known all over the Western world. It is a creamy braise of lamb or mutton, onion, herbs and potato with stock. It was originally goat or kid, for no farmer would be foolhardy enough to use his young lambs for it. When well made, it is a dish full of flavour.

For many centuries the general favourite has been pork, ham and pork products. Bacon (*tinne* or *senshaille* in early Irish) is mentioned many times in medieval

literature, particularly in the medieval poem *The Vision of MacConglinne*, where sausages are mentioned, combined with leeks (another traditional food) and oatmeal to make a savoury stew. Blood puddings, like the French *boudin,* are part of a true Irish breakfast, with bacon, eggs and sausages and, of course, brown soda bread with honey.

How much of this kind of food do you find today in Ireland? In country districts, quite a lot. The cooking can be variable, but the baking of bread and

cakes is almost always reliable. Meat tends to be overcooked for continental tastes, but such tastes are now better understood in Ireland. The food in hotels and in Dublin is much more cosmopolitan and good: also in many small owner-run restaurants all over the country, north and south.

The Irish still eat quite a lot of potatoes, far more than of any other vegetable. Originally, in the 18th Century, they were the province of the richer people. The poor lived only on the small gleanings, mostly eating oatmeal as a cereal crop. Recipes from about 1746 show that potatoes were made into an elaborate tart put into pastry. The tart was filled with sieved potatoes, butter, sugar, brandy and egg-yolks before

Left, because Ireland is an island, it includes a wide variety of fish in its cuisine. Right, the country's other culinary glory is its wonderful range of home-baked bread.

being baked. It is very delicious, and a puzzle to diners. About the last survival is the potato cake and the potato scone, which are not sweet; the former is eaten with bacon and eggs for breakfast. This is very popular in the northern parts of Ireland, whereas the fluffy potato scone is spread, hot, with butter and sometimes honey. Both are fattening and exquisite.

Irish hospitality is not a tourist phrase; it has a long and honourable tradition first formulated in the 5th Century. The Brehon Laws, or Laws of the Fianna, were laid down in about 438, in the 10th year of King Leary's reign. They were written down between the 8th and the 13th centuries, the largest and most important being called *Senchus Mor*, the Great Old Law Book. According to the Brehon Law, people in the higher stations were bound to entertain guests "without asking any questions." There were also some few hundred guest-houses scattered throughout the country in the early days of Christianity, the master of each being obliged to keep his kitchen fire constantly burning and joints boiling in his cauldron in readiness for the arrival of strangers. This tradition was upheld for several centuries.

Patrick Sarsfield, mayor of Dublin in 1554, opened his house in High Street from 5 a.m. until 10 p.m. Nobody went from his door with an unquenched thirst. In addition to malmsey, muscadel and sack, he dispensed more than 5,000 gallons of claret during what appears to have been a very hectic year. This was before the Elizabethan wars rent Ireland.

Irish clerics were often very good hosts, as shown by W. R. Le Fanu's 1894 account in *Seventy Years of Irish Life*: "Father Horgan was the soul of hospitality, and gave many a dinner-party, where all sorts and conditions of men were wont to meet: at the upper end of his table were clergy and gentry of the neighbourhood, peasant farmers at the lower. The eatables were alike for all—alternate dishes of chicken and bacon all down the table. With the drinkables it was different; there was wine at the upper end, whiskey (which they preferred) for the farmers at the lower. He said to me: 'You see, my dear friend, I don't know how to order a big dinner with all sorts of dishes; and if I did, old Bridget could not cook it. So I just have a pair of chickens and then a dish of bacon and greens, then another pair of chickens and another dish of bacon and greens, and so on all the way down. Everyone likes chickens and bacon, and when a man sees these before him he looks for nothing else. I am saved a world of trouble, and everyone seems happy and contented.' " And so they were.

What are the main occasions for hospitality, apart from conviviality with friends? Easter Day, St. Patrick's Day, Hallowe'en and Christmas Day are the days when people take a holiday, enjoy simple pleasures and an exceptional meal shared with friends and family. All these days have certain traditions attached to them.

It is customary at Easter in Ireland to serve spring lamb, which derives from the paschal lamb, and also eggs, but the latter must have coloured shells to bring luck. You should also plant parsley seeds on Good Friday and eat hot cross buns (a spiced bun with a cross on it), but never meat, on that day. In Wexford the eggs used to be dyed with the yellow blossoms of the gorse bush and little houses were made called "Easter houses" which were filled with coloured eggs. These eggs were thrown down hills before being eaten, and the one who threw furthest was the winner.

Wearing of the green: St. Patrick's Day (March 17) has always been a most pleasant mid-Lenten holiday, usually spent in the home or with friends, for until a very few years back all public houses were closed on that day and the dog show at the Royal Dublin Society was the only place in the city with an open bar. (Quite a few people are said to have developed a taste for pedigree dogs.) Today the pubs are open, but only for the restricted Sunday opening hours. By tradition, a sprig of shamrock is worn.

On Hallowe'en (October 31), a currant loaf called Barm Brack is traditionally eaten, chestnuts are roasted and other nuts eaten, also a vegetable dish called Colcannon, a mixture of hot mashed potato, kale or cabbage, butter and milk, all flavoured with a pinch of nutmeg. Apples, too, play an important part and a game called Apple Bobbing used to be popular amongst the young. It consisted of floating apples in a tub of water; they then had to be picked out with the teeth. Not as easy as it sounds. Fortune-telling was another favourite game, and portents of good luck were looked for in many places. For instance, the Barm Brack to this day has a ring in it, and whosoever finds it will be married in the year; likewise the colcannon. Other charms used to be added, such as a small silver coin which meant wealth; a thimble, a spinster; a button, a bachelor, and so on.

Bonfires are lit so all the dead leaves and twigs are burned up, thus making a fine end of the autumn season.

About this time, too, it was customary to have the Michaelmas goose, what is called a "green goose." That is, it has been feeding on the stubble after the harvest is gathered. Again, eating the goose was thought to bring good fortune all the year round. It is still the custom for children to dress up and visit neighbours' houses where they are given nuts, fruit and sometimes cakes.

Christmas is the feast that has probably changed the most during this century, but certain traditions are still upheld among the growing materialism. Christmas Eve used to be the day when meat was ab-

Tipperary the doors were never bolted on Christmas Eve; they were left open as a sign of hospitality. It was thought that those who died at Christmas went straight to heaven.

The Christmas cake was, and still is, a very rich fruit cake moistened either with whiskey or Guinness. It is often made a good month before so that it can mature before being iced. This is a custom at least 150 years old.

Does much of all this tradition remain? Considering the massive worldwide changes in behaviour, quite a considerable amount. Particularly in rural Ireland, you will always find the door open and a friendly spirit prevailing, for the Irish love to talk to people, especially to

stained from, so midnight was eagerly awaited to break the fast. Turkey was not the traditional bird except among the rich and travelled, or for those who reared them. Goose, poultry or beef were the favourites, with pork and ham following closely behind.

Straight to heaven: Legend has it that the Holy Family travel the roads of Ireland during Christmastide, so often a red candle is lighted and put in the window to show the way. Maybe nowadays it is often the lighted Christmas tree which does this. In

Above, loin of pork, colcannon and beans; the Irish are learning that visitors prefer their meat not to be overcooked.

those who might have opposing opinions! Often, nothing is thought if a friend calls at close-on midnight; the kettle is put on, or the bottle brought out, some bread and cheese spread out as though it was late afternoon. Yet those same people rise early in the morning and work hard all day on the farm.

It's well worth staying at one of the numerous guesthouses or farmhouses, where you will be assured of a massive, cooked Irish breakfast, a good home cooked "tea" with the tray laid out with the best china and plenty of brown soda bread as well, with, perhaps another important ingredient: an insight into Irish home life.

269

RACING CERTAINTIES

In County Cork in the year 1752, a Mr. Edmund Blake and a Mr. O'Callaghan raced each other on horseback across the countryside from Buttevant Church to the spire of St. Leger Church four-and-a-half miles away, jumping hedges, walls and ditches on the way. As a result of that contest, a new word, "steeplechasing," entered the English language, and a new sport was created in embryo.

Steeplechasing was soon all the rage. Races were run, like the original, across open country from one point to another, with the precise course to be taken left largely to the discretion (or indiscretion) of the riders. Early in the 19th Century, an Englishman returning from a holiday in Ireland referred to the great popularity of the sport there. It was, he wrote, "a sort of racing for which the Paddies are particularly famous, and in which, unless the rider has pluck and his prad (*horse*) goodness, they cannot expect to get well home." Fortunately, Ireland had no shortage of plucky riders and good horses. *The History and Delineation of the Horse*, published in 1809, recorded that "the Irish are the highest and the steadiest leapers in the world." So it has remained.

The pre-eminence of Irish-bred steeplechasers and hurdlers on the racecourses of Britain today is undisputed; and it is remarkable, given the legions of horses exported annually to trainers in England, that the greatest steeplechasers of the modern era have also been trained in Ireland. Perhaps the greatest of all was Arkle, who won the Cheltenham Gold Cup, British steeplechasing's equivalent of the Derby, three years in succession in the 1960s, in the process humiliating the cream of the English racehorses to the undisguised glee of all Ireland.

All horse-racing is sport, but some forms are more sporting than others. The sporting Irish prefer the reckless and often threadbare thrills of steeplechasing to its rich relation, racing "on the flat." Whereas top-class flat-racing throughout the world today is dominated by the commercial re-

quirements of the multi-million dollar bloodstock industry, this aspect is absent from racing "over the sticks" for the simple reason that nearly all jumpers are geldings. The winner of a great flat race like the Irish Derby may become worth tens of millions of dollars because he may breed future winners of great races. The winner of a great jump race earns his owner only the prize-money—modest by comparison—the proceeds of a winning bet, perhaps, and the glory. But what glory. Had Arkle been entered in a referendum

for the Irish presidency, the world might well have had its first equine statesman since the days of Caligula.

Galloping to exhaustion: Although the birth of steeplechasing can be traced with reasonable confidence to that celebrated cross-country caper in 1752, the origins of horse-racing "on the flat" are lost in prehistory. We know that the Red Branch Knights of pre-Christian Ireland raced each other on horses and that horse-racing was an essential part of public assemblies or fairs in the early centuries AD. According to John Welcome's history, *Irish Horseracing*, "these fairs were held for the purpose of transacting all sorts of business—marriages were celebrated, deaths recorded, laws debated and defined, methods of defence agreed; but always they were followed by sports and games, and of these sports and games the most popular was horseracing." The greatest of these fairs was held at the Curragh—a wide, grassy plain in what is now County Kildare, across which a horse can gallop freely to exhaustion.

Racing went on, especially at the Curragh, through Norman and Elizabethan times, and through the succeeding centuries, despite an attempt by Cromwell's Puritans to stamp it out as a work of the devil. But it wasn't until the middle of the 18th Century that the results of races at the Curragh began to be recorded. In 1790, Irish racing was organized under the aegis

who shout and signal to each other constantly, chalking up odds on their blackboards and rubbing them out again with an air of obsessive duty. Wealthy women in their finery, bowler-hatted remnants of the Anglo-Irish gentry, down-at-heel city-dwellers rubbing shoulders with red-faced farmers...all human life is there.

Just before the start of each race, there is a last flurry in the dance around the bookmakers. Then a tense stillness falls on the crowd as the race commentator's voice echoes over the stands. Batteries of binoculars are trained silently on the runners. But as the horses round the final bend, a murmuring in the crowd rises like a gathering storm until the commentator's voice is drowned in a cacophony of supplication,

of a governing body, the Turf Club, which continues to oversee the sport today.

Its headquarters, naturally enough, are at the Curragh, which remains the heartland of Irish racing. Its 6,000 windswept acres are the home of many training stables. On most days of the year, the gaunt grandstands of the Curragh racecourse overlook the plain silently, like a stranded liner; but on the day of a big race, they overflow with a restless, garrulous throng of spectators, trainers, owners, bookmakers and hucksters. A race meeting is a heady mixture: the lean, hard-muscled horses, the small, scrawny jockeys in their vivid silks, the eager gamblers thrusting handfuls of banknotes at the bookmakers,

triumph and despair. Hats are thrown in the air in delight, losers' betting tickets fall to the ground like confetti.

The Curragh is the setting for all the Irish classic races: the 2,000 and 1,000 Guineas, the Derby, the Oaks and the St. Leger. The most valuable of these, in terms of prize-money, is the Derby, sponsored in 1986 by the US brewers Budweiser after a long association with the Irish Hospitals Sweepstakes. The total prize fund is now IR£450,000, and can be expected to keep rising. Although it is invariably contested

Above, signing a cheque at the Ballinasloe Horse Fair. Right, fashion is as important as fillies at the Dublin Horse Show.

by fewer runners than its English counterpart, the race is arguably a truer test of a horse's ability, as the Curragh has none of the topographical eccentricities of the Epsom Downs. Recent winners include some of the world's greatest racehorses: Nijinsky, Shergar, El Gran Señor.

A superb shop-window: The Derby is always a thrilling spectacle. Like all classic races today, it is also a superb shop-window for the international bloodstock industry, in which Irish breeders play a vital and growing role. Ireland is now Europe's leading nursery for thoroughbred racehorses: in 1985, for the first time, more foals were born in Ireland than in Britain. In spring, the annual migration of birds from their winter quarters in

sunnier climates is paralleled by a migration of hundreds of mares (mainly from the US, Britain and France) to be mated with the many former leading males of the turf who have now retired to stallion duties at Irish stud farms.

The recent prosperity of the Irish bloodstock industry owes much to a 1969 government concession under which fees received for the services of thoroughbred stallions are fully exempt from tax. Its effect is shown dramatically in the turnover of Ireland's leading bloodstock auctioneers, Goffs of Kildare, which rose from around IR£2 million in 1974 to more than £40 million in 1984. Nice work if you can get it. Goff's managing director,

Jonathan Irwin, describes Irish horses as "a great natural resource—and, unlike something like copper or oil, you don't have to dig it up."

Horses are said to thrive in Ireland because of the moist climate, which produces some of the world's lushest pastures, and the limestone subsoil, which makes the grass rich in bone-building calcium. Less easily explained is the third element in the formula: the natural ability of many Irish people to understand and handle horses, whether as breeders, stud managers, stud and stable hands, jockeys or trainers.

This justly celebrated Irish way with horses is apotheosised in the dapper and diffident personage of Vincent O'Brien, whose training record stretches credulity and defeats superlatives. He has also had an enormous impact on the bloodstock industry worldwide through his astute preference for the progeny of the Canadian stallion, Northern Dancer (sire of Nijinsky). O'Brien's victories with sons of Northern Dancer helped to establish the horse as the world's top stallion. His remarkable talents as a trainer appear to have been inherited by his son David.

Summertime visitors to such top-class tracks as the Curragh, Leopardstown or Phoenix Park (both in Dublin) are likely enough to see runners trained by Vincent (M.V.) O'Brien, most likely two-year-olds being introduced to the duties and rigours of racing life before being sent across the Irish Sea in search of a big-race win to set them on their planned careers as classic victors and, later, top-priced stallions. But their odds are likely to be prohibitively short—and they do not always win, for, in spite of O'Brien's genius in breeding and training, Mother Nature has a way occasionally of undoing the best-laid plans of men. If you like a bet, you are more likely to find a winning wager among the runners trained by Dermot Weld, very much the up-and-coming man of recent years and the top name in the Irish trainer's table for 1985 with 120 victories. Among riders, look out for Michael Kinane, Weld's stable jockey, who set a new record of 105 winners in the 1985 season, and for Pat Eddery, now established as one of the world's best, and successor to Lester Piggott as Vincent O'Brien's retained rider.

Apart from the aforementioned tracks, there is racing "on the flat" and "over the sticks" at 25 other racecourses throughout Ireland. They include Fairyhouse, venue for the Irish Grand National, held on Easter Monday; Punchestown, which holds an historic three-day festival meeting in late April; Killarney and Galway, both of which hold meetings in holiday-time high summer with a festive, not to say Bacchanalian, tinge.

Race across the beach: Perhaps the unlikeliest venue is Laytown, a small holiday resort on the east coast, about 30 miles north of Dublin. Racing is held there on only one day a year, in July or August, on a date determined as much by the tidal movements of the Irish Sea as by the Turf Club—for when the tide is in at Laytown, the racecourse lies under a metre or more of water. The Laytown Strand Races are one of the few sporting events to justify that overworked epithet, unique: it is the only official race meeting in Europe to be held on a beach.

There is no grandstand at Laytown—and, strictly speaking, no racecourse at all; just a long, gently-sloping beach. A group of marquees erected in a field overlooking the beach serve as the racecourse offices, tea-room and bar. The racetrack is marked out with flags on the sands at low tide.

The atmosphere is extraordinary. In the field above the beach, horses parade in the paddock, owners and trainers confer, punters debate the form, bookmakers shout the odds, drinkers drink—all much like an ordinary race meeting. But down on the beach hucksters sell candy floss and fish-and-chips and fizzy drinks and toys and raffle-tickets and souvenirs; small-time bookmakers splash barefooted through small pools left by the receding tide; children run about yelling and eating ice-cream; strangest of all, huntsmen on horseback in their red-coated regalia ride back and forth, policing the crowds clear of the racetrack. At times, the races themselves seem like a sideshow.

Laytown is a world away from the Curragh on Derby Day, from big prize-money and bafflingly high bloodstock prices. It has none of the glamour of the top meetings—and little of the tension. You won't see Vincent O'Brien or his ilk there, though some of the leading jockeys may turn up (winners are winners). You won't see top-class horses: the prizes are modest. But although the Laytown Races are unfashionable by the standards of today, they are maybe not so far in spirit from the races that thrilled the people at those fairs in ancient Ireland.

A likely tail at the hospital-like laboratory at Airlie Stud in Co. Dublin.

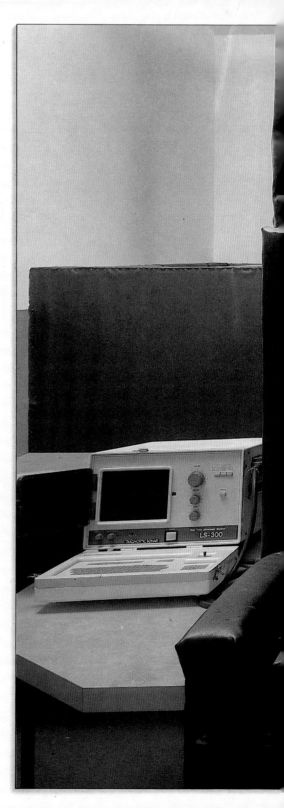

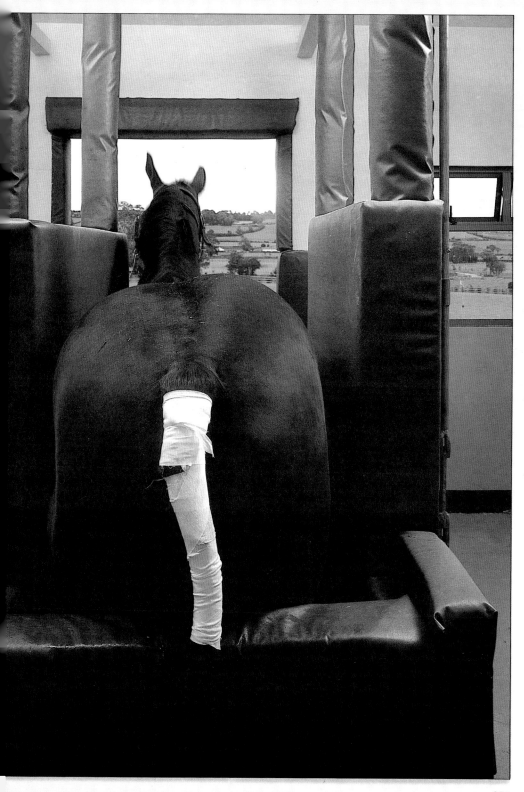

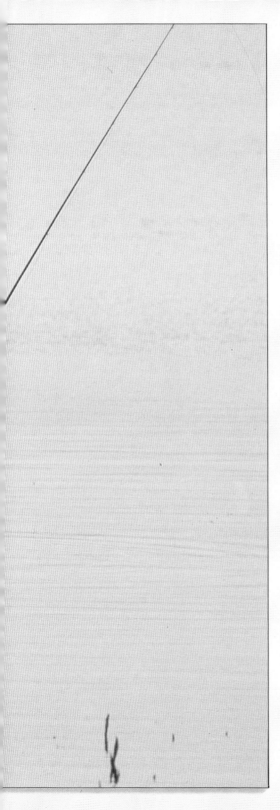

A FEW ANGLES ON FISHING

If you want to catch lots of fish, an Irishman will advise you, buy a trawler—but, if you enjoy fishing, come to Ireland. Not that you won't catch lots of fish there. The point is that an Irishman has little sympathy for the Superman who needs a huge catch to prove he's an angler, who sulks when a fish selects a rival's bait instead of his, who won't linger at table because he is so keen to get back to the pond.

In Ireland, angling is the enjoyment of all things connected with the rod and line. With sea fishing, there is the added attraction of the unexpected—like a huge fish or a British submarine straying into Irish waters. One way of telling which you've caught is to see whether, after you've been towed backwards, you get a letter of apology from the Ministry of Defence. So far, there has been at least one such apology.

Ireland is not normally thought of as a haven for big game fish, but tuna of about 1,000 lbs (450 kg) have been spotted following the rubby dubby trail of minced mackerel, fish oil and bran. Conduct an opinion poll in an Irish pub and most of the intoxicated throng will swear on the longevity of their ancient relatives that they too have seen tuna and huge shark chew their way up the line and use the rod as a tooth-pick.

Jousting with jaws: Totally sober, though, you can see huge mako shark jump clean out of the water off the wild west coast of Ireland. Any fool, of course, can catch good blue shark, but it takes an expert to get real enjoyment from the fight. Porbeagle shark are another matter: with luck and advice you can hook one of these big fish and get the kind of scrap you normally only read about in magazines.

All that shark fishermen need to do is telephone Brian Murphy at the Black Sheep Inn in Schull, County Cork, and he'll set everything up. (That's the way things are done in Ireland.) Three favourite ports are Kinsale, Youghal and Schull. There is really great sea fishing in Blacksod Bay, County Mayo; that's the place to meet a big fish. Charter boats operate out of many ports and the best boat to choose is the one with the worst smell: that's the one which

Left, in Ireland there's so much water and so many coarse fish that it's rare to see many other anglers.

catches fish. There is superb rock and beach fishing to be had all around the Irish coast, but do remember that from time to time the Atlantic sends in nasty waves.

The sea angling expert in the Central Fisheries Board—it's usually easy to get through to officials in Ireland—is Norman Dunlop. The board will provide maps showing the best locations of various species and can advise on charter boats or shore locations. Indeed, to receive the most intimate details of what Irish fishing has to offer, all you need is the board's address and telephone number: CFB, Mobhi Boreen, Glasnevin, Dublin 7 (Tel: Dublin 379206). In the Six Counties, check with the Northern Ireland Tourist Board; for such a small place, the North is

offenders risk the next best thing to the death sentence.

A salmon fishing permit can be bought from most tackle shops for IR£5 to £10 (local permit) or £15 (annual one). In addition, you'll almost certainly need to pay a fee to whoever owns the fishing rights. But the best salmon fishing still costs only a fraction of its Scottish equivalent. For example, the average cost of a rod per day on a good river is about £15, and you can hire a gillie for between £12 and £20 a day.

Best *early* rivers are the Bundrowse in County Donegal, which opens on January 1, and the Blackwater in Munster, in the south, which opens in February. The Bundrowse costs only £6 per rod per day, and the contact is Thomas Gallagher, Eden-

well served with excellent boats (especially Portrush on the north coast and Strangford in the southeast of the province). There are no serious restrictions on bait digging and most tackle shops can provide bait.

Salmon fishing is a widespread passion. Irish salmon are capable of putting up one horsepower of fight, the equivalent of two little Japanese motorcycles. Urban anglers can undertake some preliminary practice by trying to hook and land a passing Hell's Angel on a moped. In Ireland the sex life of the salmon is regulated by law; in other words, it is illegal at certain times of the year to interrupt love-ins in the spawning beds and, if the judge happens to be a keen angler with a share in local fishing rights,

ville, Kinlough, County Leitrim (Tel: 072 41208). The Blackwater is a big river, with many managers and owners. One good one is Peter Dempster at Carrigeen Hill, Conna, Tallow, County Cork (Tel: 058 56248). Later in the year other splendid fisheries come into their own. A notable one is the Errif in County Mayo; contact Des Brennan at the Central Fisheries Board.

A salmon permit also entitles you to fish

Above, part of the fun of fishing, particularly in the more remote parts of the country, is swapping tall tales with locals. Right, sometimes the tales turn out not to be so tall after all and new records are set.

278

for sea trout in the many excellent sea-trout fisheries. Newport House, in County Mayo, a good salmon fishery, has excellent runs of sea trout in the Newport River and Beltra Lake. The hotel will alert you to other fine lakes in the area, and a short drive will take you over the mountains to the magnificent Moy system, a network of rivers stuffed with salmon and sea trout. Ballina is a convenient touring centre.

For the most part fishing for brown trout is free, though there may be some restrictions on the number you can take and the way you catch them. So do ask.

For the lough fisherman, there is little better sport than that offered by the great limestone lakes of the Midlands and the West. It would be an ignorant class of bank

manager indeed who wasn't moved to poetry by the beauty of the arena in which he does battle with his fish.

Young doctors starting out in country areas often come across a condition known as *pink lung*. All that means is that their patients don't have air bags encrusted with the filth of city life. Fish like clean air, too, because the rain that falls doesn't add undissolved industrial fumes to the acid level of their water. Happily, Ireland's industrial miracle has been so spectacularly unsuccessful that the country has largely escaped the acid rain that has reduced many of Europe's fisheries to pickle pots.

Sea trout, of course, don't mind a bit of acidity in the water: that's one of the rea-

sons they go to sea. This branch of the family are actually brown trout who, finding the living hard in their native river or lake, swim out to sea to stuff themselves on the kinds of food most of us regard as *hors d'oeuvres*. Like so many Irish men and women who have travelled far from their homeland in search of fortune, they find themselves drawn back to Mother Ireland.

Resident all year round (and available to fishermen with no close season) are what have become known discourteously as coarse fish: bream, roach, pike and so on. In many Irish waters, not only do they breed with the kind of abandon that accords with Catholic views on contraception, they also grow very, very big. Farmers have discovered that they can sell anglers pints of maggots, and so a whole new industry has appeared.

Fish with ferocity: In one county alone, Cavan, it is possible to fish a different water every day for a year. There is so much water and so many coarse fish that it is rare to see another angler. Like the giant conger eels of the seas around Ireland, the pike in rivers and lakes show a quite unreasonable ferocity and, again as with the conger, the biggest ones have yet to be caught because few anglers are equipped to tackle such huge creatures. Most Irish fishing records, therefore, are wide open.

A coarse angling permit is required only in Northern Ireland. Live baiting with small fish to catch bigger fish is illegal, so use lures or dead bait. Maggots are quite legal, except for trout. Good coarse angling is available all over the country: details for Northern Ireland can be had from any branch of its tourist board; in the south the expert in the C.F.B is Hugh Gough.

Any branch of the Irish Tourist Board will supply details of hotels and guest houses where dirty, smelly anglers are welcome. And, because Irish anglers demand value in food and accommodation, the value is first-rate. It's possible to find a bed and fully cooked breakfast for just £6.

Tips for a successful trip: bring warm and waterproof clothing, a Thermos (many places can lend you one, but some don't) and a good torch, especially if fishing for sea trout after dark. Fishing tackle can readily be bought or hired, but serious anglers may prefer to bring their own. Fly anglers, however, might do well to use local flies with a proven record. Also, bring your own gaff or landing net, as often the gillie has lost his the week before. But don't bother bringing a watch: time doesn't mean much in many parts of Ireland.

GAMES PEOPLE PLAY

All the major international sports are played to some extent in Ireland and only a few are affected by the political division of the island: the main exceptions being soccer, athletics and hockey. But the most popular sports in the island are the native ones of hurling and Gaelic football. These are truly amateur games, organized on the smallest social unit of population, the parish, and controlled by an organization called the Gaelic Athletic Association.

The GAA was founded in 1884, in Thurles in County Tipperary, by Michael Cusack, a fiery nationalist from the Burren in County Clare, who was immortalized by James Joyce as "The Citizen" in *Ulysses*. Its purpose was as much political as sporting: to revive the native games, under native control, as a means of strengthening national self-respect at a time when national morale was at a low ebb. The association also organized athletic contests in opposition to the Ascendancy-controlled organization which banned "artisans" from its competitions and, because of a mixture of exclusivity and Sabbatarianism, held its contests on Saturdays. At the time, all but the professional classes worked a six-day week and Sunday was the only day left for organized games.

Hurling has been played in Ireland since prehistoric times and the oldest sagas tell of hurling matches between teams of warriors that went on for days. It is the fastest of all field team games and its rules are relatively simple, although those who see it played for the first time have some difficulty following the flight of the ball.

Played between teams of 15 a side, it gets its name from the stick, a hurley, used by the players. Made from ash, the hurley is about 3.5 feet (one metre) long with a crooked blade which is about three inches (eight cm) across at its broadest. The ball consists of yarn, tightly wound round a ball of cork and covered with hard leather, stitched along the outside in a ridge to facilitate handling. The playing pitch is 150 by 90 yards (a yard is slightly less then a metre) and the goal-posts stand 21 feet (about seven metres) apart in the centre of the end lines. They are usually 21 feet high, with a crossbar eight feet (2.5 metres) from the

Hurling, one of the world's toughest, fastest and most exciting ball games.

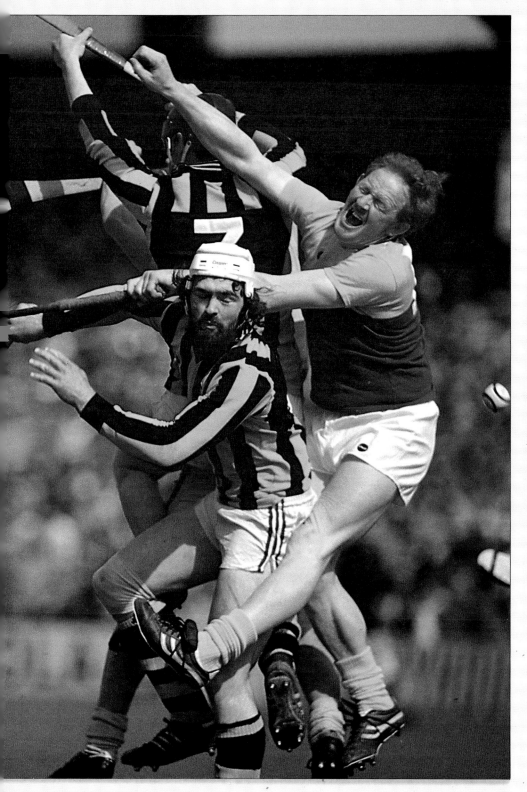

ground. A goal (three points) is scored when the ball is sent between the posts under the bar. A single point is scored when the ball goes between the posts and over the bar.

The ball can be propelled along the ground or hit in the air. It can only be taken into the hand if caught in flight, or if lifted from the ground with the stick. Skilled players are able to take the ball on to the hurley, from the ground, while running at full speed and carry it, balanced or bouncing, on the broad end before passing or scoring. Experts maintain that the skills of hurling have to be mastered when young as the use of hands, wrists and elbows must link naturally with stick and ball.

Although fostered by the GAA in all

soccer. Its main flaw is that there is no clear method, within the rules, of dispossessing a player in possession.

But it is a most spectacular game, when played attackingly, and attracts the biggest crowds of any sporting event in Ireland. Stand tickets for the big games that find their way on to the black market are sold at many times their face value.

Australian Rules, although played with an oval ball on an oval pitch, has features similar to those of Gaelic football. Irish emigrants were no doubt responsible for the long kicking and the great leaps in the air to catch the ball. In an attempt to gain an international dimension for a game played only in Ireland (with the exception of Irish emigrants in the USA and Britain),

parts of the country, the main traditional hurling areas remain south of a line from Dublin to Galway, with a small pocket in the Glens of Antrim. Cork and Kilkenny are the leading hurling counties.

Football, Gaelic-style: Gaelic football is also played by teams of 15 a side and the layout of the pitch and methods of scoring are the same as for hurling. Played with a ball smiliar to that used in soccer, Gaelic football is to a great extent an invented game. The rules are therefore imperfect and subject to constant revision. Players can handle the ball, lift it off the ground with the foot, run with it while passing it between hand and foot, kick it, or fist it, or play it with the feet on the ground as in

the GAA has recently organized tours to and from Australia, with games played under compromise rules. The fact that the Australian players are all professionals has so far given the contests more bite than was anticipated. Professional players do not like being beaten by amateurs.

Hurling and Gaelic football are organized in a variety of competitions, graded according to age up to senior level, for county and then provincial championship. The high point of the GAA year comes in September with the All-Ireland hurling and

Above, greyhound racing attracts the gambling fraternity. Right, Dublin's Hermitage Golf Club, signalling a national passion.

282

football finals in Dublin's Croke Park.

In Gaelic football, Kerry are the undisputed masters, and the ambition of every boy in the county is to win an All-Ireland medal in the famous green-and-gold jersey. In Kerry, photographs of famous teams and players hang on the walls in the company of the Sacred Heart of Jesus, the Pope and Jack Kennedy. Yet the country's best-known hurler and footballer is Jack Lynch, a Corkman and the only player ever to win six successive All-Ireland titles. His fame as a player led to an equally successful political career and he was prime minister twice between 1966 and 1979.

Bowling along: Road bowling is a strange game, played only in South Armagh, Cork and parts of Waterford and Limerick. In on individual shots. One of the interesting features of road bowling is that it is illegal, as sections of public roads are barred to traffic while the contest goes on. However, prosecutions are rare as the authorities close their eyes to the activities of the unofficial stewards.

Hares and horses: Greyhound racing, on tracks, and coursing in enclosed fields with live hares, are very popular sports in Ireland. The breeding and export of greyhounds is a minor industry and prizemoney is now increased by sponsorship. The fact that races are over in a matter of seconds is no deterrent to the small army of punters who attend. Bookmakers attend all kinds of dog- and horse-races, in competition with the more impersonal tote.

Europe it is played in a small area of Holland and on the German side of the nearby border. The game is very simple: two players throw or bowl an iron ball along an ordinary public road, and the winner is the one who covers a set distance with fewer throws. The bowl, or "bullet," can be 28, 21 or 16 ounces (between 800 and 450 grammes). One of the skills of the game is the negotiation of a bend in the road, either by lofting the bowl over the corner or by curving the throw. If the bowl leaves the road the player is penalized.

It is a great betting sport and large sums change hands when two noted players meet. Not only are bets laid on the result of the contest; side-bets are also laid

In their offices, the bookies take bets on almost any contest from the World Cup to the Papal election. Bookies' offices in Ireland are almost as numerous as pubs, but with a quaint reticence they are usually labelled, "Turf Accountants."

Coursing is a winter sport which in recent years has come under fire from animal-rights campaigners because of cruelty to hares. Two dogs are slipped simultaneously to chase a hare. Points are scored by deflecting the hare from its course, or by killing it before it gets to the escape exit at the end of the field. Frequently the animal is caught by both dogs and torn apart. But despite protests, some violent, and press photographs of savage "kills,"

coursing remains popular in rural areas.

Casual perusal of the sports pages of any Irish daily newspaper will show that an extraordinary range of sports, both national and international, is covered. And, while spectators outnumber participants by a high proportion, a surprising number excel in a variety of sports at the highest level.

World titles in the following sports are held, or have until recently been held, by Irish athletes: professional boxing, snooker, motor cycling, lawn bowling, 10-pin bowling, 5,000-metre track and professional cycling. To that list can be added two players with the most international appearances: Mike Gibson, in rugby football, and Pat Jennings, as a soccer goalkeeper.

In international rugby Ireland fields a team drawn from Northern Ireland and the Republic. It is the one international sport, with the exception of professional boxing, that unites all political elements on the island, at least temporarily.

Soccer, the great working-class game, is split by the internal political border. The island fields two international sides: Ireland, as the Northern Ireland team is officially designated, and the Republic of Ireland. While the best players from both states play with clubs in Britain or the Continent (for obvious financial reasons), the achievements of the Northern Ireland team have been noteworthy. Picking from the smaller pool of first-class players, they have succeeded in qualifying for the final stages of the last two World Cups.

Where golfers link up: Golf is another national passion. Because of the availability of courses, it is played by everyone interested enough to buy a set of clubs. The country is dotted with courses: inland courses like the Curragh (the oldest), Mullingar, Tralee (designed by Arnold Palmer) and the picturesque one at Killarney, where the scenery distracts even the most dedicated of golfers. There is also a chain of seaside links right round the coast from Rosses Point in Sligo, to Lahinch in Clare, to Ballybunion and Waterville in Kerry, Portmarnock and Royal Dublin in the capital, Beltray in Louth and Royal County Down in Newcastle.

So let the non-golfer be warned: Ireland has a higher percentage of golf bores than any other Europeans country. Most of them though, are also interested in hurling, Gaelic football, soccer, racing snooker, boxing so let the non-sportsman be warned.

Left, Gaelic football, a spectacular game; the rules, such as they are, are frequently revised.

GUIDE IN BRIEF

Travelling to Ireland

By Air

There are three international airports in the Republic of Ireland, at Dublin, Cork and Shannon. The busiest by far is Dublin, with annual traffic of about 2.5 million passengers. There are connections from Dublin and/or Shannon to many destinations in Britain and Europe, including London, Glasgow, Manchester, Liverpool, Amsterdam, Brussels, Copenhagen, Dusseldorf, Frankfurt, Las Palmas, Madrid, Malaga, Milan, Moscow, Paris, Rome and Zurich, as well as to transatlantic destinations such as New York, Boston, Atlanta, Toronto, Chicago, Los Angeles, Mexico City, Havana and Managua. Belfast Airport (Aldergrove) in Northern Ireland has flights to most main British destinations and to Amsterdam.

By Sea

Many ferry services connect Ireland to Britain and to France. These include: Larne to Stranraer and Cairnryan (both in Scotland); Belfast to Liverpool and Douglas (Isle of Man); Dublin to Liverpool (England) and Holyhead (Wales); Dun Laoghaire to Holyhead; Rosslare to Fishguard and Pembroke (Wales), Cherbourg and Le Havre (France); Cork to Le Havre and Roscoff (France). Details of services and operators are liable to change; for full details, contact a travel agent.

Getting Acquainted

Climate

Although Ireland lies at roughly the same northerly latitude as Newfoundland, it has a mild, moist climate, because of the prevailing south-westerly winds and the influence of the warm Gulf Stream along its western coast. As no part of the island is more than 70 miles from the sea, temperatures are fairly uniform over the whole country. Average air temperatures in the coldest months, January and February, are mainly between 4°C and 7°C (39°F to 45°F). The warmest months, July and August, have average temperatures between 14°C and 16°C (57°F to 61°F), but occasionally reaching as high as 25°C (77°F). The sunniest months are May and June, with an average of between 5½ and 6½ hours a day over most of the country. The sunniest region is the extreme southeast. The west of the country is wetter than the east because of the prevailing Atlantic winds.

Clothing

Casual clothing is acceptable almost everywhere in Ireland, including smart hotels and restaurants. Because of the unpredictability of the weather, pack some rainproof clothing and a warm sweater, even in summer. But bring the suntan cream as well: during a spell of fine weather, the ozone-laden winds from the Atlantic can intensify the burning effect of the sun's rays.

Time

Ireland follows Greenwich Mean Time. In spring, the clock is moved one hour ahead for Summer Time to give extra daylight in the evening and in autumn moved back again to GMT.

When it is noon according to GMT, it is 2 a.m. in Honolulu; 4 a.m. in Los Angeles and Vancouver; 5 a.m. in Calgary; 6 a.m. in Chicago, Houston and Winnipeg; 7 a.m. in New York, Toronto, Montreal and Lima; 8 a.m. in Caracas, Santiago and Halifax; 9 a.m. in Buenos Aires, Montevideo and Rio de Janeiro; noon in London, Edinburgh, Dublin, and Accra; 1 p.m. in Amsterdam, Belgrade, Copenhagen, Gibraltar, Lagos, Madrid, Malta, Oslo, Rome and Stockholm; 2 p.m. in Alexandria, Athens, Cairo, Cape Town, Helsinki, Istanbul, Leningrad, and Wellington; 3 p.m. in Baghdad, Moscow, and Nairobi; 3.30 p.m. in Tehran; 4 p.m. in Mauritius; 5 p.m. in Karachi; 5.30 p.m. in Bombay, Calcutta, Colombo and New Delhi; 6 p.m. in Dacca; 6.30 p.m in Rangoon; 7 p.m. in Bangkok and Jakarta; 8 p.m. in Hong Kong, Manila, Peking, Perth and Singapore; 9 p.m. in Tokyo; 9.30 p.m. in Adelaide; 10 p.m. in Melbourne and Sydney; 12 midnight in Christchurch and Wellington.

Many visitors find that time passes more slowly in Ireland. An overseas visitor once asked if the Irish attitude to time could be expressed by the Spanish saying, "Mañana, mañana." He was told; "Oh, we've nothing as urgent as that here." Like everything else, this attitude is changing, but the country is still reckoned to be about 20 years "behind the times" and, in certain tribally-oriented parts of the North, perhaps 300 years behind.

Shopping hours

Most shops are open from 9.00 a.m to 5.30 p.m. Outside the large cities, there is usually an early-closing (1p.m.) day once a week. Shopping centres stay open until 9 p.m. on Thursdays and Fridays. Many small grocery stores are open until late at night and there are a few 24-hour shops in Dublin.

Money

The Irish pound (or *punt*), usually written IR£ to distinguish it from the pound sterling, is divided into 100 pennies. The coins used are ½p, 1p, 2p, 5p, 10p, and 50p. The notes are IR£1, IR£5, IR£10, IR£20, IR£50, and IR£100.

In Northern Ireland, British currency is used. At the time of writing, the Irish pound was worth around 91 British pence and US$1.31.

In the Irish Republic, banks are open 10 a.m. to 12.30 p.m. and 1.30 to 3.00 p.m., Monday to Friday. Most Dublin banks are open until 5 p.m. on Thursdays. In Northern Ireland, bank opening hours are 10 a.m. to 12.30 p.m. and 1.30 p.m. to 3.30 p.m. Monday through Friday, British visitors to Northern Ireland can cash personal cheques with an ordinary bank card. But British visitors to the Republic and European visitors to both parts of Ireland will require Eurocheques and Eurocards for this purpose. Travellers cheques are acceptable to all banks, money-change kiosks and many hotels.

Access (alias MasterCard) and Visa are the most commonly acceptable credit cards, followed by American Express and Diners Club. But small guesthouses and bed-and-breakfast places will want payment in cash.

Public Holidays

The public holidays are New Year's Day (January 1), St Patrick's Day (March 17), Good Friday (March 28*), Easter Monday (March 31*), June Holiday (June 2*), August Holiday (August 4*), October Holiday (October 27*), Christmas Day (December 25) and St. Stephen's Day (December 26), Those marked * are variable and the dates given above are for 1986.

Language

The Republic of Ireland has two official languages, English and Irish (Gaelic). English is spoken everywhere, but while many people throughout the country know Irish, it is the everyday language of only about 100,000 people in areas known as Gaeltachts, mainly in the extreme West.

Electrical Current

220 volts is standard. Hotels usually have dual 220/110 voltage sockets for electric razors.

Getting Around

Buses and trains

In the Republic, the State transport authority, CIE, operates trains between the main cities and buses to many cities, towns and villages. Its information and booking office is at 59, Upper O'Connell St., Dublin 1 (tel: 787777), and you can dial a recorded timetable for most mainline rail destinations (look in the telephone directory under Coras Iompair Eireann).

In Dublin city, CIE also operates an efficient electric suburban rail service, DART—which runs, alas, only along the coastal strip from Howth to Bray—and a maddening and unpredictable bus service. Its crews seem permanently engaged in various private competitions to see, for instance, who can make a uniform look least like a uniform; who can fool the greatest number of passengers the greatest proportion of the time by arriving at stops late, early, or not at all; and who can manage nearly always to drive away from a stop just as a heavily laden would-be passenger is running towards it. Apart from the competitions, there is a general co-operative effort to show that any resemblance between the schedule described in the timetable and actual events is purely accidental. Having said all that, there is no great problem about getting around Dublin by bus; you just have to be philosophical. There are also CIE city bus services in Cork, Galway, Limerick and Waterford.

Eurailpasses are valid for bus and train travel in the Republic, excluding city services. A free ferry link is provided by Irish Continental Line from Le Havre and Cherbourg in France to Rosslare. These tickets must be bought in advance from offices of the participating railways.

CIE offers reduced-rate Rambler passes providing unlimited travel on buses and trains, excluding city services, for either 8 or 15 days. Tickets can be bought from any bus or train station in the Republic, or through a travel agent abroad.

In Northern Ireland, trains run from Belfast north-west to Derry via Ballymena and Coleraine; east to Bangor; and south to Dublin via Newry. Information from Northern Ireland Railways, Belfast Central Station (tel: 230310). Bus services in Belfast and throughout Northern Ireland are operated by Ulsterbus (tel: Belfast 220011).

Taxis

There are metered taxis at railway stations, ports and airports in Dublin, Belfast, Cork, Limerick and Galway. Elsewhere, fares are by arrangement with the driver in advance. In cities and towns you can book a taxi by telephone.

Driving

This can still be a real pleasure in Ireland, as the roads are the least congested in Europe.

Drive on the left is the rule, on both sides of the border. Drivers and front-seat passengers must wear seat belts. In the Republic, the speed limit is either 30m.p.h. or 40m.p.h. in urban areas and 55m.p.h. on country roads. In Northern Ireland, the limit for country roads is 60m.p.h., and 70m.p.h. is allowed on motorways and dual-carriageway trunk roads. There is a list of *car rental firms* in the Appendix.

Cycling

This is a excellent way to see the countryside at a leisurely pace, provided you aren't anxious to cover too much ground (the modern disease). Throughout the Republic, specially appointed Rent-a-Bike dealers hire out sturdy Raleigh Tourer bicycles: a list of them is available from the Irish Tourist Board.

Cruising on inland waterways

The three main waterways for cruising are the River Shannon, navigable for 150 miles downstream form Lough Key, Co Roscommon; the Grand Canal, which runs westward from Dublin across the central plain to the Shannon, and is joined in Co Kildare by a branch line running south to the River Barrow; and the River Erne, navigable for 50 miles from Belturbet, Co Cavan through Upper and Lower Lough Erne to Belleek, near Enniskillen, Co Fermanagh. All three waterways are marvellous for fishing, birdwatching, rowing, photography, or just pottering peacefully along.

In the Republic, 11 approved companies offer cabin cruisers for hire—nine on the Shannon, one on the Grand Canal an one on the Erne. In Northern Ireland, seven companies operate on the Erne. Cruisers range in size from two berths to eight; all have refrigerators and gas cookers; most have heating, hot water and showers; dinghies, charts and safety equipment are included. Experience in handling a boat is an advantage, but instruction is provided for novices. Full details from the respective tourist boards.

Horse-drawn caravans

Horses and caravans are available for hire in Counties Cork, Kerry and Wicklow. You can expect to cover only about 10 miles a day—but going slowly is just the point, of course, giving you plenty of time to appreciate the countryside, meet and talk to passers-by and let your inner rhythms settle down to a more sensible pace. Feeding, grooming and harnessing the horse is time-consuming too, and quite hard work. The caravans, which have gas cookers, are mostly for four people, with berths that convert into seating for daytime. Utensils, crockery, etc are provided. Fastidious people should note that caravans do not have toilets (Well, didn't you want the real thing?). Details from the Irish Tourist Board.

Accommodation

Hotels, guesthouses, home and farmhouses

It is possible to pay as much as IR£100 or more for "bed and breakfast" in a top-rated hotel, or as little as IR£10 or less in a family home which takes visitors. Dearer is not necessarily better, of course, but generally speaking the more you pay, the more facilities are on offer. Apart from what you can afford to pay, you may decide that you don't need a hotel with suites available, night service, two restaurants, a health complex and uniformed attendants at every turn. Or you may simply dislike large, grand hotels and prefer small, family-run places with a bit more character, even if the bathroom is down the hall and the menu is pot luck.

Both the Irish Republic and Northern Ireland classify hotels on the same grading system, as follows:

Hotels:
A*: *Hotels which are particularly well-equipped and furnished and offer a very high standard of comfort and service under widely experienced management and staff. A very high standard of cuisine is reflected in varied à la carte and table d'hôte menus. Night services are provided. Suites are available and most bedrooms have private bathrooms.*

A: *Hotels which provide a high standard of comfort and service under experienced management and staff, with varied à la carte and table d'hôte meals of good quality and presentation. A large proportion of bedrooms have private bathrooms.*

B*: *Hotels which are well-furnished, offering very comfortable accommodation and good service. Bedrooms with private bathrooms available. Good cuisine.*

B: *Hotels that are well kept and offer comfortable accommodation with good bathroom and toilet facilities. Limited, but good standard of cuisine and service.*

C: *Hotels that are clean and comfortable, with satisfactory service for the reception, accommodation and comfort of guests. Hot and cold running water and heating in bedrooms. Adequate bathroom and toilet facilities.*

Guesthouses: are simply small, usually family-run hotels, corresponding roughly to Continental pensions. In the Republic they are graded in three classes:

A: *Guesthouses which provide a very high standard of comfort and personal service. A very good standard of cuisine, including full meal service for resident guests. Hot and cold running water in all bedrooms. Some premises have rooms with private bathrooms.*

B: *Guesthouses that are well furnished, offering very comfortable accommodation with limited but good standard of food and service. Hot and cold running water in all bedrooms.*

C: *Guesthouses which are clean and comfortable. Hot and cold running water in all bedrooms. Adequate bathroom and toilet facilities.*

In Northern Ireland, guesthouses are graded in two classes, as follows (the language is execrable, but don't blame us):

A: *Guesthouses which are particularly well-equipped and furnished and offer a high standard of comfort including separate lounge and dining-room accommodation for the exclusive use of guests, also full board if required and normally offering an alternative for main courses at lunch and evening meals.*

B: *Guesthouses offering separate and comfortable lounge and dining-room accommodation with a minimum meal service of breakfast and evening meal—packed lunches on request. Bedrooms have heating and not less than three-quarters of letting bedrooms are fitted with hot and cold running water. Adequately furnished and equipped and with toilet/bath facilities adequate for the number of persons lodged in the premises.*

Town and country homes: These are private family houses which take visitors. Evening meals are normally provided if notice is given before noon.

Self-catering accommodation is available throughout Ireland in houses, cottages (some thatched), apartments, caravans and even a few castles (suitable for groups). There are also many caravan and camping parks for those who like to take their accommodation with them.

Information on all forms of accommodation is available from the tourist boards.

Communications

Telephones

In the Republic, telephone services are operated by a state-owned company called Telecom Eireann. It is a highly unpopular organization, for reasons that are liable to become apparent to any visitor who has occasion to make a lot of phone calls. There is no great shortage of public telephones—in hotels, shopping centres, in street kiosks, etc—but the vandals who keep wrecking them are more efficient than the engineers who come to repair them; theirs is an easier job, admittedly. When you find a telephone that seems to be working, don't relax: gremlins, crossed lines and UFO's (unpredictable fade-outs) abound.

A local call from a public telephone costs 15p. Longer-distance calls to most places within Ireland can be dialled direct; area codes are listed in the front of the telephone directories. (Directory Part One is for the Dublin area; Part Two is for the rest of the Republic.) Make sure to have plenty of coins ready. International calls can be dialled direct from private phones, but when using a public phone, dial 10 for the operator.

Telephone services in Northern Ireland are operated by British Telecom; dial 100 for the operator. Local calls from public booths cost 10p. For the weather forecast, call Belfast 8091.

Postal Services

At the time of writing, letters weighing less than 20 grammes (approximately the weight of an envelope containing up to three regular A4 sheets of paper) cost 28p within Ireland and to all EEC countries (Belgium, Britain, Denmark, France, West Germany, Greece, Italy, Luxembourg, Netherlands, Portugal and Spain). Postcards cost 24p. To all other destinations, letters cost 39p, postcards 28p.

In Northern Ireland, British postal rates apply. Since these are 17p for a letter sent first-class to anywhere in the British Isles and 12p for one sent second-class, it may pay to hold your mail for posting in the North.

Newspapers: The Irish devour newspapers, and have no fewer than six morning newspapers to serve the island's population of five million. The *Irish Times*, *Irish Independent* and *Irish Press* are published in Dublin. The Times, the most serious and comprehensive, is best for foreign news, arts and business, and has a great letters page. It has no political affiliations. The Independent broadly supports the Fine Gael party and aims for a hard-hitting style. The Press supports Fianna Fail; it is newsy but less brash than the Independent. The **Cork Examiner** is the staple diet of business and farming people in the south-west. Two morning papers are published in Belfast: the Unionist/Protestant **News Letter** and the nationalist/Catholic **Irish News**; it can be fascinating and instructive to compare their treatments of a controversial story.

There are four evening papers: the *Evening Press,* the *Evening Herald* (from the Independent stable in Dublin), the *Evening Echo* (Cork) and the *Belfast Telegraph*. All contain liberal doses of sport, gossip and showbiz.

The Press and Independent have Sunday versions; also published from Dublin are the *Sunday Tribune*, which aims to be a serious paper of political analysis, arts review, etc., and the *Sunday World*, a highly successful piece of trash (pin-ups, shocks scares, scandals, etc). From Belfast, there is the *Sunday News*, from the News Letter stable, but less politically partisan. Since all the British national dailies and Sundays are readily obtainable on both sides of the border, even the most news-hungry visitor should be satisfied.

There are nearly 100 local papers, which may be entertaining and informative if you are interested in a particular region, or interested in newspapers.

Magazines: *Magill* is best for domestic political issues; *Hot Press* is a lively local equivalent of *Rolling Stone*. *In Dublin* is useful for telling you what's on at the theatre, cinema, etc.

Radio and television: The national broadcasting service, Radio Telefis Eireann (RTE) has two TV channels and two radio stations. In addition, all British TV channels (BBC1, BBC2, ITV and Channel 4) can be received over much of the country—which accounts for the unsightly height of television aerials.

On TV, RTE2 is the more serious channel. On Radio, RTE1 is the main station for news, current affairs and drama; RTE2 has a staple output of pop music. If you want to "tune in" to the everyday concerns of people in Ireland, there is no better way than by listening to radio's "Gay Byrne Show," which is on throughout most of the year from 9.15 a.m. to 11.00 a.m., Monday to Friday.

Health and Emergencies

Medical insurance is highly advisable for all visitors. However, visitors from EEC countries are entitled to medical treatment in Ireland, North and South, under a reciprocal arrangement. Travellers from the UK to the Republic of Ireland should obtain Leaflet SA 28/July 1978 from their local social security office before departure. Travellers from other EEC countries to either part of Ireland should obtain form E111 from their own national social security office. These forms entitle the holders to free treatment by a doctor and free medicines on prescription. If hospital treatment is necessary, this will be given free in a public ward.

For **emergency services**, such as police, ambulance, fire service, lifeboat and coastal rescue, telephone 999 (in either part of Ireland) and ask for the service you need.

The **Samaritans**, who help lonely, depressed and suicidal people, can be contacted on Dublin 778833; Cork 21323; Ennis 29777; Galway 61222; Limerick 42111; Waterford 72114; Belfast 664422; Bangor 464646; Ballymena 43555; Coleraine 4545; Londonderry 265511; Newry 66366; Omagh 44944; and Portadown 333555.

Other useful numbers are: **Poisons Information Service**, Dublin 745588; **Alcoholics Anonymous**, Dublin 774809, Belfast 681084, and Londonderry 265374; **Rape Crisis Centre**, Dublin 601470 and Belfast 249696.

Food and Drink

You will find many superb natural ingredients on offer in Irish restaurants—fresh and smoked salmon, trout, prawns, oysters, succulent beef, pork and lamb—above all, perhaps, delicious and chewy wholemeal and soda bread. But you will find few dishes that are specifically Irish, because the country has no tradition of *haute cuisine* and because the people tend to associate traditional fare such as Irish stew of boiled bacon and cabbage with the poor old days. These may be humble dishes, but they are also wholesome and delicious. Keep an eye out too for the ever-growing range of Irish cheeses, many of which are first-class.

Eating out in Ireland is not cheap (though it is cheaper in the North than in the Republic). In the cities and towns there is no shortage of fast-food places offering everything from hamburgers to fish-and-chips or sweet-and-sour chicken. At the other end of the scale there are top-class restaurants that will stand comparison with the best anywhere. It is between these two extremes that the pitfalls lie. If you are lucky, you will eat superb, fresh ingredients cooked simply and well and you will find that the fresh Irish air gives you the appetite of a lifetime to match. If you are unlucky, you will pay inflated prices to eat overcooked and over-dressed food (probably from a menu with misspelt French names) in pretentious surroundings. If this happens, please complain. Many Irish people hate to make a fuss, and bad restaurants survive as a result.

The most famous Irish drink is, of course, Guinness, that dark, creamy king of stouts. Although it is sold throughout the world, it tastes incomparably better in Ireland. Irish whiskeys have played second fiddle internationally to Scotch ever since the days of Prohibition in the US, when "Irish" became associated with bootleg brews, but they are now making a deserved comeback. Brands include Jameson, Powers, Paddy, Bushmills and Tullamore Dew. So charge your glasses and "*Slainte!*" ("Health").

A curious feature of many restaurants, especially in Northern Ireland, is their reluctance to bring the wine until you are well into the main course. When ordering your vintage, therefore, it's wise to add the magic words: "We want it now." While in the North, don't forget that pubs are shut on Sundays.

There is a list of selected restaurants in the Appendix.

Things to See and Do

Ireland is renowned above all else for its scenery: often lush, sometimes bleak, always memorable. Here is a handy checklist of places of scenic interest, county by county. (Many have little to offer except beauty or tranquillity and may not be mentioned in the main text.)

Antrim: Ballintoy, Ballycastle, Carnlough, Cushendall, Cushendun, Giant's Causeway, Glenariff, Portballintrae, Portrush, Waterfoot, Whitehead.

Armagh: Jonesborough, Newtownhamilton.

Carlow: Bunclody, Hacketstown, St. Mullins, Tullow.

Cavan: Glengavlen, Shannon Pot, Swanlinbar, Virginia.

Clare: The Burren, Feakle, Kilkee, Lahinch, Lisdoonvarna, Cliffs of Moher, Mountshannon, Scarriff.

Cork: Adrigole, Ballickey, Ballymacoda, Bantry, Glandore, Glengarriff, Gougane Barra, Keimaneigh Pass, Kinsale, Millstreet.

Derry: Castlerock, Draperstown, Glenshane Pass, Magilligan, Portstewart.

Donegal: Buncrana, Bundoran, Clonmany, Dunfanaghy, Dunlewy, Glen, Glencolumbcille, Glenveagh, Gweedore, Lough Swilly, Malin More, Rosapenna, St. Patrick's Purgatory, Slieve League.

Down: Annalong, Bangor, Bryansford, Crawfordsburn, Donaghadee, Hilltown, Kilkeel, Newcastle, Portaferry, Rostrevor, Silent Valley Warrenpoint.

Dublin: Dalkey, Howth, Killiney, Kilternan, Tallaght.

Fermanagh: Belcoo, Boho, Tempo, Tully Bay.

Galway: Aran Islands, Ballynahinch Lake, Carna, Clifden, Killary Harbour, Kylemore, Leenane, Lough Corrib, Lough Inagh, Lough Mask, Lough Nafooey, Oughterard, Recess, Roundstone.

Kerry: Ballydavid, Caragh Lake, Connor Pass, Dingle, Glenbeigh, Glencar, Healy Pass, Kenmare, Killarney, Parknasilla, Valentia Island, Ventry, Waterville.

Kildare: Celbridge, Leixlip.

Kilkenny: Graiguenamanagh, Inistioge, Thomastown.

Laois: Abbeyleix, Dunamase, Mountmellick, Rosenallis.

Leitrim: Dromahair, Glenade, Kinlough, Lough Allen, Lough Gill, Lurganboy, Manorhamilton.

Limerick: Ardpatrick, Ballylanders, Kilfinane, Montpelier.

Longford: Ardagh, Drumlish, Granard.

Louth: Carlingford, Omeath, Ravensdale.

Mayo: Achill Island, Ballycastle, Belderg, Croagh Partick, Delphi, Killary Harbour, Lough Conn, Lough Corrib, Louisburgh, Mulrany, Moyne Castle, Westport.

Meath: Oldcastle, Slane.

Monaghan: Carrickmacross, Castleblayney, Rockcorry.

Offaly: Clareen, Kinnitty.

Roscommon: Boyle, Strokestown.

Sligo: Benbulben, Cliffony, Drumcliff, Easky, Lough Gill, Rosses Point.

Tipperary: Aherlow, Clogheen, The Gap, Mitchelstown Caves.

Tyrone: Gortin, Newtownstewart, Plumbridge.

Waterford: Ballymacarbry, Cheekpoint, Kilmacthomas, Lismore, Tramore.

Westmeath: Castlepollard, Fore, Glassan, Mullingar.

Wexford: Bunclody, Curracloe, Kilmore Quay, Rosslare, Scullogue Gap.

Wicklow: Annamoe, Aughrim, Avoca, Bray, Enniskerry, Glendalough, Glenmalure, Poulaphouca, Rathdrum, Roundwood, Sally Gap, Woodenbridge.

Ireland is rich in relics of its fascinating, troubled past.

From prehistoric times, there are monuments such as the extraordinary burial chamber at **Newgrange**, Co. Meath; the stone fort, **Grianan of Aileach**, Co. Donegal; the megalithic tomb of **Creevykeel Court Cairn**, Co. Sligo; or the strange carved stone figures on **White Island**, Lough Erne, Co. Fermanagh.

From the golden age of Celtic Christianity, there are the ruins of great monastic settlements such as **Glendalough**, Co. Wicklow; **Clonmacnois**, Co. Offaly; **The Rock of Cashel** and **Holycross Abbey**, Co. Tipperary; **Mellifont Abbey** and **Monasterboice**, Co. Louth; and **Boyle Abbey**, Co. Roscommon.

From the times when Gaelic chieftains and Norman barons struggled for supremacy, there are hundreds of castles and fortresses: **Kilkenny Castle**, **Blarney Castle**, **Bunratty Castle**, **Cahir Castle**, **Knappogue Castle**, **Dunluce Castle**, to mention only a few.

From the centuries of Anglo-Irish Ascendancy, there are many historic and beautiful houses and gardens, such as **Castletown**, Co. Kildare; **Damer House**, Co. Tipperary; the **State Apartments of Dublin Castle**; **Lissadell House**, Co. Sligo, celebrated in a great poem by Yeats; **Russborough**, Co. Wicklow, which houses a splendid art collection; **Birr Castle Demsne**, Co. Offaly, with over 1,000 catalogued species of trees and shrubs; **Howth Castle Gardens**, Co. Dublin; **The Japanese Gardens**, Tully, Co. Kildare; and **Mount Usher** and **Powerscourt** gardens, Co. Wicklow.

Then there are splendid national and civic parks and nature gardens, such as **Phoenix Park** and the **National Botanic Gardens** in Dublin city; **Glenveagh National Park**, Co. Donegal; **Killarney National Park**, Co. Kerry; **Fota Estate**, Co. Cork; **Lough Key Forest Park**, Co. Roscommon; **Tollymore Forest Park** and **Castlewellan Forest Park**, Co. Down; and **Gortin Forest Park**, Co. Tyrone.

The Irish Tourist Board lists a selection of places to visit in a booklet, *Ireland's Heritage*, available from tourist offices (IR£1.50 at time of writing). The Northern Ireland Tourist Board will also supply details of visitor attractions in its area.

Museums and Libraries

DUBLIN & ENVIRONS

National Museum, Kildare St., Dublin 2 (tel: 765522). Irish antiquities, arts, industry, natural history.

National Library, Kildare St. (765521).

Trinity College Library (72941). Houses countless treasured volumes, including the *Book of Kells*.

Civic Museum, 56 South William St., Dublin 2 (771642). History and antiquities of Dublin.

Marsh's Library, St. Patrick's Close, Dublin 8 (753917). Oldest public library in Ireland. Fascinating.

National Wax Museum, Granby Row, Dublin 1 (746416). Life-size wax models of historical, political, literary, theatrical and sporting figures.

Kilmainham Jail Museum, Kilmainham, Dublin 8 (755984). History of struggle for independence.

Pearse Museum, St. Enda's Park, Rathfarnham, Dublin 14 (934208). Documents, photographs, etc, connected with great patriotic leader, Patrick Pearse.

James Joyce Museum, Martello Tower, Sandycove (809265). Documents and memorabilia, housed on old tower where Joyce lived for a short time.

National Maritime Museum, Haigh Terrace, Dun Laoghaire.

Parnell Museum, Avondale House, Rathdrum, Co. Wicklow (0404-6111). Material relating to great 19th Century political leader, housed in his ancestral home.

Millmount House Museum, Millmount, Droghaed (041-36391), Folklore, local history.

National Stud and Irish Horse Museum, Tully, Co. Kildare (045-21617). The history of the horse in Ireland.

SOUTHEAST REGION

Carlow Museum, Town Hall, Carlow (0503-31759). Folklore, archaeology, natural history.

Maritime Museum, Lightship *Guillemot*, The Quay, Wexford (053-23111).

Wexford County Museum, Castle St., Enniscorthy. Housed in 13th Century Norman castle. Folklore, archaeology.

Waterford Civic Museum, Reginald's Tower, The Mall, Waterford (051-73501). Civic and maritime history.

Rothe House Museum, Parliament St., Kilkenny (056-22893). Archaeology, local history, housed in Tudor merchant's home.

Clock Tower Museum, Main St., Youghal. Local history.

SOUTHWEST REGION

Cork Public Museum, Fitzgerald Park, Cork (021-20679). National, local and social history. Cork silver and glass.

West Cork Regional Museum, Old Methodist School, Western Rd, Clonakilty. Folklore and history of region.

Ballyferriter Museum, Co. Kerry (066-56100). Exhibitions on Brendan the Navigator, the currachs of Ireland and the heritage of the Dingle Peninsula.

MID WEST REGION

Civic Museum, St. John's Square, Limerick (061-47826). Archaeology and history of the region.

Hunt Collection, National Institute for Higher Education, Plassey, Limerick. Bronze-Age artefacts, medieval art, 18th Century silver.

Interpretive Centre, Lough Gur (10 miles south of Limerick). Displays relating to many Stone-Age ruins around Lough Gur.

Bunratty Castle and Folk Park, Bunratty (061-61511). Tapestries, furniture, dwelling houses, craft workshops, agricultural machines.

Craggaunowen Project, Quin (061-72178). Full-scale model of Bronze-Age dwelling. Also, "The Brendan," a hide boat in which the explorer Tim Severin sailed to America in the 1970s.

Cosheen Folk Museum, Corbally, Kilkee. Household implements dating from 18th Century.

De Valera Library and Museum, Harmony Row, Ennis. Paintings, archaeology, history.

Burren Display Centre, Kilfenora. Three-dimensional model of Burren region. Exhibits of flora, fauna, archaeology and literature of the area.

Clonmel Gallery and Museum, Parnell St., Clonmel. Local antiquities

Damer House and Roscrea Heritage Centre, Roscrea (0505-21850). Traditional furniture collection of the Irish Country Furniture Society.

MIDLANDS REGION

Steam Museum, Stradbally (0502-25136). Railway steam engines and related items.

Birr Castle Demesne, Birr (0509-20056). Giant 19th Century telescope, once the world's largest. Astronomical drawings and artefacts.

Athlone Castle Museum (0902-72191). Folklore, archaeology.

Mullingar Museum, Market Square, Mullingar (044-48795). Local history, folklore, archaeology.

Diocesan Museum, St. Mel's Cathedral, Longford (043-46465). Religious and archaeological items.

St. John's Interpretive Centre, Strokestown. Stone-age Ireland.

FAR WEST REGION

Galway City Museum, Spanish Arch, Galway. Local history and folklore.

Mill Museum, Shop St., Tuam (093-24463). Old water mill. Craft shop.

Museum Arainn, Kilronan, Inishmore, Aran Islands. Folklore, crafts, clothes, utensils, history. Material from 1905-6 relating to Douglas Hyde's visit to the US to promote the Gaelic League.

Museum na nOilean, Inishmaan, Aran Islands. Folklore. Material relating to the playwright J.M. Synge. Books.

Belcarra Folk Museum, Belcarra, Castlebar, Folklore. Newspaper photographs of the famine.

Knock Folk Museum, Knock Shrine, Claremorris (094-88100). Folklore, archaeology, history, religion.

NORTH WEST REGION

Sligo County Museum, Stephen St., Sligo (071-2212). Folklore, archaeology, history, paintings, rare books and manuscripts. Items relating to W.B. and Jack B. Yeats, including the former's Nobel Prize medal.

Glencolumbkille Folk Museum (Glencolumbkille 17). Folklore of South Donegal.

Donegal Museum, Franciscan Friary, Rossnowlagh (072-65342). Archaeology, folklore, history, military, numismatics.

COUNTY MONAGHAN

Inniskeen Folk Museum, Inniskeen, 7 miles east of Carrickmacross (042-78109). Folklore, archaeology. Special section on the poet Patrick Kavanagh, who was born nearby.

Monaghan County Museum, St. Mary's Hill, Monaghan (047-82928). Archaeology, folklore, local history, crafts, lace. Awarded 1980 Council of Europe museum prize.

NORTHERN IRELAND

Ulster Museum, Botanic Gardens, Stranmillis Rd, Belfast (668251). Life in Ireland over 9,000 years. Treasures from the Spanish Armada.

Transport Museum, Witham St., Belfast (51519). Steam locomotives, trams, early fire engines, early bicycles and vintage cars.

Linenhall Library, Donegall Square North, facing front of City Hall (221707). Important Irish books, Robert Burns collection, old newspapers, genealogy. Founded 1788. In 1798, Chief Librarian Thomas Russell was executed for his part in the United Irishmen's rebellion.

Belfast Central Library, Royal Avenue (243233). Early printed books, photographs, old newspapers, early maps.

Ulster Folk and Transport Museum, Cultra (Holywood 5411). Old dwellings, implements, machinery.

Armagh County Museum, The Mall, Armagh (0861-523070). Library, art gallery, natural history room, Victorian doll collection.

Armagh Planetarium, College Hill, Armagh (0861-523686). Star theatre, full-scale mock-up of Gemini spacecraft, other equipment used by US astronauts, space telescope.

Royal Irish Fusiliers' Regimental Museum, The Mall, Armagh (0861-522911). Uniforms, medals, silver and a beautiful flag of the French Revolution, surrendered to the Armagh militia at Ballinamuck, Co. Longford, by the French force sent by Napoleon to support the United Irishmen in 1798.

Church of Ireland Cathedral Library, Armagh (0861-523142). Valuable collection of books— theology, science, archaeology, travel, rare manuscripts and registers of Archbishops of Armagh from medieval times. Can be seen only by arrangement with the Dean.

Ulster-American Folk Park, Camphill, Omagh (0662-45857). Old dwellings, artefacts.

Art Galleries

DUBLIN REGION

National Gallery of Ireland, Merrion Square West (608533). Weekdays 10 a.m. to 6 p.m. (Thursday 10 a.m.-9 p.m.), Sunday 2 p.m. to 5 p.m.

Hugh Lane Municipal Gallery of Modern Art, Parnell Square (741903). Tuesday-Saturday 9. 30 a.m. to -6 p.m., Sundays 11 a.m. to 5 p.m.

Gallery of Oriental Art (Chester Beatty), 20 Shrewsbury Rd (692386). Tuesday-Friday 10 a.m. to 5 p.m., Saturday 2 p.m. to 5 p.m. Guided tours Saturday and Wednesday 2.30 p.m.

Apart from the above three galleries, which anyone interested in the visual arts should see, Dublin has many smaller exhibition centres and commercial galleries which often contain interesting work. Here are a few of them:

Douglas Hyde Gallery, Trinity College (772941 ext 1116). Monday-Saturday, 11 a.m. to 5 p.m. Contemporary Irish and international painting, sculpture and photography.

Bank of Ireland Exhibition Hall, Lower Baggot St. (785744). Monday-Friday, 10 a.m. to 5 p.m. Modern Irish and international exhibitions.

Tom Caldwell Gallery, 31 Upper Fitzwilliam St. (688629). Tuesday-Friday, 11 a.m. to 5 p.m., Saturday, 11 a.m. to 1 p.m. Contemporary Irish artists, especially Northern.

Combridge Fine Arts, 24 Suffolk St. (774652). Monday-Friday 9.30 to 5.30, Saturday 10 a.m. to 1 p.m. Conventional landscapes in oil and watercolour.

Oliver Dowling Gallery, 19 Kildare St. (766573). Monday-Friday, 10 a.m. to 5.30 p.m., Saturday 10 a.m. to 1 p.m. Paintings and sculptures by Irish and international artists.

Hendriks Gallery, 119 St. Stephen's Green *[west side]* (756062). Monday-Friday, 10 a.m. to 5.30 p.m., Saturday, 11 a.m. to 1 p.m. Modern Irish art—abstract, "new expressionist," etc.

Lincoln Gallery, 4 Lincoln Place (680665). Tuesday-Saturday, 10 a.m. to 6 p.m. Work by younger Irish artists.

Oriel Gallery, 17 Clare St. (763410), Monday-Friday, 10 a.m. to 5.30 p.m., Saturday, 10 a.m. to 1 p.m. 19th and 20th Century Irish paintings, mostly landscapes. Established names such as Paul Henry, Jack B. Yeats, "AE".

Taylor Gallery, 6 Dawson St. (776089). Monday-Friday, 10 a.m. to 5.30 p.m., Saturday, 11 a.m. to 1 p.m. Contemporary Irish painting and sculpture.

Gallery of Photography, 37-39 Wellington Quay (714654). Irish and international exhibitions; postcards, prints and posters.

DUBLIN & ENVIRONS

Kilcock Art Gallery, School St., Kilcock, Co. Kildare, Tuesday-Friday 10 a.m. to 3 p.m., Saturday 2 p.m. to 5 p.m.

Portrait Gallery, Malahide Castle, Malahide, Co. Dublin (452337/452706). Monday-Friday (all year), 10 a.m. to 5 p.m., Saturday, 11 a.m. to 6 p.m. (April-October), 2 p.m. to 5 p.m. (November-March). Sunday, 2 p.m. to 6 p.m. (April-October), 2 p.m. to 5 p.m. (November-March).

SOUTHEAST REGION

Funge Art Centre, Gorey, Co. Wexford (055-21470). Contemporary paintings.

Kilkenny Castle Art Gallery, Kilkenny (056-21450). Late 19th Century and 20th Century Irish art.

Waterford Arts Centre, O'Connell St., Waterford, (051-73501).

Waterford Trade Centre, The Mall, Waterford (051-76002). Craft exhibition—glassware, brass, wrought iron, etc.

Wexford Art Centre, Cornmarket, Wexford (053-23764).

SOUTHWEST REGION

Cork Arts Society Gallery, 16 Lavitt's Quay, Cork (021-505749). Tuesday-Saturday, 11 a.m. to 2 p.m., 3 p.m. to 6 p.m. Occasional exhibitions by Irish artists.

Crawford Municipal Art Gallery, Emmet Place, Cork (021-965033). Monday-Friday, 10 a.m. to 5 p.m., Saturday 9 a.m. to 1 p.m. Irish and European paintings, sculpture, silver, glass.

Forrester's Gallery, North Main St., Bandon (023-41360).

Triskel Arts Centre, 5 Bridge St., Cork (021-506055). Tuesday-Saturday 10 a.m. to 5.30 p.m. Exhibitions, poetry readings.

Searson Gallery, 55 Main St., Midleton (021-631559). Daily, 10.30 a.m. to 5.30 p.m. Exhibitions by local and national artists.

Fota House, Fota Estate, Carrigtwohill (021-812678). Mid-March to September, Tuesday-Saturday 11 a.m. to 6 p.m., Sunday 1 p.m. to 6 p.m. Irish landscapes from 1750s to 1870s—the most comprehensive private collection in existence, containing many masterpieces of national importance. 18th Century and early 19th Century furniture.

Sheeog Art Gallery, Langford St., Killorglin (066-61111). April-Sept, December, Monday-Saturday, 10.30 a.m. to 6.30 p.m.

Sean O'Connor, Town Hall, Killarney. Monday-Saturday, 9 a.m. to 5 p.m. (Thursday 9 a.m. to 1 p.m.). Landscapes.

MID-WEST REGION

Belltable Arts Centre, 69 O'Connell St., Limerick (061-319866). Monday-Saturday, 10 a.m. to 9 p.m. Paintings by local artists.

Municipal Art Gallery and Library, Pery Square, Limerick (061-314668). Monday-Friday, 10 a.m. to 1 p.m., 2.30 p.m. to 8 p.m., Saturday, 10 a.m. to 1 p.m. Collection of oils and watercolours. Local and touring exhibitions.

MIDLANDS

Jill Whyte Gallery, Castle St., Mullingar (044-48662). Monday-Friday, 9.30 a.m. to 1 p.m., 2 p.m. to 5 p.m. Contemporary Irish art.

FAR WEST REGION

Education Centre, Castlebar (094-21769). Monday-Friday, 10.30 a.m. to 5 p.m. Irish art and crafts.

Kenny Art Gallery, High St., Galway (091-62739). Monday-Saturday, 9 a.m. to 6 p.m.

Cregal Art Centre, Ballybane, Galway (091-51247). Monday-Saturday 9 a.m. to 6 p.m. Irish and international paintings.

NORTHWEST REGION

Sligo Art Gallery, Stephen St., Sligo (071-5847). Monday-Friday, 10 a.m. to 2 p.m., 3 p.m. to 5 p.m., Saturday 10 a.m. to 1 p.m. About 100 paintings, including work by John B. Yeats and Jack B. Yeats.

Glebe Gallery, Churchill, Co. Donegal, Derek Hill collection; Hill is an English-born artist associated particularly with paintings of Tory Island.

NORTHERN IRELAND

Ulster Museum, Botanic Gardens, Belfast. Ulster and Irish artists such as Sir John Lavery, Paul Henry, Jack B Yeats, Colin Middleton.

Arts Council of Northern Ireland, Bedford St., Belfast. Exhibitions, bookshop.

Bell Gallery, 13 Adelaide Park, 19th Century and 20th Century Irish artists, Victorian paintings.

Tom Caldwell Gallery, 40-42 Bradbury Place. Living Irish artists.

Magee Gallery, 455 Ormeau Rd. Mostly conventional work by established painters.

Octagon Gallery, 1 Lower Crescent. Run by younger local artists, promotes their work.

Fenderesky Gallery, 4 Malone Rd. Contemporary and avant-garde Irish painting.

Orchard Gallery, Londonderry. Contemporary paintings.

Activities

Golf

Visitors are welcome to play at about 180 golf courses in the Irish Republic. Green fees average about IR£7 a day, but range from IR£3 up to IR£15. Some clubs offer discount rates to groups and societies. Charges in Ireland are generally by the day, and not by the round, as in some countries. Some courses have sets of clubs for hire. Caddies are not usually available, except by prior booking. Most clubs hire out pullcarts, but not electric or petrol-driven carts. Visitors are advised to bring only light golf-bags, as they may have to carry their own.

For full details of gold courses, holiday offers, or individual golf itineraries, contact J.P. Murray Golf Promotion Executive, Irish Tourist Board, Dublin 2.

Sea Angling

Shore fishing (from rocks, piers, beaches and promontories), inshore fishing (in bays and inlets) and deep sea fishing are all popular in Ireland all the year round. No permits are required. There are over 250 competitions organized throughout the country from February to November. Full details of events and of boats for hire are contained in the Irish Tourist Board publication, *Sea Angling in Ireland*. It is available for IR£1, including postage, from the Irish Tourist Board Literature Dept, P.O. Box 1083, Dublin 8, Ireland.

Coarse Angling

The species of freshwater fish in this category are pike, perch, bream, rudd, tench, dace and various hybrids. The main area for coarse fishing is the Midlands, stretching from the River Erne system in the North southwards through the Shannon basin, the Monaghan and Westmeath lakes, the grand and Royal Canals, to the Barrow River and Canal and the Munster Blackwater. There is no legal closed season. No licence is required in the Irish Republic. In Northern Ireland, anglers require an annual general coarse fishing permit and a coarse fishing rod licence (for 15 days or a season)—available from local tackle shops, local hotels, handling agents or the tourist board.

Tackle can be bought but seldom hired in Ireland. Pre-packed bait, such as pure breadcrumbs, white maggots and worms can be bought from a number of stocklists, but it is best to pre-order from Irish Angling Services, Ardlougher, Co. Cavan (tel 049-26258). If you are bringing your own bait into Ireland, do not pack it in soil or vegetable material, the importation of which is illegal.

Game Angling

The species in this category are salmon, sea trout and brown trout. The season for salmon-fishing is from January 1 to September 30, depending on district. A licence is essential, and usually a fishery permit also, though some loughs, for example Corrib and Conn, are free of permit charge. A salmon licence and permit also covers fishing for sea trout, which is in season from June to September 30 (October 12 in some areas). For brown trout, a licence is required in Northern Ireland only and much of the fishing is free.

Canoeing

This is a rapidly developing year-round sport. In winter there is slalom, downriver racing, rough water, surfing; in summer, sprint, long distance, marathon, surfing. Canoeing is also an excellent way to explore backwaters, as canoes can enter rivers and waterways barred to larger craft.

For information, contact: Development Officer, Irish Canoe Union, 4-5 Eustace St, Dublin 2 (tel 719690).

Sub-Aqua Diving

Contact: Honorary Secretary, Irish Underwater Council, 60 Lower Baggot St., Dublin 2 (785844)

Water-Skiing

Contact: Mr Sean Kennedy, President, Irish Water-Ski Association, 7 Upper Beaumont Drive, Ballintemple, Cork, (021-292411).

Surfing

Contact: Mr Roci Allan, Secretary, Irish Surfing Association, Tigh-na-Mara, Rossnowlagh, Co Donegal, (072/51261 home, 073/21053 work).

Birdwatching

There are more than 55 recognized birdwatching sites in Ireland. For details of these, and of the various species to be seen at different times of year, contact the Irish Wildbird Conservancy, Southview, Church Rd. Greystones, Co. Wicklow (01-875759). There are two bird observatories at which visitors can stay. These are Cape Clear Bird Observatory (Bookings Secretary is Mr O,O'Sullivan, 46 The Glen Boden Park, Dublin 16); and Copeland Bird Observatory, Co Down (Bookings Secretary is Mr N. McKee, 67 Temple Rise, Templepatrick, Co Antrim).

Hang-Gliding

Contact: Mr Declan Doyle, Secretary, Irish Hang-Gliding Association, c/o Irish Hang-Gliding Centre, "Wits' End," Drumbawn, Newtown, Greystones, Co. Wicklow (01-819445).

Hill-walking, rambling, climbing

There is surely no need for further propaganda about the unspoilt beauty of Ireland's hills and mountains. Few of them rise above 3,000 feet (1,000 metres), but they have great character and variety, from the soft, bog-covered domes of Wicklow to the jagged peaks of Connemara, the ridges of Cork and Kerry, the strange, basalt outcrops of the Antrim plateau or the dramatic, sweeping Mountains of Mourne. Most of Irelands's mountains command marvellous views of the sea.

The best-known long-distance walking path in the Republic is the "Wicklow Way," which extends for about 79 miles (126 kms) southwards from Marlay Park, Co. Dublin to Clonegal, Co. Carlow. The route switchbacks along the eastern flanks of the Dublin and Wicklow mountains, the largest unbroken area of high ground in Ireland, very sparsely inhabited. For information on the route and accommodation, and on hill-walking in other mountain regions of the Republic, contact COSPOIR (The Irish Sports Council), Hawkins House, Dublin 2 (714311).

One of Europe's great long-distance paths, the "Ulster Way", virtually encircles Northern Ireland, stretching for 500 miles (800 km). For information contact the Sports Council for Northern Ireland, House of Sport, Malone Rd, Belfast 9 (661222).

For information and advice on mountaineering and rock-climbing, contact the Federation of Mountaineering Clubs of Ireland, 20 Leopardstown Gardens, Blackrock, Co Dublin (881266); the Sports Council for Northern Ireland.

Events and Festivals

The number of events and festivals, big and small, seems to increase every year. There are folk festivals, music festivals, oyster festivals, regattas, angling competitions, drama festivals, chess congresses, sporting competitions of all kinds, beauty contests, song contests, parades, car rallies, boat rallies, literary festivals, jazz festivals, exhibitions, agricultural shows, horse shows, dog shows, cat shows, commemorations, celebrations, hunt meetings, marathons, summer schools, community festivals, ceilidhs... the list is endless. In many cases, dates and venues are variable and some festivals—particularly the smaller, local ones—may appear and disappear from year to year according to the availability of funds, enthusiasm, or organizers.

Here is a small selection, listed in calendar order. Tourist boards can provide precise dates and details and also supply a full calendar of events for the current year.

January Races, Leopardstown, Dublin: top-class National Hunt (jumping) meeting.

Aer Lingus Young Scientists Exhibition, RDS, Ballsbridge, Dublin—January.

Holiday and Leisure Fair, RDS, Ballsbridge, Dublin—January.

International Rugby Championship (Ireland versus England, Wales, Scotland, France). Home matches at Lansdowne Rd, Dublin—January/February.

Irish Motor Show, RDS, Ballsbridge, Dublin—February.

Ulster Harp National, Downpatrick: steeplechase—late February/early March.

Cork City Opera Season, Cork Opera House—early March.

Limerick Theatre and Music Festivals—early March.

Irish Dancing Championships, Mansion House, Dublin—early March.

St. Patrick's Day (March 17): Festival of Ireland's national saint. Celebrated throughout Ireland and much of the world, notably and noisily in New York city.

Dublin Irish Music Festival: in a variety of venues, mostly licensed. Around St Patrick's Day.

World Irish Dancing Championships: venue variable—late March.

Irish Grand National (steeplechase), Fairyhouse—Easter Monday.

Circuit of Ireland Car Rally—Easter weekend.

Dublin Grand Opera Society Spring Season, Gaiety Theatre—late March/April.

Cork International Choral and Folk Dance Festival—late April/May.

Belfast Civic Festival and Lord Mayor's Show—May.

Belfast City Marathon road race. Mass masochism—May.

Northwest 200: fastest motorcycle race in Britain or Ireland. Starts from Portstewart, Co Derry—May.

Irish 2,000 Guineas (for 3-year-old colts) and 1,000 Guineas (for fillies), both run over one mile. The first classics of the flat racing season staged on consecutive Saturdays at the Curragh in May.

Ulster Classic Fishing Festival, Fermanagh Lakeland. Anglers' cornucopia—May.

Spring Show, RDS, Ballsbridge, Dublin. Major agricultural exhibition and social occasion, with many sideshows for the city slickers—May.

Pan-Celtic week, Killarney. Gathering of Celts from Brittany, Cornwall, Wales, Scotland and the home turf—May.

Royal Ulster Agricultural Show, Belfast—May.

Listowel Writers' Week, Listowel, Co. Clare—late May/June.

Music in Great Irish Houses Festival: held in various mansions near Dublin—early June.

Bloomsday Literary Festival, June 16, Dublin. Held on the date on which Joyce's "Ulysses" takes place. Strictly for Joyce buffs, but there is no shortage of those.

Sligo Midsummer Festival, Sligo—mid-June.

Ballybunion International Batchelor Festival, Ballybunion, Co. Kerry. Irish manhood's answer to the Miss World contest. Seeing is believing—late June.

Irish Derby (1½-mile flat-race for 3-year-old colts). Most glamorous day in the Irish racing calendar. Held at the Curragh—late June.

Westport Sea Angling Festival, Westport, Co. Mayo—late June.

Irish Oaks, the Curragh, Equivalent of the Derby for fillies—early July.

Willie Clancy Summer School, Miltown Malbay, Co. Clare (uileann piping) —July.

Ulster Harp Derby, Downpatrick, Co. Down —July.

Orangeman's Day, all over Northern Ireland —July 12.

International Rose Trials, Sir Thomas & Lady Dixon Park, Belfast—July-September.

Galway Races—heady, often hilarious, holiday horse-racing—late July/August.

Mary from Dungloe International Festival, Dungloe, Co. Donegal—late July/August.

Ulster Steam Traction Rally, Shane's Castle, Antrim—July, Huffing and puffing.

Stradbally Steam Rally, Stradbally, Co. Laois—early August. More Huffing and puffing.

Dublin Horse Show, RDS, Ballsbidge. Greatest event in the show-jumping calendar—August.

Puck Fair, Killorglin, Co. Kerry. Ancient pagan festival at which a goat is crowned—August.

Ulster Flying Club International Rally, Newtownards, Co. Down—August.

Yeats International Summer School, Co. Sligo. A two-week course of study and discussion of the great poet—August.

The Ould Lammas Fair, Ballycastle, Co. Antrim. The North of Ireland's most popular old fair, at which you traditionally "treat your Mary Ann to some dulse and Yellow Man." For elucidation, go to Ballycastle—last Monday and Tuesday in August.

All-Ireland Amateur Drama Festival—August.

Ulster Grand Prix (motorcycling), Dundrod, near Belfast—August.

Merriman Summer School, Lisdoonvarna, Co. Clare. A week of intense intellectual debate about the nation's culture, liberally laced with drinking and partying.

Rose of Tralee International Festival, Tralee, Co. Kerry—late August.

Fleadh Ceoil na hEireann (All-Ireland festival of Irish music, with competitions therein). Venue variable—August.

Matching Festival of Ireland, Lisdoonvarna, Co. Clare. More fun than computer dating—September.

Hurling and Gaelic Football: All-Ireland finals, Croke Park, Dublin—September.

Galway Oyster Festival, Falway city—late September.

Irish Hot-Air Balloon Championships, Ballymahon, Co. Longford—late September.

Dublin Theatre Festival—late September/October.

Dublin Cat Show, RDS, Ballsbridge—October.

Wexford Opera Festival, Wexford town—October.

Cork Jazz Festival, Cork city—October.

Dublin City Marathon, More self-inflicted punishment—late October.

Belfast Festival, Queen's University, Belfast, Ambitious, event-packed two weeks of music, drama, folksong, cinema, etc—November.

Dublin Grand Opera Society Winter Season, Gaiety Theatre, Dublin—December.

Spectator Sports

Music

Ireland has arguably the most vital traditional music in the world. You can hear it in pubs almost everywhere in the country, but visitors who want to be sure of hearing some good stuff are best advised to attend an organized session, such as one of those presented in summer on Wednesdays and Thursdays at Culturlann na hEireann, the headquarters of Comhaltas Ceoltoiri Eireann (the traditional music association). The address is Belgrave Square, Monkstown, Co Dublin (800295). Buses no 7 and 8 from Dublin city centre stop nearby and the Monkstown and Seapoint DART station is only a short walk away. CCE at the address given or from local tourist offices. Dublin's leading folk music club is at Slattery's of Capel Street. Details of sessions there appear in *In Dublin* magazine.

In Dublin also carries detail of jazz, rock and classical music events. The top venue for the latter is the National Concert Hall in Earlsfrot Terrace, off St Stephen's Green, Dublin.

Theatre

Dublin's chief theatres are: **The Abbey Theatre**, Lower Abbey St., Dublin (744505), Ireland's national theatre. Founded in the early years of the century by Yeats, Lady Gregory and their collaborators, it quickly won a world reputation with some outstanding plays and a unique style of acting. Many Irish classics feature in its programme. The Abbey's sister theatre, the **Peacock**, is used to try out new and experimental work.

The Gate Theatre, Parnell Square (744045), was founded by Micheal MacLiammoir and Hilton Edwards. Orson Welles made his first professional appearance here as a teenager. Productions are of a consistently high standard.

The Gaiety Theatre, South King Street (771717), is a fine Victorian building, recently restored. The programme includes opera, ballet, pantomime, variety concerts and serious drama.

The Olympia Theatre, Dame Street (778962), has a similar programme to the gaiety. It was once a Victorian music hall.

Theatres elsewhere in the country include:

Belfast: Grand Opera House, Great Victoria ST. (241919); Lyric Theatre, Ridgeway St. (660081); Arts Theatre, Botanic Avenue (224936).

Cork: Opera House, Emmet Place (270022); Granary Theatre, Grenville Place (276871); Ivernia Theatre, Grand Parade (272703).

Limerick: Belltable Arts Centre, 69 O'Connell St. (319866); Granary Tavern, Charlotte Quay (47266).

Galway: Druid Theatre Company, Druid Lane Theatre, Chapel St. (68617); Taibhdhearc na Gaillimhe, Middle St (62024).

Sligo: Hawk's Well Theatre, Temple St. (61526/61518).

Appendix

Places to stay

The approximate prices, quoted in IR£s, are for per person sharing a room; the cost of breakfast is included. A single room usually costs more. In most places, prices vary according to season.

DUBLIN

Egans House, 7-9 Iona Park, Glasnevin, Dublin 9, (tel 303611). First-class guesthouse on Northside, convenient to airport and near the Botanic Gardens. 24 rooms. £17. 50-£20.50.

Gresham Hotel, 23 O'Connell St Upper (746881). One of the city's oldest and best-known hotels, close to cinemas, shops, theatres and galleries, 180 rooms, £29.25-£58.50.

Jury's Hotel, Pembroke Rd. (605000). Modern hotel in suburb of Ballsbridge, close to US Embassy. Popular banqueting and conference centre."Jury's Irish Cabaret" attracts coachloads of tourists., 300 rooms, £44.50-£48.50.

Lansdowne Hotel, Pembroke Rd. (684079). Small family-run hotel in Ballsbridge, £30-£35.

Mount Herbert, Herbert Rd. (684321). Family-run guesthouse/hotel in Ballsbridge. Excellent value, £17.50-£26.

Powers Hotel, Kildare St. (605244). Nicely situated in the same street as Dail Eireann (the Irish Parliament), the National Museum and the National Library. Nightclub. £26.50-£31.

St. Aiden's Guesthouse, 32 Brighton Rd., Rathgar (970559/902011). Excellent guesthouse serving gourmet dinners. Great value. £13.

Westbury Hotel, Grafton St., Dublin 2 (791122). Dublin's newest luxury hotel, handily sited for the city's top shops, Trinity College, St Stephen's Green. A small-scale architectural horror, but a well-equipped place to stay, with its own shopping mall including Chinese and Indian restaurants, bookshops, beauty salon, etc. £56.75-£57.30.

Shelbourne Hotel, St. Stephen's Green (766471). For years one of the city's best-known hotels, and still more stylish than its newer competitors. £56.25-£73.25.

SOUTH OF DUBLIN

Royal Marine Hotel, Marine Rd., Dun Laoghaire (801911). Close to ferry terminal, pier, yachting marina, shop. Grand Victorian building, recently refurbished. £22.50-£33.75.

Dalkey Island Hotel, Dalkey (850377). Situated on rocky coastline, overlooking small island with Martello tower, close to charming village of Dalkey. £22.50-£32.50.

Court Hotel, Killiney (851622). Grand old building, decently extended, overlooking broad, sweeping bay. £33.50-£36.50.

Downshire House, Blessington (045-65199). Family-run hotel on main street of attractive Wicklow village, 18 miles (29 kms) from Dublin. Good food. £22.

Royal Hotel, Glendalough (0404-5135). Beautiful riverside setting beside celebrated ancient monastic ruins, Good food. W19-W22.

La Touche Hotel, Greystones (874401). Seaside hotel in the grand old style, recently refurbished. Good value. £18.

Hunter's Hotel, Rathnew (0404-4106). Old coaching inn with delightful riverside gardens. An old-fashioned treat. £23.50.

Old Rectory Country House, Wichklow (0404-2048). Tranquil, old house, nicely restored. Gourmet food. £25.50.

NORTH OF DUBLIN

Howth Lodge Hotel, Howth (390288). Family-run hotel overlooking the sea, close to Howth Castle. £19.50-£25.50.

Conyngham Arms, Slane (041-24155). Stonefaced Victorian inn in beautiful 18th-Century village on River Boyne. £15-£17.50.

Ballymacscanlon House Hotel, Dundalk (042-71124). Converted and extended old country mansion. Swimming pool, sports complex. £23-£27.50.

McKevitts' Village Hotel, Carlingford (042-73116). Family-run small hotel. £12.

WEST OF DUBLIN

Moyglare Manor Hotel, Maynooth (286351/286469/286501). Beautifully furnished Georgian manor surrounded by parkland. Comfortable. £42.15

Curryhills House Hotel, Prosperous (045-68150). Georgian farmhouse near Grand Canal. Good food. £20.

Barberstown Castle Hotel, Straffan (288157/288206). Dripping with historic atmosphere—includes medieval, Elizabethan and Edwardian features. £27.

SOUTHEAST REGION

Courtown Hotel, Courtown Harbour, near Gorey, (055-25108). Indoor heated pool. £18.70.

Marlfield House, Gorey (055-21124). Grand Regency house with first-class restaurant. £42.60-£49.50.

Cedar Lodge Hotel, Carrigbyrne, Newbawn, near New Ross (051-28386). Small, modern, family-run hotel. Good food. £22.

Hotel Rosslare, Rosslare Harbour (053-33110). Squash court, sailboarding, good food. £21-£25.

Ferrycarrig Hotel, Ferrycarrig Bridge, near Wexfor (053-22999). Fine setting by Slaney River. £23.50-£25.50.

Whitechurch House Hotel, Cappagh, near Dungarvan (058-68182). Classical Georgian house in Blackwater River valley. £17.

Richmond House, Cappoquin (058-54278). Guesthouse in fine Georgian residence in timbered parkland. Good value. £11.

Dooley's Hotel, Waterford (051-73531). Family-run hotel in centre of town. Good food. £22-£27.50.

Hotel Kilkenny, College Rd., Kilkenny (56-62000). Modern hotel and leisure complex built around old home. Conservatory, indoor pool, jacuzzi, £28.25-£29.75.

Lacken House, Dublin/Carlow Rd., Kilkenny (056-65611). Family-run guesthouse with emphasis on cosiness and good cooking. £13.20.

SOUTHWEST REGION

Arbutus Lodge Hotel, Montenotte, Cork (021-501237). Small hotel in early 19th century town house with fine gardens and collection of modern Irish arts. Celebrated food and wines. £31.25-£33.

Jury's Hotel, Western Rd, Cork (021-966377). Large, modern hotel five minutes' walk from city centre. £39-£41.

Metropole Hotel, MacCurtain St, Cork (021-508122). Typical Victorian grand hotel in city centre. £39.

Moore's Hotel, Morrison's Island, Cork (021-271291/2/3). £21.50.

Ashbourne House Hotel, Glounthane, Cork (021-953319/953310). 19th century country house by River Lee. Swimming pool, tennis. £24-£25.50.

Ballymaloe House, Shangarry, Midleton (021-652531). Large Georgian house, owned by farming family, built around Norman castle. Swimming pool, tennis, small golf course, modern paintings. friendly. Good food. £29.40-£35.25.

Grand Hotel, Fermoy (025-31444). Busy, friendly place, popular with fishermen. £22.

Blue Haven Hotel, Kinsale (021-772209). Small, cosy, family-run hotel. Good food. £21-£23.

Assolas Country House, Kanturk (029-50015). Grand 17th century with sweeping riverside gardens. Idyllic. £28.60-£30.

Barley Cove Beach Hotel, Goleen (028-35234). Good seafood in restaurant. £17.50-£30.

Cahernane Hotel, Muckross Rd, Killarney (064-31895). Splendid, ivy-clad manor house, former residence of the Earls of Pembroke. Tennis croquet, reserved fishing, good food. £27.50-£33.

Great Southern Hotel, Killarney (064-31262), Grand Victorian railway hotel. Swimming, tennis, sauna. From May to September, *Siamsa*, the national folk theatre, performs four nights weekly. £38.25-£47.25.

Kathleen's Country House, Tralee Rd, Killarney (064-32810). Well-appointed guesthouse. £16.

Ard-na-Sidhe Guesthouse, Caragh Lake, Killorglin (066-69105). Rambling Victorian mansion with antiques, open fires. £26.50.

Caragh Lodge, Caragh Lake (066-69115). Lovely gardens, swimming, tennis, fishing. £22-£27.50.

Park Hotel, Kenmare (064-41200). Luxurious hotel in grand old greystone building. Excellent food. £52-£64.

Great Southern Hotel, Parknasilla (064-45122). Rambling, 19th Century mansion with extensive semi-tropical gardens. Private golf-course, swimming, horse-riding, tennis, fishing, water-skiing. Good food. £42.75-£51.75.

Butler Arms Hotel, Waterville (0667-4144). Fine, family-run hotel overlooking the sea. Golf, tennis, fishing. Good food. £23-£27.

Smuggler's Inn, Cliff Road, Waterville. Small, family-run guesthouse. Good food. £16.50.

MIDWEST REGION

Jury's Hotel, Ennis Rd, Limerick (061-55266). Modern hotel with pleasant bar and classical French cuisine. £32-£34.50.

Woodfield House Hotel, Ennis Rd, Limerick (061-53023). Small, cosy hotel, recently refurbished. £21.70-£23.

Dunraven Arms Hotel, Adare (061-94209). Attractive old inn in beautiful village. £29-£34.50.

Kilcoran Lodge Hotel, Cahir (052-41288/41465). Converted hunting lodge with splendid view of Galtee Mountains. £26.50-£31.

Cashel Palace Hotel, Cashel (062-61411). 18th Century Palladian mansion, formerly a bishop's palace. £38.

Dundrum House, Cashel. 18th Century Georgian mansion, family-run. £24.20-£30.25.

Hotel Minella, Clonmel (052-22388). £22.

Rectory House Hotel, Dundrum (062-71115). Small, family-run country house hotel. £17-£21.

Ballykilty Manor Hotel, Quin (065-25617). An appealing first stop for Shannon arrivals. Georgian manor in wooded country on river Rine, which has good trout and salmon fishing. Knappogue Castle and the Craggaunowen Bronze Age sites are nearby. £22.30-£25.50.

Old Ground Hotel, Ennis (065-28127). Spacious, ivy-clad hotel partly 17th Century. £29.50-£34.

Auburn Lodge Hotel, Galway Rd, Ennis (065-21247). Modern family-run place. Squash, tennis, jacuzzi, etc. Good value. £18.50-£20.

Falls Hotel, Ennistymon (065-71004). Family owned and managed Georgian house near waterfalls on River Inagh. £16.50-£18.70.

Keane's Hotel, Lisdoonvarna (065-74011). Small, old-style hotel owned by five generations of the Keane family. Present owner is author of book on the Burren. Groups only March 1 to April 30. £13-£14.

Sheedy's Spa View Hotel, Lisdoonvarna (065-74026). Cosy, family-run. Turf fires, tennis court. £14.50-£16.

Cregans Castle Hotel, Ballyvaughan (065-77005). Not a castle, but a country house in the strange and fascinating Burren country. Comfortable. Good food. £25.87-£31.50.

MIDLANDS REGION

County Arms Hotel, Birr (0509-20791). Small, owner-managed hotel in converted Georgian mansion. £20-£25.

Prince of Wales Hotel, Church St, Athlone (0902-72626). Though the hotel dates from 1848, the present building is modern. Good value. £19.50.

Village Hotel, Tyrrellspass (044-23171). Family-runs small hotel in picturesque village. £13.50-£15.50.

Bloomfield House Hotel, Belvedere, Mullingar, (044-40894/5/6). Friendly hotel in old, castellated house that once served as a convent boarding school. Good value. £18.50-£20.

Royal Hotel, Bridge St, Boyle (079-62016). Friendly, family-run old village-centre hotel alongside river. £19.

Abbey Hotel, Abbeytown, Roscommon (0903-6505). Modern hotel in venerable old shell. £26-£28.

FAR WEST REGION

Great Southern Hotel, Eyre Square, Galway (091-64041). Grand old railway hotel on city's main square. Indoor pool, health complex. £38.25-£42.75.

Connemara Gateway Hotel, Oughterard (091-82328). Well-run, large modern hotel. Swimming, tennis. £22.50-£28.75.

Currarevagh House, Oughterard (091-82313). 19th Century country mansion in woodland by Lough Corrib. Good food. £28.60.

Ballynahinch Castle Hotel, Ballinafad (095-21269). Splendidly sited in the wilds of Connemara at the foot at one of the "Twelve Bens", overlooking the Owenmore River. £34-£39.

Abbeyglen Castle, Clifden (095-21070). Beautiful site on outskirts of "capital of Connemara." Outdoor heated pool. Good food. £22.50-£26.

Rock Glen Country House, Clifden (095-21035/21493). Converted shooting lodge. Cosy. Good food. £22.50-£28.

Cashel House Hotel, Cashel (095-21252/31001). Elegant country house in lovely gardens over-looking bay. Good food. £28.50-£33.

Crocnaraw Country House, Moyard (095-41068). Grand, white Georgian house, colourful decor. Good food. £26.40-£29.15.

Rosleague Manor Hotel, Letterfrack (095-41101). Fine Georgian house. Good food. £24-£30.50.

Doonmore Hotel, Inishbofin Island (Inishbofin 104). Small, family-run hotel on beautiful offshore island. £11-£13.20.

Ashford Castle, Cong (094-22033). A splendid former residence of the Guinness family, standing on the isthmus between Lough Corrib and Lough Mask. Private golf course, tennis, fishing, boating and shooting. Ronald and Nancy Reagan stayed here on their visit to Ireland in 1984. £60.

Olde Railway Hotel, The Mall, Westport (098-25090/25166). Family-run hotel, more than 200 years old. Thackeray called it "one of the prettiest and comfortablest inns in Ireland." £15.40-£17.60.

Breaffy House, Castlebar (094-22033). Stone-built mansion on outskirts of Mayo's county town. £22-£23.

Belleek Castle Hotel, Ballina (096-22061). Set in a forest by a Salmon river, close to the sea, Medieval great hall, suits of armour, Nightclub. £30-£35.

Mount Falcon Castle, Ballina (096-21172). Greystone mansion. Farm cooking. Fishing. £33.

Ostan Gob A'Choire (Archill Sound Hotel), Archill Island (098-45245). You don't need a boat to get here: this splendidly scenic island is connected to mainland Mayo by a causeway. £14-£16.

NORTHWEST REGION

Rock House Hotel, Lough Arrow, Castlebaldwin (079-66073/66077). Family-run converted farm-house. Good value. £15-£17.

Sligo Park Hotel, Pearse Rd., Sligo (071-60291). Modern hotel, formerly part of the Jury's chain. Reasonably priced. £24-£26.50.

County Hotel, Carrick-on-Shannon (078-20042). Family-run town centre hotel. £18-£20.

Ernan Park Hotel, St Ernan's Island, near Donegal Town. (073-21065). Beautifully situated on a small, wooded island reached via a causeway. Peaceful and friendly. £17.50-£20.

Ostan Radharc na Mara (Seaview Hotel), Bunbeg, (075-31159). Good value. £18.15.

Carrigart Hotel, Carrigart (074-55114). Roadside hotel offering excellent value. Heated pool, squash, sauna, solarium. £17-£20.

Carrig-Rua Hotel, Dunfanaghy (074-36133). Efficient, family-run hotel. Good value. £13.50-£17.50.

Port-na-Blagh Hotel, Port-na-Blagh (074-36129). A grand setting overlooking Sheephaven Bay. Good value. £17-£19.60.

Rathmullan House, Rathmullan (074-58117/58188). Country house on shores of Lough Swilly. Beautiful gardens. £26-£27.50.

NORTHERN IRELAND: The approximate prices, quoted in £s sterling, are for per person sharing and include breakfast.

BELFAST

Conway Hotel, Dunmurry (612101). £27.50.

Culloden Hotel, Holywood (02317-5223). Mock-baronial building. Good food. £37.50.

Forum Hotel, Great Victoria St. (245161). Modern, business-style hotel in city centre. £31.75.

Wellington Park Hotel, 21 Malone Rd. (661232). Popular with the rugby set. £30.

Eglantine Guest House, 21 Eglantine Ave. (667585). £8.50

COUNTY ANTRIM

Dunadry Inn, Templepatrick (08494-32474). Attractive old building. Close to airport. £27.50.

Leighinmohr House Hotel, Ballymena (0266-2313/56669). £15.50.

Adair Arms Hotel, Ballymoney Rd., Ballymena (0266-3674). £21.

Londonderry Arms Hotel, Carnlough (0574-85255/85458). Old coaching inn that once belonged to Sir Winston Churchill. The present proprietor was a devotee of the great steeplechaser, Arkle, and set up a miniature museum in his honour. It includes a portrait of the horse by the Glens of Antrim painter, Charles McAuley. £16.

Thornlea Hotel, Cushendall (02667-71223/71403). £12.

Antrim Arms Hotel, Castle St., Ballycastle (02657-62284). Fairly basic. £13.

Atlantic Guest House, The Promenade, Ballycastle (02657-62412/62768). £8.

Rathlin Guest House, Rathlin Island (02657-71217/71216). Reached by boat from Ballycastle, weather permitting. £7.

COUNTY DERRY

Edgewater Hotel, 88 Strand Rd., Portstewart (026583-3314/3688). Overlooks magnificent sandy beach. Jacuzzi. £17.75.

Lodge Hotel, Lodge Rd., Coleraine (0265-4848/9), £15.

Bohill Auto Inn, Bushmills Rd., Coleraine (0265-4406/7). Modern motel, £12-£16.

Glen House Hotel, Main St., Eglinton (0504-810527). £18.

Everglades Hotel, Prehen Rd., Londonderry (0504-46722). Good food. £19.

White Horse Inn, 68 Clooney Rd., Campsie, Londonderry (0504-860606). Good food. £13.

COUNTY DOWN

Old Inn, Crawfordsburn (0247-853255). Good food. £26.

O'Hara's Royal Hotel, Bangor (0247-473866). £16.

Abbey Lodge Hotel, Downpatrick (0396-4511). £15.

Cranfield House Hotel, Kilkeel (06937-62327). Good food. £12.

Kilmorey Arms Hotel, Kilkeel (06937-62220). £12.50.

Burrendale Hotel, Castlewelland Rd., Newcastle (03967-22599). Good food. £15.

Enniskeen Hotel, Bryansford Rd., Newcastle (03967-22392). Good food. £15.

Brook Cottage Hotel, Bryansford Rd., Newcastle (03967-22204). Good food. £12.

COUNTY ARMAGH

Silverwood Hotel, Kiln Lane, Silverwood, Lurgan (07622-27722). Good food. £16.50.

Carngrove Hotel, Charlestown Rd., Portadown (0762-339222). Good food. £13.75.

Seagoe Hotel, Upper Church Lane, Portadown (0762-333076). Good food. £17.50.

COUNTY TYRONE

Inn on the Park Hotel, Moy Rd., Dungannon (08687-25151). Good food. £14.

Valley Hotel, Fivemiletown (03655-21505). Good food. £14.

Royal Arms Hotel, Hight St., Omagh (0662-3262). £13.

Fir Trees Lodge Hotel, Melmount Rd., Strabane (0504-883003). Good food. £16.

COUNTY FERMANAGH

Brooklands Hotel, Main St., Ballinamallard (036581-515/6). £12.50.

Killyhevlin Hotel, Dublin Rd., Enniskillen (0365-23481). Good food. £24.

Mahons Hotel, Enniskillen Rd., Irvinestown (03656-21656). £14.

Lough Erne Hotel, Kesh (03656-31275). Good food. £10.50-£12.

Ortine Hotel, Lisnaskea (03657-21206). £14.50.

Where To Eat

Irish Republic

The symbols at the end of each entry provide a rough guide to prices, based on the average cost of a three-course evening meal, excluding wine, £ = less than IR£6 per head; ££ = between IR£6 and IR£17 per head; £££ = more than IR£17 per head. Lunch is usually cheaper. The symbol T means that the restaurant offers a special-value, three-course Tourist Menu, priced at either IR£5 or under. Where no area code is given, the telephone number is in the Dublin exchange (01- prefix when dialling from another area).

DUBLIN

Bad Ass Cafe, 9-11 Crown Alley [*behind Central Bank*] (tel 712596). Loud, informal pizzeria popular with young people. Blaring rock music from video-jukebox. Big helpings. ££ T.

Berkeley Room, Berkeley Court Hotel, Lansdowne Rd (601711). The Berkeley Court is ugly outside and pretentious within, but the French cuisine is first-rate. Private alcoves in the restaurant. £££.

Bernardo, 19 Lincoln Place (762471). The main attraction here is *not* the food, which is run-of-the mill Italian, but the comfortable atmosphere of a warm, dingily elegant room with faded old oil paintings on the walls, where you can feel at home for an evening's conversation. The house wine is pleasant and reasonably priced. ££.

Bewley's Cafes, 11-12 Westmoreland St., 13 South Great George's St; and 78-79 Grafton St. The cafes — big, old-fashioned tearooms with stained-glass windows — are at the back of Bewley's venerable tea, coffee and bakery shops. They are much used by Dubliners as places to meet for a chat or to grab a quick breakfast and a look at the newspaper before dashing into work. The food is mostly plain and unremarkable, but the atmosphere is an essential part of Dublin. £ T.

Cafe de Paris, The Galleria, 6 St. Stephen's Green [*north side*] (778499). Determinedly French bistro/brasserie with wine bar and railway-carriage bench seating. Daily specialities of game, fish and seafood. £££.

Captain America's, 1st floor, Grafton Court [*arcade at top of Grafton St*] (715266). American-style family restaurant with bar serving American cocktails and beers, Hamburgers, "Tex-Mex," barbecues, etc. £.

Ernie's Restaurant, Mulberry Gardens, Donny brook, (693300). Small restaurant designed around large mulberry tree. Charcoal grill, seafood specialities, shellfish, game. £££.

George's Bistro, 29 South Frederick St. (603177). Off-beat place open late and popular with show-biz types. Live jazz or crooning. ££ T.

Golden Orient, 27 Lesson St. (762286). Long-established Indo-Pakistani restaurant. Chef's special Thali dishes and children's portions. ££.

Kapriol, 45 Lower Camden St. (751235/985496). Small, family-run Italian restaurant. First-rate food, extensive wine list. £££.

Kilkenny Kitchen, Nassau St. [*above Kilkenny Design shop*], Popular self-service lunch-spot, always crowded, Home cooking, nice salads, fruit crumbles, etc. Closed in the evening. £.

Le Coq Hardi, 35 Pembroke Rd. (684130/689070). Roomy French restaurant offering seasonal specialities, nouvelle cuisine. Outstanding wine list. £££.

Locks, 1 Windsor terrace (752025). French provincial-style restaurant specializing in cuisine moderne. £££.

Lord Edward, 23 Christchurch Place (752557). Pleasantly old-fashioned seafood restaurant in the city's oldest quarter. £££.

Mamma Mizzoni, 91 Rathgar Rd. (970537). Busy family-run Italian restaurant with pianist and guitarist at weekends. ££.

Municipal Art Gallery, Parnell Square North. Cheap, tasty hot lunches (looking at pictures is hungry work). Closed in the evenings. £.

National Gallery, Merrion Square. Spacious self-service restaurant with statues, pot plants and a baby grand piano. Tasty hot lunches, wholefood, salads. Closed in the evenings, except for Thursdays (8.30pm). £.

Old Dublin, 91 Francis St. (751173/752236). Russian and Scandinavian cuisine with emphasis on fish; intimate. ££.

Patrick Guilbaud, 46 James Place (764192). First-rate French cuisine. £££.

Periwinkle Seafood Bar, Powerscourt Townhouse Centre, South William St. Bar-service. Closed in the evenings. ££.

Rudyard's, Crown Alley [*beside Bad Ass Cafe*] (710846). English-style restaurant — bentwood chairs, big pot plants — serving tasty, good-value food. ££.

Tandoori Rooms, 27 Lower Lesson St. [*downstairs from Golden Orient*] (762286/688618). First-rate North Indian cuisine.

White's on the Green, 115 St. Stephen's Green (751975). One of Dublin's newest and best. Elegant French food, excellent wine list. £££.

Wild Geese, 10 Lower Camden St. (757107), Friendly atmosphere, experimental food such as salmon in green pepercorn sauce. ££.

SOUTH OF DUBLIN

The Abbot of Monkstown, Monkstown Crescent [*on main Dublin-Dun Laoghaire road*] (805174). Stylish restaurant with traditional and modern Irish cooking. £££.

Roly's, Monkstown Crescent, The Abbot's cheaper and less formal sister-restaurant — no booking required. Tasty, garlicky hot dishes. ££. T.

Captain America's West, Shopping Centre, Dun Laoghaire (804688). Similar to parent restaurant in Grafton St. £.

Digby's, 5 Windsor Terrace, Seafront, Dun Laoghaire (804600/809147). Comfortable, tented dining-room, international cuisine. £££.

Pavani's Bistro, 2 Cumberland St., Dun Laoghaire (809675). Cosy, Italian-style restaurant on main road into Dun Laoghaire. ££.

Restaurant na Mara, Dun Laoghaire harbour (800509/806767). Converted Victorian stationmaster's offices — elegant high-celinged rooms. Fresh chowder and seafood dishes. £££.

The Archive, 21 Castle St., Dalkey (850552). Interesting decor and paintings, including one of James Joyce's Molly Bloom in a brass bed. Good value table d'hote. ££-£££.

Tree of Idleness, Seafront, Bray (863498/828183). Greek-Cypriot food and wines. ££.

Enniscree Lodge, Cloon, Enniskerry (863542). Tudor-style inn set in forested hillside. Good soups, fondue. ££.

Hunter's Rathnew (0404-4106). One of Ireland's oldest coaching inns, with lovely gardens running down to Vartry river. Old-world politeness. ££.

NORTH OF DUBLIN

Abbey Tavern, Howth (390307). Stone walls, flagged floors, turf fires, gaslight — olde-worlde atmosphere, in other words. Fish dishes, folk music. £££.

King Sitric, East Pier, Howth (325235/326729). Stylish, harbourside restaurant. Fish, game in season. £££.

Dunderry Lodge, Dunderry, Robinstown, Navan (046-31671). Converted barn and byre. Cooking emphasises lightness and simplicity — no heavy garnishes or sauces. Herbs and vegetables from restaurant garden. £££.

The Gables, Dundalk Rd., Ardee (041-53789). Fresh seafood catch of the day, game in season. ££.

WEST OF DUBLIN

Rea House Inn, Newbridge (045-31316/31657). Cosy atmosphere in old inn with turf fires. ££.

Country Shop, Mill St., Maynooth. Craft shop/restaurant; pleasant place to stop for lunch or coffee-and-scones. Closed in the evenings. £ T.

Moyglare Manor, Maynooth (286351). Magnificently furnished Georgian manor at the end of a tree-lined avenue. Popular with huntin', shootin' 'n' fishin' parties and with the Curragh set for after-racin' celebrations. £££.

Curryhills House, Prosperous (045-68150/68336). Family-run hotel/restaurant in Georgian country house. Irish traditional music on Wednesday and Friday nights. ££.T.

Barberstown Castle, Straffan (288206/288157). Hotel/restaurant in 12th Century castle. French cuisine, pianist on Friday and Saturday nights. £££.

SOUTHEAST REGION

Marlfield House, Gorey (055-21124). Regency house in 35 acres of woodland and gardens. Fish specialities. Booking essential. ££.

Galley Cruising Restaurant, New Ross (051-21723). Dine while cruising on the River Slaney. £££.

Casey's Cedars Hotel, Rosslare (053-32124). Lobster a speciality. ££.

Merry's, Lower Main St., Dungarvan (058-41974). 17th Century wine merchant's. ££. T.

Candlelight Inn, Dunmore East (051-83215/83239). Family-run; seafood specialities. ££. T.

Dooleys Hotel, Waterford (051-73531). Family-run, city-centre hotel/restaurant. ££. T.

The Maltings, Inistioge (056-29484). Family-run place in attractive village by River Nore. French cuisine. ££.

Lacken House, Carlow Road, Kilkenny (056-21329). ££.

Step House Restaurant, Borris (0503-73209). Old-style restaurant in Georgian house. Mussels, prawns, game, etc. ££.

Searson's Seafood & Eat It, Main St., Midleton (021-631123). Whatever about the title, the food's fine. Booking essential. £££.

SOUTHWEST REGION

Arbutus Lodge, Montenotte, Cork (021-501237). Renowned both for its food and its extensive wine cellars. The Gallery Bar and patio (lunchtime only), specialising in seafood, is cheaper than the main restaurant. £££.

Lovetts, Churchyard Lane, off Well Rd., Douglas, Cork (021-294909/932204). Late-Georgian house. French cuisine specialising in rare fresh fish. £££.

Barley Cove Beach Hotel, Goleen (028-35234/35100). Large seafood selection. ££. T.

Blairs Cove, Durrus (027-61127). Stone-walled restaurant in stables of Georgian mansion overlooking Dunmanus Bay. Grand piano doubles as sweet trolley. Dining in summer on heated and covered terrace with fountain. Open-fire rotisserie. Need we say more? ££.

Shiro Japanese Dinner House, Ahakista, Durrus (027-67030). Sublime food and scenery. £££.

Blue Haven, Pearse St., Kinsale (021-72209). Small, cosy, family hotel. Seafood specialities. ££.

Longueville House, President's Restaurant, near Mallow (022-27156). Splendid 1720 Georgian mansion with Victorian conservatory. Food mainly from farm, garden and river. Wine from Ireland's only vineyard. £££.

Doyle's Seafood Bar, John St., Dingle (066-51174). Bright red exterior, cosy kitchen restaurant within. Speciality lobster, chosen live from tank in the bar. Menu chosen daily from catches landed by the Dingle fishermen. One of the country's best seafood restaurants. ££.

The Half-Door, John St., Dingle (066-51600). Another first-rate, family-run fish restaurant with good wine-list. ££.

Park Hotel, Kenmare (064-41200). First-class French cuisine, piano in season. £££.

Deenach Grill, College St., Killarney (064-31656). Unpretentious, good value. Children's portions. £ T.

Butler Arms Hotel, Waterville (0667-4144). Seafood, bar snacks. ££.

Smugglers Inn, Cliff Rd., Waterville (0667-4330). Family-run beach restaurant with fine views. Seafood, meat, poultry. ££. T.

MIDWEST REGION

Gregans Castle Hotel, near Ballyvaughan (065-77005). Country house hotel in the bleak Burren country of Clare, commanding fine views over Galway Bay. Seafood speciality. Live entertainment nightly in high season. £££.

MacCloskeys, Bunratty House Mews, Bunratty (061-74082). Restored cellars of 17th Century house overlooking Bunratty Castle and Folk Park. French-Irish cuisine. £££.

Maryse & Gilbert's, Corofin (065-27660). French and Italian dishes. ££ T.

Killilagh House, Roadford, Doolin (065-74183). Varied menu. ££ T.

Dunraven Arms, Adare (061-94209). Attractive old inn in one of Ireland's loveliest villages. ££.

Bulgaden Castle, Kilmallock (Kilmallock 209). Restored 18th Century tavern. Irish cabaret Mon, Wed & Thurs in summer. ££ T.

Jury's Hotel Coper Room Restaurant. Attentive service, classical, rich French cooking. £££.

Matt the Thresher, Birdhill [*on Limerick-Nenagh road*] (061-379227). Old pub/restaurant. Impromptu music "sessions", £.

Kilcoran House, Cahir (052-41288/41465). Old hunting lodge. Traditional fare, good views. ££.

Four Seasons, Cashel Palace Hotel, Cashel (062-61411). First-class food. £££.

La Scala, Market St., Clonmel (052-2147). Rustic limestone building. Italian specialities, steaks and desserts flambeed at table. ££.

MIDLANDS REGION

Royal Hotel, Bridge St. Boyle (079-62016). Friendly, family-run riverside restaurant, Generous helpings. ££ T.

Le Chateau, Abbey Lane, Athlone (0902-4517). ££.

Crookedwood House, Mullingar (044-72165). Family-run cellar restaurant. ££.

Bridge House, Bridge St., Tullamore (0506-21704). Fresh fish and game in season. ££.

Moorhill House, Clara Rd. Tullamore (0506-21395). Converted stables of old country house. ££ T.

FAR WEST REGION

Cashel House, Cashel, Co. Galway (095-21252). Old country house in 50-acre estate of gardens and flowering shrubs at head of Cashel Bay. Booking essential. £££.

Abbeyglen Castle, Sky Rd. Clifden (095-21070). Excellent restaurant serving locally caught salmon, lobster, prawns, mussels, scallops. ££ T.

The Pantry, Westport Rd. Clifden (0945-21389). ££ T.

Eyre House Restaurant, 10 Eyre Square, Galway (091-62396/63766). On city's main square. ££ T.

The Malt House, Olde Malte Arcade, High St., Galway (091-67866/63993). £££.

Moran's Oyster Cottage, The Weir, kilcolgan (091-96113). Beautifully situated cottage bar, seafood specialities. ££ T.

Drimcong House, Moycullen (091-85115). 300-year-old country house with polished oak tables, Adventurous cooking. £££.

Chalet, Keel, Achill island (098-43157), You don't need a boat: Achill is linked by a bridge to mainland Mayo. Fresh shellfish, splendid views. ££ T.

Enniscoe House, Castlehill, near crossmolina, (096-31112). Small restaurant in Georgian country house, inherited by present owner, with family portraits, antiques, open fires. ££.

Chalet Swiss, The Quay, Westport (098-25874). Seafood, veal, steak specialities. ££ T.

NORTHWEST REGION

Dragon Restaurant, Rock House Hotel, Lough Arrow, Ballindoon, Castlebaldwin (079-66073). Country house on shores of Lough Arrow, Antique rooms, turf fires, home produce. ££ T.

The Moorings, Rosses Point (071-77112). Cosy seafood restaurant. ££.

Knockmuldowney restaurant, Culleenamore, near Strandhill (071-68122). Ivy-clad Georgian house in Sligo's "Yeats Country". Local produce, ££ T.

Country Hotel, Cattick-on-Shannon (078-20550). ££ T.

Mooney's, Bunbeg (075-31147). Cosy, thatched restaurant with turf fire, Seafood. ££ T.

Water's Edge, Rathmullan (074-58182). The water is Lough Swilly, Seafood, boned duckling, steak specialities. ££.

St. John's, Fahan (077-60289). Home-cooked food in restored Georgian house overlooking Lough Swilly. ££.

Northern Ireland: The symbols at the end of each entry provide a rough price guide, based on the average cost of a three-course evening meal including a 10% service charge and VAT, but not wine.
£ = under £10 sterling; ££ = £10-£15; £££ = over £15.

BELFAST

Archana, 13 Amelia St., (247875). Indian and European. ££.

Ashoka, 363 Lisburn Rd., (660362). Indian and European. £.

Backstage bistro, 8 Clarence St., (247636), Gaspacho, spaghetti, steaks. £.

Beaten Docket, 48 Great Victoria St., (242926). £.

Belmont Court, 45 Park Ave (659724). Live Jazz Thursday evening. ££.

Bosco, 12 Brunswick St., (248398). Pizzas, grills kebabs. £.

Capers, 63 Gt Victoria St., (247643). Italian-style food, especially pizzas. £.

Chez Delbert, 12 Bradbury Place (223244). Cheap french food — peppered steaks, crepes, garlic bread. £.

Dragon Palace, 16 Botanic Ave. (223869). Peking-style cuisine. £.

Forum Hotel, Gt Victoria St., (245161). ££.

Four Winds Inn, 111 Newtown Park (701957). Huge portions. £££.

Friar's Bush, 159 Stranmillis Rd., (669824). Casseroles, pork in cider. £.

Giaciglio, 117 Gt Victoria St. (257891). Italian-style. £.

La Belle Epoque, 103 Gt Victoria St. (223244). French — lobster, pheasant, steaks. ££.

Manor House, 47 Donegal Pass (238755). Authentic Cantonese cooking. £.

Mews, 3 Univesity St., (225137). ££.

Pips International, 43 Dublin Rd., (233003). Garlic prawns, barbecue steaks. ££.

Pierre, 78 Botanic Avenue (223230). French — steak, seafood, pike. ££.

Restaurant 44, 44 Bedford St., (24844). Game, fish. £££.

Strand, 12 Stramillis Rd., (682268). First-class cooking, informal atmosphere. ££.

Tramps Bistro, 50 Dublin Rd., (232995). £.

Truffles, 3a Donegal Sq., West (247153). £.

Welcome, 22 Stranmillis Rd. (681359). Cantonese. £.

Wellington park, 21 Malone Rd. (661232). Popular with blazer brigade. £.

Zero, 2 University Rd. (233218). Vegetarian, wholefood. £.

COUNTY ANTRIM

Ballygalley — Ballygally Castle (0574-83213). ££.

Ballymena — Adair Arms, Ballymoney Rd (0266-3674). ££. Leighinmohr House. Leighinmohr Ave (0266-2313). ££.

Bushmills — Auberge de Seneirl, 28 Ballyclough Rd (02657-41536). French. ££.

Carnlough — Londonderry Arms (0574-85255). £.

Carrickfergus — Dobbins Inn, 6 High St (09606-63905). £.

Cushendall — Thornlea (02667-223/403). ££.

Dervock — North Irish Horse, 15 Main St., (02657-41205). £.

Giant's Causeway — Causeway Hotel (02657-31226/31210). £.

Glenariff — Laragh Lodge (026673-221/383). £.

Glengormley — Chimney Corner, 630 Antrim Rd. (02313-44925). ££. Swiss Chalet, 81 Ballyclare Rd., (02313-48630). £.

Larne — Magheramorne House, 59 Shore Rd., (0574-79444). ££.

Lisburn —Hansom Cab, 35 Railway St., (08462-7465). Pianist, open fire, Victorian decor, ££, Moghul-E-Azam, 58 Bow St (08462-71099). Indian, £. Pizzarelly's, 10 Bachelor's Walk, tel: 08462-71980. £.

Newtownabbey — Corr's Corner, Ballyhenry (02313-2118). ££. Sleepy Hollow, 15 Kiln Rd., (02313-44042). Art gallery, first-class food. ££.

Portballintrae — Bayview (02657-31453). £.

Portrush — Dionysus, 53 Eglinton St., (0265-823855). Greek. ££. Harbour Inn, 5 Harbour Rd (0265-825047). £. Ramore and Lobster Pot, The Harbour (0265-823444). ££.

Rathlin Island — Rathlin guesthouse (02657-71217). £.

Stoneyford — Ballymac, 7a Rock Rd. (084664-313). £.

Templepatrick — Dunadry Inn (08494-32474), Smokedeel, game, ££. Pig'n Chick'n (08494-32310), £.

COUNTY DOWN

Annalong — Fisherman, 43 Kilkeel Rd., (03967-66733). Local seafood. £. Glassdrumman House, 224 Glassdrumman Rd., (03967-68549). £££.

Ardglass —Downs, 7 Castle Place (0396-841315). Italian-style. ££.

Ballynahinch — Primrose Bar, 30 Main St., (0238-563177). £. Woodlands, 29 Spa Rd (0238-562650). Seafood. ££.

Bangor — Cartwheel, 44 High St., (0247-456362). £. The George, Crawfordsburn Rd., (0247-853311/852884). ££.

Comber — Old Crow, Glen Rd., (0247-872255). ££.

Crawfordsburn — Old Inn, 15 Main St., (0247-853255). Thatched inn with 18th-Century minstrels' gallery. ££.

Crossgar — Villager, 1 Downpatrick St., (0396-830385). £.

Cultra — Culloden (02317-5223). ££. Cultra Inn (02317-5840). £.

Downpatrick — Rea's 78 Market St., (0396-2017). Old-fashioned bar. ££.

Dromara — O'Reilly's, 7 Rathfriland Rd., (0238-532209). Seafood. ££.

Dundrum — Buck's Head Inn, 7 Main St., (039675-228). £.

Gilford — Pot Belly, Tullylish Pottery, Banbridge Rd., (0762-831404). ££.

Hillsborough — Hillside Bar, 21 Main St. (0846-682765). ££. Marquis of Downshire, 48 Lisburn St., (0846-682472). £.

Holywood — Chiccarino's, 49 High St., (02317-6439). ££. Schooner, 30 High St., (02317-5880). Recommended. ££.

Kilkeel — Cranfield House, 57 Cranfield Rd., (06937-62327). ££.

Killinchy — Balloo House (0238-541210), Fresh fish and game, Recommended, ££, Nick's, 18 Kilmeed Church Rd. (0238-541472), Converted church building, Recommended. ££.

Newcastle — Brook Cottage, 58 Bryansford Rd., (03967-22204). £. Burrendale, Castlewellan Rd., (03967-22599). ££.

Newry — Henry T's, 74 Hill St. (0693-4647). ££.

Newtownards — Athena Taverna, 29b Frances St., (0247-819090). Greek. £. Ganges, 69 Court St., (0247-811246). Indian. £.

Portaferry — Portaferry, 10 The Strand (02477-28231). Recommeded. ££.

Saintfield — The Barn, 120 Monlough Rd., (0238-510396). Recommeded, booking essential. ££.

Strangford — Lobster Pot, 11 The square (039686-288). £.

Waringstown — The Grange, Main St., (0762-881989). Recommended, booking essential. ££.

Warrenpoint — SS Schooner, Newry Rd., (06937-72255). £.

COUNTY DERRY

Aghadowey — Brown Trout Inn, Mullaghmore (026585-209). £.

Ballyronan — Gaugers Inn, St., Helena Point. Fresh fish. £.

Coleraine — McDuff's 112 Killeague Rd., Blackhill (026585-433). Highly recommended, ££, Salmon Leap, 53 Castleroe Rd., (0265-2992). ££.

Eglinton — Glen House, Main St., (0504-810527). ££.

Londonderry — Eveglades, Prehen Rd., (0504-46722). ££. White Horse Inn, 68 Clooney Rd (0504-860606). £££.

Magilligan — Ballymaclary House, 573 Seacoast Rd (05047-50283). 18th Century country house. £.

Portstewart — Edgewater, 88 Strand Rd., (026583-3688). £.

COUNTY ARMAGH

Armagh — Charlemont Arms, 63 English St., (0861-522028). £.

Loughgall — Bramley Apple, Main St., (318). Highly recommended. ££.

Lurgan — Sliverwood, Kiln Lane (07622-27722). ££.

Portadown — Carngrove, 2 Charlestown Rd., (0762-339222). ££. Seagoe, Upper Church Lane (0762-333076). ££.

COUNTY TYRONE

Dungannon — Inn on the Park, Moy Rd., (08686-25151). ££.

Fivemiletown — Valley, Main St., (03655-21505). £.

Omagh — Royal Arms, 51 High St., (0662-3262). £.

Strabane — Fir Trees Lodge, Melmount Rd., (0504-883003), £.

COUNTY FERMANAGH

Ballinamallard — Brooklands, Main St. (036581-515). £. Encore Steak House, Main St., (036581-606). £.

Belleek — Carlton, Main St., (036565-282). £.

Bellanaleck — the Sheelin (036582-232). Buffet £, gourmet evenings (booking essential) £££.

Enniskillen — Crow's Nest, 12 High St., (0365-25256), £ Killyhevlin, Dublin Rd (0365-23481). £. McCartney's Inn, 17 Belmore St., (0365-22012). Beoth. Irish stew. £.

Kesh — Lough Erne, Main St., (03656-31275). £. May Fly, Main St. (02657-21206). ££.

Lisnaskea — Ortine, Main St., (02657-21206). ££.

Car Rentals

Irish Republic

All the companies listed here are members of the Car Rental Council and operate a code of practice drawn up by the council and the Irish Tourist Board. Note that all Dublin area telephone numbers need an 01 - prefix if dialled from outside the area.

Argus Automobiles, Terenure, Dublin 6 (906129/904440). Deliveries to Dublin airport, ferry ports and hotels.

Avis Rent-a-Car, Hanover St. East, Dublin 2 (776971); Jurys Hotel, Ballsbridge (683394); Dulin Airport (372369); Shannon Airport (061-61643); Cork Airport (021-965045); Galway (091-68901). International franchises; Avis Worldwide.

Boland's-Inter Rent, New Ross, Co. Wexford (051-21213); Pearse St., Dublin (770704); Dublin Airport (379900 ext 4744); Shannon Airport (061-61877); Wexford (053-23711); Cork (021-508766); Rosslare Harbour (053-33288/051-21533); Waterford (051-76558). International franchise; Inter Rent and Dollar.

Budget Rent-a-Car, Lower Abbey St., Dublin (787894/747816/741147); Dublin Airport (370919); Shannon Airport (061-61361); Ballygar, Co. Galway (0903-4571); Rosslare Harbour (053-33318); Waterford (051-21550); Dun Laoghaire (854129), International franchise: US Budget Rent-a-Car.

Bunratty Car Rentals, Caherdavin, Limerick (061-51741); Shannon Airport (061-62549); Dublin Airport (379900 ext 4730).

Cahills Car Rentals, North Strand, Dublin (747766); Lower Glanmire Rd., Cork (021-506744).

Dan Dooley Rent-a-Car, Knocklong Co. Limerick (062-53103); Cathal Brugha St., Dublin (720777/787496); Cathal Brugha St., Dublin (720777/787496); Shannon Airport (061-61098). US contacts: Box 426, Whitestone, N.Y. 1137 (718-767-0524).

Flynn Brothers Rent-a-car, Ballygar, Co. Galway (day 0903-4668, night 0903-4689); Lower Drumcondra Rd., Dublin (379611/379802); Dublin Airport (420793); Shannon Airport (061-61361), US contacts: F.H. Fleming, 15 Crescent St., Walton, Mass. (617-899-7733); D.J.Flynn, P.O.Box 1511, Mineola, New York 11501 (516-294-6537). International franchise: Budget Rent-a-Car.

Hamill's Rent-a-Car, Dublin Rd. Mullingar, Co Westmeath (044-48682/40508/41274/41026),

Delivery to Dublin and Shannon Airports and Dublin ferry terminals, US contacts; C, Hughes, c/o The Dubliner, 4 F St., Washington D.C. (202-737-3773).

Hertz Rent-a-Car, Hertz House, Grand Canal St., Lower, Dublin (765594/765921); Leeson St Bridge, Dublin (602255); Dublin Airport (371693); Dun Laoghaire (801518); Shannon Airport (061-61369); Cork Airport (021-965849); Headford Rd., Galway (091-66674). International contacts; Brussels 5136761; Paris 7885151; Frankfurt 730404; London 6791799; US: 800-223-6537/800-654-3090.

Irish Car Rentals, Ennis Rd., Limerick (061-53049); Dublin Airport 9379900 ext 4795); Dublin (761311); Shannon Airport (061-62649), US contacts: Lismore Travel, 106 E 31 St., New York, N.Y. 10016 (212-685-0100).

Johnson & Perrott, Emmet Place, Cork (021-273295); South Leinster, Dublin (767213); Dublin Airport (370204/379000 ext: 4031); Shannon Airport (061-61094); Cork Airport (021-963133), US contacts: 800-522-5568/212-758-4375. Canada: Zenith 00910.

Kanning Car Hire, Westland Row, Dublin (772723); Dublin Airport (371156); Shannon Airport (061-61819); Cork Airport (021-276611); Western Rd., Cork (021-276611); Western Rd., Cork (021-276611), US contacts: American International Rent-a-Car, UK contacts: Kenning Car Hire, Chesterfield (77241).

Murrays Europcar Rent-a-Car, Baggot St. Bridge, Dublin (681777); Dublin Airport (3781790); Shannon Airport (061-61618); Cork Airport (021-966736); Rosslare Harbour (053-32181); Galway (091-62222); Wexford (053-22122), UK contacts: Godfrey Davis/Europcar (01-950-5050); Europe: Europcar (Paris 043-8282); US: National Car Rental (800-Car-Rent); Canada: Tilden (416-925-4551); Australia: Nat Car (436-3852).

O'Mara's Rent-a-Car, Galway Rd. Athlone, Co Westmeath (0902-2325/4310); Shannon Airport (061-61702).

South Country Self-Drive, Rochestown Ave., Dun Laoghaire (806005), Delivery to Dublin, Shannon and Cork airports, Dublin, Dun Laoghaire and Rosslare ferry terminals.

Tipperary Self-Drive, Limerick Rd., Tipperary (062-52526/51320); Dublin Airport (376348); Shannon Airport (061-61532); Cashel (062-61544), US contacts: 212-937-5636.

Treaty Car Rentals, William St., Limerick (061-46512/41128); Shannon Airport (061-62342).

Westward Garage, Strokestown, Co Roscommon (078-33029/33183); Russell St. Dublin (73540/735144); Sligo (071-2091/2).

Windsor Rent-a-Car, South Circular Rd., Rialto, Dublin (540800); Bachelors Walk, Dublin (732609); Nassau St., Dublin (775775/711733). Delivery to Dublin Airport and to Dublin and Dun Laoghaire ferry terminals.

Norther Ireland

Avis Rent-a-Car Great Victoria St., Belfast (240404); Belfast Airport (08494-52333); Coleraine (0265-3654); Londonderry (0504-3654).

Hertz Rent-a-Car, Belfast Airport (08494-53444); Londonderry (0504-260420).

Godfrey Davis Europcar, Linenhall St., Belfast (233773); Belfast Airport (08494-53444); Larne (0574-79360).

Budget Rent-a-Car, Lisburn Rd., Belfast (682439).

McCausland Car Hire, Grosvenor Rd., Belfast (227211/224411).

Roman Motors, Ramoan Rd., Ballycastle (02657-62534).

Mid-Ulster Self Drive, Gortalowry, Cookstown (06487-62953).

Lochside Garages, Tempo Rd., Enniskillen (0365-24366).

Diplomatic And Consular Missions To Ireland

Embassies

Argentina: 15 Ailesbury Drive, Dublin 4 (691546). Ambassador's residence: 694290.

Australia: Fitzwilton House, Wilton Terrace. Dublin 2 (761517).

Austria: 15 Ailesbury Court, 91 Ailesbury Rd. Dublin 4 (694577). Ambassador's residence: 694625.

Belgium: Shrewsbury House, Shrewsbury Rd. Dublin 4 (692082/691588). Ambassador's residence: 694332.

Britain: 31 Merrion Rd., Dublin 4 (695211).

Canada: 65 St. Stephen's Green, Dublin 2 (781988). Ambassador's residence: 851246.

China, 40 Ailesbury Rd., Dublin 4 (691707).

Czechoslovakia: call London, 031-229-1255

Denmark: 69 St. Stephen's Green, Dublin 2 (760122). Ambassador's residence: 860556.

Egypt: 12 Clyde Rd., (606566/606718). Ambassador's residence: 802586.

France: 36 Ailesbury Rd., Dublin 4 (694777).

Germany (Federal Republic): 31 Trimleston Ave., Booterstown (693011).

Greece: 1 Upper Pembroke St., Dublin 2 (767254).

Hungary: call London, 031-235-7191.

India: 6 Leeson Park, Dublin 6 (970843).

Iran: 72 Mount Merrion Ave., Blackrock (880252/882967).

Iraq: call London, 031-584-7141.

Israel: call London, 031-937-8050.

Italy: 12 Fitzwilliam Square, Dublin 2 (760366).

Japan: 22 Ailesbury Rd., Dublin 4 (694244).

Lebanon: call London, 031-229-7265.

Malaysia: call London, 031-245-9221.

Mexico: call London, 031-235-6393.

Netherlands: 160 Merrion Rd., Dublin 4 (693444).

Ambassador's residence: 984638.

New Zealand: call London, 031-930-8422.

Nigeria: 56 Leeson Park, Dublin 6 (604366).

Ambassador's residence: 962412.

Norway: 69 St. Stephen's Green, Dublin 2 (783133). Ambassador's residence: 698127.

Poland: call The Hagur, 16-31-70-602806. Portugal; Knócksinna House, Dublin 18 (893375/894416).

Qatar: call London, 031-235-0851.

Singapore: call London, 031-235-8315.

Spain: 17a Merlyn Park, Dublin 4 (691640/692597). Ambassador's residence: 692131.

Sweden: Sun Alliance House, Dawson St., Dublin (715822).

Switzerland: 6 Ailesbury Rd., Dublin 4 (692515).

Ambassador's residence: 692689.

Tanzania: call London, 031-499-8951.

Turkey: 60 Merrion Rd., Dublin 4 (685240).

United States of America: 42 Elgin Rd., Dublin 4 (688777).

USSR: 186 Orwell Rd., Dublin 6 (977525).

Yugoslavia: call London, 031-370-6105.

Foreign Consular Offices in Dublin

Brazil: Honorary Consul — P.J.Murphy, Shottery, Saintbury Ave., Killinery (851971).

Cyprus: Consul — Phoebus S. Moussoulides, 11 Shrewsbury Park, Dublin 4 (691397).

Ecuador: Honorary Consul — Dr. Julio Guash y Julia, 3 Hamilton Court, Seaview Terrace, Dublin 4 (695448).

Finland: Honorary Consul General — John Donnelly, Fitzwilliam House, Wilton Place, Doblin 2 (765153).

Iceland: Honorary Consul — Thomas P. Hogan, 6 Monkstown Ave, Monkstown (808103).

Malta: Honorary Consul — Noel Judd, 1 Upper Fitzwilliam St., Dublin 2 (760333).

Monaco: Honorary Consul — A.G.Quirke, 27 South Frederick St., Dublin 2 (682530).

Pakistan: Honorary Consul General — Dr. Said A. Yasin, 8 Millbrook Court, Milltown, Dublin 6, tel (698234).

Peru: Honorary Consul — T.C. Clifford, 20 Wellington St., Dun Laoghaire (800256).

Philippines: Honorary Consul — William Sandys, Stephen Court, 18 St. Stephen's Green, Dublin 2 (760150).

Thailand: Honorary Consul — P.J. Dineen, 18 Harcourt St., Dublin 2 (781599).

Tunisia: Honorary Consul — Louis J. Maguire, 15 Rathgar Rd., Dublin 6 (976735).

Booklist

Acton, **Charles:** *Irish Music and Musicians,* Eason.
Arnold, **Bruce:** *A Concise History of Irish Art,* Thames & Hudson.
Bardon, **Jonathan:** *Belfast, Blackstaff Press.*
Beckett, **J.C.:** *The Making of Modern Ireland,* Feber.
Bord Failte: *Ireland Guide.*
Boylan, **Henry:** *A Dictionary of Irish Biography.* Gill & Macmillan.
Boyle, **Kevin,** and Hadden, **Tom:** *Ireland: A Positive Proposal,* Penguin.
Brown, **Terence:** Ireland: *A Social and Cultural History 1922-1985,* Fontana Press.
Catto, **Mike:** *Art in Ulster, vol 2.* Blackstaff Press.
Cleeve, **Brian:** *A View of the Irish,* Buchan & Enright.
Constitution of Ireland, Stationery Office, Dublin.
Craig, **Maurice:** *The Architecture of Ireland,* Batsford.

Crookshank, Anne: *Irish Art from 1600,* Department of Foreign Affairs.

Danaher, Kevin: *In Ireland Long Ago.* Mercier Press.

D'Arcy, Gordon: *The Guide to the Birds of Ireland.* Irish Wildlife Publications.

Delaney, Frank: *James Joyce's Odyssey — A Guide to the Dublin of Ulysses.* Hodder & Stoughton.

Department of Foreign Affairs: *Dublin· Facts About Ireland.*

Evans, Estyn: *Irish Folk Ways.* Routledge and Kegan Paul.

Fitzgibbon, Theodora: *A taste of Ireland,* Pan.

FitzSimon, Christopher: *The Irish Theatre.* Thames & Hudson.

FitzSomon, Christopher: *The Arts in Ireland.* Gill & Macmillan.

Gogarty, Oliver St John: *As I Was Going Down Sackville Street.* Sphere.

Guinness, Desmond: *Georgian Dublin,* Batsford.

Hewitt, John: *Art in Ulster, vol 1.* Blackstaff Press.

Kearney, Richard (ed.) *The Irish Mind.* Wolfhound.

Kee, Robert: *Ireland — A History.* Weidenfeld.

Lehane, Brendan: *Dublin.* Time-Life.

Lehane, Brendan: *Companion Guide to Ireland.* Collins, Prentice-Hall.

Lydon, James and MacCurtain, **Margaret** (eds.): *The Gill History of Ireland (12 vols.).* Gill & Macmillan.

Lyons, F.S.L.: *Ireland Since the Famine.* Collins.

McDonald, Frank: *The Destruction of Dublin.* Gill & Macmillan.

MacLysaght, Edward: *Irish Families and their Names and Origins.* Figgis.

MacLysaght, Edward: *Surnames of Ireland.* Irish Academic Press.

Murphy, Dervla: *A Place Apart.* **Murray.**

Murphy, John: *Irish Shopfronts.* **Appletree** Press, Belfast.

O'Brien, Maire and Conor Cruise: *Concise History of Ireland.* Thames & Hudson.

O'Canainn, Tomas: *Traditional Music in Ireland.* Routledge & Kegan Paul.

O'Connor, Frank: *A Book of Ireland.* Collins.

O'Connor, Ulick, illus. **Bewick, Pauline:** *Irish Tales and Sagas.* Granada.

O'Faolain, Sean: *The Irish.* Penguin.

O Murchú, Máirtín: *The Irish Language.* Department of Foreign Affairs.

O'Riada, Sean: *Our Musical Heritage.* Dolmen.

O'Sullivan, Maurice: *Twenty Years A-growing.* OUP.

Potterton, Homan: *The National Gallery of Ireland.*

Praeger, Robert Lloyd: *The Way that I Went.* Allen Figgis.

Sandford, Ernest: *Discover Northern Ireland.* Northern Ireland Tourist Board.

Somerville-Large, Peter: *Dublin.* Hamish Hamilton.

Somerville-Large, Peter: *The Grand Irish Tour.* Penguin.

Stephens, James, illus. Rackham, *Arthur: Irish Fairy Tales.* Gill & Macmillan.

Wallace, Martin: *100 Irish Lives.* David & Charles.

Woodham-Smith, Cecil: *The Great Hunger.* Hamish Hamilton.

Irish Tourist Board Offices

General postal enquiries: Irish Tourist Board, PO Box 273, Dublin 8, Ireland.

The following are the principal offices for the various regions and are open throughout the year. Many other local offices are open only in the summer months. A full list is available from any tourist information office.

DUBLIN & ENVIRONS

Dublin City: 14 Upper O'Connell St., Dublin (747733).
Dublin Airport: 376387/375533.
Dun Laoghaire: St Michael's Wharf (806984/5/6).

SOUTHEAST REGION

Rosslare Harbour: 053-33232.
Wexford: Crescent Quay (053-23111).
Kilkenny: Rose Inn St. (056-21755).
Waterford: 41 The Quay (051-75788).

SOUTHWEST REGION

Cork City: Tourist House, Grand Parade (021-23251).
Skibbereen: The Square (028-21766).
Killarney: Town Hall (064-31633).
Tralee: Aras Siamsa, Godfrey Place (066-21288).

MIDWEST REGION

Limerick City: The Granary, Michael St. (061-317522).
Shannon Airport: 061-61664.
Cashel: Town Hall (062-61333).

MIDLANDS REGION

Mullingar: Dublin Rd. (044-48650).
Athlone: 17 Church St. (0902-2866).

FAR WEST REGION

Galway City: Aras Failte, Eyre Sq. (091-63081).
Westport: The Mall (098-25711).

NORTHWEST REGION

Sligo: Aras Reddan, Temple St. (071-61201).
Letterkenny: Derry Rd. (074-21160).

Irish Tourist Board Offices in Northern Ireland and abroad

Northern Ireland: 53 Castle St., Belfast (227888); Foyle St., Londonderry (0504-269501).

Britain: 150 New Bond St., London W1Y OAQ (01-493 3201).

Europe: 9, Boulevard de la Medeleine, 75001 Paris (01-261 8426); c/o Aer Lingus-Irish, Via Galleria Passarella 2, 20122 Milan (02-700080/783565); Untermainanlage 7, 6000 Frankfurt-am-Main 1 (69-236492); Rue de l'Industrie 4, Box 6, 1040 Brussels (02-513-7874); c/o Co petance Special Service, Store Strandstraede 19, 1255 Copenhagen K (01-158045); Irlandska Statens Turistbyra, PO Box 8305, 10420 Stockholm (08-502028).

US And Canada: 590 Fifth Ave, New York, NY 10036 (212-869 5500); 230 North Michigan Ave, Chicago, Illinois 60601 (312-726 9356); 625 Market St., Suite 502, San Francisco, California 94105 (415-957 0985); 10 King St., East, Toronto M5C 1C3 (416-364-1301).

Australia and New Zealand: MLC Centre, 37th Level, Martin Place, Sydney 2000 (01-232 7460); 2nd Floor, Dingwall Building, 87 Queen St., PO Box 279, Auckland 1 (09-793708).

Argentina: 2036 Conde, 1428 Buenos Aires (01-552 0950).

Japan: c/o Taiyo Enterprises, Yamaga Building, 3rd Floor, Azabu-dai, Minato-ku, Tokyo (03-582 8886).

Northern Ireland Tourist Board

The following offices are open all year:
Belfast: River House, 52 High St., (246609); Belfast Airport; Crumlin 52103.
Armagh: Council Office, Palace Demesne (0861-524052).
Newry: Arts Centre, Bank Parade (0693-66232).
Londonderry: Foyle St., (0504-269501).
Ballycastle: Sheskburn House, 7 Mary St., (02657-62024).
Cookstown: Town Hall, Burn Rd., (06487-63359/63441).
Enniskillen: 0365-23110/25050.

NITB offices in the Irish Republic and abroad

Dublin : Tourist Information Desk, Clery's Department Store, O'Connell St., (786055).

Britain : Ulster Office, 11 Berkeley St., London W1X 6BU (01-493 0601).

Europe : Northern Ireland Tourist Board, Neue Mainzerstrasse 22, 6000 Frankfurt-am-Main (069-234504).

North America : 3rd Floor, 40 West 57th St., New York NY10019 (212-756 5144).

ART/PHOTO CREDITS

Backcover Pictures: G.P. Reichelt (Top right corner); Peter Lavery (Horses); Bruce Bernstein (History); Billy Strickland (Hurling); Thomas Kelly (Sea); Bob Hobby (Solitude); NITB (Singalongs); Jeremy Nicholl (Drummers); George Wright (Drink); Antonio Martinelli (Doorways); G.P. Reichelt (Traders); Antonio Martinelli (Towers); Thomas Kelly (Travellers).

Spine (from top to bottom) : Bob Hobby; Joseph F. Viesti; Tony Stone Worldwide; Tony Stone Worldwide; Tony Stone Worldwide.

Index